SPECIAL TRUST

SPECIAL TRUST

ROBERT C. MCFARLANE

WITH ZOFIA SMARDZ

CADELL & DAVIES
NEW YORK

Cadell & Davies™
An imprint of Multi Media Communicators, Inc.
575 Madison Avenue, Suite 1006
New York, NY 10022

Jacket design: Tim Ladwig and Jim Hellman
Cover photo: The White House

Library of Congress Cataloging-in-Publication Data:
McFarlane, Robert C.
    Special Trust / Robert C. McFarlane, with Zofia Smardz
        p. cm.
    Includes bibliographical references and index.
    ISBN 1-56977-880-9 : $25.00
     1. McFarlane, Robert C. 2. Iran-Contra Affair, 1985-1989.
    I. Smardz, Zofia. II. Title.
    E876.M394   1994
    955.05'4—dc20   94-32882
                                          CIP

10 9 8 7 6 5 4 3 2 1

Printed in the United States of America by Berryville Graphics with special thanks to Jackie Rhine.

To my wife Jonda,
partner, lover, mentor and friend
"To know how very much..."

ACKNOWLEDGMENTS

Almost seven years ago I committed to write a book—half history, half memoir—and ended up five months later in a white-knuckled name-calling rage when it became clear that sensationalism was that publisher's only goal. Perhaps the best tribute I can make to those who have assisted this time around is to say, "You've made it all worthwhile." The difference that has made this effort feasible—indeed much more, an immensely fulfilling experience—has been the professional excellence and shared sense of purpose of a few good friends. First among them is my wife of 35 years, Jonda. Only she could have mastered and moderated the Manichean mood swings that threatened to undo the effort so many times. Only she kept the real focus—the kids and future generations—foremost in my mind.

With no experience in either the mechanics of publishing or the marketing of memoirs, I was terribly fortunate to have been led by Doug Holladay, a man whose faith—and whose faith in me—inspired me to take this on. There cannot be many publishers with the courage to say, "This is your book. Write it the way you want, and we will publish it." Thanks Doug, I hope you won't change your mind. Doug took me to Multi Media and Ron Friedman—the key individual who has given this book whatever topicality and read-ability it has. Further, to whatever request I made for support, Ron's answer was always "Yes." The same applies to Ron's wife Laura Carr, who notwithstanding delivery of their first child, didn't miss a beat. So too was the entire Multi Media team—Karen Santiago, Sam Chapin and so many others—always there for me.

The "doing of it," however, relied on Zofia Smardz, my co-author. Zofia, a respected journalist, brought to the preparation of this manuscript more than writing skills. As an experienced observer of the political life of Washington, she, as perhaps no other, could translate the complexity, nuance, passion, anguish and anger of my recitation of each episode into accurate historical—and often lyrical—prose. Thank you, Zofia, more than my words can say.

Finally, there are my closest co-workers here in my office cum writing studio—my extraordinarily talented Executive Assistant of seven years, Caroline Scullin, and my eternally cheerful and literarily insightful secretary, Karen Stiver. You were indispensable.

For the rest—judgments, criticisms, errors, and all else—I alone am responsible.

CONTENTS

PREFACE   xi

Part One   CRISIS: IRAN-CONTRA   1

  Chapter 1   THE RIGHT THING TO DO   3
  Chapter 2   AN OPENING TO IRAN   17
  Chapter 3   ARMS FOR HOSTAGES   37
  Chapter 4   IN THE BELLY OF THE BEAST   53
  Chapter 5   THE BATTLE FOR THE CONTRAS   67
  Chapter 6   SCANDAL   89

Part Two: DREAMS AND DUTY   109

  Chapter 7   GRAHAM, TEXAS   111
  Chapter 8   'NAM   133
  Chapter 9   REGARDING HENRY: THE NIXON-FORD YEARS   149
  Chapter 10 ON THE SHIP OF STATE   171

Part Three: IN THE REAGAN WHITE HOUSE   191

  Chapter 11 MAKING THINGS WORK   193
  Chapter 12 STAR WARS   215
  Chapter 13 THE EMERGING NEW WORLD ORDER   237
  Chapter 14 TAKING CHARGE   257
  Chapter 15 TO THE FUTURE   275
  Chapter 16 A TURNING POINT IN HISTORY   291
  Chapter 17 A TIME TO GO   323

Part Four: A PUBLIC HEALING   335

  Chapter 18 COMING BACK   337
  Chapter 19 TRUTH AND LIES   349
  Chapter 20 THE PRICE OF POWER   355

AFTERWORD   367

APPENDICES   369

APPENDIX A: Letter from President Gerald R. Ford
                concerning the *SS Mayaguez.*   371

APPENDIX B: National Security Decision Directive
                Seventy-Five, January 17, 1983
                (declassified July 16, 1994).   372

APPENDIX C: Commission of Robert C. McFarlane
                from President Ronald Reagan to be
                National Security Adviser.   381

APPENDIX D: Note from President Reagan regarding
                the recovery of the *Achille Lauro.*   382

APPENDIX E: Secretary of State's Distinguished
                Service Award.   383

APPENDIX F: Selected Correspondence:

                - President Nixon's reaction to the
                  foreign policy initiatives Robert McFarlane
                  proposed to President Reagan in
                  January 1987.   384

                - Note from President Nixon following
                  Robert McFarlane's attempted suicide.   385

                - Note from Zgibniew Brzezinski, National
                  Security Adviser to President Carter.   386

                - Note from Prime Minister Margaret
                  Thatcher.   387

                - Letter from President Ford.   388

                - President Nixon's response to Robert
                  McFarlane's letter of January 1991
                  regarding Boris Yeltsin and issues in
                  U.S.-Japanese relations.   389

INDEX   391

PREFACE

The President of the United States of America
To all who shall see these presents, greeting:

Know Ye, that reposing special trust and confidence
in the patriotism, valor, fidelity and abilities of Robert
Carl McFarlane, I do appoint him: Second Lieutenant,
United States Marine Corps (June 1959), Captain
(February 1964), Major (November 1967), Lieutenant
Colonel (June 1975), Special Assistant to the
President for National Security Affairs (December
1976), Counselor of the Department of State
(February 1981), Deputy Assistant to the President
for National Security Affairs (January 1982), Personal
Representative of the President in the Middle East
(July 1983), Assistant to the President of the United
States of America for National Security Affairs
(October 1983).

Over the course of the past two centuries, the idea of representative democracy has been adopted by Americans as the definitive
model of governance. Rather than holding referenda on each major
policy issue as some countries such as Switzerland do, we choose
people—and empower them to choose others—to represent us, to
consider alternatives, to use judgment, occasionally to take risks,
ultimately to decide for us and to govern. We repose enormous trust
in these individuals, yielding to them authority to spend huge sums
and charging them with the conduct of affairs of state, including
even the declaration of war. Over time, their character, ideas, and
judgments, as well as the overall vindication or breach of this "special trust" by them, are an important determinant of whether we
prosper or decline as a nation.

This concept of "reposing special trust" is a reciprocal covenant in which the electorate yields part of its sovereignty in exchange for the official(s)' commitment to live up to certain rules—not to break the law, not to lie, cheat or steal or in any other way violate the public trust.

We don't do this haphazardly. Understanding human failings, we built accountability into the concept and structured the branches of government and their relationship to us through such things as periodic elections and daily press scrutiny as the means to keep the ship of state on course; or at least to keep things from going too far wrong. When an official or a group has done something corrupt or foolish, our approach has been to enact new law to circumscribe the authority of public servants, to tighten the rules, to limit their freedom to act, or to increase their reporting responsibilities, in an effort to better assure against future sin or ineptitude.

For most of our history, this idea of reposing special trust in others has worked well. At least we can say it has helped us avoid catastrophe, although it must be acknowledged that for the first 150 years, the government's role was a much smaller part of our lives. It didn't have the authority to get into very much trouble. As the scope of government has broadened and its power and influence have spread both at home and internationally, our country has been blessed with scores of men and women of superior intellect and an elevated sense of patriotism who have enabled us to keep the peace, win the wars and over time, prosper. Such men as Paul Nitze come to mind, a man who has devoted 50 years of his life to public service and made historic contributions to our victory in the cold war, the control and ultimate reduction of nuclear weapons and many other landmark achievements.

This book is about my attempt to vindicate the special trust I was privileged to take on as an officer in the Marines, as a senior official of the Department of State and as a member of the White House staff for nine years, culminating in my appointment as President Reagan's National Security Adviser. I look back on my life as a great adventure, filled with challenge, controversy, risk, danger, and achievement, as well as failure and near-tragedy. It is all here—as objectively as I can recall it. A few episodes stand out in my mind and therefore consume more space: the Vietnam War, during which I commanded a unit in the first landing of U.S. forces in March

1965, and a second tour two years later; the opening to China in the early 1970s, a historic, geopolitical stratagem conceived by President Nixon and executed through the brilliant diplomacy of Henry Kissinger, in which I was privileged to play a supporting role; the failure of Communism in the 1980s and the U.S. role in accelerating that collapse, which occurred while I served as President Reagan's National Security Adviser. I treat the failures as well as the successes with as much objectivity as possible—again the Vietnam War and the Iran-contra fiasco.

With nine years distance from government and, I believe, a better perspective on the substantial changes over the past forty years in how it functions, I have tried to do two things in this book. The first is to record my version of history, relying on notes taken at the time and from extended reference to my personal papers from those years, held at the Ronald Reagan Presidential Library, at the National Archives and at the National Security Council. Occasionally I excerpt from those papers; where oral statements are involved, I have recorded the quotations from notes or as I remember them based upon notes. My second goal is to convey through a hundred stories—from the jungles of Vietnam to the cloistered corridors of the Kremlin, from the Byzantine chambers of the Middle East to the pristine yet somewhat tarnished West Wing of the White House—how the concept of "reposing special trust and confidence" has been eroded and why.

I will also add a word on how to restore the special trust to its original status as a covenant that has stood us successfully through more than two centuries of greatness and, if renewed, can enable us to vindicate the American role of leadership into the third.

Finally, in the course of providing my comment on these temporal events, I hope to convey my belief in and understanding of a larger "special trust" we all enjoy. And that is the trust from God to develop ourselves to the limit of our endowment, to apply the skills thus honed to the benefit of others, and in all things to be humble.

PART ONE

Crisis: Iran-Contra

Chapter 1

THE RIGHT THING TO DO

Early one afternoon in February 1987, without telling anyone where I was going, I left my office in Washington, D.C., got into my car, and went to look for a place to die.

As I drove up Canal Road along the Potomac River, a terrible pall hung over me. I struggled with feelings of shame and despair, feelings that were more than just a state of mind. Strange physical sensations gripped me. I felt an acute pressure, as though the world were bearing down upon me, squeezing me into a ball that would grow smaller and smaller until at last it would violently implode. My toes and fingers began to tingle, and I found myself absurdly worrying that I might have an accident that would thwart my plans to kill myself.

For this is what I fully intended to do. In two days, I would end my life, a life of accomplishment, recognition and service, a life full of blessings—loving family, good friends, useful work, years of promise still lying ahead. The life of a man with everything to live for. A life, therefore, that would compensate for the wrong I believed I had done my country.

The trip this day was a reconnaissance mission. I had determined how and when to die; today I would determine where. I had served in the U.S. Marine Corps for 20 years; planning to the last detail for the execution of every operation had become a matter of habit.

I yearned to die because I knew that dying was the right thing to do. Driving along the Potomac in the fading light of a cold winter day, I thought how fitting a river setting would be for my last moments. My wife, Jonny, and I had always loved the river; for years, we had dreamed of owning a house with a view overlooking the Potomac's rolling waters.

I turned into Carderock recreational area, a large park located on a bluff above the Potomac just beyond the Beltway in Montgomery County, Maryland. The south end consists of ball fields and a number of covered pavilions for large parties. We had had a picnic there several years before with many of my classmates from the U.S. Naval Academy. As I circled the grounds, it occurred to me that the Park Police probably patrolled the south end so frequently that I would be discovered before the pills I intended to take would have time to act. I drove on.

To the north, the park is natural wilderness, dotted with only occasional family-sized picnic areas. Trails wind through the woods and along the bluff overlooking the river. On weekends, the bluff is a popular place for rock climbers and Outward Bound veterans. One or two spots boast a 50 to 60-foot rappel.

I left the car in the parking lot, bothered again by the thought that it would serve as a tipoff for the Park Police. I struck out northward on the trail, hoping to find a secluded spot overlooking the river but hidden from the view of passersby. Unfortunately, the terrain between the C&O canal and the river narrows to no more than 200 yards in this area, and the number of small trails increases. In winter, there is no cover, so a person is visible almost anywhere.

Dismayed, growing anxious, I clambered onto the rocks and began searching for likely hiding places. Surely somewhere in this vast space there was a concealed spot where a man could die in peace, undiscovered and undisturbed. I found one or two niches that I thought might work, and sat in each of them for five minutes or so, crouching awkwardly in my business suit and overcoat. But each time, I was flushed out by couples who were obviously seeking the same privacy, only for more constructive purposes.

My sense of despair deepened. The park apparently would not work. The threat of discovery before I had achieved my goal was too great. The wind whipped through the trees and whistled past my head, stinging my eyes and bringing tears. In the gathering dusk, my heart weighed down, I headed back to the car. In my mind I turned over a handful of other possible scenarios for my death, but each had some drawback I could not overcome.

Finally, reluctantly, I gave in to the truth—that what I really wanted to do was simply to go to sleep as always with Jonny—and not wake up. The thought of having her discover me in the morning gave me pause, yet I selfishly rationalized that at least in the years to come, she might be comforted by the fact that I had wanted to be with her to the very end.

What was a man like myself doing in that desolate park on that gray day, contemplating and planning his own demise? I was a prominent and respected figure in the nation's capital. I had been a highly-placed government official—National Security Adviser to President Ronald Reagan. Fourteen months earlier, I had left that post on a high note of achievement that included helping to negotiate the first reductions in U.S. and Soviet nuclear weapons in history. Now privately in residence at a Washington think tank, I was still much in demand on the lecture circuit, in academia and in media circles for my knowledge of foreign policy. Over 30 years, I had built up a career and reputation that placed me among the top ranks of the nation's foreign policy professionals, which brought me power, status and regard. A few short months before, my future had appeared only bright. What could have happened to make me so determined to end my life? What could have happened to alter everything, to make me so anxious, to plunge me into the abyss of suicidal depression?

Before that February of 1987, I had never imagined suicide as a conceivable act—for me or for any other McFarlane. If I had even contemplated its possibility, it would have been solely in the military tradition, to prevent being caught in a compromising situation as a prisoner—self-destruction as a lesser evil than betrayal. Otherwise, like most people, I would have thought of suicide as an irrational act, the last refuge of the hopeless.

Yet in recent days, the thought of taking my own life had overpowered me; it had gripped me with an unassailable logic and had taken on legitimacy as a just and fitting duty—the right thing to do. After weeks of deepening anguish and despair, it had come to me with an illuminating clarity from the most distant corner of my mind. The spiritual pulse was clear: "Go ahead. This is the way." Not the way out—out of my predicament, out of the spotlight in whose glare I stood exposed, out of the hearings and the news reports and the gossip columns, out of the sidelong glances of strangers in the street, out of life. I was not looking for escape, not that. But for the way to make things right.

For nearly 30 years, I had been a public servant, dedicating my life's labors to the good of my country in the manner of my father before me. I had shaped my life according to the principles taught me first by him, then re-emphasized at the U.S. Naval Academy, and finally by the U.S. Marine Corps. "Duty, honor, country"—these were the real values I had honestly striven to sustain in all my endeavors, the absolutes I cherished and wished to uphold. In the course of my career, I had risen steadily from one position of trust to another, first through the Marine Corps, and then in government, where I had ultimately chosen to concentrate my skills. I had worked hard, believing what I was doing was not simply work, not primarily a career, but over and above all service, a genuine dedication of myself, my work, my life to the good of the country and its people.

For this, I had been generously rewarded. I had left government at the zenith of my career, believing I had a great many more contributions to make even from the private sector. But now, everything seemed in jeopardy—my future, the government, the country. And I believed that for this, I was responsible.

I believed the Iran-contra scandal, which had in the last three months all but engulfed the Reagan administration, and by extension the country, was all my fault. Certainly the "judges" of Washington—from the broadcast bureaus to the halls of Capitol Hill—said so.

Since the previous November, I had appeared time and again before the congressional committees investigating the so-called arms-for-hostages deal by means of which the President and his men had sought to rescue the seven Americans then held captive by Shia Muslim terrorists in Beirut. I had told the presidentially-appointed Tower Board, which was also looking into the affair, the story of how our approach to Iran had begun while I was National Security Adviser, and how it had gone astray after I left the government. I had appeared on *Nightline,* the *Today* show, the *CBS Morning News* and countless other television news shows, and granted a dozen newspaper interviews, to explain that we had never intended a simple ransom arrangement; that our goals at the beginning had been larger, geostrategic, aimed at finding an opening to pragmatic elements in the regime of the fanatically anti-American Ayatollah Khomeini, an opening to people who might ultimately replace him.

The trouble was, this was not what the journalists wanted to hear, and so the stories were always boiled down to a simple equation: arms-for-hostages, Reagan Deals with Terrorists. And the trouble was, I was the only one talking. No one else had come forward to back me up. Not the President who had approved and backed the Iran initiative from the very beginning. Not the Secretaries of State and Defense, George Shultz and Caspar Weinberger, who had known of all the developments. Not the men with whom I had worked so closely as National Security Adviser and who had carried on the Iran dealings after I resigned from that post—John Poindexter, who had been my deputy and had taken over as the top man after I left, and Oliver North, the zealous young Marine lieutenant colonel who had served as my right-hand man on so many occasions.

John and Ollie had taken the Fifth, George and Cap had distanced themselves from the whole imbroglio, and the President remained sealed behind a wall of advisers who had allowed him only the occasional miscast statement on the matter.

I had been devastated by the news stories that were leaked out of Ronald Reagan's first session before the Tower Board in late January. They made the claim that the President had denied knowing of or approving the first shipments of arms to Iran by the Israelis in 1985. They made it appear that I had run a renegade operation against the President's will.

Shaken by the headlines, I had called Brent Scowcroft, one of the three panel members. I had worked with Brent in the Ford administration, when Brent was National Security Adviser.

"Brent," I asked anxiously. "Are these stories true?"

"No, no. To the contrary," he had replied. He told me that the President, asked about his knowledge of that first shipment, had actually handed the panel a copy of my earlier sworn testimony on the issue and said, "There you are. Bud's got it right."

I hung up feeling both agitated and relieved. I did not doubt that Don Regan, the President's controversial Chief of Staff, had been responsible for the distorted version of the leaks, and that he was trying to protect the President. The stories' damage had been done, though, at my expense. To the public at large, watching television, reading the newspapers, I was coming across as the lone aberrant, the source of the problem, the guilty party.

The fact of the matter was, I felt guilty—not for what I had recommended as I resigned, or for the coverup, for I had told the truth—but for having, as I saw it, copped out. I had advised Reagan to turn off the Iran initiative as I prepared to leave government, yet part of me had known that, given his deep desire to do something about our hostages in Lebanon, he would never take that course. Yet I had left just the same.

In the late 1970s, while I was still with the Marines, my family and I had lived in Japan. In that time, and through the ensuing years, I had come to admire that country, its culture, its people, its traditions. Among those traditions is one called *seppuku*. This is the ceremonial rite in which a samurai who believes he has disgraced his country commits suicide in atonement.

I believed I had disgraced my country.

———

The turning point came with the President's State of the Union address on January 27.

Up until that night, I had clung to the belief that I could compensate for the damage I had caused. I believed that the country, diverted by the succulent scandal unfolding in Washington, was about to miss a historic opportunity in foreign affairs. At that time, midway through Ronald Reagan's second term, I believed we had an opportunity to restore our leadership of the Western world with the full cooperation and support of the American people. Concerned about Soviet expansionism and the need for strengthening our defenses, the public, for the first time in more than a generation, since the war in Vietnam, had been willing to back a more assertive foreign policy with expanded financial resources.

I was convinced that if only the President would step up to the podium, admit that the Iran initiative had been a mistake, take responsibility and appeal to Congress to join him in putting this episode behind us and moving forward in pursuit of specific goals, we could still salvage something of this rare moment—when public and fiscal support converge with a competent President—and focus the country on a positive agenda.

It is a hallmark of depression, I later learned, that the mind plays tricks and distorts perspective, blowing certain aspects of life out of proportion while suppressing others, and often leading the sufferer to believe that he or she has a singular grasp of the critical nerve pulse of life. Simultaneously, by assuming all responsibility for things that have gone wrong, the depressive comes to believe that he or she can "own" a problem, and therefore by corollary solve it. In my case, I had convinced myself that I alone was responsible for the scandal before us and for the losses our country was about to suffer as a consequence. Depression led me to exaggerate that sense of responsibility and to take on a deep burden of guilt and sadness. In my despair I reached the conclusion that only I could save the situation—again, as I have since learned, a manifestation of advanced depression. The need to act then became an obsession, one which I pursued by falling back on skills I had used a thousand times before. Simply stated, they were: analyze the problem, define the solution and get it in the hands of the decision makers.

In that misguided hope, I had conceived a plan of drawing up a series of concept papers that would provide the basis for new initiatives, which would allow the President to make lasting gains in the remaining two years of his second term. I saw four areas of foreign policy where the President could move decisively: to consolidate reductions in nuclear weapons; to reach a compromise with Congress after a long, divisive struggle over Central America; to reach a compromise budget agreement and seriously tackle the deficit; and to advance the peace process in the Middle East. I had worked every free moment on the papers—weekends at our cabin in the Shenandoah Valley, evenings and nights at home in front of the PC—and believed then and now that had the concepts in the papers been adopted, they could have resulted in very substantial gains for the United States.

Finished, I delivered them: to Senator Sam Nunn, the Georgia Democrat with whom I had established a good relationship when I worked on the staff of the Senate Armed Services Committee (if any of these initiatives were to succeed, they would need the backing of a respected Democrat), to Vice President George Bush, and to George Shultz at State. The copy for the President I sent to Mike Deaver, a longtime Reagan confidant and his former Deputy Chief of Staff, with whom I had enjoyed a certain rapport when we were both at the White House.

Mike called me later to report that he had passed the papers along to the President, and that Reagan had liked them, thought they were sensible and worth pursuing and had sent them on to George Shultz for him to develop. This heartened me, as did a note from Nunn, who said that if the President were seriously interested, Nunn would be willing to sit down with someone in authority and talk about the proposals.

From Shultz, however, came a perfunctory note: thank you for your ideas, always value your insights, over and out. It was clearly a brush-off, and I should of course have understood it to be the most predictable response of all. What it reflected was the brutal reality of official Washington, which I had shied from accepting: that when you're out, you are really out, and no one listens to you anymore, certainly not those who themselves had failed to conceive of any proposals to move us beyond scandal.

I believed there were no men around the President now who had a depth of knowledge of history or an understanding of how other cultures behave—essential qualities for effecting a workable and creative foreign policy. George Shultz was a steady Secretary of State but not an original thinker. But he and Defense Secretary Cap Weinberger were still in the magical inner circle, and I had removed myself from that sanctum. My words had lost their weight; to all but Reagan, I was little more than a small, disembodied voice lost on the winds of Washington's raucous political stage. Absorbing the reality of being deserted deepened my already profound sense of despair— again, a predictable consequence of severe depression.

Nonetheless, on the night of the 27th, I sat down in front of the TV set in the family room in a state of heightened expectancy. I still believed it was possible that some *deus ex machina* would descend to rearrange the scenery and alter the outcome of the morality play in which we were engaged. As Reagan came out into the House of Representatives chamber, to far less thunderous applause than he had enjoyed in the past, I leaned forward hopefully. But as he spoke, I began to sink farther back into the couch. Later, Jonny told me how she watched the dismay spread palpably over my whole person.

Reagan spoke of "errors" made in the course of the Iran initiative, but refused to disavow the policy itself, or to admit that it had in fact deteriorated into nothing more than a swap of arms for hostages. He reasserted his backing for the contras in Nicaragua.

Of my initiatives, there wasn't even the hint of a mention.

When the speech was over, I shook my head. "Well, that's that," I said. And I truly felt as though all hope was lost, as though it were all over.

It was a jolt, this sudden collision with reality. I realized I had been foolish in thinking I might have effected any difference in policy.

In the days that followed, I thought often of my father, whose devotion to public service had been the ruling tenet of his life. I thought of how hurt he would be by the damage I had done to the family name. I thought of my wife and children, and the burden placed on them by the glare of publicity that went everywhere with me and affected every aspect of my life.

One day, I got a call at my office at the Center for Strategic and International Studies, a Washington policy institute where I was a counselor specializing in arms control and the Soviet Union. The call was from Ed Budd, the chairman of the board of Travelers Insurance, a board on which I sat as a director.

"Bud, I'm a little concerned about the criticisms we may receive for having someone in the public spotlight who bears a fiduciary responsibility to our shareholders," Ed said.

For some minutes he continued in that vein, addressing the issue in a backhanded manner, and never expressing any regard for my situation. After a little of this, I found myself stiffening and said: "Now let me get this straight, Ed. You're calling a member of your board who has not been charged, nor indicted, nor otherwise found culpable of any act of moral turpitude or civil breach, and you are asking him to resign. Is that right?"

"Well," he said, clearing his throat again and sounding uncomfortable, "you know how things are, Bud. People worry."

I did, of course, know how things were. Stifling my anger, I said, "All right. I'll resign."

In letters dated February 9, I handed in my resignations from all the boards on which I sat, to spare the other chairmen the burden of having to make the kind of call that Budd had made. To his credit, John Birkelund, chairman of Dillon Read, refused to accept my resignation and said he would be glad to take whatever flak came his way. I was grateful for the show of support.

More and more often in those days, I found myself thinking what had been on my mind from the first hours that the Iran affair had become public: "This is likely to be the salient event of your life, McFarlane. Nothing will ever quite measure up to this sustained scandal. You're at the center of a great national loss. Had it not been for your errors, it would not have happened. Try as you may to spend your time each day righting this wrong, it isn't working. And five years from now, you're going to be carrying this same burden; you're going to be the person who brought this embarrassment on the country."

I felt acute shame at this thought. I felt dismay that all the achievements of my career in public service were likely to be eclipsed forever by the dark shadow of this senseless scandal. My role in conceiving and advancing the Strategic Defense Initiative, in accelerating nuclear arms reduction agreements between the United States and the Soviet Union; all this would forever be subordinated to this error in judgment that had arisen not from venality, nor ambition, but from worthy motives, from a belief that we might find a successor to Khomeini and ultimately restore relations with a vital country.

Moreover, I was a McFarlane. My father had raised me and my brother and sisters with a sense of obligation to serve, a responsibility to use the blessings God had bestowed on us to lead. He had taught us to see ourselves, in Plato's term, as "guardians," chosen servants of talent, obliged to advance the human condition at whatever the cost. That obligation was one I took very seriously.

I had been endowed with a special trust, and in an important way, I had failed it. Now it was my duty to atone for that. In a metaphorical sense, this commitment to atone was a presentiment of suicide. The acts of abandonment by my former colleagues in government and private life and my public shaming deepened my already exaggerated vulnerability to the next step in the downward spiral of depression; that is, to conclude that I must move from guilt to atonement—to suicide—thus sparing others the discomfort of my presence by withdrawing from life. By so doing, I believed, I would be performing a service to the country.

—

Of course, being raised a McFarlane also meant that you never talked about your feelings or shared your emotional turmoil or your difficulties with others. In my family, men, especially, were supposed to be self-reliant, strong figures, and in times of stress or error were expected not to acknowledge vulnerability. We were trained to figure out the problem, solve it, and go on. It had been the same in the Marines. That is what I had always done, and it had always worked.

All my life, I had kept a tight rein on internal conflicts, on doubts or worries or fears. I did not open the door onto that sphere of my nature easily, not even to Jonny.

Now was no exception. While worries and anguish boiled inside me, I strove as much as possible to spare Jonny the full brunt of my despair. This was not always easy, but I almost always succeeded. We had had a handful of long conversations about the Iran scandal as

THE RIGHT THING TO DO

it unfolded, and she was aware that I was distraught about its implications, not so much for myself as for the country. But she could not have known the true darkling depths of my emotions.

One day, however, I very nearly exposed them. It was early morning and I was heading out the door to meet Len Garment, my lawyer, and proceed to another round of Iran-contra hearings and interviews by investigators. Jonny came to the door to kiss me good-bye. She must have noticed some greater strain than usual in my face and asked what was wrong. I leaned against the door frame and put my head in my hand.

"I just have a bad feeling about all this," I confessed, and my voice was shaking. "I'm afraid this whole thing isn't going to end very well." I was close to tears, barely holding on and holding them back. I was on the verge of breakdown.

"You're doing what's right," Jonny reassured me, supporting me as she had all through our married life. "Just keep on doing it, and everything will be all right."

I managed to pull myself together and go on. But it was not long after that that I determined how to solve the problem. My solution, as I saw it, bore two advantages. It would, first of all, serve as atonement. But secondly, I believed that the death of a public figure such as myself would be an event dramatic enough to shake the nation, to awaken it from its absorption with scandal and recognize that there was still so much work to be done, that important opportunities would be lost while it wallowed in sensationalism.

With the burden of finding the solution lifted, I found it almost a relief to apply myself to its execution. My Marine training clicked in, and I ran through the checklist of things to do.

Thinking of Jonny, I determined to avoid a violent death. I believed, absurdly, and as only a mind steeped in depression can, that a benign passing would be less upsetting to her. I remembered the bottle of Valium in my medicine cabinet, a prescription for back pain, and decided that pills would do as a way to die. Deciding where to die was more problematic, but after my trip to the park, I realized I wanted to be with Jonny until the last possible moment.

———

I hoped my last weekend with Jonny would be as private and satisfying as possible. Even though I had left government, Jonny and I still had precious little time together, especially now, with all the hearings and Jonny's job teaching English at Bethesda-Chevy Chase High School.

I was scheduled to appear before the Tower Board once again on Monday, February 10, and later so many of the analyses would insist that I had been unable to face the panel anymore, but this simply was not true. The truth was that the Tower Board was not even on my mind. My first two appearances had gone easily, smoothly. I was unconcerned about the next one.

While Jonny was off at school on Friday, February 6, I worked at the computer, writing some final letters. Among them was one to Meg Greenfield, the *Washington Post* columnist with whom Jonny and I had enjoyed a friendly relationship. To Meg I tried to explain the magnitude of the loss I thought the country would sustain if we allowed Iran- contra to overwhelm all other foreign policy considerations.

"The absence of any apparent intention to try to translate the precious cycle of American sacrifice that we have enjoyed for the past six years into a more enduring framework for stability is a loss of such magnitude as to leave anyone in abject despair," I wrote. "This is especially so for me, for it is undeniable that but for my personal failures and shortcomings, there might still have been a chance. It is true. In the sense that if I had prevented the Iran initiative from ever getting started, and even before that, if I had been more attentive to what surely must have gone on in support of the contras, this historic failure would not have occurred. I deserve the full burden of criticism. By this time it will have become apparent how remorseful I feel about this."

I outlined for her the four initiatives I had sent to the President with such a desperate sense of expectation a few weeks before. If only he would take responsibility, we could move on beyond this, I wrote. I hoped she would see my reasoning and publish my thoughts. Then, in turn, if the President and a bipartisan cadre of Congressmen adopted the ideas, a few important points might still be made.

Len Garment called that afternoon. We chatted for a few moments, and then I said to him, very deliberately: "I want you to know, Len, how grateful I am for everything you've done for me."

The words resounded portentously in my own ears, but Len, of course, had no idea that I thought this would be the last time we would ever speak.

The rest of the weekend passed uneventfully, as I had hoped it would. After church on Sunday, I headed over to the Bethesda Y for my habitual three-mile jog. On the way, I dropped the letters I had written, all but Jonny's, into a mailbox.

Jonny and I spent the rest of the day around the house. I felt curiously peaceful, almost optimistic, all day. Late in the evening, when Jonny announced she was heading upstairs, I said I would join her shortly. Then I went and got her letter, and the pills.

My actions on that February 8 were calm, deliberate, almost mechanical, unaccompanied by fear, regret or second thoughts of any kind.

My only vestige of guilt was towards my wife and children. As I took the bottle of pills from the medicine cabinet, I experienced again a recurrent qualm that what I was doing was unjust to Jonny, that I was leaving her with burdens she should not have to bear. Yet in my letter, I had tried to explain what had brought me to this extreme act of, as I saw it, sacrifice and atonement. And in the long reach, I believed, my family, who knew me thoroughly, who understood as no one else did the sort of person I was, would understand why I had acted as I had.

So, too, I was convinced, would the nation. And in understanding me perhaps it would forgive its leaders, and allow them to forgive each other and move on out of the quagmire that had engulfed them.

It has taken me a long time to recognize the futility of this sort of thinking, and the pointlessness of attempting to destroy oneself in an effort that would bear no fruit. I was attempting to transpose onto our society an ethic that simply doesn't exist here, an ethic of personal responsibility for bringing shame on the country. I still believe we would have a better country if we did have such an ethic, if those who failed their responsibility to the nation and failed to live up to the trust placed in them by those whom they serve were moved to atone for this failure—not irrationally, not by suicide, but by the public contrition that enables them to take responsibility and the public to learn from their mistakes.

Shortly after 11 p.m., I went into the kitchen, carrying my briefcase in one hand and the bottle of Valium in the other. I placed the briefcase on the red Formica breakfast counter, cleared off and spotless as usual, opened it, and propped a sealed envelope addressed to my wife against the lid. I placed the bottle of Valium beside the sink and poured myself a glass of wine. With a deep breath, I reached for the Valium, pried off the cap and, with rhythmic determination, proceeded to swallow the pills—30 or more. Finished, I stood for a moment there in the kitchen, head bowed, and prayed—for my family, for forgiveness.

Then I went upstairs to bed.

Jonny was still puttering about the bedroom and bathroom, getting ready for the night. Sitting up against the pillows, I watched her, the woman with whom I had shared my life for 33 years, who was as much a part of me as one of my own limbs, but who had no inkling of the path down which I had just embarked. I studied her in a way I never had before, recording her movements as if somehow to etch this last image of her in my heart.

While she moved about the room, we exchanged small talk, about the Tower Board hearing the next day, about her agenda. Finally, I urged her to hurry and come to bed.

As she slipped in on her side, I reached over to her.

"Come here for just a minute," I said. "I just want to hold you for a little while."

Smiling, she leaned against me, her back against my chest, and we sat that way in silence. She could not have known that I was silently bidding her good-bye. It didn't feel like good-bye; I could not feel I was truly leaving her. I was at peace, sure of my course. After a moment, Jonny turned and kissed me, all unknowing, going through the motions of our usual bedtime routine.

"'Night," she said, putting her head on my chest, as she had countless thousands of times before. Thinking, see you in the morning.

"Goodnight," I murmured back. Nothing more. I turned off the light, stretched out and closed my eyes.

I never expected to open them again.

Chapter 2

AN OPENING TO IRAN

"A man," wrote Sir Francis Bacon 400 years ago in his treatise *Of Expense,* "ought warily to begin charges which once begun will continue." These are surely words to live by, and there is no better example of their validity than the Iran affair and how it developed.

I argued at the time it was launched, and I argue now, that to have ignored the Iran opening when it occurred, never even to have explored the possibilities of making contact with potential opposition elements in the Khomeini regime, would have been as grave a mistake as ignoring Chinese overtures to re-establish relations in the 1970s. There's no question, however, that once the demands for arms entered the equation, and once the deal began to smell of ransom for captives and little else, the administration, myself included, should have become as wary as the most fastidious housewife sniffing chops at an open-air butcher stall.

There was, however, no mention of weapons at the start.

—

It was a typically hot, muggy Washington afternoon when David Kimche, the Director General of the Israeli Foreign Ministry, came by to see me in my White House office on July 3, 1985. I had been President Reagan's National Security Adviser for almost two years. After a general talk with several Israeli embassy officials and some members of my National Security Council staff present, David asked to see me alone. The others left, and David turned to me.

"You know, Mike Ledeen came and asked us whether we had any judgments about an Iranian opposition movement," he said. "Well, we told him that we do, but frankly I am here because I wanted to make sure that you really did send him to ask us this."

In fact, I had not officially charged Ledeen with any specific mission to look into Israeli contacts with possible Iranian dissidents. Mike worked for the National Security Council as a consultant on the Socialist International, a worldwide organization of socialist parties with which he was well connected. He made frequent trips to the Mediterranean and the Middle East, a region on which he considered himself an expert. Mike was a gregarious fellow, the sort who wandered in and out of your office unannounced, wanting to schmooze even when you were busy. He was an engaging raconteur and never let slip an opportunity to tell the tales of his visits with various prime ministers and other VIPs.

In the spring of 1985, as he was planning a trip of his own to Israel, he had come to my office. "So, are you worried about Iran?" he'd said in his teasing manner, and then, unbidden, sat down and talked with me about my concerns about the region. He knew that I was indeed interested in exploring whether there might be an opposition of some sort forming to the radical theocracy of the Ayatollah Khomeini.

There were good reasons to expect such a development. At that time, Iran had been at war with Iraq for five years, half a million people had died, and there appeared to be no end in sight to the carnage. The war had destroyed Iran's oil-producing—and thus its revenue-earning—capacity. Unable to buy food and staples, peasants had begun streaming into Tehran from the countryside, putting political pressure on the government.

Moreover, the Soviets had 26 divisions stationed on the northern border, in the trans-Caucasus hills, conducting daily exercises that involved the same tactics that would be used in a thrust toward the Persian Gulf. And to the East, 100,000 Soviet troops in Afghanistan could only heighten Iranian concerns about historic Soviet ambitions to achieve unfettered access to the open ocean and control of the Persian Gulf, the avenue that, because of the flow of oil through it, literally constituted a global lifeline.

I had long focused on the Persian Gulf and Iran as a vital region of strategic importance to the U.S. As early as 1981, when I arrived at the State Department to work with then-Secretary Alexander Haig, I had put the Persian Gulf, with particular reference to Iran, at the top of a list of proposed National Security Council study directives for developing administration strategy in various parts of the world where our interests were at stake.

Since then, a number of other administration studies had further stressed the importance of the Gulf, most recently a CIA Special National Intelligence Estimate on Iran. That SNIE, prepared by

Graham Fuller, the Middle East intelligence officer at the time and an acknowledged expert today, had raised a hue and cry within the administration when it appeared in draft form in June of 1985. Not only did it outline the same reasons I held for theorizing that an opposition either outside or inside Khomeini's regime was within the realm of possibility, it also boldly suggested that the only means of appealing to such a cabal would be to offer it support in the form of weapons. Cap Weinberger at Defense had vehemently denounced the report, and particularly the latter idea, as "absurd." George Shultz at State had offered slightly milder but equally clear opposition.

The fact of the matter was, though, that the President himself had for years been disappointed with his State Department's performance on Middle East issues. His highly-touted Middle East peace initiative, launched with flourish and fanfare in September 1982, had gone nowhere. It had fallen, to be blunt, flat on its face, and he wasn't happy about the way we had floundered in our Middle East policy ever since.

So it was no secret to Mike Ledeen or anyone else that I was interested in exploring options in the region. And when Mike offered to talk to the Israelis about their intelligence on the situation inside Iran, I said, "Sure, go ahead. Please do, and let me know what they say."

I learned later that Mike had taken that offhand encouragement and presented it in Tel Aviv as an official charge from the White House that would grant him greater credibility with the Israeli government than he would otherwise have enjoyed. It was a piece of brashness that later cost me an angry phone call from George Shultz, who saw Ledeen as having acted at my express behest to undercut State on the foreign policy stage.

But there was no question that I wanted to know what the Israelis had to say, and I encouraged Kimche to give me his views.

"A year or so ago, we began talking with Iranians who are disaffected by all the turmoil in their country," David began. "We believe we have made contact with people who are both willing and able over time and with support to change the government.

"Recently, these Iranians have said that they recognize that if they are ever going to be able to gain real power, they are going to need outside support. And they believe this support can only come from a country large enough to deal with Iran, which is the United States, and with the ability to deter any Soviet involvement, which is the United States."

He said these dissident Iranians had, at some risk, provided concrete intelligence concerning the military situation in the Iran-Iraq war, as well as the vulnerabilities of the incumbent leadership, from Khomeini to Khamenei to others in the power constellation in Tehran, and that the intelligence had been validated by the Israelis themselves. He believed further evidence of their legitimacy was their willingness to engage with Israeli agents at taped meetings in Germany and elsewhere, all the while running the risk of public disclosure.

But he said that the Iranians also recognized the need to present the U.S. with some sort of bona fides, some evidence that they indeed possessed a level of influence in Tehran. And the evidence they offered was the release of all the American hostages in Beirut.

"They are confident they can do this," David said. "All they want to know is, where do you want them?"

The offer was to release the hostages in Lebanon, either Beirut proper, or just outside, in a town called Junieh, or further north, along the coast, and have them picked up by U.S. forces.

There was no request for arms or *quid pro quo*.

I listened to David hopefully. I had known and respected him since first meeting him in Israel in 1981, when I was Al Haig's point man on the Middle East. Oxford-educated, extremely well-spoken, Kimche had had a distinguished career in the Mossad, the Israeli intelligence agency, where he had had a reputation as a highly intelligent and experienced policy analyst and practitioner.

What he was telling me now was certainly intriguing and provocative. I could not deny that I was interested in what he had to say, and that I believed the President would be, too. I told him I would put the matter before Reagan at the earliest opportunity.

David nodded in understanding. He said nothing for a moment. Then he leaned forward in his seat and fixed me with an intent look. What he said next made it clear that the Israelis had ideas with regard to Iran that went beyond the scope of U.S. goals or my interests in the region.

"You know, Bud," he said meaningfully, "things could get violent at some point."

"Well, yes, they often do in the Middle East," I replied blandly.

"I mean," he said archly, "what if Khomeini should die?"

I looked at him. "Are we talking about old age, or some other less natural cause?" I asked.

"Well, accelerated perhaps by one means or another."

His meaning, of course, was clear. "David," I said forcefully, "we could not possibly be party to anything of that nature. Period. Do you understand me?"

"Yes, yes," he said, nodding, "but what if someone were to do something to accelerate matters?"

I enunciated my words carefully. "I don't want you to have any illusions that you and we can cooperate in any venture in which the U.S. government is witting that you intend to kill Khomeini."

Kimche was not easily discouraged and persisted in this exchange for some minutes more, artfully pressing his point. However, I pressed back as decisively, finally growing quite heated. "Understand me, David," I said at last, "that we cannot engage with you in an enterprise in which anyone's purpose is to assassinate the Ayatollah."

At that he yielded, saying, "All right, that's clear."

We agreed to talk by telephone in a few days, using a code that we made up on the spot, so that I could inform him of the President's reaction to his proposition regarding the Iranians and the hostages. Then he left.

The Ayatollah Khomeini died four years later of natural causes relating to old age.

———

Everyone who worked with Ronald Reagan was acutely aware of his great concern for the fate of the seven men held hostage in Beirut in the summer of 1985. One by one, they had been captured off the streets of the war-torn city by the Hezbollah, a terrorist faction of fundamentalist Lebanese Shia Muslims with ties to Iran. Most had already been held for many months, and one, CIA Station Chief in Lebanon, William Buckley, was known to have been interrogated and tortured by his captors.

The President's attention had been turned irreversibly toward these seven men by events of just the previous several weeks. On June 14, TWA Flight 847 had been hijacked in Lebanon and the passengers all taken hostage. One young sailor, Robert Dean Stethem, had been brutally murdered and his body dumped on the airport tar-mac. Fourteen days later, the President met with relatives of the hostages in Chicago Heights, Illinois, to reassure them of our efforts to gain the release of their loved ones. Among the families present was that of Father Lawrence Martin Jenco, a Catholic missionary who was one of the seven "forgotten" hostages, as they were some-times popularly described in the press. They peppered Reagan with questions about what was being done for Jenco and the other six, as it was for the TWA hostages, who were close to being released. Reagan was visibly shaken and moved by the travails of all the fami-lies, but the Jencos' comments appeared to touch him in a special place. After the meeting, he said to me, "It's an awful thing that these parents and loved ones have to live with."

Reagan is a very sentimental man. In public, he took a hard line on policy, declaring the United States would never negotiate with terrorists—it was what he had to say, for hadn't he defeated President Jimmy Carter in 1980 partly with rhetoric denouncing the Democrat's inability to bring home the American hostages in Tehran and to deal decisively with the captors? However, his personal expe-riences with the hostages themselves and now with the new hostages' families softened him, just as he was always softened by the suffering or plight of an individual.

The day before Kimche visited my office, the President and Mrs. Reagan had visited the grave of Seaman Stethem at Arlington National Cemetery, and then gone to Andrews Air Force Base to greet the released TWA hostages as they arrived home. Anyone with him that day, as I was, could not have failed to see the emotion that overcame him both at the graveside and on the plane with the hostages. The arrival was supposed to be a quick, ten-minute cere-mony, but it stretched to half an hour or more as the President and First Lady lingered with the hostages, listening attentively and empathetically to descriptions of their ordeal.

Reagan's compassion was a quality that anyone would have to admire; it was genuine, human—what made him a warm and likable man. But it was not a sound basis for governance; it held the danger of leading him into labyrinths of policy devoid of logic or legitima-cy. The President is the steward of our larger interest, and to allow himself to be vulnerable to foreign exploitation of human suffering can be a serious flaw.

More than once I had tried to warn him of the consequences of such a weakness. "You know, Mr. President," I would say, "when you are portrayed by the hostages' relatives and others as extremely anguished about their loved ones, that can have the effect on terrorists of encouraging them, making it clear there is real leverage."

And he would reply, in reluctant but emphatic tones: "Well, I understand that. But I have a responsibility to these people, and I just can't ignore their suffering."

All this was on my mind when I went into the Oval Office for the regular 9:30 a.m. national security briefing a day or so after my meeting with Kimche. Nevertheless, I believed that the prospect of a genuine opening to Iran held sufficient potential to be worth examining, and that the President, too, would understand its geopolitical significance. I saw no reason to disbelieve or distrust Kimche on what he had said, although clearly Israeli interests and ours were not congruent. A cynical Israeli leader, for instance, could see an opportunity to damage our relations with Arab states—a high risk if this initiative were prematurely disclosed—as benefiting Israel. Apart from that, it was conceivable that Israel saw this channel as offering a way to exfiltrate Iranian Jews. I considered these and other plausible Israeli motives and concluded that they had to be kept in mind each step of the way, but that at this stage (prior to any mention of arms in the arrangement) Israel and the Iranians were risking more than we. Public exposure of the idea in July 1985 would have been far more damaging to them than to us.

When I reported Kimche's comments, the President was in fact interested and pleased at the idea that there was a chance of working toward nurturing an opposition element that could change the policies and ultimately even the government of Iran. "Well, that sure would be good," he said when I described this to him. But he was clearly more pleased at their offer to validate their bona fides by releasing the hostages. This aspect had a much more marked effect on his adrenaline level than the geopolitical upside of what we were discussing. "Gosh, that's great news," he said, perking up at its mention. "How would they do it, and how soon?"

He agreed that I should contact Kimche and give him the go-ahead for the release, leaving up to me the decision as to where and how it should be effected. I passed all this along to Cap Weinberger, who in turn discussed it with General Jack Vessey, chairman of the

Joint Chiefs of Staff. After examining the various options, they determined that it would be safest to have the men turned over to U.S. Navy forces on the beach north of Junieh, a location that would be easier for our military to access and control than anyplace inside or immediately around Beirut.

I called Kimche and relayed the President's message in the code we had established. The President would be pleased to engage with Israel's Iranian contacts, I said. As a precondition to opening any dialogue, however, we would need evidence of their genuine power in the form of a release of all our hostages. I told him where we wanted them, and then said: "After you report back to your intermediaries, let me know when this will be feasible and we will be there." He promised to get back to me and signed off.

I heard nothing more on the matter for a week or more, and thought little about it, for I was preoccupied at the time, as I would be for most of the rest of the year, with preparing for the first summit meeting between Reagan and the new Soviet leader, Mikhail Gorbachev. This was the subject that dominated the administration's foreign policy agenda for most of 1985. To my own mind, our relations with the Soviet Union and the opportunity to translate the huge investment of the past five years into results that would last were of paramount importance to the United States, and indeed to the world order. I concentrated the greater part of my energies that year to putting in place negotiating positions and a strategy that would assure success, particularly with regard to our wish to reduce the level of nuclear weapons for the first time in history.

On July 12, President Reagan entered Bethesda National Naval Hospital for a routine physical examination. Unexpectedly, the hospital visit became anything but routine. Doctors discovered a cancerous growth in his intestine that required immediate surgery. For eight hours on July 13, for the first time in history, the President transferred his powers, as outlined in the Twenty-fifth Amendment to the Constitution, to his Vice President, designating George Bush acting President for the duration of the operation and until the general anesthetic wore off. Vice President Bush was vacationing at his summer home in Kennebunkport, Maine, at the time, and I received a phone call from him when the news of Reagan's surgery was announced. Bush and I had a solid, personal relationship; he was calling now for my advice on whether he should return to Washington.

"Would my coming back look like I'm trying to pretend to be President?" he asked, worriedly. "Or does my staying up here look like I'm too blasé?"

"Mr. Vice President," I said, "I don't see any alarming clouds on the horizon that could require your presence here. And if they come up, the communications links are good enough to enable us to get your decisions until you're back in the White House."

He agreed, and remained in Kennebunkport.

Meanwhile, the same day the President was in surgery, Mike Ledeen came to see me in my office once again with some unsettling news. He said that an emissary of Israeli Prime Minister Shimon Peres, an arms merchant named Adolf Schwimmer, had arrived in town with a message from the Iranians he and Kimche were dealing with. Upon further consideration, it seemed, they had decided that as they demonstrated their bona fides by releasing our hostages, they also wanted proof of our good faith in this transaction. Since they were civilians who could not act against the Ayatollah's government without support from the military, they wanted U.S. weapons, the only currency that would be persuasive to the Iranian army of the United States' serious intentions toward the Iranian opposition. Specifically what they wanted, Ledeen said, were 100 TOW missiles, state-of-the-art antitank weapons made in the United States.

I was sorry but not surprised at this addition to my earlier agreement with Kimche concerning the hostages. Clearly our lives would have been made easier by a unilateral release of the hostages by the other side. And yet, as I thought back over other coups and power grabs that had been mounted over the past generation in the Middle East, it was clear to me that strength in arms had been the common factor in their success. There are no primaries, party caucuses or nominating conventions in the Middle East. There, might still makes right. Consequently, I believed it was important to explore the opening, and it seemed reasonable to expect that any coup faction worthy of the name would need the support of the army.

Ledeen told me that the chief Iranian contact was a man named Manucher Ghorbanifar, described by the Israelis as a businessman working with an opposition cell of pragmatists in the Iranian government, including one or two advisers to the speaker of the Iranian parliament, Hashemi Rafsanjani. Mike described Ghorbanifar enthusiastically to me as a "genius," and "a mastermind of Iranian

politics." I couldn't have known then how wildly off-base his char-
acterizations were, how poor his judgment, and that we were about
to head into a covenant with a man who was a pathological liar and,
when all was said and done, a self-serving criminal, not a patriot.

On that July day, I told Mike I would have to study the matter of
the TOW missiles. The next day, I cabled George Shultz, who was
traveling in Australia, informing him of the request for the TOWs. I
told him I thought we ought to be wary, since the whole thing could
be an elaborate con simply aimed at extracting weapons from us.
But I also said I did not feel we should simply close off the entire
possibility of a dialogue with the Iranians without probing a little
further. "We could make a tentative show of interest without commitment and see what happened," I cabled, "or we could just walk
away. On balance I tend to favor going ahead."

George cabled back his essential agreement: "I do not think we
could justify turning our backs on the prospect of gaining the release
of the other seven hostages and perhaps developing an ability to renew
ties with Iran under a more sensible regime—especially when presented to us through the Prime Minister of Israel." It was a message rather
at variance with all Shultz's later protestations that he had firmly
opposed the Iran initiative from the very outset, and it has always
galled me that he later refused to acknowledge his early support.

The President was still recuperating in the hospital, and I had not
yet wanted to bother him. Nancy Reagan, who was fiercely protective of her husband, discouraged the idea of any visitors for a number of days after the operation. I agreed; there was nothing to report
that couldn't wait. I did talk to Cap Weinberger on the secure phone
and met briefly with the Vice President to explain the new development. On July 18, Don Regan called me to say I should come in to
give the President a foreign policy briefing. I went in that morning
and, with Regan in the room, first brought the President up to date
on U.S.-Soviet arms control negotiations.

The President was sitting up in his hospital bed, in good spirits
and listening attentively, although he still looked a little weak. I
wrapped up the arms control material in about 15 minutes. Then I
told him of the new twist in the Iranian matter, the request for
TOWs. His face seemed to fall and he pursed his lips.

"What do you think?" he asked me.

I went over the pros and cons as I had in my cable to Shultz. At the end, I said: "Arms will be essential to any ultimate effort to change the government, but at this point, I don't think we know enough about the people we're dealing with to take that risk.

Reagan thought for a few seconds. Then he nodded. "We can't do it," he said. The U.S. authority to sell arms is precisely prescribed in law. An exception in a situation such as we were considering would require that the President make a "Finding," a special presidential order justifying a covert operation deemed important to the national interest. The law also required that the Congress be notified, although the time limit for such notification was not prescribed at the time.

But it was clear the President was disappointed. He had hoped the hostages were going to be released; apparently, it was one of the first things he had asked about when he awakened from his surgery. And now he didn't quite want to let go of the idea that they could still be gotten out.

He said he thought the Iranians' arguments about needing a show of good faith in order to win army backing seemed plausible. "I'm not put off by the idea," he said, "but we can't do it. We don't have any firsthand experience with these people, and until we do, it wouldn't be wise to begin shipping weapons to people we don't know.

"But tell them again," he said, "we do want to talk, we want to exchange our thoughts with them, and we'll work toward the day when our confidence in each other can grow."

The next day—Friday, July 19—I went to the hospital at 10 a.m. for a national security brief. George was scheduled to come in at 11. The day before, I had told the President of Shultz's cabled reaction to the latest Iran feeler. I'd termed it "cautious support" for at least taking the matter one step further.

Reagan had apparently been thinking about that matter overnight. Now he asked me if there weren't some way "to help these guys you were talking about." I encouraged him to ask George's opinion.

Shultz had already called me twice on the private line before even setting out for the hospital to say that he had begun to have misgivings about the idea set forth in my cable. When he arrived at the hospital, however, he had other issues he wanted to discuss with the President. But before he left, Reagan asked him what he thought about the idea I had raised. Shultz's reply wasn't emphatic, but he made it clear that he saw serious risks in it and had reservations.

The next day, I went to breakfast at the State Department thinking we might discuss the matter, but it hardly came up.

The President left the hospital that same afternoon, July 20. The entire White House staff turned out on the South Lawn to welcome him as his helicopter landed. As we walked through the ground floor of the residence, he asked me, discreetly, to "get the guys together to talk about that matter you mentioned at the hospital."

I scheduled a meeting of the National Security Planning Group for the following Monday right after the morning brief. The NSPG is made up of the Secretaries of State and Defense, the Director of the Central Intelligence Agency, the Chairman of the Joint Chiefs of Staff, the Vice President, and the National Security Adviser. No assistants attend, and no notes are taken.

In the days that followed, we met several times in the residence, where the President was still recuperating. Present at those meetings were, variously, the President, the Vice President, myself, Don Regan, George Shultz, Cap Weinberger, CIA Director William Casey, and General Jack Vessey, Chairman of the Joint Chiefs of Staff. In the course of these meetings, I outlined to all of them the Iran initiative from its origins with Kimche's visit to me through the current Iranian request for TOW missiles.

Most vocal, immediately, in opposition to the idea of sending any arms to Iran was Weinberger. It was out of the question, he said, maintaining that the President would be running an enormous risk, that any shipment of arms was probably illegal. He was categorically opposed to it.

Less vehement but also opposed to the arms shipment idea was Shultz. Also voicing doubts about the arms sales, albeit more mildly, were Don Regan and George Bush. On the other side of the issue sat Bill Casey.

Unlike his predecessors at the CIA, who had viewed their job as being one of providing objective analysis rather than making policy recommendations, Casey was never shy about saying what he thought was the right course of action on any issue. He was a self-assured, well-read, devoted Reaganite. But as early as 1982, and certainly by the spring of 1984, it had become clear to me that Casey, convinced that Ronald Reagan lacked the passion for foreign affairs that would lead him to tackle issues on that front decisively, and believing that the palace guard—the famous troika of Jim Baker,

Mike Deaver and Ed Meese—was shielding the President from difficult issues, began to act more autonomously, taking on the responsibility for accomplishing things he believed the President would
agree with but would not do himself.

Gruff but affable, Casey had a very low regard for Shultz, thinking him to be severely lacking in depth when it came to history and
to understanding international politics, especially in the Middle East.
As for Weinberger, while Casey liked him and saw in him an ideological soulmate, he also thought him naive and untutored in the
ways of clandestine political warfare. And on the law in this matter,
he thought Cap was just dead wrong.

Casey believed, in short, that sending arms to an Iranian opposition cell was both legal and sound policy. "There's a strong basis for
believing that there is an opposition element there in Tehran, and
history tells us that governments in the Middle East often change
through this very kind of aggregation of power by some opposition
elements," he said. "It's not without many, many precedents. It's
just a question of whether or not these people are real and can do the
job."

Looking back on these meetings now, I fault Casey for not having
given me, the President or the other members of the NSC any warning, any indication about the sort of person we were dealing with in
Ghorbanifar. For it turned out that the CIA had had earlier dealings
with him. He had approached the agency about becoming an operative for them a year earlier, and had been given a lie detector test
which he failed with flying colors. This is not to say that effective
coup plotters don't need to be shrewd, tough and street smart. They
do. But they must also be intelligent, and have a political platform
worthy of the name. Ghorbanifar had neither.

Yet Casey, who knew all this, never came forward with the information when it might have made a difference in how we proceeded.
I assume that he was sufficiently impressed both by Ghorbanifar and
by the Israeli recommendation to keep the truth to himself; clearly,
he saw the prospect of subverting Ayatollah Khomeini. And, at the
end of the day, he could always say, "It was McFarlane's idea."

The normal course to follow when our country receives a proposition such as we did from the Israelis in July is to refer it to the CIA
to explore, both in order to get covert operations professionals
involved and to avoid political interference in quasi-legal activities.

That had, indeed, been my inclination when David Kimche presented the original proposal to me. But he had specifically asked that the CIA not be involved. He had said that the Mossad was not involved, and that if the CIA were, the Mossad would inevitably find out and cause problems within the Israeli government. Instead, he said, Prime Minister Peres had chosen to set up a cell outside the government to handle the matter. He did, however, say that the Israeli foreign minister, Yitzhak Shamir, had requested that Shultz be informed and involved, as he was.

In this case, I doubt that if I had referred this matter to the CIA, that agency professionals would have recommended proceeding, even though their national intelligence officer for the region, Graham Fuller, had authored the SNIE that had urged just such a course 30 days earlier. Indeed, in the wake of the Church and Pike investigations of 1975-76, the operational side of the agency had atrophied to such an extent as to be virtually incapable of and generally unwilling to undertake more than very limited forms of political work. In this case, though, a refusal to do anything would have had a beneficial effect.

It may, however, have been precisely because he knew that no one in the agency would want to undertake an operation in Iran even with the best of interlocutors that Casey, who was instinctively inclined to act against radical groups (and who, at this point, may already have known that he was dying of brain cancer, making him even more determined to accomplish as much as possible) agreed, even urged, that the Iran initiative be handled by the White House.

It is important to underscore that it is occasionally essential for the White House to handle sensitive foreign issues, primarily if the foreign party insists upon this. Specifically, if we are asking a foreign party—be they Chinese, Russians or Iranians—to adopt a fundamentally different course in a given area, we are in effect asking them to take risks. Their politburos and revolutionary command councils often include men who aspire to the leader's job. Coup plotters cannot afford to be exposed before they are ready to act.

Related to this reason for secrecy is the other side's need to know that we are truly committed to it. Dictators tend to believe that only the President of the United States can make commitments for our country. Before going down a dangerous path, therefore, they will almost always insist that the White House be involved.

The fact remains, however, that in this case, the White House involvement was a mistake. The other side was simply insufficiently organized and too weak to act. It still is.

At the July meetings the general consensus was not to act on the Iranian arms request. The President, however, urged me to remain in touch with the Israelis and their contacts; he thought it important that we keep talking to them.

That was the message I conveyed back to Schwimmer and Kimche through Mike Ledeen later that week. Reagan wanted to keep the channel open. But a U.S. shipment of arms, I said, was a no go.

—

The next weekend, July 27 and 28, Reagan went to Camp David, the rustic Presidential retreat in the Catoctin Mountains of Maryland. That Saturday, I was in the office as usual, working on a laundry list of issues, when the secure phone rang.

"Hello, Bud," said the familiar, throaty voice on the other end. The President was calling.

He had been thinking about that "Israeli thing," he said, and the more he thought about it, the more he liked it. "Couldn't you use some imagination and try to find a way to make it work?" he asked.

"You remember, Mr. President, your Secretary of State and Secretary of Defense were opposed to this," I reminded him.

"I know," he said, "but I look at it differently. I want to find a way to do this."

I said I would think about it.

"Please do," he said.

—

On August 2, David Kimche came to see me again in Washington.

The Israelis had received my response via Schwimmer, he said, but he wanted to hear everything from me personally. "Are you sure about this?" he asked.

"Yes, that's the President's position," I replied.

"Well," David said, "what if *we* ship these weapons?"

"David, that's a distinction without a difference," I said. "The issue is whether or not these people are of sufficient power and inclination to get results."

"All right. You say you're not going to do it. But if we do it, can we buy new weapons from you?"

"Israel will be able to buy weapons from the United States forever," I said. "You know that. So that's not the issue."

"Nevertheless, I am under instructions to determine whether, if we go ahead with this, we will be able to replace the weapons from the United States."

"I'll get an official response for you," I said.

I told the President the thrust of the new proposition the following Monday morning. "Good," he said. "Get the guys together."

———

The next morning, I talked the matter through with George Shultz by secure telephone. A meeting at the White House had already been scheduled an hour hence to allow Cap Weinberger and Jack Vessey to brief the President on proposed changes to our nuclear targeting doctrine. The Vice President was to attend that session, and I thought we could deal with the new Israeli proposal at the same time. No staff subordinates attended. We gathered at the west end of the second floor of the residence, in the hallway beneath the rose window that looks out over the press office and the colonnade.

I reported on Kimche's visit and his request for U.S. replacements for any weapons Israel might ship to Iran. He was asking, in effect, for approval for just such a shipment.

Weinberger voiced his opposition emphatically at once. He repeated his concerns that even if a third country shipped American weapons, the law required that this third-country transfer be reported to Congress. Earlier, on the phone, Shultz had also been against an Israeli transfer. He worried that it would inevitably take on the appearance of an arms-for-hostages deal, which would contravene our public position to embargo all arms sales to Iran and, if it ever came out, would damage the President dramatically.

Casey was not present at this meeting, but he had previously challenged Weinberger on the matter of legality. "I don't think it's illegal, Cap," he had said on one occasion. "We do a lot of things under CIA authority with the President's approval. You know that." He believed that the President's approval would constitute a covert action Finding that would make the transfer legal (much later, in November 1986, Attorney General Ed Meese would tell me the same thing: that even a onetime oral authorization by the President was sufficient to legitimize subsequent actions taken pursuant to that authority).

As for the arms-for-hostages risk, Casey had thought the initiative was worth a try regardless.

Regan and Bush were both mildly supportive of an Israeli shipment, terming it a reasonable risk by a third party. "It's Israel, not we, doing this," was a theme that was echoed by various participants.

For my part, I was wary, but not wary enough. Although I saw the real risk of the Iranians' merely tricking us, or the Israelis, into an arms sale and never coming through on their end of the bargain, I maintained rock-solid confidence in Kimche's assurances about the people involved. I was inclined to believe that it was worth the risk to allow Israel to go ahead with a one-time shipment if it achieved a real opening to this strategically vital country, countered the Soviet influence there, and created an opportunity to work toward a change in the Iranian government.

We tend to forget that many of those places where democracy has never been tried and may never be tried are extremely important to us, as well as to our friends and enemies. Iran, in 1985, was clearly one of those places. In that period, the Soviet Union was still our determined rival for power, control of resources and political influence on the world stage. Moscow had seized every opportunity in the previous 15 years to promote its interests wherever an unstable climate existed by identifying a faction willing or eager to adopt the totalitarian Leninist model and backing it, with success from Angola to Ethiopia to Vietnam to Nicaragua. Now Soviet troops had taken over in Afghanistan, just a frontier away from Iran. There were no guarantees in 1985 that Iran was not next on Moscow's list. So I was willing to go ahead with the initiative, and said so. Yet despite this rationale, I recognize that we should never have considered sending arms to anyone in a radical state that we knew was sponsoring terrorism and holding hostages until we were absolutely certain about the people involved—specifically that they were opposed to the government's policies and in a position to act decisively. And on this we had no first-hand basis for confidence.

Our discussion that day was spirited, vivid, forceful. The disagreements were sharp, and with a split in the group, President Reagan did not make a decision. He never did like to decide things whenever there were people in the room who were arguing. He didn't want to disappoint anyone to his face. However, his own inclination to try to keep this initiative on track was not difficult to discern. He repeated his earlier statement that he would prefer not to have our own weapons or inventory involved, and seemed to fixate on the way Casey stressed that it would be Israel taking action, not the United States.

"I think we must do everything we can to support people like this," the President said. But he ended the meeting without reaching a conclusion. "All right, I'll think about it."

———

A little after noon of the same day, I was called to the Oval Office again. Unaware of the subject to be discussed, I hadn't brought the notes I had taken during the Kimche meeting, but it turned out this was what the President wanted to talk about. I went back to my office and fetched them.

At the President's request, I ran through the Israeli proposal again. "In short, Mr. President, the Israelis are proposing that they ship weapons from their stores to opposition elements in Iran as needed to develop support and cohesion within a group that aspires to succeed Ayatollah Khomeini," I said. "In addition, they want your assurance that if arms are transferred, they will be able to purchase replacements from the U.S."

If he chose to authorize this plan, I said, I believed he ought to impose certain restrictions on the types of weapons sold: for instance, no major "end items" (Pentagonese for large equipment such as tanks, aircraft, or ships), and no quantities sufficient to affect the military balance in the war with Iraq.

The President brooded quietly for a few moments. He pressed his fingertips together reflexively and stared at the carpet. Finally, he looked up. "Well, I've thought about it," he said, "and I want to go ahead with it. I think that's the right thing to do."

"All right, Mr. President," I said. "I want to remind you, though, that George and Cap were opposed to this. You remember that?"

"Yes, I understand how they feel. But I have to think about what's at stake here. I believe it's the right thing to do."

"Fine," I said. "I'll notify the others."

———

I was convening a secure conference call later that day with the Vice President, Shultz, Cap, Casey, Regan and Vessey to discuss contingent measures that might be taken to apply pressure to renegade Libyan leader Moammar Gadhafi. As that discussion wrapped up, I brought up the morning conversation about the Israeli proposal. The President, I announced, had approved Israel's going ahead, with the one or two restrictions I had suggested.

Shultz was chagrined at the President's decision and grumbled that the whole thing was "a bad idea." I urged him to call the President and express his views once again, and he said he would think about it.

Weinberger was even more vexed. "It's a terrible idea," he railed. "Awful."

"Well, Cap, you ought to call the President and say so," I suggested.

"I may do that," he replied curtly, and hung up.

Later, when the Iran initiative became public and turned to scandal, both these men would deny having had this discussion or having known the details of the Iran initiative as it developed. Of course, it became evident—as recorded in Weinberger's handwritten notes and the notes of Shultz's executive assistant, Charles Hill—that they had both deceived the Congress under oath concerning the fact that they had been fully informed. I always thought it odd that as Weinberger issued his denials, no one seized upon the glaring illogic in his claims of having been left in the dark. The Israelis were asking for replacement weapons, and *I* certainly had no weapons to supply them. There is only one source from which they could have hoped to replenish their stock of arms: the Pentagon, and it was presided over by Caspar Weinberger.

It would have been inconceivable for me to have made commitments to Israel on my own that would have led immediately to their placing requests with the Pentagon. Clearly at that point, Weinberger would have refused to honor such requests unless the President had sanctioned them. Apart from the logic of my explanation—with which the Tower Board, the Joint Congressional Investigating Committee and the Independent Counsel came to agree—my version of events and especially the fact that I had kept Weinberger fully informed was finally, albeit ironically, vindicated by Weinberger himself. In the meticulous notes he had kept of all meetings and telephone conversations with me and the President, which he withheld from all of the investigating bodies, he had recorded my invitations to him in August 1985 to send a Pentagon representative to meetings in Europe with Ghorbanifar and the Israelis—graphic evidence, in his own hand, of his knowledge, and his perjury.

Soon after my conversation with the President, I notified David Kimche of the President's decision. I also informed him that as I was soon to be heading out to California with Reagan for the congressional recess, the two contacts in my office for Iran matters would be my deputy, John Poindexter, who had been in several of the meetings with the NSPG when the issue was discussed, and my staffer in charge of counter terrorism, Lieutenant Colonel Oliver North. I authorized Mike Ledeen to convey messages as well.

We left for the Reagans' ranch near Santa Barbara aboard Air Force One on August 11, 1985. I was preoccupied with South Africa; there was growing public and congressional pressure for economic sanctions against the Pretoria government, and our policy toward the country of apartheid needed concentration and development. As for the Iran initiative, it was in Israeli hands now, and the U.S. had no active role to play for the moment. As the press of other events crowded upon me, I filed it far at the back of my mind.

Chapter 3

ARMS FOR HOSTAGES

Ollie North was calling, his voice, as usual, full of energy and urgency.

"Bud, we think Weir is coming out this weekend," he said.

"That's good, Ollie."

"We have a hostage support team in Europe ready to meet him, get him through a physical examination in Germany. Then they'll bring him back to Norfolk and sequester him for a couple days of debriefing."

"All right," I said. "I'm going to be down in the Shenandoah Valley. Call me when you know something."

I hung up and sat for a moment, thinking . I could not feel as upbeat as North at the prospect of Weir's release. The Rev. Benjamin Weir was a Presbyterian missionary who had been held captive in Beirut since May 8, 1984. Certainly obtaining his freedom after such a long captivity was gratifying, but I was disturbed by the manner in which it had come about. Try as I might to cast the best light on the developments of the last month, I had to concede that it looked unhappily as though we were heading down the road of swapping arms for hostages. Nothing more, at least not so far. And nothing less.

Mike Ledeen had come out to see me in mid August while I was in Santa Barbara with the President. He had come from a meeting in Germany with the Israelis—Kimche, Schwimmer and another arms dealer named Yaakov Nimrodi—and Ghorbanifar and some of his people. The Israelis, he said, were ready to ship 100 TOW missiles to Iran. The Iranians, for their part, would see to the release of one hostage—and I was to choose which one.

This news was mortifying. It was far from what I had hoped for after my first talk with Kimche, and a clear sign that matters were unfolding in unpredictable fashion. Moreover, it distressed me to be put in the position of playing God, of deciding who would be rescued and who would be left behind.

I told Mike we would take hostage William Buckley first, knowing that because he was the Beirut CIA station chief and had report-
edly been tortured, he was the hostage about whom the President
was most urgently concerned.

It wasn't until after Labor Day, when we were all back in
Washington, that I heard any more on this front. I asked North to
inquire about the status of the Israeli transfer, which Mike had
reported as imminent. North, a hard-charging staffer with energy to
burn and a passion for causes which at the time I found only
admirable, was actively involved in the Iran matter and with Ledeen
had met several times with the Israelis and Ghorbanifar. Now he
reported back to me in somewhat garbled fashion that there was a
hitch in the TOW transfer, that the Iranians and Israelis had argued
about the number of missiles to be shipped. But, he said, the Israelis
thought the Iranians would ultimately agree to 100.

A bell should have gone off for me right then; I should have seen
the prospect of getting suckered into nothing more than a rug merchant exchange. But we are all brilliant when armed with hindsight.
At the time, I simply did not focus as critically as I should have on
the potential significance of what Ollie was telling me.

Then came the message that Buckley's physical condition was too
poor to allow him to be moved, and that another hostage would have
to be selected for release instead. After thinking about it, I picked
Weir, because he was the longest-held hostage and, truthfully,
because his family had been the most loudly and persistently critical
of us. I thought if we brought him home, it might enable us to work
in an atmosphere of less vulnerability to Iranian demands.

Ollie called again on Sunday morning, September 15. Jonny and
I were at our cabin in New Market, Virginia.

Weir had been released, North said. He was with Reg
Bartholomew, our ambassador in Beirut, and arrangements were
being made to fly him to Wiesbaden, Germany. Only one snag.

"We want to tell Mrs. Weir, but we're afraid she's going to resist the
idea of this two-or-three-day debrief. We think you ought to call her."

I agreed, but first I called the President.

"Weir's coming out," I said.

"Golly, that's great. Glad to hear it," Reagan answered. "What
about the others?"

"We only got one," I said, and walked him through the chronology of events that had transpired. "We're a little concerned that the news of Weir's release will provoke a response from his family," I said.

"Let me know if you want me to do anything," he offered graciously.

Mrs. Weir was a little tougher call to handle. Upon hearing her husband was free, she went into effusions of relief and happiness, but soon stiffened when I told her we wanted to debrief her husband for a few days.

"I'm not going to be manipulated by you people," she asserted. "You've made a mess of things up to now, and I see no reason why I should cooperate with you at all."

She had always been a difficult person to deal with, sharply challenging the administration for what she considered its wrongheaded view toward Arabs and Palestinians generally. It was our misguided policy, she charged, that had led to the capture of the hostages, and nothing else.

Now she and I went through two or three exchanges, she having none of the notion that there ought to be anything but an immediate, open reunion with her husband, that they were free agents and could do as they pleased. As it happens, I have a tendency to get fairly firm after a few rounds of this sort of thing, and finally I found my voice rising as I spoke to her.

"Mrs. Weir, I understand how you feel. However, there are a lot of lives at stake here besides Ben's. You and I have a responsibility to them, too. Now this is what we intend to do. I hope that you'll see fit to stay with us on this, but that's your decision to make. Is that clear?"

There was a pause. Then she said, "All right, I'll get ready to go and we'll talk about this later." In the end, I suppose she won the skirmish. She never did make any promises.

On the other hand, we did manage to debrief her husband without any publicity. Yet what he had to say was deeply discouraging. He knew little about the other hostages. His assignment from his captors, he said, was to tell us that they insisted upon the immediate release of 17 Shia Muslim prisoners, known as the Dawa prisoners, jailed in Kuwait for terrorist acts including the bombing of the U.S. Embassy there. It was a hopeless situation. The President had publicly declared on numerous occasions that he would never negotiate for the release of those prisoners with American hostages' lives.

It wasn't until the next day that Ollie told me the other bad news that accompanied the Weir release. When I came into work on Monday morning, he informed me that the Israelis had transferred an additional 408 missiles to the Iranians. "The price," as he put it, "went up."

The President, when I passed this on to him at the national security briefing, seemed far less disturbed by it than I.

"That's a different number than we thought, isn't it?" he remarked.

"Yes, it is," I said. "And I believe it's a bad signal. Plus, we didn't get everybody out."

Yet Reagan was obviously pleased that we had managed to obtain at least one hostage. That meant a great deal to him. To me, it was more significant that we had just received a rather dramatic signal that we were being duped. I had a sharp sense that this deal did not match the image Kimche had painted of a serious group of pragmatic people devoted to changing Iranian policy who were in a position to release the hostages as a means of demonstrating their good faith. Rather, it sounded to me like an attempt to leverage us by means of the very high value that Reagan put on the hostages.

Still, I must concede that I wasn't yet absolutely convinced of that. I rationalized that it was plausible that our cabal of pragmatists was not demonstrating bad faith at all; that, rather, they found themselves subservient to a cell of army generals who were demanding more weapons than originally agreed upon. And I reminded myself once more that matters seldom go the way one thinks they will in the Middle East. So once again, I sent the Iran file to the back of my mind—not yet fully cognizant that I was storing away a ticking time-bomb.

———

The fall of 1985 was an extraordinarily busy time, crowded with activity and preparations for the November summit between Reagan and Gorbachev. The week after Weir's release, the President was scheduled to go to the United Nations to attend a meeting of the General Assembly. Later, he was to meet with Soviet Foreign Minister Eduard Shevardnadze, a visit requiring a great deal of staff work and preparation. Apart from that, I spent nearly all my time chairing meetings on our arms control position and on four major addresses we wanted the President to deliver in support of our goals at the summit. Shultz and I were scheduled to travel to Moscow in early November, in advance of the summit, to meet with Gorbachev, confirm the agenda and hopefully obtain his prior agreement to the outcome of the arms control sessions. In the meantime, the President was to meet with a dozen or more visiting heads of state in the period from late September through early November.

And in the middle of all this, there was the *Achille Lauro*.

This Italian cruise ship was hijacked in the Mediterranean on October 7 by four terrorists who murdered a wheelchair-bound American citizen, Leon Klinghoffer, then cold-bloodedly tossed his body, wheelchair and all, into the sea. The hijackers managed to escape and make their way to Egypt, where they boarded a flight to Tunisia. But my NSC staff, led by John Poindexter and Oliver North, hatched a plan to intercept their plane in the air and force it to land in Sicily, where the terrorists were arrested. It was a moment of soaring glory in the President's war against terrorism, a euphoric victory that lifted the spirit of the administration, and the nation.

In the midst of that crisis, however, I had a disturbing visit from Mike Ledeen. A self-appointed guru on Italy, having lived in Rome for many years, Mike came in ostensibly to discuss the *Achille Lauro* hijacking. But soon enough he was telling me that he had had yet another exchange with Ghorbanifar, whose contacts in Iran had told him that the generals were in need of some very sophisticated hardware. Specifically, they were requesting Phoenix missiles, air-to-air missiles fired from F-14 fighter jets at enemy aircraft. These were at the time the most sophisticated air-to-air missiles in the world. The loss of one, especially to the Soviets, would have been extremely damaging. More's the point, this upping of the ante took us well beyond the original need to validate our bona fides. This was extortion on a grand scale. In addition, they were asking for Harpoon and HARM (Hypervelocity Anti-Radiation Missile) missiles, the former an anti-ship missile, and the latter a prime anti-radar missile.

I listened to Ledeen in disbelief. What he was describing was out of the question. When he finished, I exploded.

"Mike, this is just nuts, forget about it," I shouted. "You've got to be crazy to even suggest such a thing. We will not have any part of this. You can go back and tell them emphatically that this is not on, it will never be on, that our purposes here are to engage in a political dialogue, not to supply the Iranian military!"

"All right, all right." Mike rose and sidled to the door. "I had to tell you, that's all. I promised I would," he said, and got out.

My earlier concerns were beginning to blossom into full-blown doubts. More than a month into the Iran initiative, we had yet to make any sort of real contact with the supposed pragmatists in Tehran, there had been no further indications that any more hostages were going to be freed, and the demands for weaponry were becoming ever more extravagant. It didn't take a genius to see the trend that was developing. I had a distinctly bad feeling about the whole enterprise and came near to shutting it down. Why I did not do so at this point is a question I will always ask myself. Sure, I was tired, I was seriously thinking of leaving government, and I was still occupied from morning till night with a thousand and one matters, all of more pressing concern. But perhaps most of all, where Iran was concerned, I still had hope. And there is no more powerful blinding force.

———

Israeli Defense Minister Yitzhak Rabin called me in Geneva, on an open line. He had a problem, he said, and needed some help. I could imagine what he was referring to. I said I'd have one of my people in Washington call him.

Rabin had visited me at the White House a couple of days earlier, while he was stateside for the annual negotiations of Israel's military assistance package. He hadn't mentioned any imminent plans to ship more arms to Iran, but he did want to know whether President Reagan was still in support of the initiative and would still replenish any Israeli arms that were transferred to Tehran. I had assured him that this was still the case.

Now from New York he was evidently overseeing another shipment. But preoccupied as I was in Geneva with the summit and all its attendant turmoil, the labor and the fanfare, I could hardly afford to take time out to deal with this, nor could I handle the matter very effectively on an open long-distance line. I tried to reach Poindexter. He was unavailable, so I asked for Ollie, and told him to call Rabin, then let me know what was going on.

The next day, Ollie called back. The Israelis were planning a shipment of 80 Hawk missiles, he said, but the logistics had become bollixed up. "They don't even have planes big enough to carry these things, though I think I can solve that problem," he reported.

They also did not have proper clearances through Portugal, where they hoped to land in transit to Tehran. He said he thought it might be necessary for me to place a call to expedite those clearances. Finally, he said, if everything came together, the Iranians had purportedly agreed that all the remaining hostages would be released in a phased fashion over the next few days. There would be three sorties of two planes each delivering the Hawks, and as each sortie passed the point of no return between Portugal and Iran, two hostages would be released to the U.S. ambassador in Beirut.

This I reported to the President the next morning before the first summit session. Only Don Regan was in the room with us. The President was pleased and hopeful, although I cautioned him that there were many risks that events would not unfold as described. He nodded. "Well, I hope it works," he said. "Keep me informed."

I imparted the same information to Shultz privately later at his suite at the Intercontinental Hotel. He was dubious. "You're skating on thin ice here," he said. "This is very high risk, could do a lot of damage to the President."

"George, you ought to say so, if you think so," I said. "Tell the President." I was, effectively, telling him to fish or cut bait. But he evidently was not ready to fish. He was not going to interfere, he said.

I informed Cap of the developments by telephone, after briefing him on the summit and on how well I thought the President had done that day, how he was not going to give away the store (in spite, I thought wryly, of the fears to that effect he had expressed in a letter to President Reagan leaked to *The New York Times* on the day we had left Washington). After hearing of the Israeli shipments and the planned delivery of the hostages, Weinberger began to rag at me. "It sounds very unlikely to me that things will happen that way," he said skeptically. "It's a bad business." But when I urged him to talk to the President, he backed off just as George had done.

It's reasonable to ask why these two men, who opposed the shipping of weapons to Iran so strongly, did not speak out against the Iran initiative more forcefully and continually. It's not hard for me to imagine the answer.

It is difficult to tell the President that he is wrong. As a Cabinet officer, if you have done it once, you tend to tell yourself: "He knows what I think. Why nag him? He was elected, not I." The Secretary of State may tell himself that he has an obligation to stay on to tackle the myriad other problems that confront the United States all over the globe. I must say that both Shultz and Weinberger, and particularly the latter, were deeply loyal to President Reagan and would have done virtually anything for him within the law. They knew that possible successors would not necessarily feel the same way. They profoundly wanted for the President to succeed, they wanted to help him succeed, and they also wanted to share in his success. At the end of the day, this was not a matter of sufficient import to either of them to prompt their resignations. I am sure that if Shultz had threatened to resign, this move would have convinced the President to halt the Iran initiative. But the central responsibility for initiating it was undeniably mine, and I am equally sure that if I had not left the government, as I was soon to do, I could have brought the initiative to a close by orchestrating the persistent resistance of these two Cabinet officers and feeding it into the Oval Office. And so the fault for all that subsequently happened was most heavily my own.

———

The Geneva summit was a success. After three days of complex, contentious and often heated talks, Reagan and Gorbachev reached an unprecedented agreement to reduce each of their nation's nuclear arsenals by 50 percent. After the weeks, months and years of backbreaking preparations, and the arduous 20-hour days of the event itself, it was a triumph that vindicated all the elaborate, exhausting effort.

We wrapped up in Geneva on a high note of accord and celebration. Jonny had flown out on the government plane that would carry us on my leg of the post-summit "victory lap"—a series of high-level briefings to our European and Japanese allies on the summit results. It was a generous gesture on Reagan's part to include the spouses, generally left behind on trips and indisputably neglected in the normal course of our turbocharged, 80-hours-a-week existences. Having had the Gulf Stream all to herself on the trip across the Atlantic, Jonny had arrived in Geneva bubbling like a little girl about the pampered treatment she had received: the door-to-door service, the vintage wine and the sterling silver, the bed with the turned-down sheets. As we headed across the airport tarmac the next day for our flight to Rome on the same plane, I glanced at her impishly. "I'm surprised it doesn't have a new name across its nose—the Jonny-Lou," I teased.

In Rome, I made the rounds of scheduled meetings with the Italian Prime Minister, Pope John Paul II, and various other officials to discuss the summit. In the midst of this activity, I received a message to call Oliver North.

The Portuguese were not allowing the Israelis to land. I called the foreign minister in Lisbon and requested the necessary clearances on behalf of the President of the United States. He agreed to grant them, we chatted politely, exchanged greetings, and said goodbye.

The Iran initiative thus tugged at my attention for only a few minutes in the course of a period of extraordinary, highly-concentrated and extremely absorbing activity. It absorbed a total of perhaps 20 minutes over the three weeks spanning the summit, the briefings in Rome, a weekend at British Prime Minister Margaret Thatcher's country home of Chequers, to Thanksgiving and beyond. I could never have guessed then how thoroughly it would come to dominate my attention and my life later, after I thought I had done with it. I could not have known how minutely every moment I had spent on it would be scrutinized, analyzed, investigated and interpreted, how my actions would be dissected and described by people who had been neither party nor witness to them. We think we can recognize history while we are living it, but fate, perhaps, is another matter and much less distinct in design.

I had been thinking for some time, for manifold and complex reasons I will go into later, of leaving government, and by October 1985 had reached a final decision to resign my position once the summit with Gorbachev was concluded. The day after I arrived back in Washington from Europe, I flew out to California, where the President was to spend the Thanksgiving holidays, and handed him my resignation.

The President was as pained as I at the prospect of my departure, but, since I couched my reasons in personal and family terms, he felt obliged to accept it. A year before, when I had offered to resign, he had said that he found me to be the only truly indispensable man he'd ever known and that he would only consider my resignation if I felt I had to leave in order to spend more time with my family. Now he had to honor my request.

Shultz and I had already discussed potential successors to my post and had agreed to promote my deputy, John Poindexter, when the discussion came up with the President. I called John to tell him of this when I got back to my office in Washington. He, meanwhile, had some more discouraging news for me: The Hawk shipment, it appeared, had gone completely, resoundingly awry. The Israelis had not only shipped the wrong type of missiles, but the ones they had sent were stamped with the Star of David, hardly the most auspicious symbol to be sitting on the tarmac in Muslim Iran. The Iranians were infuriated, believing themselves to have been not only cheated, but insulted as well. Not surprisingly, no hostages had been released.

Before I left the White House for good, I now knew, I had to try to turn off the Iran arms deals. In my last President's Daily Brief, I informed Reagan of my thinking .

"You should know, Mr. President, that this is not working ," I told him. "Our hopes at the beginning of this were to be talking to Iranian politicians and to have a political agenda. It has ended up that we are talking to arms merchants, with no apparent prospect of establishing a political agenda.

"I think you ought to review this matter once again with your Cabinet officers."

"OK," the President agreed. "Get the guys together."

We met on Saturday, December 7, in the residence at the White House. I reviewed the Iran matter from the first TOW shipment in August and described how I believed the operation had gone off course. Shultz and Weinberger, as ever, quickly spoke up and pressed for a discontinuation of the initiative. They both expressed their fears that we were sending Iran, and other terrorist nations, signals that Americans could be kidnapped for profit.

The President listened to them attentively, lips pursed. He sat leaning forward against the table, pressing his fingertips together in his habitual gesture of impatience.

"I just don't see it that way, George," he said when Shultz had finished speaking. "The way I look at it, we're trying to reach opponents of Khomeini, and I'm willing to defend it on that basis. We're not dealing with terrorists."

The discussion went on, with arguments on both sides, for upwards of an hour. John McMahon, Bill Casey's deputy at the

CIA, brought up the subject of formal authority, asking whether the initiative were going to become official policy. Don Regan voiced his opinion that the twin aims of talking to Iranian moderates and trying to free the hostages ought still to be pursued.

It was clear that the President himself was not convinced he should abandon this channel, that he badly wished to find a way to keep it open, keep it working, and extract the rest of the hostages if possible.

Earlier in the week, I had asked Poindexter and North to arrange a tentative meeting with Ghorbanifar in London for this weekend, anticipating what I now suggested to the President. I would go to London, I said, and meet with the Iranian intermediaries and tell them that while Washington continued to be interested in a political dialogue with any pragmatic elements in Tehran, we would not sell them any American arms, and would not allow or encourage anybody else to do so either. I would size up the situation, get a first-hand reading on the kind of people with whom we were actually conducting transactions, and make a personal determination regarding their reliability and the viability of any further dealings.

Everyone agreed this was a reasonable course of action. "Go ahead," the President said briskly. I left that same night for London. It was the eve of my wife's birthday.

—

The apartment in London's West End, in an old Victorian building, belonged to Al Schwimmer. The room where we met in mid-afternoon on Sunday, December 8, was dark, filled with heavy Baroque antique furniture, and lined with bookshelves. I sat in an armchair with a small, high table in front of me. Around the room sat David Kimche, Yaakov Nimrodi, Schwimmer, and North. Also present, although I was unaware of it at the time, was Richard Secord, a retired Air Force major general who, North had told me when I arrived in London, had been "helpful" in arranging transportation in the convoluted and ultimately botched Hawk shipment.

Across the small table from me sat Manucher Ghorbanifar.

He was a small, squat, burly man with a great deal of curly black hair and glinting black eyes. His round face was puffy, his complexion swarthy. We had exchanged pleasantries when introduced, since he spoke in understandable but essentially pidgin English. We eyed each other a little warily.

The mood in the room was charged, tense. I knew that Kimche, with whom I had met earlier in the day, was unhappy with my intentions. He remained confident, he had said, that Ghorbanifar and his associates, including a man named Karrubi, were committed to change and over time could produce it. "David, I'm leaving government," I had told him, "and quite honestly I have no confidence that this can be successfully carried out after I'm gone." Kimche had expressed his hopes that we would reconsider, but had not pressed the point any further.

Now I addressed Ghorbanifar, speaking slowly so that he would be sure to understand.

"I am here representing the United States and under instruction," I began, using the term of diplomacy that conveyed that what I said was official U.S. policy.

I went through the history of the Iran dealings and how we saw their development from our perspective. We had entered into them, I said, with the hope that there might be an opportunity to establish contact with pragmatic people committed to change in Iran, and that, although we were reluctant, we understood that if such people existed and were to become strong enough to take action, they would need the support of the army, and we had consequently condoned the transfer of arms to them. In short, we had fulfilled our part of the commitment. For their part, their obligations were to demonstrate their commitment to change and their power to effect change by releasing the hostages. This they had not done, however. Our government had therefore reconsidered the situation and decided the following:

"That, first, we are interested in establishing contact with political figures committed to changing Iranian policy. Secondly, the agenda we pursue with these figures will be a political one that will focus on bilateral relations and the means by which we might work toward a renewed formal relationship. The agenda will treat regional issues, to include Iran's relationship to its neighbors—the Soviet Union, Afghanistan, Iraq—as well as our bilateral relationship.

"Whenever your colleagues are ready for this," I said meaningfully, "they should say so. But until that time, we have no interest in transferring arms, and cannot encourage others to do so."

There was a pregnant pause. The silence in the room was absolute, nearly palpable.

Then Ghorbanifar blew. As the popular phrase has it, he went ballistic. He leaned over, pressed his palms on the table, and fixed me with a burning look.

"What are you talking about? Are you crazy?" he shouted, and brought his fist down on the little table so that it wobbled on its thin legs. "You just left a mess behind and now you want something else?

"Don't you understand? My contacts are desperate people! They want to change, but they are too weak now for political talk with you. They have no interest in such talk. They must first get strong and take power!

"They are expecting that you understand that, that you will help them get strong with weapons. Only after we finish the war, then we think about all this nice political science!"

Again, the fist came down onto the table with a resounding bang. His next words were delivered with studied deliberation.

"If I take this news back to my colleagues, they will go mad! They might say, 'To hell with the hostages! Let the Hezbollah kill them!'"

In retrospect, I have wondered whether he and North did not perhaps collude in that suggestion, for North certainly knew that it would have leverage with President Reagan, although I personally did not believe the hostages would be in any greater danger from our having cut off talks with the Iranians. I knew, too, that Ollie was unhappy about my instructions for this meeting. When I had told him of them earlier, he had not hesitated to express his dissent. "I think that's just going to blow things sky high in Tehran," he had said. "Khomeini's got to go first. If you tell them this now, it'll set things back a long way."

Clearly North had suspected what Ghorbanifar's reaction was going to be. The Iranian was positively bellicose, roaring over and over: "This is crazy! I cannot believe what you are saying!"

As his tirade, like a crashing wave, washed over me, I listened calmly. "I don't believe we have anything more to talk about," I said at last, rising from my chair even as he continued to rant and fume: "This is incredible! I cannot believe you will do this!"

I spoke formally, perhaps a little coldly. "If your position changes, and you become interested in what I have outlined, let us know." I left the room without shaking his hand; behind me he continued to mutter in anger.

"Let's get out of here," I said to North, and we left the building military-style, in echelons.

Heading back to the hotel, I finally let off my own steam. "This is finished," I said to North. "I'm leaving government, Ollie, and I don't have any confidence at all that this guy is legitimate."

North began to defend him. "Well, you know, there aren't an awful lot of elevated thinkers wandering around Tehran right now, and this is the best we could do," he said. "I still think this thing can be made to work."

My anger got the best of me at that. "Ollie, this is not somebody that the United States government ought to be dealing with!" I snapped. I could feel my face growing hot. "All he could talk about was arms! 'We need arms!' 'You promised us arms!' He could no more organize a coup—much less govern—than the man in the moon. He's nothing more than a *bazaari!*" This is the Middle East term for an unscrupulous trader.

I did not know that North was already relaxing his own scruples and making private plans to connect his newly-minted Iranian channel with a bank for the contras. His plan had little relation to the official position I had just laid out to Ghorbanifar. As we prepared to leave London, he asked if Dick Secord could accompany us on the jet back to Washington. I said yes, not thinking much about it, since Secord was a retired military man and entitled to ride military aircraft. I did not inquire about his connection with North beyond what North had told me about his help with the Hawk shipment. In the light of hindsight, it's clear that North was already making his plans, laying the groundwork, for a project of which he knew I would disapprove, which I would never have permitted him to pursue. But I was a lame duck, on my way out, and all he had to do was to bide his time. Poindexter, he had no doubt concluded, would be more receptive to his ideas.

Back in Washington Monday morning, I debriefed in the Oval Office. I gave my views on Ghorbanifar, much as I had voiced them to North, except more calmly. I urged the President to shut the whole Iran initiative down. As soon as I had finished speaking, Weinberger, seated opposite me on one of the two large sofas in the room, leaned forward in his seat.

"Yes, Bud's right, Mr. President," he said avidly. "It's what I've been saying all along."

Shultz was out of the country, but his deputy Michael Armacost dutifully laid out what he knew to be his boss's objections to the initiative. For the first time, too, Don Regan concurred that it was time to call the whole thing off. I had had many problems with Regan in the course of his one-year tenure as the President's Chief of Staff. Our relationship had turned abrasive on more than one occasion, and he was undeniably part of the reason I was leaving the White House. Yet it was gratifying now to hear him back me up on a point about which I felt strongly. "I think we should listen to Bud," he said. "I think it's not worth the risk anymore."

George Bush echoed his words. "Yes, Bud's probably right," he said in his mild, nonassertive way. It was not a forceful endorsement of my position; forcefulness was not Bush's style, at least not while he was Vice President. But his opinion was significant, and he, too, deserves credit for believing that the Iran initiative was headed in the wrong direction and should have been called off.

But that decision, of course, belonged only to the President. And Reagan, at that point, was evidently still looking for the pony. It was his favorite story, about the little boy who, confronted with a roomful of manure on Christmas morning, shouts, "There must be a pony in here somewhere!"

Reagan listened noncommittally, obviously reluctant to accept all the bad news he was receiving.

"I'm sorry to hear all this," he said, more than once. "I think this has real promise."

It undoubtedly did not help that Bill Casey would not back off from the initiative. "It's risky," Casey said, "but most things worth doing are."

The meeting ended, as they so often did, inconclusively. "Well, OK," the President said, signaling our adjournment. But nothing more. No decision was taken, and I remember thinking as I left the room that I really did not know where matters stood.

Weinberger, for his part, thought we had convinced the President to give it up. He wrote in his notes for that day that "the baby has been strangled in its crib." Armacost reported a similar impression to Shultz.

They were, however, wrong.

—

As I bade my last farewell to the President a few days later at a reception he kindly held in my honor, I reiterated to him what I had said the day I resigned: that I was ready to continue to be of service to him in the future if ever he should have need of me. Already, I regretted my decision to resign. I felt, in a way, as though I were leaving the President in the lurch. I knew that, given the personality clashes and conflicting political philosophies that prevailed in the Reagan administration, no one would be able to keep the national security machinery running as well as I had. Poindexter was a good man, intelligent and competent, but he had no stomach for the internecine Cabinet squabbling that was such a large portion of the job's daily routine. And he shared the disdain that both the President and the Secretary of Defense felt toward the Congress, a disdain that I knew could cost us a great deal in the national security and defense arena. Was I copping out, I wondered, by leaving?

Moreover, just a few days after my negative report on the London trip, I had the sense that the President had not, in fact, let go of the hope that he could still make something of Ghorbanifar and the Iran initiative, if only to win back the hostages. I knew that what I had said had disappointed him. Having been the one who had rained on his parade, I now felt keenly that I wanted to leave his employ with a positive message. Privately, I told him that if ever the Iran initiative should develop to the point where a real political dialogue were possible, I would be glad to help him with it in any way I could. He shook my hand. "Thanks, Bud. I'll call on you," he said.

And so it was that five months later I found myself sitting beside some spare weapons parts in an unmarked plane headed for Tehran, carrying a passport that identified me as a citizen of Ireland by the name of Sean Devlin.

Chapter 4

IN THE BELLY OF THE BEAST

From the hotel balcony at twilight, the muggy evening haze that spread over downtown Tehran stretched outward toward the distant Elburz mountains. A phrase floated up from a distant corner of my mind—"light thickens"—and fast on its heels came the realization that it was a line from *Macbeth*. Appropriate. I smiled wryly to myself.

Below the mountain skyline at closer range, building cranes, all of them rusting, rose above the torpid urban oasis that was Tehran in May 1986. Occasionally, a nesting hawk would leave a crane and circle slowly overhead. Below, a scene of Brownian motion unfolded. Here and there, a few old cars zigzagged wildly down the wide boulevards built by the Shah, exhausts smoking, all going at breakneck speed in comic contrast to the general languor of the city.

The sultry summer scene mirrored my own subdued mood. After three days in the Iranian capital, it was clear that my mission here—to open at last a dialogue that might with time lead to the renewal of normal relations between the United States and Iran, and to win the release of the remaining five American hostages in Lebanon—was not to be. Certainly not yet.

John Poindexter had contacted me in late April. A computer linking me to the White House national security office, on which I could continue to send and receive encrypted messages, still remained in my home, as did a classified telephone line. From time to time, I had received notes from Poindexter or North apprising me of what was going on in the Iran initiative. My gloomy forebodings on leaving the White House had proved accurate: Far from giving up on the Iran arms shipments, the President had stepped them up instead. In January 1986, barely a month after my departure, he had signed a Finding authorizing shipments of U.S.—not Israeli—arms to Iran, and finally involving the CIA in the transfers. Shultz and Weinberger had apparently made one last stab at dissuading the President from this course, but having failed, had apparently decided to cease bucking the tide. Now the U.S. was shipping weapons directly itself, no longer relying on the Israelis to act as intermediaries. Already, two large shipments of TOWs had been delivered. But they had yielded no more hostages.

The frustration level at the White House was high. Around late March, early April, I had had the sense that John was ready to end the Iran operation. But then he called with a different message: the Iranians were ready at last, he said, to undertake a political dialogue with the United States. High-level officials were willing to meet in Tehran with similarly high-level Americans to discuss a political agenda. The names of those with whom I might meet included Rafsanjani, the speaker of the Majlis, or the Iranian parliament; Prime Minister Hussein Musavi, and even President Ali Khamenei. The Iranians promised that all hostages would be released upon the arrival of a delegation in Tehran. The President, John said, wanted me to go.

For all of my professional life, it had been a foundation principle that when the President asks you to do something, you do it. I couldn't not do what the President wanted. Now, perhaps, after everything that has happened, I could refuse. But not then.

Further, I saw the trip that John had outlined as holding out two possibilities. On the one hand, it was conceivable that the Iranians did want to talk seriously at last, although I believed there was only about a 20 percent probability that this was the case. It was more likely, I thought, that this was just another elaborate con, of the sort I had tried vainly to bring to an end before I left government.

But perhaps, I told myself, just perhaps, if I were to go on this mission and come back with that same message, based this time on firsthand experience and dialogue in Tehran, the President would finally see the light and discontinue the Iran operation once and for all. At a minimum, I thought, better that I go—someone who understood the issue and was bearish on it—rather than a cheerleader who might color events to feed into the President's eternal optimism.

For all these reasons, I agreed to go. I prepared with a series of CIA briefings on the internal situation in Iran. One was conducted by a retired analyst named George Cave, who would accompany me on the actual trip to Tehran. A few weeks went by as several delays occurred; the Iranians were bickering over the time and terms of the meeting and, as it turned out, over a concurrent arms delivery. Finally the call came: the meeting was set for May 25 in Tehran. I was to leave at once.

There was only one modification from the first description of the mission. My team and I would be taking one pallet of spare Hawk parts with us on our flight to Iran, the first segment of a large shipment the administration had apparently agreed to provide. It would be the last shipment, John insisted. In fact, the pallet we took with us, John said, as well as the remaining 11 pallets of the shipment, which would wait in Israel until I signaled that they could be released, would not be turned over to the Iranians until the hostages had been freed. I was unhappy with this development. Here we were again, dealing in arms and caving into demands for arms, before we achieved our objectives. I could have used this as an excuse to back out of the mission. But I didn't.

Jonny was justifiably concerned about the trip. As I packed, she watched me anxiously. I was after all, heading into a country with which we had no formal relations, that considered itself a sworn enemy of the United States, and whose government looked upon our government and our President as the Great Satan. Apart from Jonny and the people at the White House, the only other person who even knew I was making this trip was Caroline Scullin, my executive assistant.

Jonny drove straight to the point. "What makes you think they'll ever let you leave again?" she asked. But I told her I didn't believe there was any reason to worry. I was a prominent American, entering the country on a diplomatic mission. Even the most fanatical Iranians had to understand that they ran a severe risk if they tried to take me prisoner, or to harm me in any way. If they believed we were helping Iraq in the war before the trip, how much more would we be likely to do if a former National Security Adviser were taken hostage or killed? All the same, I recognized that the risk I was running was real. Before I finished packing, while Jonny was out of the room, I walked into the bathroom and retrieved a bottle of Valium my doctor had prescribed some months before for back pain. I hid it carefully among my folded travel clothes. As it turned out, this would not be the occasion when I would feel impelled to make use of it.

We left Washington on a corporate Canadair 600 jet. Accompanying me were NSC staffer Howard Teicher, Cave and a couple of CIA communicators. We flew to Rhein/Main Air Force Base in Frankfurt for a brief layover, then on to Tel Aviv. There, we were met at the airport by North and Dick Secord. I was not fully aware of all of Secord's activities at the time, but he had by then become a full-time CIA cutout, or private contractor, providing logistical support on the Iran arms shipments. And other shipments, too, as later came out.

North introduced me to Amiram Nir, who he said had replaced David Kimche as the Israeli prime minister's Special Adviser on Terrorism. (Kimche had left his post in the Israeli government not long after I left the White House.) Later, at the hotel where we went to rest, North told me that Nir had asked to be taken along to Tehran. I thought this was odd, both because of the danger that faced an Israeli in Iran, but also because I believed this to be a strictly U.S. diplomatic mission, aimed at exploring the possibility of future bilateral relations. What an Israeli had to do with such a discussion, I did not see. But North insisted that a refusal to allow him to join us would offend the Israeli Prime Minister. I finally agreed to allow Nir to come along, undercover as one of our communicators, after North assured me that Reagan had approved it.

We had several hours to wait in Tel Aviv until our flight to Tehran, which was to leave at midnight. We all went to dinner together at a seafood restaurant on the beach. Afterwards, unbeknownst to me, North and Nir went off to a bakery to buy the now and forever infamous cake—a chocolate cake with a skeleton key on top, like some eccentric ornament.

Ollie showed it to me later on the plane, with some delight. He explained that it was a reference to an earlier meeting with Ghorbanifar in Frankfurt, when the talks had become deadlocked and someone had commented that what was needed was a key to unlock the disagreement. "We're going to show them we've found the key," North said, laughing.

It was the sort of sophomoric prank Ollie would enjoy, and I took it in that spirit, but I told him that I wanted no part of it. "That's not what I'm here for," I said.

"Don't worry, Bud," Ollie replied jocosely. "It's a private joke. We'll take care of it out in the hall."

We went out to the airport, where three slicks waited on the tarmac. These were unmarked 707 cargo planes, white with no identifying lettering or numbering, flown by American crews. Secord had made all the arrangements. Our flight took off, flying over the Negev desert, into the Gulf of Aqaba, down the Red Sea and out the

Bab-el-Mandab Strait, then around the Arabian peninsula and back up the Persian Gulf. We entered Iranian air space as the sun came up, and landed in Tehran at about 9 A.M. There was no one at the airport to meet us.

This was, of course, the first bad omen. A ramp guard ushered us into a VIP lounge, where we sat, staring at each other and cracking uneasy jokes, cooling our heels for the next two hours. At last Ghorbanifar appeared, trailed by a sidekick, looking harried and unsettled. He made his excuses, said we had not been expected until later. But to me, in my already suspicious state of mind, and obviously because of my opinion of Ghorbanifar, it all sounded like double-talk. He led us through the terminal to a couple of broken-down cars that hardly looked like an official motorcade for diplomatic visitors. Even Iran, I thought to myself, ought to have better rolling stock than this.

At least the drive through town was interesting. Tehran, even after the revolution and the subsequent years of decline, was still a handsome city, with the mountains rising steeply to the east, and the Persian elegance of the buildings and architecture. It seemed, however, half-deserted, with very little traffic. Few people were on the streets, most of them heavily-veiled women.

We arrived at the former Hilton, now the Independence Hotel, and Ghorbanifar ushered us at a brisk pace through the somewhat seedy lobby, as though, understandably, he wanted to minimize the visibility of our group. We rode the elevator to the top floor, where he ensconced me in a suite at one end, and assigned the rest of the team individual rooms along the hall. An Iranian security guard stood watch at the top of the stairs.

We proceeded to hold a brief session then and there. I wanted to know when I would be meeting with the Speaker and Prime Minister. Ghorbanifar equivocated, saying it wasn't clear just whom I would be seeing. The alarm bells went off in my mind. This was a distinct departure from everything I had been told about the mission. I listened to Ghorbanifar and North going back and forth and it occurred to me that North's assurances to me that I would be meeting with principals had been exaggerated, to say the least. North would prod Ghorbanifar about the meetings with Rafsanjani, saying, "Well, maybe tomorrow or the next day." And Ghorbanifar would respond, "I told you that's very unlikely." I was still too close to and too fond of Ollie then to acknowledge that he had been deceiving

Poindexter and the President, and now me. In fact, the collapse of this entire mission was due to lies and deceptions on the part of both North and Ghorbanifar. At the time, however, I was willing to believe that the perfidy was all on the Iranian's part.

Ghorbanifar left, saying someone would arrive to hold a first meeting with us at 2 P.M. I motioned Ollie out onto the balcony, where I hoped there was no bugging equipment and we could not be overheard. "What's going on?" I demanded.

He shrugged. "They told us we'd be meeting with these people," he insisted.

"That's not what Ghorbanifar is saying now."

"He's lying," North said, "and he's probably lied to his side about what we want."

He went on to speculate that perhaps the Iranians had actually changed their minds and gotten cold feet because they did not have the necessary control over the Revolutionary Guards. I agreed that this could be true, but if it were, it told us that our supposed pragmatists were not strong enough to act, and that it was therefore pointless for us to be there.

"Let's play it out," Ollie urged.

And we had, but to no avail. I was so discouraged by what we encountered that I sent a very pessimistic cable to Poindexter describing Iran as I saw it:

"It may be best for us to try to picture what it would be like if after nuclear attack, a surviving cobbler became Vice President; a recent grad student became Secretary of State; and a bookie became the interlocutor for all discourse with foreign countries. While the principals are a cut above this level of qualification, the incompetence of the Iranian government to do business requires a rethinking on our part of why there have been so many frustrating failures to deliver on their part."

For two days, we saw no senior officials of any kind. All our dialogues were carried on with third- and fourth-level officials, led by a strident young functionary from the Foreign Ministry, who insisted that there had been no prior commitment to release the hostages, and launched repeated diatribes at us for not having brought enough of the Hawk spare parts. To my chagrin, in fact, I learned that the parts we had transported in our plane had been unloaded at the airport in defiance of what I believed had been the agreement.

Either I was under a misimpression, or, as I then believed, we had been had, by either Ghorbanifar or his contacts, who had simply said what was needed to get us there and bring them the weapons they desired. All our discussions were at cross-purposes. I was angry at the waste of time and frustrated by the absence of anyone in authority. I had not traveled all this way, and at all this risk, to meet with low-level bureaucrats. Finally, I withdrew from the meetings with the Foreign Ministry functionaries and left them to my staff.

At last, the Iranians had produced an official at sub-minister level to speak with me. Hadi-Najafabadi was a member of the Majlis and foreign affairs adviser to Rafsanjani. He was a short, urbane, bewhiskered man in his early sixties, apparently Western-educated, who spoke excellent English. Unlike the insecure young fellow from the Foreign Ministry, Najafabadi was at ease and spoke with the self-assurance that comes from depth and breadth of knowledge and a relationship of trust with a decision-maker.

We had had a one-on-one meeting in my suite that morning, a meeting that approached a fairly normal diplomatic exchange. We had actually discussed politics and our countries' relative positions on a range of issues of common interest, including the Soviet Union, terrorism, the Iran-Iraq war and the politics of the Middle East. Najafabadi had struck me as a reasonable, even peaceful man. He recognized that though the Iranian revolution had succeeded internally, it had come at great cost. He understood that the Iranians needed time to consolidate their revolution, and that it was thus not in Iran's interest to promote terrorism or to continue the war, both of which worsened its isolation and led ultimately to economic ruin. I found talking to him heartening, for his words seemed to validate the original premise of our whole Iran undertaking—that there should have been sensible people in Tehran interested in ending the war, relieving their isolation and restoring a measure of normalcy to relations with the West.

But it was also clear that Najafabadi and those like him who might have been our partners in a dialogue were far from a position of sufficient strength to act on their views. At best, they were part of a fractious circle around Rafsanjani that was still dominated by radicals. They no doubt remembered that the last official who had dealt with the Great Satan, former Prime Minister Bazargan—who had met with President Carter's National Security Adviser Zbigniew

Brzezinski in Algeria in 1980—had been unceremoniously stripped of his post and had fled into exile.

Contrary to our expectations, the Iranians had not made any overtures to the Hezbollah in Lebanon regarding our hostages before our arrival in Tehran. When they did, the terrorists listed a number of extreme conditions for their release, such as Israeli withdrawal from the Golan Heights and southern Lebanon and, most outrageous of all, that someone pay the bills the hostages had accumulated. "How's that for *chutzpah*," I had cabled Poindexter. After our meeting, Najafabadi had hurried off to work on the hostage question. He had returned several hours later, fired up and accompanied by an entourage that included the Foreign Ministry official of the first two days, as well as an assistant to the Prime Minister who was a former cobbler. This man could never seem to get the front of his shirt to contain his "unrevolutionary" stomach and stay tucked into his trousers. He arrived at each meeting out of breath, looking as if he had been called out of the shower. Which, judging from his fragrance, was clearly not the case.

Najafabadi reported that they had succeeded in persuading the Hezbollah to drop all the conditions it had posed for release of our hostages, except for the freeing of the 17 Shia Muslim prisoners in Kuwait. Knowing this was a non-starter with me, however, he quickly changed the subject and said that the Iranians had come to accept that a misunderstanding had occurred and believed that the best course was to avoid recriminations and get on with more important things.

"If the plane [with the balance of the Hawk spare parts] arrives before tomorrow morning, the hostages will be free by noon," Najafabadi promised. "We do not wish to see our agreement fail at this final stage."

Mindful of the three similar commitments that had been made—and broken—in the past, I endeavored to turn things around. "Can we separate the issue, as a humanitarian gesture?" I asked. "You can release the hostages, then we'll deliver the weapons."

Najafabadi hesitated. "OK," he said at last, but added that Rafsanjani wanted the final agreement down in writing. That might be difficult to accomplish tonight, he said; couldn't I perhaps stay a bit longer or leave staff behind to work it out? It seemed to me that the Iranian side was facing toughness for the first time. Ghorbanifar had apparently told Najafabadi that my staff was more flexible than I.

It was not surprising that they wanted to get me out of the picture.

"Had this spirit existed in our first encounter a year ago, it would have been clear that we could reach some agreement," I replied. "Unfortunately, we have reached this point after a year and three efforts in which you failed to honor any agreement.

"This has affected the President's view of our ability to rely upon any commitment. He has kept trying, due to his belief that there were larger interests at stake, but the several failures have clearly lowered his confidence that we will ever be able to work together.

"Even so, he was willing to try once more," I went on, "and last week, he was told that we had once more come to an agreement. But his instructions in sending me here were firm: If the hostages aren't returned, we are to discontinue the talks."

I made clear that I would leave the following day, with or without an agreement.

After Najafabadi left, I gathered the team for dinner in my suite. We didn't talk much, assuming that we were being monitored. Probably the Shah's Intelligence Service's leftover gear; ironic.

After dinner, we had come out to the balcony. All the staff— Howard, Ollie, Nir and Cave—believed that the hard line I had taken was working, and that in the end, the Iranians would yield on the hostages. I stressed to all that there could be no backing down on our position: all hostages must be turned over to us before one more item was delivered in Iran. All nodded agreement, but I noticed that Nir was unenthusiastic. I had had to take him aside the day before and in no uncertain terms tell him that his separate corridor dialogues with the Iranians between meetings were undercutting the mission and that he had to stop them at once.

Najafabadi was due to return at 9:30 p.m. with the agreement to release the hostages, prepared to work with my staff to write down a memorandum of understanding for the first steps toward reducing tensions. I instructed Howard and Ollie to follow up on two ideas designed to build confidence on both sides. One was a proposal that, after our hostages were released, and subject to an Iranian commitment to bring an end to terrorism against the West, both sides would commit to lowering the rhetoric toward one another in the coming months. Such a move would begin to alter the climate in both countries with regard to the other and over time make possible the acceptance of a more normal relationship, especially by their people, who

had been subjected to the proselytizing of extremists for five years.
In addition, bearing in mind that the Soviet Union had undoubtedly
been monitoring Ghorbanifar's telephone communications from
Europe to the United States, and in the interests of eliminating the
middle man, I proposed that we establish a two-man secure communications station in Iran so that we could sustain a direct and secure
exchange of information. Finally, in an effort to bring matters to a
close, I directed Ollie to say that we had to have their answer by 4 a.m.
the next morning, in about eight hours.

The guys went off to organize the meeting. I turned again toward
the mountains, trying to frame the breathtaking scene in my mind so
that I could describe it to Jonny. The ridge line to the east of Tehran
in many respects resembles the sculpted Sandia range northeast of
Albuquerque.

—

Najafabadi arrived back on time and the staff set to work with
him, trying to hammer out the terms of an agreement. Almost
immediately, the Iranians began to backpedal on their earlier commitment to releasing the hostages. There was still a lot of work to
do to convince their Hezbollah clients in Lebanon, they insisted.
They wanted to known what we were prepared to say about the
Dawa prisoners in Kuwait. Believing that they were looking more
for a face-saving gesture than actual results in a release of the
Dawas, Ollie proposed a paragraph of bureaucratic rhetoric to the
effect that the United States would work with international bodies
and private individuals (he had in mind Terry Waite, the Anglican
Church emissary who had been endeavoring to arrange a "humani-
tarian action" involving a sequence of prisoner releases by Israel,
Hezbollah and the Kuwaitis) to seek the just treatment of Shia
Muslims everywhere.

The Iranians were dissatisfied, and said they would think about it.
But by 11 p.m., the talks had reached an impasse. I asked that
Najafabadi come to my suite. I wanted to try to determine from him,
in the absence of his henchmen—who came from other political
camps—how much he had been able to accomplish with his superiors and what the real prospects for making headway were.

He was bone-tired, but not dispirited. He wanted more time, he
said. I wasn't sure whether all the delays were the result of pure

bloody-mindedness and his bosses' desire to up the ante, or whether a combination of fear, confusion and ineptitude simply required time to sort out. But it seemed to make little difference in terms of the proper course to follow. If the relationship between Washington and Tehran were ever to develop, it would be necessary to establish some discipline and ground rules at the outset. This was our first meeting with Iranian officials, and certain standards had to be set. For starters, from our perspective, you don't invite a Cabinet-level emissary to your country based on understandings that certain events will take place and then leave him to meet with low-level functionaries for three days.

I held to the 4 a.m. deadline for their answer. Najafabadi left.

I called John Poindexter on the secure radio set up by the CIA team to report where matters stood. I restated my recommendation of earlier in the day, that we hold to our original understanding of the agreement and not negotiate new terms, and asked that he let me know if the President disagreed. Later, John informed me that he had given the President my earlier reporting cable, and that after having thought about it, the President had said: "Bud's the one on the scene. Only he can judge what is best. He should do what he thinks is right."

That was good guidance. I went to bed.

At about 2 a.m., Ollie and Howard awakened me. Najafabadi was back. He looked as though he'd been through the wringer. Yet his voice was steady and sober as he informed me that although his government was working as hard as it could, they could not possibly have an answer for us before 6 a.m. I told him that I had directed my staff to prepare to leave; if, however, he could give me a firm time when the hostages definitely would be released, I could launch the plane from Israel before then, so that it would arrive two hours after the hostages had been turned over to Ambassador Bartholomew in Beirut. I wanted to keep the pressure on him by not accepting his request for delay and not agreeing to stay on longer than I had said I would. But I did want to express some goodwill as well.

Najafabadi pondered my offer briefly, then said he would be back before 6. He hurried off, and I went back to bed.

Just before 6 a.m., Ollie woke me again. He said he had called the second aircraft forward from Tel Aviv on the outside chance that Najafabadi would produce results by 6, in which case the aircraft could arrive in Tehran by about 10 a.m. With no results to report, Ollie assumed that I wanted the aircraft turned around; it was nearing the point of no return on fuel.

"Yes," I said. "Turn it around, Ollie."

I found it hard, in those days, to get mad at Ollie. I saw him then as a resolute, hardworking and well-intentioned professional who gave every task assigned to him every ounce of heart that he had. We had worked together for four years, and in that time had become very close. Like me, he was a Marine and a veteran of the Vietnam War, and I believed that the latter had encouraged the development of the sentiments that seemed to me, believing the best of him, to drive him in his work: a certain cynicism toward politicians combined with a passionate devotion to saving human lives. I thought that for Ollie, the lesson of Vietnam had been that once you put someone at risk, you never run out on him, not ever. This credo, I believed, was what was causing him anguish now as he watched the string run out on one more failed effort to save the hostages. I anguished with him, choosing to believe his heart was in the right place, that he had told Ghorbanifar he was launching the plane in the hope that it would somehow give the Iranians enough of a push to get the hostages out. If he had asked my consent before acting, I would have stopped him, since I believed launching the plane would have the opposite effect and show irresolution on our part. But I did not criticize him for taking the initiative. The scales over my eyes were still in place; it would be a long process before they fell away, one by one, to reveal the real Oliver North.

In a different context, I was disappointed for Najafabadi as well. Since his brief visit four hours ago to ask for more time, I had slept only fitfully. His face kept rising before me, as it had looked when we finished our first meeting the day before. He had made clear that he did not fully support Khomeini's theocratic crusade and delusions of empire, and that he believed that efforts to stimulate fundamentalist uprisings in other countries were wrongheaded and a waste of energy and resources. He was a realist on international matters who had joined forces with the most pragmatic faction in Iran—Rafsanjani's circle—but recognized that even in that cabal radicals predominated. Perhaps he had hoped that over time he could get the Americans involved diplomatically to help Iran find a face-saving way out of the war and, in the bargain, establish a modicum of cooperation on Afghanistan, to deter any broader Soviet ambitions regarding Iran. "This has been a most important meeting," he had said as our first talk ended. "It is a beginning that we must keep alive." Yet despite his hopeful words, his face had mirrored resignation, the foreknowledge that the mistrust bred by Ghorbanifar's self-serving mendacity, and the fear and fractiousness that reigned in his government, had together aborted my mission before it even began.

Now, I caught his eye and we shared a look of mutual, and sad, recognition that it was too soon. There were sensible people in Iran, people who would have wished to reach out to the international community and end Iran's isolation, but they were too insecure—too weak—to act.

I asked Ollie to arrange for cars to get us to the airport. We had packed the night before and left our bags in the hallway, hoping to lend credibility to our pledge to leave. Just before 8 a.m., the cobbler-turned-"emissary" arrived with some new information. "They think they can get two out now," he reported, "but it will require 'joint action' on the other two."

Ignoring him, I signaled the team to head downstairs for the motorcade to Mehrabad Airport. Soon after, Najafabadi arrived with the same offer.

"You have our position," I told him. "When you can meet it, let us know."

He didn't respond or even try to keep matters going. He understood. It was too soon.

At the airport, I told the adviser to the Iranian Prime Minister to remind his superiors that this was the fourth time they had failed to honor our agreement. "Our lack of trust will endure for a long time," I said. "An important opportunity has been lost."

The little man seemed genuinely surprised. He had apparently expected me to consider the offer of two hostages. Only later did I learn that during the early morning hours, in another "corridor conversation," Nir had suggested that if they could not get all four hostages, I might be persuaded to accept only two. This was an outrageous action. But of course it was consistent with the approach Israel has always followed regarding prisoners. Get the best deal you can and cut it.

So we left Tehran.

———

As the wheels of the 707 slammed up after takeoff, I gazed out the window at the city receding behind us. My hopes for a genuine opening to Iran remained there on the ground with it, growing smaller and fainter, until at last everything was lost in the swirling mist of time. I turned and studied the faces of my team members, and Nir. Everyone was downcast. They had all hoped that things would go better. Each probably believed that a preparatory trip—which Poindexter had nixed—would have helped matters. Undoubtedly so. Such a trip presumably would have exposed Ghorbanifar's duplicity to Najafabadi and the rest of the hierarchy, and the Iranians might have reacted by starting all over again. And yet, the central issue on the Iranian side would have remained unchanged: the government was sharply split between those who looked at the United States with total hostility and sought to exploit us for weapons, and those who took a longer view and wanted our help in ending the war, helping Iran break out of isolation and get its economy back on its feet. The White House had no business trying to influence events in that climate. But it had been right to find out—and to let them know where we stood.

Time weighed heavily on the trip back from Tehran. We landed first at Ben Gurion airport in Tel Aviv. I stepped out onto the sunlit tarmac and asked the CIA radioman to set up his transmitter for a call to Poindexter. It was time to tell him that the mission had failed; he should tell the President how sorry I was, and warn him that I was bringing no happy news home with me—and no hostages.

North tapped me on the shoulder as he passed and grinned at me. "Don't worry, Bud, it's not a total loss," he quipped enigmatically into my ear. "At least we're using some of the Ayatollah's money in Central America."

And he was off, hurrying into a car for a rendezvous with someone in Cyprus regarding the status of a separate effort he had set in motion to gain the release of the hostages.

I stood there, caught flat-footed. In a moment, the radioman was handing me the headset; Poindexter was on the line. I turned to speak with him just as the full import of Ollie's comment sank in.

Chapter 5

THE BATTLE FOR THE CONTRAS

In the spring of 1984, the Nicaraguan contras were fast running out of money—and luck. The rebel movement was just about to lose the official support of the United States government, via the CIA, in its guerrilla war against the Communist-backed Sandinista regime of Daniel Ortega. The Democrat-controlled U.S. Congress, chafing at Ronald Reagan's disdain for its role as foreign policy overseer, irate over the secret CIA-sponsored mining of Nicaraguan harbors—and no doubt hoping to hurt the President in his re-election effort—was debating a new version of the Boland amendment, legislation that would disallow any financial, material or logistical aid whatsoever to the rebels from the CIA "or any other agency or entity involved in intelligence activities." Congressman Ed Boland, chairman of the House Select Committee on Intelligence, was determined to end U.S. support for the freedom fighters in Nicaragua.

The contras were one of President Reagan's personal causes. In his eyes, the anti-Sandinista rebels were modern-day minutemen, heroic revolutionaries, patriots whose struggle on behalf of liberty and democracy deserved America's wholehearted and unflagging support. Sustaining the cause of those fighting Marxism was part of a deliberate, global administration doctrine (popularly referred to as the Reagan doctrine) a commitment to roll back and reverse the territorial gains of communism. It was not a matter merely of pride or vanity, but a belief that if we could turn the tide, whether in Afghanistan or Nicaragua or Angola or Ethiopia, it would send a dramatic signal to the Kremlin that their imperial ambitions were doomed to fail and would lead to a greater willingness on the part of our allies to join in reversing Soviet expansionism around the world. In Nicaragua and El Salvador, they were endeavoring to establish a beachhead on our own continent, and working from there to spread communism virtually all across our backyard. To Reagan, this state of affairs was intolerable.

So it was with chagrin that the President read the briefing paper on the contra situation that I gave him in late May. Prepared by Ollie North and the National Security Council's Latin America staff, it set forth the bleak prospects facing the movement as its $24 million appropriation from the previous year ran out, and as congressional opposition to further funding mounted.

A day or two after I had given him the paper, the President handed it back to me as we wound up the daily brief. "We've got to find a way to keep doing this, Bud," he said, fixing me with an intent look. "I want you to do whatever you have to do to help these people keep body and soul together. Do everything you can."

The NSPG had already held a number of discussions on the contra question, and one of the ideas repeatedly floated was that of asking other countries to make donations to the contra cause. The idea was on the whole favorably considered as being a legal way of coping with a congressional prohibition on direct U.S. aid. Heretofore, however, no firm decisions or action had been taken. Now, as I talked over the President's mandate to me with John Poindexter and Ollie North, it surfaced once again. Ollie suggested that Saudi Arabia might be a sympathetic candidate for a contribution; I thought Israel, which had been suggested several times by Bill Casey, would be worth a try first. Israel and the United States shared a broad "strategic partnership" that had been codified in 1983 in a memorandum of understanding signed by Cap Weinberger and the Israeli Defense Minister. Within the framework of this partnership, Washington had on several occasions assisted Israel in concluding contracts for projects in Central America and Africa exploiting Israel's acknowledged excellence in water resource development and training of internal security forces. We had also helped in restoring diplomatic relations between Israel and at least one African Muslim nation.

It seemed reasonable, therefore, that in the spirit of this same strategic partnership, Israel would be willing to tide us over on the contras until the administration was able to reorganize its congressional lobbying effort for more aid, get through the upcoming Presidential election, and finally persuade the contras to improve both their image and their organization to make themselves a more appealing recipient of U.S. support.

When we approached the Israelis with our request, however, they turned us down. The political situation in their own country, they said, made such assistance impossible at that time. I was disappointed, but understood, and turned my sights instead on Saudi Arabia.

For several years, since becoming Deputy National Security Adviser in 1982, I had made a practice of meeting regularly—usually about once a quarter—with the Saudi ambassador in Washington, Prince Bandar bin Sultan, to discuss the agendas of our respective governments and matters of interest that were transpiring in our respective capitals. Saudi Arabia is an important player in the Middle East, a strategically vital country with the largest oil reserves in the world, and a strongly anti-Marxist country highly aware and wary of Soviet imperialist ambitions and the historic Soviet objective of achieving a warm-water port. The presence of 100,000 Soviet troops in Afghanistan since 1979 had heightened Saudi concerns and led to massive U.S. arms sales to Saudi Arabia, including the politically costly campaign of 1981 to sell them AWACS aircraft. The Saudis understood that our interests in rolling back Marxism coincided closely with their own. Toward that end, in fact, we were already working together on what ultimately became a $500 million-a-year program of support to the *mujaheddin*, the freedom fighters conducting a guerrilla war against the Soviet puppet regime in Afghanistan.

Now I called Bandar and said I would like to have one of our meetings. He invited me out to his lavish home on Chain Bridge Road, across the Potomac River in McLean, Virginia, and one late May morning, before work, I stopped by. We discussed some general affairs and then I ran through the prospects for the President's re-election, pointing out that he was vulnerable on one major issue—the contras. Because he was being attacked and criticized on the Central America front, I said, the likelihood was high that he would not get any more money for the contras from the Congress this year, and if the movement collapsed, it would be a major defeat for the President's platform.

Bandar listened knowingly. When I had finished, he said, "I believe that His Majesty, King Fahd, would understand the importance of this both to us and to President Reagan and that he would probably be pleased to help."

He asked what I thought it would take to keep the contras going, and I told him that their usual costs ran to about one million dollars a month.

Within a week, he called me back. He had sent a courier to
Riyadh, he said, and the King had responded that he was willing to
help. They wanted to know where to send the money. I called
North.

"There is going to be a contribution," I said. "Where should it be
sent?"

From Adolfo Calero, the Nicaraguan businessman who was political director of the FDN (Nicaraguan Democratic Front), the largest
contra force, North got the number of the contra account in a Miami
bank, and I delivered it personally to Bandar in a handwritten note
one day in mid-June. The deposits would begin on July 1, he said,
and continue for the remainder of the year. The contras had won a
reprieve.

I passed the news to the President a day or two later on a notecard
I slipped into his morning briefing book. After the briefing, I was
called back in to retrieve the card with his notation, which expressed
his great pleasure and satisfaction at the development, along with the
admonition, "Mum's the word."

I told Weinberger and George Shultz about this reprieve at one of
our weekly Wednesday breakfast meetings. With staff, there were
usually about a dozen people in the room, but they were generally
solid, productive working sessions. Throughout the spring, we had
all been receiving intelligence on the contras indicating that their
money was running out, but within the first couple of weeks of July,
the tenor of the reports changed. Now, they said, the contras seemed
to be getting a new supply of rations and clothing, they had launched
one or two new probes or patrols; there was every indication of a
resurgence of effort.

Someone in the Pentagon dining room that day commented on the
change, saying it looked as though the contras had gotten well and
were beginning to present the kind of image needed to win votes—
both in Nicaragua and in the U.S. Congress. At that, I gave a visual
signal to both Shultz and Weinberger, indicating that we should
move on quickly to other matters. But once breakfast was over, I
asked to see them alone for a moment. After everyone else had filed
out, we stood together at one end of the table. I said:

"We've bought some time on the contras, and that problem is
solved through the end of the year. But we're going to have to prepare ourselves to win this in the Congress. If we can't, we ought to

shut it down. It's not fair to ask the contras to keep risking their lives if we can't match the Soviet level of support."

Shultz and Weinberger were both pleased at the good news, and asked what had happened to reverse the contras' fortunes. "You don't want to know," I said. And they agreed. It was better, in a case like this, to preserve a certain amount of deniability. Even though the Saudi contributions were not illegal, they involved the sort of evasion of restrictions that would anger our congressional opponents and which they would seek to cut off if they could. The fewer the people who knew the details, the less likely that Congress would be able to sniff them out. Weinberger and Shultz congratulated me on keeping the contras going, but didn't ask for any more specifics.

I had received a charge from President Reagan to keep the contras together body and soul, and I respected that charge, as well as his belief in the contras and the cause for which they were fighting. That was why I had pursued the course I had. At the same time, however, I had doubts about the wisdom of pursuing that course indefinitely. I knew that any help we received from foreign parties was not going to be given gratis, and that some sort of *quid pro quo* would be requested sooner or later—whether that meant a certain vote in the United Nations, or a sale of more arms or some other favor.

But beyond the debt we were incurring, I was concerned about the policy in the field. How realistic was it to look to foreign, non-appropriated monies to run our policy, when the opposing side was being funded by the Soviet Union at a level of $400 million a year? The crux of the matter, I knew, was to come up with a strategy for winning Congress over to the contras. We needed to rally the contras to improve their image, first as an army capable of winning battles, and then as a democratic reform movement with a political agenda that would make them a viable alternative to the ruling Sandinistas, and not just a ragtag paramilitary organization bent on destroying the government but unable to replace it with a solid governing framework of its own.

I believed that if we could not win Congress's support, then we should discontinue the policy. To do otherwise would be wrong, even immoral. It was the lesson etched on my conscience by the experience of Vietnam. It was wrong to ask people—in this case the contras—to risk their lives, promising to support them, but then failing to do so, abandoning them and leaving them to their fates. No one who went to Vietnam could have come out of there without realizing that the single most important reason for our failure in that war was the President's inability to explain his goals, define the problem, and the solution, and evoke popular support for that solution. I had watched hundreds of men—many of them close friends—lose their lives in that war, and the experience had forged a fundamental tenet of my subsequent public life: Policy officials must acknowledge the responsibility to explain what they are trying to do, and if they cannot explain it, then they should not do it. As heart-rending as it might be not to win, it would be far more tragic, as measured in other people's lives, to lead people on with false hope.

I explained my conviction to the contras themselves. In January 1985, after the President had been re-elected, George Shultz and I agreed that Central America, along with U.S.-Soviet relations, should be one of the administration's priorities for the second term, the areas on which we would concentrate our time and effort and resources, promoting new initiatives aimed at achieving concrete gains. We presented our views to the President, and he agreed with them. And in that context, I prepared a swing through Central America two months after the election to reaffirm for the countries there what the President's second-term policy would be, and to rally enthusiasm for it among the populace.

I traveled with several staffers, including North, Alan Fiers from the CIA, and Nestor Sanchez from Defense. With the exception of Nicaragua, we visited the President or Prime Minister of each of the Central American countries to deliver the same message regarding Reagan's continuing political and economic commitment to the region, to each of the nations individually, and to the freedom fighters in Nicaragua.

In our last stop, Honduras, U.S. Ambassador John Negroponte arranged a meeting for me with Adolfo Calero. The contra chief and I had a long talk in the library of the Ambassador's residence in Tegucigalpa, and I laid out for him, with the bark off, the realities of the contras' standing in Washington and the scope of change they would have to accomplish if they hoped to reclaim significant assistance from the United States in their struggle.

"Improve your military performance," I urged. "There are a lot of people on Capitol Hill who are sympathetic to the contra cause, but simply do not like backing losers and are hesitant to vote for funding until you can demonstrate that you are capable of some military victories.

"But more importantly, you must draw up a political agenda and bring credible political figures into your movement to show that if you win the war, you'll be capable of governing."

This was not, of course, what Calero wanted to hear. But he received my counsel with good grace and promised his movement would make every effort to polish its performance and its image.

By this time, the Boland amendment had been in effect since October, and the Saudi money for the contras had stopped. The outlook for the movement was truly bleak, especially as the new legislation effectively proscribed any effort on the administration's part to raise funds for the rebels. As far as I knew, everyone in my shop was abiding by that proscription. I had repeatedly addressed to them what became a kind of litany at Wednesday staff meetings: They were not to "solicit, encourage, coerce or broker" financial contributions for the contras. I knew that Ollie North, for one, as a vigorous supporter of the contra cause, was champing at the bit over this restraint. He was more motivated by the presidential charge to keep the contras together "body and soul." But what that meant now, I said, was providing political and moral support. I knew he didn't like it, but I didn't believe he would willfully disobey an order. In the fall of 1984, for instance, he had sent me a memo stating that a private citizen had contacted him to express willingness to pay for a helicopter the rebels needed. I had squelched that proposal, writing in the margin: "I don't think this is legal," and Ollie had agreed not to pursue it.

In February, I had a call from Prince Bandar for another meeting, as Saudi King Fahd was preparing a state visit to Washington. It was to be the first visit to the United States by a Saudi monarch in nearly 30 years. Bandar was anxious that the visit include some distinguishing event indicative of special respect, so we agreed on a private meeting between the King and President Reagan in the family quarters of the White House, something that is almost never done. In the course of our conversation, Bandar asked me the latest about the contras and their funding. I confirmed that they had been denied any more money by Congress, and he asked what would happen as a result.

"I don't have an answer for you," I said, "but right now it looks as if we're going to have to close down." He received the news without comment.

King Fahd's private meeting with the President turned out to be a breakfast, of all things, a mildly gaffish case of the United States putting its left foot forward. It is the King's custom to receive his peasant and Bedouin constituents in the early hours of the morning, from 1 or 2 a.m. to about 5 a.m., and then to retire. Even when traveling away from the kingdom, Fahd was known to hold meetings until the wee hours and sleep in afterwards. So a summons for breakfast at 8 a.m. must have appeared to the King to be highly uncivilized.

He came, however, with good grace, and as the meal drew to a close, he requested a few moments alone with the President. There were seven or eight of us in the room, including the Vice President, Shultz and me, and we all left, except for Bandar, who stayed behind to act as interpreter. The three of them remained behind closed doors for about five minutes.

The next day, Bandar invited me over to his residence for a brief meeting with Fahd. When I arrived, he pulled me aside in the library and disclosed that the King had offered President Reagan $25 million more to aid the contras.

In the salon, I turned to the King. "I've been informed of your generosity, and I'm sure the President is deeply touched," I said. "This is an important policy to him. However, it is a policy that we should be able to carry out on our own. In the President's behalf, I must commit to you that we cannot continue to rely upon you to make possible the conduct of an American policy."

The King nodded and assured me that he was, nevertheless, glad to help. The contras, to be sure, would be glad of that.

———

Soon afterward, we in the administration rolled up our sleeves to begin the campaign for renewed congressional support of the contras. I conveyed to North and to Don Fortier, my deputy and Senior Director for Policy Development, that the President continued to harbor a strong wish that we not break faith with the contras, and that our mission was to win the vote in Congress the next time around. We conducted a round of interdepartmental meetings involving the NSC, State, Defense, the Joint Chiefs and the CIA on the feasibility of developing a broader platform for the contra movement. One result of this was the establishment of a political umbrella for the rebels, an anti-Sandinista coalition known as the United Nicaraguan Opposition, which North coordinated with Calero and other contra leaders. North had been the NSC point man on the contras since 1981, when he was appointed the staff liaison to the CIA as the agency started up its covert operations in Nicaragua. In late March, UNO issued a peace proposal that included a call for a cease-fire and Sandinista agreement to set a date within 60 days for new elections. The proposal resonated favorably on the Hill, boosting our hopes that we might win a positive vote on funding in the spring.

Around the same time, the intelligence reports were beginning to show once again an increase in deliveries of material and other supplies to the contras, as well as a surge in their field activities, all indicating a fresh infusion of funds from some source. One day, Cap Weinberger called in some excitement. "Bandar came to see Jack Vessey," he said conspiratorially. "He told us the Saudis provided the President with $25 million for contra support." He was very pleased, though ironically he would later deny ever having been informed of the Saudi contribution. I was concerned, however, about Bandar's spreading the information too widely, since I feared it could cause a gratuitous backlash in Congress and make our task that much more difficult. Shortly afterward, General Vessey told me the same news as well. "Well, let's keep it under our hats," I said. "We're going to have to go and do our own heavy lifting on this with the Congress from now on."

Despite our best efforts, however, we lost the vote on the Hill that spring. It was a narrow defeat, and we still had the possibility of attaching an amendment to another bill later in the year. Still the loss agitated Ollie North. Earlier, he had sent me a memo proposing a fallback plan for just this contingency. Among its provisions was the suggestion that I go back to the Saudis one more time to ask for yet another contribution, a notion I had disapproved out of hand. I was prepared to see the contra operation ultimately shut down if we failed to rally Congress behind it, but Ollie didn't seem to be able to accept such a prospect. He couldn't, or wouldn't, accept that in Vietnam, many more lives had been lost than needed to be simply because we pretended we were going to be able to sell the war at home when we manifestly weren't. I also believed that by refusing to take the easy way out—going to friendly countries—it would make Ollie and others work harder.

I knew that North was making periodic trips to Central America and that he met routinely with Calero and other contra leaders in Miami. He told me, however, that these were little more than morale-boosting, handholding trips, in which he assured the rebels that the United States was still 100 percent behind them, and urged them to hang tough while we worked to pass legislation supporting them on the Hill. Whatever logistical assistance he provided consisted, according to him, of fundamental tactical advice and pointers—how to secure a perimeter, where to conceal trucks—small unit leadership advice of the sort that any self-respecting infantry officer would pass on. A far cry, at any rate, from "running a war," from deciding which regions of the country you would seek to control, or how you would deploy your troops in the field, or any of the larger elements of strategy which we took to be covered by the intent of the congressional prohibition.

I knew, too, that North was much in demand by the White House public liaison office as a speaker before VFW conventions and Chambers of Commerce and Lions' and Rotary clubs, where his role was to explain U.S. policy, both in general and specifically toward the contras. He went with my blessing, but also with the stricture that he was not to use these occasions as fundraising opportunities for the rebels. He always insisted that he never did. There was a lot of support in the heartland for the contras, he said, and people invariably approached him at the conclusion of one of his speeches to offer assistance and contributions, but his response to them was always the same: "I say, 'I am an official of the United States government and I cannot take any contributions,' and then I tell them to contact the contra leadership in Miami and tell them they're in the phone book," he told me. Still, at Wednesday afternoon staff meetings, I continued to stress frequently to my subordinates the realities of the law and the prohibition against soliciting or brokering any money for the Nicaraguan opposition.

In the summer of 1985, however, news reports began to appear charging that the NSC staff was doing precisely that, and more. Many of the stories focused on Ollie, alleging that he was helping the contras conduct their war and obtain supplies, both lethal and non-lethal, as well as actively engaging in private fundraising for their cause. When I asked him about these charges, he assured me as ever that there was nothing to them.

The stories would not go away, however, and in August, there was a more serious development. I was in Santa Barbara with the President when John Poindexter called to inform me that the office had received two letters from Hill Democrats demanding more information on my staff's activities regarding the contras. The letters, from Congressmen Lee Hamilton of Indiana and Mike Barnes of Maryland, asked for any NSC documents that would provide either evidence or explanation of the staff's involvement in support of the opposition movement.

I directed John to have all the contra documents that had come through my office, all the memos and reports, collected for my inspection, and when I returned to the office after Labor Day, I found an inch-and-a-half thick file on my desk. From this stack of papers, I gleaned six memos from North to me that appeared on their face to present evidence of his having engaged in activities that might arguably have been in violation of the law. They concerned matters such as his meeting with representatives from China to urge them to allow the delivery of anti-aircraft weapons to the contras, and a plan to seize a Nicaraguan merchant ship preparing to deliver a load of arms to Nicaragua. I remembered disapproving of the latter proposal, but I did not recall having seen all of these memos earlier. The fact is, though, that the volume of paper that flows through the National Security Adviser's office is so great—more than 30,000 pages in an average year—that I probably had seen them, but simply not reacted to them. Now I called Ollie in for an accounting.

"What's the story here?" I said. I told him that the memos looked damaging to me, that if I were a member of Congress looking at them without any context, I could certainly interpret them as proof that the NSC staff was indeed providing direct and/or indirect support to the contras. "Yesterday, I would have told anyone that we haven't been pursuing any activities in violation of the law," I said. "But today, there's a question in my mind about that."

North shook his head. "You're misreading these," he said, and launched into an elaborate explanation of how each memo said something different from what I thought it said. One, for example, stated that the contras were "responding well to our advice." That, he said, referred to the advice of a former Marine colleague on how to set up a staff. I listened to him, unconvinced. Accepting this and other explanations would have required a great stretch of the imagination. And I knew that most congressmen wouldn't be up for imagining anything.

At the same time, I was still mindful of Reagan's personal charge to me about sustaining the contras, body and soul. While I respected the Congress and believed in following the law to inform and consult with them—indeed, I had devoted far more time to consulting with the Congress than any of my predecessors—I did not believe that this required a wholesale abdication of the President's authority to conduct our foreign policy.

"Look, Ollie," I said. "You and I both have a responsibility to respect the separation of powers and to protect the President's prerogatives in this domain. But we also must not get him into an untenable position. So it's going to take some thorough understanding on our side and a careful engagement with the Congress to respond to their requests without prejudicing the President's rights or getting him into trouble."

I looked at him intently. "This is not a judge sitting here, Ollie, or your father confessor. It's me, Bud. Now tell me truthfully, one Marine to another. Have you been doing anything against the law?"

North did not hesitate. He looked me in the eye and told me a boldfaced lie. "Bud," he said. "I never did anything illegal."

And despite my suspicions, because I trusted him, I took him at his word.

———

My relationship with Oliver North has been a painful lesson in the power of human affection to blind one to the truth of another person's nature and the harm that this can do. The extent of my misjudgment of this man's character caused damage not only to myself, but to the administration I served and to the very image of responsible government that all public servants should strive to project to our young people, our citizens, and the world.

Marine Lieutenant Colonel Oliver L. North joined the staff of the National Security Council in 1981, a year before I came to the White House as deputy to the newly-appointed National Security Adviser, Judge William P. Clark. By then, North was already a figure of office folklore. He had already built the reputation of a real workhorse, staying at the office late in the day, producing papers more prodigiously, advocating the President's position in interdepartmental meetings more effectively than many of his colleagues.

His work habits, as it happened, were not very different from mine, starting with the five years I worked for Henry Kissinger and continuing today. Often we were the only two in the office late in the evening after everyone else had signed off for the day. He tended thus to gravitate toward my office to discuss or consult on various issues that we were working on. We were also both Marines— although I had retired from the Corps years before—and felt that sense of fraternity the Corps engenders in its members. There are no ex-Marines.

Early on, North also mentioned to me that he had served as S-3, or operations officer, under then-Lieutenant Colonel (now retired Major General) John Grinalds in a Second Marine Division battalion for six months in the Mediterranean in the mid-1970s. Grinalds, as it happened, was an old friend; in 1971, he and I had been the first Marines ever selected as White House Fellows. John was a West Point graduate and Rhodes Scholar, the type of person referred to among Marines as a "water walker." He and I were both promoted early on the same list—to lieutenant colonel—a year ahead of our classmates, and were viewed as two of the rising stars in the Corps. A devout and evangelical Christian, John had grown very fond of North and had exercised a strong influence on him, to the extent that I believe he was instrumental in North's being "born again." I asked John about Ollie not long after North mentioned him, and his response was one of unqualified praise for the young lieutenant colonel. "Ollie's terrific," he said. "A good guy, resourceful, energetic. The hardest-working guy I ever had." That was pretty persuasive to me. If John Grinalds thought Oliver North was good, then he undoubtedly was.

There was much else that recommended North to me at the time, that made me identify with him. Like me, he had come from middle-class roots, attended the Naval Academy, joined the Marines, served with distinction in Vietnam. Having shared the experience of that terrible war, I believed we shared many of the same beliefs and convictions about responsibility and public service. We were both hard-working, action-oriented individuals who seemed to share the same criteria for judging U.S. interests abroad and how to promote them.

One day in 1983, North approached me with a personal issue. After two years of civilian service at the White House, he wondered if it were time to return to the Marine Corps and pursue his ultimate objective of commanding a battalion; he worried that staying away longer might hurt his chances of doing that. In addition, he confided, he was having difficulties with his wife, Betsy, over the amount of time and energy he was putting into his work at the expense of his young family.

I understood acutely the dilemma he was facing. It was one I had confronted myself. I had served outside the Fleet Marine Force for five years during the Nixon and Ford administrations, and it had affected my career, causing vast ill will among the Corps' generals and costing me the opportunity to command a battalion. In that period, too, I had worked 85 hours a week or more, seven days a week, and often only saw my children when they got up to have breakfast with me at 5 o'clock in the morning or when I returned home after 10 at night. In spite of this, I did not believe North needed to apologize for his work habits; the assignment he was now engaged in would undoubtedly be the only one in his Marine Corps career he would be able to look back upon and say that he had influenced national policy and made a real difference, and that, I told him, was vindication of his investment in it. But I advised him that he should probably not extend his White House tour for more than another year, for the sake of both his career and his family.

A year later, Ollie was back with the same problem. By this time, however, I had been appointed National Security Adviser, we had established a close working relationship, and I had come to rely on him to a great extent for superior work on those issues that fell within his brief. For his part, he felt that in his involvement with the contras, he had gradually assumed the stature of a sort of "father confessor," and that to break off that relationship now would be difficult both for him and for them. Once again, I advised him that extending his time at the White House would undeniably hurt his career in the Marines, that once he passed the point of no return, he would forfeit any chance of becoming a general. At the same time, I assured him that if he chose to stay, I would use all my influence to get him command of a battalion whenever he returned to the Corps. He thought this over for a few days, and then told me he had decided to stay. I was pleased, for selfish reasons, and told him so. But he extracted a promise from me that I would hold to what I had said, and in a year, help him get a battalion. "I just don't want to go out and be a staff pogue somewhere," he told me pointedly.

Sure enough, a year later, he was headed for just that fate. In the spring of 1985, he told me that he had spoken with his Marine Corps monitor, or personnel detailer, who had indicated that when he returned to the Corps, he would be sent for a year to the War College, after which he would be assigned to a staff job somewhere. Remembering my promise to him, I arranged to have lunch with Marine Corps Commandant P.X. Kelley. P.X. and I went back a long way, having served together in headquarters in 1968 to 1970, when we were both execs to general officers, and I considered him an old friend. I broached the subject of North. Kelley listened attentively.

"Well, Bud, we can get North a battalion," he said when I had finished. "But are you aware of North's history in the Marine Corps?"

I didn't know what he meant. I had never heard of anything untoward regarding North.

"It was in the mid-1970s," Kelley said. "He had come back from Vietnam, and apparently was having great trouble with his family life. He and his wife were under great stress, and he turned himself into Bethesda. For psychiatric care."

I had never heard this before. "Tell me about it," I said.

"There isn't much more to tell. He recovered and went back to being an infantry officer. But you and I, Bud, both have watched promotion boards all our lives, and I'm telling you that North is not going to make general because of that experience. Call it unfair, but we both know that's how promotion boards act."

He paused for a moment. Then he added: "That isn't the only thing. Ollie just rubs a lot of people the wrong way. He has an air of superiority and he's a self-promoter, and that makes a lot of folks mad.

"I know that people who are destined to lead and get ahead are often like that, it's the nature of things. But in North's case. . . . Well, he's got more enemies than you would imagine. I think he also has trouble with the truth sometimes."

For some time afterward, I turned all of this over in my mind. I was concerned about the revelation of North's episode of depression; I thought it certainly possible that someone with that history, working under the enormous stress we experienced at the White House, could suffer a recurrence. This persuaded me that I ought to send Ollie back to the Marine Corps and I determined to do that in the long run. But in the short run, I had a selfish interest in keeping him on at the White House. I rationalized to myself: "Let's just get through this last struggle to get money for the contras. Then in the fall, you've got to think about this again and send him back."

As to Kelley's other comments about North, they did not make a deep impression on me at the time. I would never have said, then, that North's work ethic was fueled by personal ambition, by a need to make points with the boss, or anything other than dedication to his job and his constituents, like the contras, and later the hostages in Lebanon. He looked and sounded to me, as he appears to look and sound to so many today, like a genuine patriot, sincerely devoted to American ideals and their promotion and protection around the globe. As to his honesty, it had never occurred to me that he would lie. But appearances can be radically deceiving, as I learned the hard, but definitive, way. I was clearly seeing what I wished to see, because I liked this man. As a result, I did not see what was really there, the manipulative skill, the easy betrayal, the hubris, and the fierce ambition for personal advancement.

—

Ollie suggested he rewrite the memos that worried me to clarify their intent. I agreed to let him try. Yet the revised versions he brought me were ludicrous. They were for the most part grossly at odds with the original texts. In a couple of cases, he clearly altered the facts of the original, made black into white, as it were, and vice versa. I threw the rewritten versions away, and prepared to make my own explanations to Congress of what I believed to be true.

Throughout my government career, I had considered sensitive and timely consultations with the Congress to be one of the most important functions of the various posts I had held, and as vital to the success of any administration endeavor in the foreign policy arena as it was to the domestic legislative agenda. In approaching this body on Capitol Hill in which my father had served, however, I had also always adhered to certain unwritten rules of engagement that had traditionally governed executive-legislative communications and relations. According to these rules, you never lie; at the same time, Congress recognizes that a complete and thorough written answer to requests for information is not to be expected. Whatever letter one sends in response to such requests is generally intended by the congressman for public consumption in his district, where he can use it as an exhibit for his constituents, or in his subcommittee, as a demonstration of his zeal in pursuing this or that controversial issue. After providing the representative with Exhibit A, however, it is necessary to follow up in person to fill in the details, to reveal as truthfully as possible any material facts that had not been included in the written missive. This had been the practice for as long as I could remember, reaching back to when my father was a congressman. It was a practice long respected on both ends of Pennsylvania Avenue, and it was a practice I respected.

That was why I did not feel serious compunctions about signing the replies Ollie drafted to send to Hamilton and Barnes, despite the fact that their contents, looked at now, are admittedly categorical: "I can state with deep personal conviction that at no time did I or any member of the National Security Council staff violate the letter or spirit" of congressional restrictions on aid to the contras. (At the end of one of the letters, Ollie had added a poignant postscript: because of the news stories about his involvement with the contras, someone had poisoned his family's dog, it said. I found it touching, though slightly schmaltzy, myself. Much later, of course, the truth came out: The dog had died of old age and cancer. It was a vintage North flight of fancy, a small but telling example of his deceit and manipulativeness.)

After the letters were sent in early September 1985, I called Hamilton and Barnes and offered to come to their committees to testify further about what I knew North was doing, or to invite them to the White House to look at the contra documents themselves. Hamilton chose the first option, and I consequently paid a visit to the House Permanent Select Committee on Intelligence, where I talked about the morale-boosting trips North was making to Central America, and what he had told me about the many offers of financial support that he received from citizens whenever he went out on the stump. It's interesting that in this closed-door meeting, and one or two others that I held with senators and representatives at the White House, many of the congressmen, Republicans especially, actually applauded the activities I described. Henry Hyde, for instance, a Republican from Illinois, was a genuine bomb-thrower in private; he went so far as to say that the U.S. ought to find a private way to fund

Cardinal Obando y Bravo, the head of the Roman Catholic Church in Nicaragua and a fervent anti-Sandinista. Yet when the Iran-contra scandal broke in November 1986, and with it the revelations of third-country contributions to the contras and the like, Hyde was among the first and loudest to beat his breast in outrage at this violation of the public trust.

After my testimony, Dick Cheney took me aside for a private word. "The staff here is really convinced that North is doing more than you are saying he is, so you'd better watch your 6 o'clock on this," he warned me, using the fighter pilot's expression for watching one's back. His words, of course, were prescient. Yet on that day I had not the slightest inkling that North was already starting up his private, off-the-shelf enterprise for providing logistical and material support to the contras. I had my suspicions that he was not coming completely clean on the fundraising question, but it would have been inconceivable to me to imagine that he was getting ready to run a full-fledged rogue operation out of the White House. It was hard for me, later, to know with what a light conscience he had betrayed my trust, to listen to him lie, to say that I knew and approved of it, and gave him the authority to start it. This is not to say that I shouldn't have known; I should have. However busy I was with other issues, however many balls I had in the air, however many problems rested on my shoulders—I was his superior and I should have known what he was up to. I have always been willing to take responsibility for not knowing, for trusting him too much, and to be held accountable for that. But I wasn't going to know the truth from him. If I had known of his schemes, I never would have approved them. North was much too canny not to have known that; it's no doubt why he waited until I was out of office to get things into full swing.

Mike Barnes chose to come to my office to take a firsthand look at the contra documents himself. Before he was scheduled to visit, I called Dante Fascell, who was chairman of the House Foreign Affairs Committee. Dante and I had worked together for a long time and knew each other well; right after the release of the TWA hostages about two months earlier, he had sent me a gracious congratulatory note. What I wanted from him was a frame of reference: How much concern was there within the committee about the contra stories? How far was Barnes's inquiry going to go?

Dante conceded that Barnes believed my staff was providing support to the contras, and that he was serious about wanting answers from me. At the same time, he said, "[Barnes] is running for the Senate, and he's trying to get some ink. There's no big storm in the committee about this issue, and it's probably going to stay in [Barnes's Latin American affairs] subcommittee." It was the assurance I needed that the issue would most likely go away if I could meet Barnes's demands, and that these demands probably had more to do with his wanting to be able to say that he had gone to the White House on the matter, than with his being willing to sit down and spend hours going over a stack of papers in my office.

It turned out this was right. Barnes arrived for his appointment at 8:30 on the morning of October 17. "I've been rather categorical in my letter about what we are not doing," I began. "We are not violating the law. But I want you to know what we are doing, and I don't think it departs from the spirit of the prohibitions." And once again I went through my overview of North's activities. But, I said, if he wished to go through the documents himself, he was welcome to, and I pointed at my conference table. On it was the original stack of contra memos, a couple of inches thick, that my staffer Brenda Reger and the NSC legal counsel Paul Thompson had pulled for me to examine. Among them were the six problematic memos I had discussed with North, and which I now worried that Barnes might actually read.

Barnes looked at the stack of papers. He looked at me.

"I've got to have them up on the Hill," he said, knowing, of course, that this was not going to happen. Knowing that the President of the United States was not going to send memoranda from the White House staff to a legislative subcommittee. It was a *pro forma* request for which Barnes got credit and against which he could posture, but he could not have had any serious expectation that we were going to send highly classified advice given to the President by his White House staff to the Hill. I declined his request, he thanked me formally, and left.

———

It was by now September 1985. The work days were long and full of activity with the Geneva summit only weeks away, and I already had in mind to leave the White House at the end of the year. Partly in the knowledge of that, partly out of concern for North's own health and career, partly because I had my suspicions that he was doing more with the contras than he was letting on, I made myself a promise that when I left, he would leave, too. And after I had handed in my resignation, I met with John Poindexter and urged that he send Ollie back to the Marine Corps. It was in North's own best interests, I said, noting that I thought he was tired and that if he hoped to maintain his career in the military, he had already been too long away. I did not tell John about North's psychiatric history, but perhaps I should have.

For in fact, Ollie didn't leave when I left. He stayed on at the White House and his activities clearly multiplied. Around March of 1986 came another flurry of news stories about congressional angst over White House staff support for the contras in violation of the law. North, again, was at the center of most of them. Hesitantly, because I didn't want to seem to be telling him how to do his job, I sent John a note. I knew that Poindexter didn't like the Congress and didn't understand how quickly a congressman can develop an issue with great effect. And I thought he might have been missing the fact that Ollie's activities and all the attention they were attracting could create a vulnerability for him, Poindexter—and the President.

Send Ollie back to the Marines, I urged once more. He's become a lightning rod.

By this time, my own suspicions about North's activities had crystallized into a near-certainty that he was actively engaged in supporting the contras. Since leaving government, I had received one or two PROFs electronic mail notes from him asking me for help with some contra-related issues. On one occasion, he asked if I knew where it would be possible to get some artillery for the rebels. I rationalized to myself that he himself was not procuring the artillery, but only advising the contras as to where they should go themselves to look for it. Since my resignation, the law had been changed to allow that sort of advice. Similarly, when he mentioned Dick Secord in a message as having been helpful in supplying the contras with weapons and logistical support, I reasoned that perhaps the contras had approached Secord of their own accord, since he had become a weapons dealer after leaving the military. In my heart, though, I suspected worse.

Some may say I should have acted more forcefully on my suspicions. Yet I had reasons for not doing so. For one thing, I was out of the government by then, no longer a policy or decisionmaker with clout. Those on the inside would rightly resent my trying to perform their jobs from the outside. Secondly, our efforts to politicize the contras and make them more appealing to the Hill were having the intended effect, and it appeared Congress might reinstate funding for the contras on a significant scale—as much as $100 million. To have popped off at that point, as an outsider, and said, "You've got to come to a full stop here," and later to have been proven wrong in such a recommendation, went against my grain.

I have always respected the separation of powers and in my work recognized that Congress's control of the purse strings is a legitimate check on the executive's operation of foreign policy. The framers of the Constitution understood the dangers that would spring from an unbridled ability to raise private funds for the purpose of waging war and provided Congress with the reins to slow any such runaway steed. On the other hand, the unrestrained and partisan use of that check, which we certainly confronted during the Reagan years, points up a flaw in the doctrine. Later, in his testimony, one of North's more accurate lines was that in five years there were nine changes in congressional authority regarding the contras. This much, at least, was true. This sort of seesawing commitment makes it impossible to support a policy, makes it impossible to build confidence *vis-a-vis* allies who are risking their lives predicated on such support, and to provide an adequate basis for day-to-day planning when it is unclear whether the support will endure from year to year. This, too, came into my reasoning whenever I read the reports from North. If the President is going to conduct the nation's foreign policy, it cannot be under a constantly changing set of ground rules. In that respect, for the contra conspiracy that formed in the White House, Congress must bear some responsibility, too.

I made one more stab at getting Ollie sent back to the Marines. It came after he dropped his bombshell on the tarmac in Tel Aviv in May 1986. The news that money from the Iran arms sales was being siphoned off and sent to the contras was alarming, but I didn't know that there was much I could do about it. John Poindexter was North's superior now, and it was up to him to oversee the policing of his staff. Nonetheless, I suspected that Ollie probably found it easier to bully John than me. John was an extremely intelligent officer, but had no experience in combat, which probably made him more susceptible to North's occasionally cockamamie ideas about field operations and strategy. I could see that the combination of a more freewheeling North and a National Security Adviser who didn't like the Congress or the press was going to put the President in a very vulnerable position, and I thought that removing North from the picture might relieve that problem to some extent. Moreover, I thought North was tired, and consequently experiencing lapses in judgment.

So, once more, I pressed the point. In June of 1986, about a week after my return from the mission to Tehran, after I had urged the President once more to discontinue the Iran initiative, I sent Poindexter another note, urging *him* to relieve North of his duties and send him back to the Marines.

But if John heard me, he didn't listen.

Chapter 6

SCANDAL

I heard the news on the radio first.

I can no longer remember exactly where I was. This I find strange, because it seems it should be the kind of moment permanently frozen in my memory, the details of my whereabouts and actions forever vivid, as they are for people who remember precisely where they were and what they were doing when they heard about the attack on Pearl Harbor, or the assassination of John F. Kennedy. I can only remember the announcer's voice on the radio and the words I dreaded to hear:

A Lebanese newspaper, *Al Shiraa,* had published a report alleging that I, Robert C. McFarlane, former National Security Adviser, had recently visited Tehran as a secret envoy of the President of the United States, to deliver arms to Khomeini and negotiate for the release of the American hostages in Lebanon.

It was November 4, 1986. That was the beginning of the Iran-contra scandal.

That it would be a scandal, and a huge one, was the first thought that came to me. There were plenty of details the story had wrong: the date of my visit; the report that I carried a Bible signed by Reagan—there was no Bible on my trip; apparently North later carried one to a meeting; that I traveled disguised as an airline crewman—I wore a coat and tie, as suitable to a diplomatic mission; and above all, the exact nature of what had transpired in Tehran—that I was dealing with Khomeini, for instance. But the gist of it rode close enough to the truth that as I listened to the radio broadcast, I knew without a shadow of a doubt that the spotlight was about to be turned full force on the White House and the President, and that the heat from it would be withering.

We had engaged with the enemy. In the beginning, we had had legitimate reasons for doing so. But over the last 10 months, the Iran initiative had deteriorated into a pure arms-for-hostages deal with no redeeming value. In all that time, only two more hostages had been released, while the Iranians had squeezed from the United States three more overgenerous shipments of arms. My last effort at dissuading the President from continuing down this perilous path, after the failure of the Tehran mission in May, had come to naught. Someone had "blown" the operation. It could have been any of several disaffected or venal Iranians, Syria's President Hafez al-Assad or the Russians. It mattered little. The point was that Ronald Reagan's Teflon had been torn and his legions of critics were about to have revenge.

The reporters wasted no time in calling. Besieged, I stalled them at first, not lying, but merely saying that the story was inaccurate. I told one reporter it was "fanciful," as indeed many of the details were. As soon as I had a chance, I put a call through to John Poindexter. I wanted his read on how the White House was handling the news. John asked me to refrain from making any comment for as long as I could. "We still think there's a serious chance of getting some more hostages out in the near future," he said. That seemed unrealistic to me. But I loyally agreed to withhold comment for the time being.

It was the day before the midterm elections, and Jonny and I had been invited by Vice President George and Barbara Bush to join them for a reception to watch the returns. The evening passed in a surreal haze. I had felt, all day, caught in the middle of a firestorm, brimstone falling all about me; yet that evening I felt enveloped in a sort of false cocoon. The word Iran did not fall from a single pair of lips; no one mentioned the news reports, asked about them, acknowledged them in any way. It was the most momentary of respites, however. Soon enough Iran, and its offspring Iran-contra, would be dominating all our lives.

In a bizarre sidelight to the main activity, I received a phone call from former President Jimmy Carter within a day or so after the story broke. Far from being critical of the Iran operation, he asked whether I could seek the release of an individual, a Georgia businessman being held in Iran, as part of our "negotiations." I gave him no basis for optimism but agreed to pass the name to Poindexter.

Over the coming days, the White House's attitude toward the growing controversy struck me as both wrong and foolish. Stonewalling had obviously been adopted as the technique with which to handle the tidal wave of press inquiries that engulfed the administration. I wasn't privy to the mechanics of what was going on inside the White House at this stage; yet the silence that issued forth from the sanctum was unsettling. It was, most of all, not smart. I had been through Vietnam, through Watergate, and I knew that simple denial, unbacked by any further explanation, ultimately would not wash.

It ought to be a working principle in politics—when in trouble, promptly acknowledge error and apologize. Americans don't admire politicians, but they admire even less those who dissemble, equivocate or make excuses. Humility is respected; after the Marine bombing, Reagan's acceptance of responsibility had the effect of engendering sympathy and respect from the public. I believed that though the Iran scandal surely wasn't going to go away within a few days, acknowledging error would have the effect of engaging the public in a way that would appeal to their values.

Not long after the story broke, I heard from Brent Scowcroft. He said he had been getting a great many calls from journalists asking for his comments on the affair, and the clear picture he received from them was that Don Regan, my old nemesis, was indicating to one and all that the whole Iran business had been my idea.

"Regan is hanging you out to dry," Brent said.

This news did not surprise me, but it did anger me. I was willing to take the responsibility for having initiated the talks with Iran, but not against the backdrop of utter and official White House silence and disapproval, or anyone else's knowledge of the matter. Everyone in the White House national security circle, as well as several people outside it—notably Don Regan—had known about and supported, or acquiesced to, the Iran opening, but now chose to sit sphinx-like in the face of the media onslaught. Moreover, Regan had maligned me with the press on a past occasion, and this smacked of a repeat of that earlier performance. In a moment of anger, I sat down and sent John Poindexter a PROFs note complaining about Regan's actions. "This will be the second lie Don Regan has sown against my character, and I won't stand for it," I wrote heatedly.

In an effort to explain the genesis of the Iran initiative, I sat down and wrote two articles which I sent to Meg Greenfield at the *Washington Post*. One was a straightforward analysis of the situation facing Iran and the reasons why I had believed that an opening to that country was worth exploring. The second piece was more clever in its approach. It asked readers to imagine themselves as government officials faced with the question of whether or not to engage in talks with an enemy nation of great strategic importance that has sent a diplomat to Washington to suggest an exploratory dialogue. The theoretical dilemma was "whether or not to take a risk that if successful will provide enormous benefits for the country, but which if unsuccessful and misunderstood could result, at a minimum, in great embarrassment and, more likely, in a considerable setback to U.S. relations with allies and to your relations with Congress."

"You are concerned," I wrote, "for this involves a country whose government has recently gone through a very violent revolution in which the government killed literally hundreds of thousands of its own people, and where there is no certain basis for confidence that the people you might deal with carry real authority, or will deal in good faith, or will be able to make good on their commitments.

"Furthermore, it is a government that at this very moment is involved in supporting elements in third countries that are engaged in killing Americans. And the diplomat urging you to [open a dialogue] also makes clear that there will undoubtedly be a *quid-pro-quo* involved—you will have to pay something for this, probably in the domain of security assistance of some kind, for the country in question is locked in a strategic struggle with its neighbor. At the same time, there is no question but that if such a dialogue were to develop and be kept clandestine for long enough to identify a set of milestones for renewing stable relations, the strategic interests of the United States would benefit enormously."

Would the reader, I asked, agree to go to a first meeting with this country as suggested by its diplomat?

Naturally readers would assume that I was talking about Iran and the Iran initiative, but the piece ended with a twist. "Of course the scenario isn't theoretical," I wrote. "It has happened, and the government decided to go ahead with the clandestine contacts. The country was China, and today most people credit the secret diplomacy of Dr. Henry Kissinger with giving us one of the most dramatic diplomatic triumphs ever achieved in our history."

Although I believed my first piece was the better, more substantive work, Meg chose to publish the second. The effect, unfortunately, was to reinforce an impression building in the media that I had looked upon the job of National Security Adviser as my opportunity to be a

Kissinger—a man for whom I had worked and whose accomplishments, if not character, I admired—and to replicate his success and achieve his status. It implied that I was a vain, overreaching person.

The China analogy occurred to others besides myself. In the weeks after the scandal broke, a letter to the editor in the *Wall Street Journal* argued that if the Iran opening had worked, as China did, it would have been hailed as a brilliant stroke of diplomacy; having failed, it was being denounced as a foolhardy exploit of no saving grace that would forever henceforth be the butt of jokes and stories. The piece was signed by a John Taylor. Later, it was revealed that "John Taylor" was actually Richard Nixon.

In the 20 years that had intervened between China and Iran, however, much had changed in the way that American foreign policy could be conducted. Vietnam and Watergate had shaken the political landscape, and secrecy in government, particularly surrounding major policy initiatives, was no longer acceptable to the American people. Having decided to commence direct U.S. arms sales to Iran after I left, the administration should have advised Congress of the President's Finding within a few months. Yet it had never done so, no doubt out of an astute realization that Congress, reflecting the almost certain disapproval of the public, would never have gone along with the scheme. Today, a China diplomacy of the sort Nixon and Kissinger pulled off is no longer feasible. But it took the trauma of Iran-contra to teach us that lesson once and for all.

—

Finally buckling under legitimate pressure from the press, the White House at last decided to send Ronald Reagan forth to make a public statement about Iran on November 13. In the meantime, I was busy in my work with the Center for Strategic and International Studies, traveling and giving speeches on U.S. foreign policy. I was also fencing daily with the press, all the while reflecting privately on how to put this squalid affair into context for the evening sound bite. On the day of the President's address to the nation, I was traveling to Mexico City for a scheduled speech before the Young Presidents Organization there. But the media clamored for my time and attention, and I agreed to do a live interview with NBC's Tom Brokaw once I arrived in Dallas, where I was to change planes.

As I took my seat on the flight to Texas, a man approached me and asked if I minded if he sat down next to me. I agreed, and he introduced himself as Art Kent, a national security correspondent for *NBC News*. I had never met Kent before, and perhaps it was a measure of my eagerness to get my side of the story out that I was willing for the next two hours to sit and discuss with him the whole history of the Iran affair, knowing that he would use anything I had to say.

When we landed in Dallas, Kent disembarked quickly and raced off to file his story. Meanwhile I walked out of the jetway into a crush of reporters and floodlights and microphones. A United Airlines representative managed to guide me away to a private suite where I sat for the interview with Tom Brokaw. After that, I called my office, and Caroline Scullin, my executive assistant, told me that ABC's *Nightline* staff had arranged to charter an airplane to take me to Mexico City the next day if I would agree to stay overnight in Dallas and appear on *Nightline*.

On *Nightline*, I tried to represent the Tehran trip as the diplomatic mission I had intended it to be. I told Koppel that we and the Iranians "held four days of talks that went reasonably well. We were received hospitably and treated with the normal practice that surrounds meetings like this."

"Did you bring in a cake?" Koppel asked me, zeroing in on the farcical details of the trip, as so much of the press was. I bristled a bit at the thought that North's ridiculous cake was getting so much attention, as though it were some weighty and significant aspect of the trip.

"You know me better than that, Ted," I replied. "I didn't have anything to do with a cake. I didn't buy it, bake it, present it or eat it."

"Bible?" Koppel asked.

"No Bible," I said, and it was true. Yet there are still people today who insist that McFarlane took a Bible to Tehran.

Dispelling such notions was difficult, but it was just as difficult to get the press to tell the story straight. Disappointingly, the product of my two-hour heart-to-heart session on the plane with Art Kent was a slanted story that refused to give any plausibility to the idea of there being any opposition to Khomeini in Iran and simply averred that I had acknowledged the transfer of weapons for hostages.

It was frustrating to me in all the coverage of events that fall, and despite my countless appearances on all the morning shows and network newscasts, that little distinction was made between what I saw as two separate phases of the Iran initiative—one while I was in government, the second after I had left. It is accurate to say that while I was in government, no U.S. weapons were transferred to Iran, no documents were shredded or altered, or any illegal acts committed. Yet over the years, the truth of this has become lost in time and journalistic lapse.

The President's address to the nation was likewise frustrating to me. It showed no real change in the bunker mentality that appeared to have settled over the White House, and was just this side of an outright lie. While acknowledging that we had pursued a diplomatic initiative with Iran, the President stated that only a small amount of defensive weapons had been shipped, all of which could have fit into a single cargo plane. Again, I felt compelled to send Poindexter a note, stressing that it was time for the White House to get the story out.

"I lived through Watergate, John," I wrote. "Well-meaning people who were in on the early planning of the communications strategy didn't intend to lie but ultimately came around to it. I don't know how [Don] Regan will tend. He might choose two courses; either to push it off on someone outside the White House, which is fine with me, or he might go ahead with a "sell it on its merits" strategy. If the latter is the course followed, it must not be confrontational, but open and candid.

"The judgments made on this and other matters in the next four or five days will be crucial."

By now, even the White House had to acknowledge that it was time to put out some facts. A presidential press conference was scheduled, and the NSC staff planned to put together a chronology of the Iran initiative for Reagan to follow. Poindexter asked whether I would be willing to help out, and I agreed to come in and critique what had been prepared.

On the evening of November 18, I skipped a dinner party to which Jonny and I had been invited and went downtown about 8 p.m. to Ollie North's office in the Old Executive Office Building. The scene was chaos. In the outer office, Ollie's secretary, Fawn Hall, was typing away feverishly. In the inner office, Howard Teicher, Bob Earl, a Rhodes scholar, and Craig Coy, a Coast Guard officer in Ollie's branch, were seated around the conference table. The table itself was strewn with dozens and dozens of scraps of paper. Everyone was writing, cutting and pasting. It looked as though a grenade had gone off in the room.

Ollie rushed up and handed me a sheaf of papers. It was a draft chronology, he said, put together by the agency. "The people across the street," he said, referring to the White House, "believe there's a problem with the first Hawk shipment."

He looked hard at me, and I remember he spoke his next words very carefully. "Remember, Bud," he said, "you and I didn't learn until January '86 about these Hawks."

That didn't sound right to me, and I must have looked perplexed, because he went on quickly: "Remember, when you were in Geneva and we had to call the third country to get clearance for transfer? We thought it was oil drilling equipment. We didn't find out it was Hawks until later."

I was hesitant to acknowledge that this was correct, but in all honesty I couldn't at that moment clearly recollect what had transpired more than a year ago in a five-minute telephone conversation while I was in the middle of the Gorbachev summit, one of the most intense and all-consuming events of my government service. And I did vaguely remember having seen intelligence reports back then that stated the Israelis considered shipping oil drilling equipment as an alternative to weapons in the Iran initiative.

North, for his part, was not about to let me consider this question for very long. "Bud, I promised John a revised draft an hour ago," he said urgently. "I really need your help. We've got to hustle."

Today, I see that as a vintage North snow job: Give the guy the bum's rush, don't let him think, get him to take Amiram Nir to Tehran, give him some artificial reason for why it's not arguable and get on with it.

At the time, I sat down and went to work on the chronology. I could see immediately that it was a serious cut-and-paste job. Right off the bat, I identified what I thought were a number of mistakes. For instance, there was a reference to Ghorbanifar's having had contact with the CIA in 1984, a full year before he came to my attention in connection with the Iran initiative. "Is this right?" I asked North, and he shrugged, saying, "yes, it was," and he hadn't known about it either. It was the first I learned that Casey had withheld that information from me and the NSPG.

Overall, I could see that the chronology was a slanted account of the facts, designed to minimize the President's exposure to the scandal. I was not opposed to protecting the President; I still felt loyal to him, and I agreed that the truth should be presented in as favorable a light as possible. It was important, however, that it basically be the truth, or at least something one could defend as truth. That was my aim in commenting on the chronology. Where the Hawks versus oil drilling equipment was concerned, because I had been confused by North moments before, I contented myself with striking the words "oil drilling" and leaving only "equipment," which I thought was vague enough to be defensible if challenged.

The other point that concerned me was the description of Reagan's reaction upon learning of the initial Israeli shipment of TOWs. The President, the draft said, had been "upset." That statement struck me between the eyes. I didn't recall the President being upset at all; rather the opposite, in fact. I asked Ollie if he knew to whom the President had expressed any displeasure, but he said no. I could not prove that this had not happened, that the President might not have been upset with *someone.* So I merely made a note to John that I knew nothing about this, and that the President had never expressed displeasure about the TOW shipment to me, and that it seemed at odds with his support of the idea from the beginning.

I knew that the chronology was not going to be enough for the President to go on in answering questions at a press conference the next night. So after I had finished with the chronology and sent that note off to John, I began working on an opening statement for the President to make. As it was getting late, however, I decided to finish up at home and bring the completed product by in the morning.

When I returned the next day, Florence Gantt, John's secretary, told me that Ollie, John and several others were in a meeting. She looked in and came back out to say they were just breaking up. I went into John's office just as he, North, Teicher, and Alton Keel, who had taken over as deputy National Security Adviser when Don Fortier had died in August, were getting up.

Howard passed me with a greeting as I walked into the office to hear North say, "So other than the CIA involvement, we don't have a problem."

I blurted: "The heck you don't. You've got a problem with that diversion to the contras."

At that, North winced and reached past me to shut the door.

"Howard doesn't know about that," he said.

"Well, you've got to deal with it," I said shrugging. "It's not going to go away."

But I believed then that North was going to try to keep the diversion secret and sweep it under the rug if humanly possible.

———

The President's press conference was, by all measures, a disaster. He didn't use the opening statement I had prepared. He appeared nervous, bumbling, got his facts wrong and contradicted information that had already been acknowledged in the press, but still refused to admit that a mistake had been made. I was distressed.

Months before, an old friend, Gene Counihan, had invited me to speak to the Gaithersburg Chamber of Commerce on November 20, the day after Reagan's press conference. Although my appearance had been scheduled even before the Iran story broke, word that I would be speaking had leaked out and when I arrived I found a host of reporters on hand hoping to grill me.

In this atmosphere, I decided the speech I had prepared on general aspects of U.S. foreign policy would be irrelevant. So I put it aside and spoke instead, extemporaneously, about Iran. I explained the initiative, the original motivation behind it, how it had evolved. And then I said that it had been a mistake, an error in judgment for which I, and no one else, was responsible.

I wasn't prepared for the reaction that hit me when the papers hit the stands the next day. The White House was up in arms for what it deemed my treasonous remarks. Don Regan was especially vocal, complaining to the press and all who would listen about my disloyalty, even though it was he who had been leaking stories that everything was all my idea. Privately, word got back to me that he was furious that I wasn't defending the Iran initiative, as all the rest of them were. To say something was a mistake, he believed, was always the wrong thing to do.

At least one voice, however, spoke up in my favor. John Poindexter told me later that the President didn't agree with his Chief of Staff. "I understand why Bud said that," Poindexter quoted Reagan as saying. "I don't blame him a bit."

By now, almost three weeks after the storm had broken, even the chiefs in the White House had realized that action was needed to protect the President's reputation. In a public show of accountability, Reagan accordingly instructed Attorney General Ed Meese to conduct an internal investigation into the Iran initiative.

Meese called me in on the 21st for my version of events. He greeted me in his Justice Department office along with Charles Cooper, an Assistant Attorney General who was helping with the investigation. Once again, I told the lengthy tale, starting with the fateful summer day when David Kimche had come to my office. When we got to the November 1985 shipment, I described my sketchy role from Geneva and said: "I've been told that the Israelis then shipped these oil drilling parts."

Meese stopped me. "Well now, was it oil parts," he queried me purposefully, "or was it Hawks?"

"Well, it was in fact Hawks," I replied, "but I'm told that we didn't learn that until January of the following year."

Meese leaned forward. "George Shultz says that you told him in Geneva that it was Hawks, and he made contemporaneous notes about it."

"I'm sure he's right," I said without hesitation. I wasn't insisting that it was oil drilling parts; I didn't even really believe it myself, but had repeated what North had told me. Until that moment, I had not known Ollie to lie to me. And I still wasn't ready to believe that he would do that. Later, Meese testified that I was completely open on this score, but that got lost, too, in the tumultuous months that followed.

We wrapped up the interview, and Cooper left the room. I turned to Meese.

"Can I talk to you for a minute?" I asked. "Ed, the responsibility for this is mine, and I deserve the burden of that. But you should know, as the President's counsel, that he approved this at the beginning and was entirely supportive of every step along the way."

Meese nodded. "I know that, Bud," he said. Those words brought me a sense of immeasurable relief. Meese had obviously talked to Reagan before he ever got me in the room, and he knew that Ronald Reagan had approved the first Israeli shipments. In all the speculation and obfuscation surrounding that point in the weeks to come, I would be able to remember that Meese had confirmed the truth.

Now, he was thanking me for confirming it for him. "It puts things in a different light," he said, and explained that his predecessor, William French Smith, had previously determined that even oral approval could constitute a legal Finding, which would provide legitimate authority for subsequent events flowing from the original decision, and would also justify waiving the requirement to report to Congress.

I left Meese's office feeling slightly more encouraged than I had in days. Outside, I found a pay phone and called Ollie North. I wanted to pass on what I thought was good news, that Meese was encouraged by the fact that there was a legal defense for our actions. I also told him about George Shultz's notes regarding the Hawk shipment. I thought it important that he and the others get the story right, because that very day both Poindexter and Regan had held press backgrounders in which they claimed the November shipment was oil drilling parts, a claim that was about to be exposed as untrue.

The ox was in the ditch, and I still had a sense of loyalty toward North and Poindexter. I knew they were in a good deal of trouble, and that the best thing I could do was to give them my soundest judgment, which continued to be to get the facts out, and to present them in as good a light as feasible, although they were inherently bad. At the time, of course, I didn't think anyone was doing anything illegal.

It was freezing outside, an uncommonly cold day for Washington, and I shivered as I talked. Ollie thanked me for the information. Then he said he had been advised to get a lawyer. "So we'd better not talk, because I'm probably being monitored right now." My ears were numb from the cold. I was only too happy to hang up.

The next day, I was surprised to receive another call from Meese. He had some more questions; something new had come up.

I went in to his office on Monday. He informed me that in a search of North's offices the previous Saturday, his team had uncovered a memo that made clear that money from the Iran arms sales was going to the contras.

"Did you know that?" Meese asked.

I nodded grimly. "Yes, I was told by North on the tarmac in Tel Aviv," I said. I told Meese how North had enlightened me. His news had astonished me, I said, but having no reason to think otherwise, I had assumed that it was, for better or worse, approved policy.

"Did you ever hear any more about it?" Meese pressed. "About the President knowing about it or approving it?"

"No," I replied. "That's all I know."

———

That same evening, I flew to London, where I had a speaking engagement before the United Israel Appeal. I was in my hotel room the next day when the host of the group telephoned. "Have you heard?" he said. "There's going to be a White House press announcement at noon, coming on very soon here."

I switched on the television and watched as Ed Meese announced that his investigation of the Iran initiative had revealed that funds received from the sale of weapons to Iran had been diverted to the contras in Nicaragua. The Iran scandal had become the Iran-contra scandal.

The *only* individuals witting of the diversion, Meese went on to say, were National Security Adviser John Poindexter, National Security Council staffer Oliver North, and former National Security Adviser Robert McFarlane. I shook my head. It was true; I was witting of it, but no more than that. I felt a pinprick of anger at what seemed a gratuitous calling of attention to me when I had had no substantive role in this episode of the affair.

To spare my hosts the onslaught of press inquiries I could foresee coming, I sat down immediately and wrote out a truthful account of how I had learned of the diversion. I managed to get the statement out to the wire services and went off to my dinner and speech at the Dorchester Hotel. When I emerged several hours later, a mob of reporters was waiting for me at the curb. I declined to comment, jumped in a taxi and went straight back to my hotel. The scandal had clearly reached the level of an international event.

At the airport the next day, British Airways upgraded my return ticket to a seat on the Concorde. As I walked into the Concorde lounge, the first person I saw was my longtime friend, Clare Boothe Luce.

She looked at me. "What are you doing here?" she demanded.

"Going home," I replied anticlimactically.

She gazed at me for a moment, then flashed an impish smile. "Well, you're in a lot of trouble . . ." she drawled, "but give 'em hell."

I had a lot of time to think about her words on the flight back to Washington. I assumed we were heading for some sort of congressional hearings and investigations, and it seemed to me that I had to be very energetic in trying to tell the whole history of the matter as well as I knew it to help get this crisis behind us as quickly as we could. I knew Mrs. Luce was right; I was in a lot of trouble, and it was likely to be severe.

I closed my eyes and prayed, acknowledging error and asking for guidance and strength to do the right thing.

—

The congressional hearings came, as I'd anticipated, both in the Senate and the House. In addition, the President appointed a Special Review Board, headed by former Texas Senator John Tower, to do an independent investigation of Iran-contra from a policy perspective, and soon thereafter an independent counsel, Lawrence Walsh, was appointed to look into possible criminal violations. The days of December loomed as a forest of interviews, interrogations and hearings.

I was determined to go forward and tell the story to the best of my ability. I believed it was my duty. I had been a public official. I had been paid by the government. I owed the government, and the people, the truthful history of what I had done.

This, I know, makes me sound like a Boy Scout. And in retrospect, I can see that it might have been wiser, certainly more shrewd, to wait, to gain access to all my government records first, to be sure of what I was saying before I testified under oath. Yet I believed that my memory was good; I saw that no one else was willing to testify; and, in truth, I didn't feel vulnerable. I didn't believe I had done anything criminal, and for what I had done, I was willing to be held accountable.

What's more, I could not imagine my father condoning any other course. He himself had been a man of integrity and absolute, *in toto*, devotion to public service. He had taken the notion of the special trust granted to him very seriously, and in his wake I did the same. I cannot recall his ever even thinking of a way to avoid responsibility.

It was not the route that others were choosing. North and Poindexter were taking the Fifth Amendment, and later agreed to testify before the congressional committees only after being granted immunity. Others, higher up, were telling half-truths at best, out-and-out lies at worst. Reagan, after first supporting me on his approval of the Israeli shipments, was soon convinced by Don Regan and White House counsel Peter Wallison that he hadn't approved them and finally ended up saying he just couldn't remember much about the whole affair, a thoroughly plausible explanation, coming from Ronald Reagan.

Nevertheless, I still felt a loyalty to him and his ideals, and to the government I had served. Despite my best intentions, the hearings did not all go smoothly. Early on, as I testified before the Senate Intelligence Committee, staff director Bernie McMahon brought up rumors that a third country had provided financial support to the contras.

"What do you know about that?" he asked.

I was on the hot seat. The Saudi contribution had not been illegal, but it was the sort of thing that would cause an outcry if disclosed and embarrassment both to our government and the Saudis. Furthermore, this very committee had caused us problems in the past by not respecting confidentiality of information. During the seizure of the *Achille Lauro* in 1985, one prominent senator had been briefed by the CIA on how we had learned the whereabouts of the terrorists who had seized the ship and then escaped. The source was an agent in Egyptian President Hosni Mubarak's office. The senator had left the briefing and promptly reported to a morning television news show. "Through sources in President Mubarak's office, we have learned . . . ," he had unhesitatingly and self-importantly intoned on the program. It was enough to endanger a valuable intelligence source. I'd been burned once by these guys and didn't want me, the Saudis or the U.S. government to be burned again. So even though the hearing was closed, I decided to try to finesse the question until I could get some guidance from the administration. I responded that while I had seen the reports of the contribution, "the exact nature of it is beyond my ken." That was technically true, since I did not know the precise dollar amounts or the details of distribution. But the inescapable fact is that I did withhold information.

As the hearings ground on, and as, repeatedly, I was the only witness who turned up to testify, I began to experience a growing sense of isolation, and a slow depression began to engulf me. Even just a month before, when the scandal first erupted, there had been moments of lightness when I had still been able to laugh at the absurd aspects of the situation. Once, after a speech in Chicago, Jonny and I had had a very early morning plane to catch. We had stepped out of our hotel into the pitch blackness of the city and got into a waiting black limousine. As the big car moved silently into the night, a deep, heavily-accented voice came out of the darkness, speaking slowly: "Mr. McFar-r-lane, I am from I-r-ran. . . ."

Jonny seized my hand, and my own heart thumped.

"... and I believe it is excellent what you have done."

We broke into relieved laughter. The chauffeur was an Iranian exile who had fled Khomeini's revolution and now yearned to see the Ayatollah discredited.

There were still people who came up to me to say they were behind me, to lend me moral support. But just as often, as time passed, it seemed that people avoided me, or said nothing, or looked the other way in the street. Washington at the best of times is a curious, competitive town. Harry Truman knew what he was talking about when he said that if you wanted a friend in Washington, you should get a dog. In times of scandal, the city can turn vicious. As the central figure in a public scandal, you find yourself exposed to a surreal, all-encompassing spitefulness that issues even from unlikely quarters. Some people take a nearly gleeful delight in seeing the mighty brought low. Others seize the opportunity to flaunt their own dubious superiority.

Later, when I appeared before the Select Committee formed in January 1987 to look into Iran-contra, I was confronted by a young associate counsel on the Senate side who was a relative of Lyndon Johnson. This man spent the greater part of his time rather arrogantly throwing up to me the superior conduct and ethics of the Johnson White House. It was a performance that made me grit my teeth. Lyndon Johnson—for whom I confess my father campaigned quite vigorously—was one of the most deceptive men ever to occupy the Oval Office, a man of so few scruples as to have zero inhibitions about lying to the Congress, or to his wife, for that matter. To have this young functionary invoking the name of Lyndon Johnson as a model of virtue grated badly on me; for all Johnson's qualities, devotion to the truth was not one of them.

Beyond these sorts of confrontations, I also was disappointed by the behavior of the men I had worked with in the White House, with whom I had believed I shared a set of basic values, and who now were running for the nearest cover. I had not been in touch with North or Poindexter since the lawyers decided that we should not communicate with one another while the various investigations were under way. I ran into Ollie at the Army-Navy game in Philadelphia, though, when we were both invited to a half-time reception hosted by Secretary of the Navy John Lehman.

It was a bittersweet day for me. My son Scott was Brigade Commander that year, the highest position of student leadership at the Naval Academy, and we were so proud to watch him lead the parade before a stadium jammed with thousands of spectators. At the reception, though, I felt as though I were living in a time warp. No one seemed to know what to say to me. People kept their remarks neutral, anodyne, limiting them chiefly to praise for Scott, for which I was grateful. Ollie was there, meeting and greeting, being clapped on the back and roundly commended by all, even though he was not at this stage testifying. Our paths crossed momentarily and we talked. I said what I'd said to him the day he told me he was going to hold a "shredding party" at the White House: "Just tell it like it was, Ollie, and I'll back you up and everything will be OK."

North and Poindexter were clearly shrewder than I in choosing not to tell, to bargain for immunity, but it was not how I would have expected them to act. Especially on North's part—he was behaving in a way that Marines don't behave, evading responsibility, seeking shelter. That John was caught in this mess I saw as partly my fault. John was a man of high intellect and discipline, especially as applied to science and engineering, areas in which he had achieved superior results for 25 years. But asking him to be the National Security Adviser, a position requiring entirely different skills, had been an injustice to him. It was like asking Edward Teller to run HUD.

Once you put a person like this in a new environment, he continues to apply the same old skills as best he can. In John's case, these were discipline, loyalty to his boss, disdain for Congress and the press. I was disappointed that his response to the scandal was to refuse accountability, since it seemed out of keeping with his character. Yet I understood the policy judgments he had made, and I felt a measure of responsibility for having put him in a position for which he was unsuited.

As for Ronald Reagan, I couldn't bring myself to be really critical of him. It was a curious phenomenon for me to have wanted to shield a President who legitimately deserved to be held accountable for his mistakes. Yet I believed that if not for my mistakes, he would not have made his. Of course, Reagan did not believe that he had made any mistakes. In his heart, he felt his motives had been pure. To be pure, they had to rely on a version of events that was pure.

For Reagan, the construct was that in Iran, he had been dealing with a group of Iranians who wanted to take over the government and change its policies, and that in order to do that they needed to be armed. He never acknowledged that the Iran initiative had long since deteriorated into an outright swap for hostages. He clung to the original proposal I had developed for him on the basis of the first Israeli proposition. That box had been filled in, in July 1985, and nothing was going to change it. This was analogous to his habit of repeating stories about welfare queens in Cadillacs long after they had been discredited, or adhering to false accounts of Lenin's doctrine simply because they bolstered his motives and policies.

His refusal to acknowledge the facts was a combination of age and isolation, as well as the shield of advisers around him, who lacked the moral courage to urge the President to step forward and do the right thing. The objective fact that Ronald Reagan did not stand up and engage the Congress in a reasoned debate on the separation of powers and his constitutional authority to conduct foreign policy, but instead allowed a policy difference to become a legal struggle, was disappointing. But it was in fact late in the day for that. I had known signing on with Reagan in 1981 that he was a man with strong views and certain principles, but not someone who was going to charge the hill or to sustain an intellectual struggle, especially a prolonged one. He was not someone who could extemporaneously engage on any subject and be persuasive. He was firmly committed on several policy issues, and on them he was very good, but his mind did not manifest great agility or depth beyond them.

He had other admirable qualities, however. He was quite stubbornly principled and unwilling to equivocate. That predictability and strength of will are very uncommon in politics. And more, he was a very likable person. For my part, I had undeniably benefited from his largesse. He gave me an opportunity to influence national policy and to make an important contribution and was generous in supporting me. That was a blessing, a huge trust, and I could never be anything other than grateful to him.

Moreover, I felt a sense of duty toward him. In the world I had inhabited, a subordinate always takes responsibility for his boss; his job is to make the boss look good and to distance him from trouble. A good officer, doing his duty, adheres to the concept of loyalty, which, however, must flow downward from the superior as well as upward. In

that context, I felt guilt and responsibility for having left government—for having left Reagan—in the lurch, so to speak, and with a
fixation on an initiative that I already saw was doomed to failure.

That was the guilt I felt for the Iran fiasco, and that guilt deepened as December melted into January and Iran-contra dominated
the news, paralyzed the administration, and permeated the lives of
all involved. I could see Iran-contra becoming my legacy, and the
legacy of the entire Reagan administration. All the good that had
been accomplished, that could still be accomplished, would be wiped
out by this single policy failure, this one bad call. The daily press
accounts and television reports seemed to bear this out. In the thousands of words written about me as Iran-contra unwound, there was
little if any scrutiny of all the positive achievements of my 26 years of
public service. There was no perspective on my career, no balance,
just the immediate events and the distorted reflection they cast.

I began to think how I could set things right. The situation was
still salvageable, I believed and hoped, but it required positive and
decisive action. Though I didn't realize it, I was already caught in
depression's web, flailing for a way out and ready to assume all the
blame for everything that had gone wrong—even though I had not
even been privy to more than half of the actions that comprised the
Iran-contra crisis.

I was convinced that Reagan had to seize the moment or a golden
opportunity in foreign affairs would be lost. We had been poised on
the threshold of a new and productive era in foreign policy, one in
which the government would enjoy the support and financial backing of the American people to a degree unmatched since the Vietnam
War. All this would be lost unless the President acted quickly now.

I identified four areas where the administration could make great
strides—in relations with the Soviet Union; in Central America policy and our workings on that front with Congress; in advancing the
Middle East peace process; and in nuclear arms reduction. And I set
to work formulating a specific policy for each of them that the
President could present to the American people and the Congress, in
an effort to rally the country and remind it not to lose sight of what
was truly important.

It didn't seem foolhardy to me to do this, nor vain, nor pointless.
I was still operating from a plateau—albeit a shrinking one—of
hope. I believed that fixing what had gone wrong was up to me, as it

had been so many times in the past.

And I still believed that if I only applied myself, heart and soul, to finding a solution to the problem, it could be done. I had always done it before.

And yet, a small voice inside me was casting doubt. Looking about me sometimes in those days, I was at a loss to explain how I had come to such a pass. For most of my life, I had moved steadily along an ever-ascending trajectory, toward a summit that seemed always eminently reachable. Yet now, the ground was shifting unexpectedly beneath my feet. And just a step away loomed the precipice.

PART TWO

Dreams and Duty

Chapter 7

GRAHAM, TEXAS

I am a Texan by right of roots and heritage, but I can claim President Franklin Roosevelt as the reason that I was born in Washington, D.C.

My father, William Doddridge McFarlane, was the Democratic congressman from the 13th district of Texas, a rough rectangle stretching some 200 miles eastward along the Red River from the panhandle, southward another 75 miles and back west to the panhandle. Dad used to say you could cross it twice in a day in a pickup, if you didn't have a flat or stop to make too many speeches.

I should have been born in Graham, our hometown of about 8,000 people in the south center of the district. Usually, right after school let out in June and the Congress went into recess, Dad would pack up Mother and the four children and leave Washington to return to Graham for the rest of the year. My older brother and sisters would go to school in Graham through the fall, then move back to Washington after the Christmas holidays and finish out the school year there. It was a chaotic, itinerant existence for the family, but my father believed it was best for everyone to be together. And since he was a force of nature, the sort of man who had gone on a cattle drive up the Chisholm Trail and, in only his third term in Congress, was being touted as "Presidential timber," things usually went as he decreed. Besides, the Washington schools taught vital subjects unavailable to his children in Graham.

In 1937, though, Franklin Roosevelt was embarking on his notorious effort to pack the Supreme Court. That summer, Congress was forced to stay in session to consider his proposal to expand the court's size. Dad was stuck in Washington, so the family was stuck, too.

My mother, the former Alma Ellen Carl, was expecting her fifth child and prepared to have the new baby in a Washington hospital. It was a hot, sticky, miserable summer, as summers in the former malarial swamp that is the site of the nation's capital are wont to be, and back then, it had to be endured without benefit of air-conditioning.

My parents hoped for another boy, having already one son and three daughters, and planned to name the newborn Robert Carl, after each of his grandfathers. Still, the choice of name caused my mother some concern, as the large extended family already included at least six Roberts. "What will we call him if his name is Robert Carl?" she asked her 12-year-old, Mary Ellen, one day. Mary barely paused before responding. "Oh, Mother, he's going to be such a little buddy to the four of us, let's call him that." And so, before I was even born, I became "Bud."

As for my father, he had wished that I would be born on his own forty-third birthday, July 17, but I didn't wait. I arrived on July 12, five days early. I, at least, could hardly be expected to understand that the congressman always got his way.

—

My father was the third of four children of Robert William McFarlane, a Texas Ranger who later became a judge, and the former Maggie Harris. From his earliest days, young William—later known as "Mac"—was his father's favorite. In 1922, after Mac had finished college and law school and done a hitch in the Army, the two opened a family law practice, McFarlane and McFarlane, in Graham. Immediately thereafter, on the strength of my grandfather's advice that running for office was a good way of meeting people, Dad campaigned for a seat in the Texas legislature—and won. He spent six years in the House of Representatives and another four in the state Senate. Then, in 1932, at the age of 38, he was elected to the United States House of Representatives.

My father was a truly dedicated public servant of the New Deal. As a young man, before he turned to the practice of law, he had worked in the family mining business in Arkansas. There, he had experienced what he always thereafter referred to as the "healing power" of government. By 1914, the soft coal of northwest Arkansas was no longer competitive, and the business was at the point of receivership. With the First World War, though, there came a need for smokeless coal to fuel both our Navy and those of our allies, and the business was saved. Whenever Dad talked about that experience afterward, he always maintained it was the government, not the war, that had turned things around.

He registered and ran as a Democrat, yet my father was in reality the quintessential populist. He saw himself as the representative of the people, and he viewed his job as one of helping the government solve the problems of his constituents.

He was undeniably good at it. By the summer of 1937, not quite three terms into his tenure, he had secured federal funding for a post office, a new court house, and a new high school in Graham, and equivalent public works projects for virtually every other county seat in the 13th district. In addition, he had secured appropriations for the Brazos River Water Conservation and Reclamation program, which created Possom Kingdom Lake, one of the largest artificial lakes and power projects in Texas. Equivalent projects that he made possible throughout the district for six years in the 1930s employed tens of thousands of people and kept getting Dad re-elected and returned to Washington every two years.

My father had a very simple, and by today's standards perhaps naive, approach to politics. He believed that if you met all the voters and told them how you believed their government could help with their problems, and if you then did what you had said you would do, the voters would re-elect you. In the 1920s and early 1930s, a candidate didn't have to worry excessively about his opponent's warchest. You could reach just about every voter from the back of a pickup truck, with a loudspeaker mounted nearby on the roof of your Ford coupe.

By the end of the 1930s, however, things were changing. Money was beginning to make a difference. Soon after his arrival in Washington in 1933, my father had taken an interest in electrical power generation under various governmental regimes. The Canadian experience was particularly impressive to him, for providing each kilowatt hour at about a third of what it cost those of his constituents in Texas who were even equipped with electricity. Canadian power, of course, was government-owned and heavily subsidized, to stimulate economic growth.

Dad became a fervent advocate of public ownership of utilities. And this became his downfall.

Electrical power generation in the 13th district was privately owned, and although it was regulated, it was highly profitable. In 1938, the "power trust," as Dad called the Texas Electric Company, put all its money and muscle behind an undistinguished lawyer named Edward Gossett, who challenged my father for the 13th district seat. And won.

My father's defeat was a telling comment on the political strength of the privately-owned companies. In his three terms on Capitol Hill, Dad had become well known in Washington as one of President Roosevelt's staunchest lieutenants in the House. He was a vocal advocate for every New Deal program and followed through to ensure that his constituents received their benefits from every one. By the summer of 1937, Roosevelt had fallen out with his Vice President, John Nance Garner, over Roosevelt's refusal to rein in any of his New Deal spending programs, and his efforts to pack the Supreme Court. Democratic politicians were beginning to talk about dumping Garner in the next election. Someone, however, would be needed to help carry the President's message to Garner's home state of Texas. Among the leading choices, along with Congressman Maury Maverick, another dedicated populist, was my father. In 1938, Roosevelt took his famous train trip across the country in an effort to help those incumbents who had supported him. He traveled the length of the 13th district with my father on board.

It wasn't enough.

My father, Maury Maverick, and others lost their House seats, thanks to the power trust. Edward Gossett served seven unremarkable terms in the Congress. But the power trust has never been seriously threatened to this day.

———

Dad's loss of his House seat, however, paled in the shadow of a far more crushing loss that had already occurred. In April of 1938, my mother, suddenly and unexpectedly, died at the age of 38. She suffered an aneurysm one morning, an hour after my father left for the Hill, and just after my brother and sisters departed for school. She was dead before Dad reached the hospital. I was nine months old.

My father was shattered by her death. His pain was magnified by vicious, unfounded gossip, spread by his opponent Edward Gossett, that Dad had somehow been inattentive on the day my mother died, and that this had contributed to her passing.

In June of that year, my father loaded all of the kids into the car for the return trip to Graham—except for me. I had fallen ill with double pneumonia. Herman and Florence Reiling, old friends of my father's from his law school days, offered to take care of me after I was released from the hospital. Florence wanted to adopt me, as my father's new job in Texarkana would keep him away from our home in Graham except for occasional weekends. Dad, however, wanted all the children to be together.

After I recovered, Florence flew with me to Texas. By then, Dad had found a young woman schoolteacher, Mary Jane Choate, to live with us and take care of us.

—

I have no real memory of my mother. She was by all accounts a loving and devoted mother and wife, a gracious, lovely and intelligent woman who was popular with all who knew her in both Graham and Washington. She was the daughter of Judge and Mrs. Frank Carl of Edinburg, Texas. She had graduated from the University of Texas in 1922 and was a teacher at Brackenridge High School when she met my father. In the manner of most women of her time, she gave up a career in favor of raising a family, and poured her energies into volunteer work in the community and church.

More than 2,000 people came to her funeral service in Graham, and expressions of sympathy and tributes arrived from President and Mrs. Roosevelt and many other Washington political luminaries. I look at my three sisters, the fine, accomplished women they are, and know that I see her reflected in them.

No one, however, talked about Mother when I was growing up. If there were pictures of her on display in the family home, they were never pointed out to me as pictures of my real mother. In spite of this, I never felt anything remotely like a motherless child. I didn't even know that I didn't have a mother. I thought I did. I thought she was Mary Jane Choate.

This young woman, in her late 20s when she came to us, was the center of my world until I was eight years old. Mary Jane had been raised on a farm outside Graham, in the Tonk Valley. Determined to get an education despite her rural roots, she had attended the University of Texas, where she earned a master's degree in literature. Yet she gave up the promise of a career in her field to care for five young children as if we were her own. For eight years she was our mother, our housekeeper, the milkmaid to our cow, disciplinarian, comforter, nurse and tutor all rolled into one. She ran the household and tended to all our material and spiritual needs without any domestic help of any kind. That she performed these tasks so well and so selflessly for all those years always has and always will seem like the most remarkable gift to me.

I called Mary Jane "Momma," and no one ever corrected me or told me that she was anything other than that. We had a very strong and very loving relationship. She was my confidante and my source of security. She set high standards of conduct and courtesy and personal behavior, while at the same time encouraging curiosity and inquisitiveness in all areas. She insisted I take piano lessons and quite firmly expected that I practice and perform to the best of my ability. It's always been one of my great regrets that after we parted ways I let the music lessons lapse; Mary Jane, I know, would never have allowed me to do that.

Growing up in Graham, I felt fully and completely loved, both at home and in the community at large. Graham's population was mostly cattle ranchers and independent oil operators, and it was a warm small town where the old-fashioned values of community and sharing and caring for one's neighbor still prevailed. My memories of life there are uniformly positive and idyllic—picnics in Fireman's Park, Sunday school and vacation Bible school, pony rides and trips to the oilfields, going crawdad fishing and spending summers at the pool. And always, I remember being held, by everyone—roughnecks and ranchers and the ladies from the church. It has always seemed to me that everyone must have thought a great deal of my father and mother because they went to so much trouble to take care of me and my siblings after our mother died.

Throughout these early years, Dad took legal work wherever he could find it. Usually it was not in Graham, and I remember seeing him mostly on weekends. Then in 1945, he met a young high school Spanish teacher in Paris, Texas, named Inez Bishop. That same year, they decided to marry.

Several days before my father made the announcement to us children, my sister Barbara corrected me for the first time when I called Mary Jane "Momma." She pulled me aside and gave me some stunning news. Mary Jane, she said, was not my momma.

"Yes, she is," I retorted. I was eight years old, and of course I knew everything better than everyone else. "You don't know," I snapped.

But Barbara insisted she was right. We argued for a minute, until she finally flounced off, leaving me to absorb the astounding fact she had imparted. I was completely downcast. I *wanted* Mary Jane to be my mother, because I felt such absolute love for her, and thought her such a wonderful person. How was I to absorb this devastating revelation that she was not who, for eight years, I had believed her to be?

Perhaps it was fortunate that from my earliest days, I had always been taught never to show emotion, never to contribute to a "scene," never to misbehave. It was the fortitude instilled by these lessons, no doubt, that led me soon to conclude that as awful as I felt, I had to contain that feeling and go on; it wouldn't be proper to do anything else.

Luckily, I was almost immediately smitten with Inez, who was a charming, beautiful 38-year-old woman who went out of her way to engage me and to listen to me and immediately build a foundation for a good relationship. I was fearful about leaving Texas and all my anchors there, for my father had gotten a new job in Washington and we were preparing to move again, but Inez calmed me with her quick display of commitment and devotion to me and the family.

Nonetheless, it was painful to leave the surrogate mother of my earliest childhood. Mary Jane remained in Texas for a few years after we left, then married a professor and moved to Buffalo, New York. For nearly 50 years, we have stayed in touch, and Mary Jane, true to the bonds we forged in my childhood, has always been entirely supportive of me—in good times and bad.

—

My father's new job was with the Justice Department's antitrust division. It was tailor-made for him. He had always been on the side of organized labor and the "little man" and against big business, and he saw the work as an almost spiritual charge to slay the "power trust" once more. He was assigned all the tough cases—those certain to involve outstanding defense lawyers hired by clients with no concern for expense. He soon became one of the department's leading antitrust attorneys, often arguing cases before the Supreme Court. In more than 25 years at Justice, in antitrust and later in the lands division, he never lost a case.

Housing was scarce and expensive in postwar Washington, and Dad was only able to find us a small, two-bedroom apartment on

New Hampshire Avenue downtown. My brother Bill entered the Naval Academy in Annapolis as a plebe soon after we arrived, but that left the three girls and me to share one room. Mary, who had finished college and was working, still lived at home and had the single bed. Betty and Barbara, 14 and 12, were in bunk beds. And each night, we would pull out a rollaway bed and wedge it between the single bed and the bunks and that was where I slept. There was only one small closet in the room, and though it seems mind-boggling from today's perspective, the four of us—a college graduate, two adolescents and an eight-year-old—managed to fit all our clothes and beloved artifacts (i.e. junk) into that single cramped space.

Life in Washington was the polar opposite of life in Graham. I had been transplanted from a wonderful but homogeneous and provincial town to an exciting, fast-paced, multiethnic urban setting. There might have been one black person in Graham, but here I was surrounded by them. Our apartment was on the edge of the black nightlife district of Washington. Just across the street stood the old Portner Hotel, a black establishment that often hosted famous black entertainers. From our window, I spied Lionel Hampton, Billy Eckstine and Nat King Cole there more than once.

For the first time in my life, I became aware of racial segregation. We lived in an essentially black neighborhood, so I met and often played with black children, but there were still clear lines in the sand—segregated schools, neighborhood enclaves, movie theaters and even drinking fountains. It wasn't until I entered the Marine Corps 15 years later that I began to work and live closely and make real friends with African-Americans.

Four years after we came to Washington, we moved into a private home in the Chevy Chase area of the District of Columbia. By now, Mary was married and Betty was in college, so Barbara and I were the only two at home with Dad and Inez in the house on Western Avenue.

I attended Alice Deal Junior High School and then Woodrow Wilson High School, both premiere schools not only in Washington but in the nation, and attended by the children of the capital's political elite. My geometry teacher at Wilson, Ruth Lane, Ph.D., a classics scholar, spent no more than two or three weeks on traditional geometry; the rest of the time she taught us logic, the scientific method, philosophy, and the lives and legacies of Socrates, Pythagoras, Plato, Aristotle, and Alcibiades. This was no exception.

Wilson then offered the equivalent of most first-year college courses and superb teachers in all of them. Sadly, with the downturn in America's public schools over the last decades, this reputation is now little more than a relic of the past.

———

Outside of school, my teen years centered around the church and my Scout troop. The latter, especially, was a unique and extraordinary organization, the likes of which I have never seen before or since. The leader of Explorer Scout Troop 54 was Dick Ellinger, a young bachelor who had been a bomber pilot in World War II. When I knew him, he worked for the telephone company and devoted virtually all his free time and most of his money to the Scouts. Dick had belonged to the same troop as a teenager and believed that it was his duty to pay back all that he had received. He taught us all the basics—how to camp and get along in the wilderness and how to truly enjoy the outdoors. But he also took us on trips from Washington to California to teach us something about the United States, what our forebears had lived through and how richly endowed we are with all manner of resources. We hiked in the Rockies, explored the Grand Canyon, crossed Death Valley to the Pacific, up to Yosemite and back to Salt Lake and Yellowstone. We skied all over the Eastern United States and in Canada, built igloos in New Hampshire, canoed through Maine, built a house and ran a summer camp in Pennsylvania, and explored caves in West Virginia.

In the process, Dick instilled in us fundamental leadership skills and a sense of obligation to use them for the benefit of others. His not always subtle message was that each of us was a highly privileged person but that many others—with whom he took pains to bring us into contact—were not, and that we had a responsibility to the less fortunate. Dick never cast this message in spiritual or philosophical terms, but rather as an expression of his private creed. In those years, my father was stressing the potential of government for doing good; Dick was promoting a more personal framework of values.

In Chevy Chase, I began to attend the Presbyterian Church on Sunday evenings for the social opportunities it offered. We still went downtown to Mount Vernon Place Methodist Church for services every Sunday morning; it was a requirement with my father, and in fact at age 18 I received a pin from that church testifying to my nine years of perfect attendance. But in the evenings I was drawn to the Presbyterian Church near our home.

In the early 1950s, the high school youth church group was large—almost 100 members—and very active. Most of my friends belonged to it. And there were lots of girls.

The group, which was called Firesides, was led by Dr. and Mrs. Jack Angerman, a young couple who were the most solid of role models, devoting hours of their time to us, patiently conducting one-on-one conversations on everything from the meaning of marital fidelity to forgiveness. We were also blessed to have a phenomenal group of temporary Sunday school teachers, accomplished people living in Chevy Chase while professionally based in Washington. One of them was Commander (later Admiral) Jim Calvert, who was the first person to transit the North Pole in a nuclear submarine, and later became superintendent of the Naval Academy.

The Firesides president was a winsome brunette with a well-turned ankle who impressed me with her good sense and her ability to dominate meetings and get results. Her name was Jonda Riley. She was a student at Bethesda-Chevy Chase High School, a grade behind me, and dated a BCC classmate for the first two years we knew each other, while I dated three or four different girls. But we moved in the same circle of 20 or so young people from the church group, and gradually I felt myself drawn more and more exclusively to her.

I can't say whether the feeling was mutual from the start, and looking back, I don't blame Jonny if she was initially indifferent. It was the early 1950s, after all, and my barber, Mr. Milton Pitts, had successfully convinced me to succumb to a flat-top as the "in" adolescent haircut of the day. Mr. Pitts, who would later become the White House barber and groom the Presidential locks of Richard Nixon, Gerald Ford and Ronald Reagan, had a shop near the zoo—an appropriate location, some might have said, looking at me. I could have been an early *Far Side* prototype, with my generally untrimmed cut topping a rather plain and acne-covered face. It's a good thing sometimes that love is blind.

Jonny broke up with her boyfriend in her junior year, and I decided it was time to make my move. Through the good offices of a friend, I succeeded in getting a date with her to my senior prom. It was a magical evening, not least because it turned out that Jonny shared my feelings after all. It ended in a drive up to the Chesapeake and Ohio Canal near Great Falls for a few minutes of spooning and eternal pledges to write.

Two weeks later, I reported to the U.S. Naval Academy in Annapolis and Jonny and I began our long-distance but enduring love affair.

———

The decision to seek nomination to the Naval Academy as a prelude to a naval career was a natural outcome of my upbringing, during which my father had so often stressed the value of public service. Both my uncle, a World War II destroyer skipper, and my brother, a Korean War fighter pilot, had graduated from the Academy. And I was inspired by the example of various historical figures whom I counted as personal heroes. In grade school, I had read the biographies of a dozen or more prominent political figures of the late 18th century. I found the foreign missions of Jefferson, Adams, and Franklin fascinating, and dreamed of carrying out diplomatic missions on behalf of my country someday.

I worried when I was only able to get a fifth alternate nomination from my Texas congressman, Frank Ikard, who had replaced Ed Gossett. But I was lucky, winning a perfect 4.0 score on the English/literature entrance exam and a 3.87 overall, to be admitted as a qualified alternate. As it turned out, I was the only candidate admitted from the 13th district that year.

At noon on June 27, 1955, as a plebe midshipman, I took the oath of office in Memorial Hall. I memorized it then and have never forgotten it:

> "I, Robert Carl McFarlane, do solemnly swear that I will support and defend the Constitution of the United States against all enemies, foreign and domestic, that I will bear true faith and allegiance to the same, that I take this obligation freely without any mental reservation or purpose of evasion, and that I will well and faithfully discharge the duties of the office on which I am about to enter, so help me God."

The Naval Academy, notwithstanding its recent troubles and scandals, was and is one of the most remarkable institutions in the country. When I was there, from 1955 to 1959, it was scholastically narrow, but strong in teaching "by precept and example" the leadership skills essential to waging war and keeping the peace successfully. The Navy and Marine Corps sent their finest officers to the Academy to serve as instructors and role models. Even the Army sent one officer to the Academy each year. Among those who taught there during my four years were Captain George S. Patton III, the son of the famous general, and a young captain named Alexander M. Haig.

The Academy's task was to teach us to inspire others to do, and do well, things that they would not otherwise choose to do at all. This was accomplished both by means of assigned readings, through which the midshipmen absorbed the written legacies of heroes past who acted on their sense of duty, honor and country, and by means of firsthand example provided by the living heroes, tacticians and strategists who served on the Academy staff and visited as lecturers. In addition, from first day to last, each midshipman is placed on a track on which he is given as much responsibility for the performance of others as he can handle, as quickly as he can handle it. This starts out modestly, when you might be put in charge of your two- or three-man room at inspections, and progresses ultimately to the possibility of being named Brigade Commander—the senior midshipman officer—who is responsible for the movements and performance of the 5,000-man brigade both away from the Academy and at home. It was one of the proudest moments of my life when our son Scott was named Brigade Commander of the Class of 1987.

A career in the military, especially since the development of nuclear weapons, requires a special turn of mind. Most professions offer the possibility of innovation, discovery, or other measures of excellence immediately visible to society at large. At college reunions, doctors can bask in legitimate praise for their efforts at healing; engineers for the buildings or highways or communications systems they have designed and built. But if you are extremely good at your profession as a naval officer, you will never be tested. Certainly all of us take pride in having contributed to a condition of peace. And it is certainly true that most Americans understand that there is a correlation between strength and deterrence that justifies "the service."

That basically positive impulse is always in tension, however, with skepticism toward those who are seen as feeding at the public trough. We see that ambivalence in the boom or bust way we pay servicemen, and always try to reduce their benefits between wars. I fear that this attitude toward military service will worsen for as long as the all-volunteer policy continues. Because of it, young people no longer have to contemplate service. And gradually, they will tend to forget that there is a price to be paid for freedom. It should be paid by all in some fashion, even if the payment is only to walk around for a few years considering the possibility of having to serve. Only about 10 percent will ever be needed, and almost all of those will be volunteers. But simply thinking about the possibility that one might be needed leads most people to recall just how unique and fortunate our country is. And that process goes a long way toward preserving our heritage and assuring our future.

—

By the fall of my third year, I found myself thinking hard about the future and what I would ultimately do with my life. By this time, I had traveled abroad a little and been exposed to different cultures. After having for most of my years enjoyed the upside of life, I had come to see some of the downside—social inequities, the uneven distribution of resources. And I had seen and thought about the ways in which different professions can be used to better the human condition.

At the same time, I was experiencing, through attendance at chapel and private prayer, my first thoughtful acknowledgment of God's power and grace. Although I had been brought up in the Methodist church, I was more familiar, through Jack Angerman's and Jonny's explanations, with Presbyterian doctrine. I had accepted the concepts of predestination and free will and was finally wrestling with the first serious choice of any young life: the choice of profession to which I would devote myself and my energies.

Over time, I had developed a framework within which this thought process took place and which molded and guided my considerations. I believed that God intends for every person to develop his or her intellectual and other skills to the fullest possible degree, and that not to do so is a sin. In choosing a profession, therefore, one should choose something at which one excels, and which concomitantly makes one happy. But above all, what one chooses to do should not be merely self-interested, but should benefit others, and certainly never cause them any harm.

In all this, I was overcome with a sense of obligation to God. And gradually I persuaded myself that the highest calling, the most fitting fulfillment of the challenge implicit in the blessing of life, would be to undertake the ministry of God's word. I decided I should become a pastor.

I felt, at first, thoroughly at ease with this decision, which I pondered for weeks and which I believed to be right. Yet I knew that it meant that I would have to leave the Naval Academy, and this would not be received favorably by my father. In my family, you were supposed to finish whatever you started.

As a third-year midshipman, I was allowed one weekend when I could travel outside the seven-mile radius to which we were normally limited in our off-campus ventures. I wrote to my father and told him I would be coming home for a weekend and that I needed to discuss a serious matter with him.

My father was a wonderful man and an excellent parent, devoted to his family and its well-being, and he provided for us beyond measure and loved us completely. But he was not a demonstrative person. Perhaps in keeping with his Scottish background, he did not engage in overt displays of emotion or sentiment. Nor did he discuss things with us or make himself available for long talks and encouragement at times of crisis or uncertainty. His philosophy of parenting was simply to set a good example, from which his children would absorb how to live and conduct themselves and make choices in their lives.

There was no reason why he should have behaved differently on this occasion, and true to form, he didn't. In fact, he seemed to want to avoid the situation. When I arrived in Washington, I told him once again that there was something I wanted to discuss, and he replied, somewhat gruffly, "All right, we'll make time." But we never did. The weekend slipped by and we never talked. Finally, on the ride back to the bus station, I pressed the point. I told him that I was thinking about leaving the Academy and going into the ministry.

Not surprisingly, Dad would have none of it. "You have a good start at the Academy, why do you want to change?" he demanded. Dad's approach to life was simple: Work hard, do your best, be somebody. It was a good approach, yet it seemed to me to be lacking in an acknowledgment of any spiritual obligation. He believed going to church was important, but more as an ethic, a part of life that was good, than for the doctrine or spiritual guidance you might receive. And his notion of doing your best and being somebody always seemed to lack the *why*. It seemed to me that being somebody, for my father, was more a matter of pride than of vindicating a spiritual trust. To me, there was a hint of vainglory in saying that you wanted to be somebody without any further moral purpose. You should be somebody for the benefit of others.

Yet the truth was, I had always somewhat feared my father and didn't like the idea of doing something he didn't want me to do. Dropping me off at the station, he gave me my marching orders. "Go back, study hard, get good grades, graduate and get a commission! I don't want to hear any more about this," he said.

Nevertheless, I tried talking things over once more, this time with my brother. Bill by this time was a Navy fighter pilot, stationed in Washington, and a hero of mine. But he was pretty much his father's son. He was less abrupt than Dad, but told me essentially the same thing. He pointed out that I had an opportunity to lead and influence others in the military, and that since I seemed to have a facility for what I was doing—I was a four-striper at this point, a member of the brigade leadership—I ought to stick with it. As for my doubts, he said, "We all go through this." Although I've always wondered whether he really did.

The upshot was that I came to think that perhaps Dad and Bill were right, and that I was supposed to be in the Navy. In any event, I took away, once again, the lesson that there was no leaning on others in times of crisis, but that you had to find the strength to resolve difficulties within yourself. I even came to the conclusion that it was wrong to ask for help. "I mean, here you are, 20 years old," I thought. "Come on, grow up! Get on with it!"

And I did. I went back, studied hard, got good grades, graduated, got a commission. From then on, I was almost always first among my peers in anything I did. And for the next 30 years I applied my father's rigorous, self-sufficient and taciturn approach to life with nearly constant success.

———

The summer of 1958, following my junior year at the Academy, I was assigned to what is called "first-class cruise" on board the

USS Essex, an aircraft carrier in the Mediterranean. We midshipmen were apprentice officers, standing watch as junior officers on the bridge, or serving in the combat information center; in short, acting in the capacities that we would soon fill after being commissioned. It was an exciting summer, a summer of challenges in performing actual skills of navigation and ship handling and in applying both our technical and human skills in a real world context.

It was also the occasion that offered us our first graphic lesson in the development of national strategy and crisis resolution. On July 12, we were anchored off the Greek port city of Piraeus. It was my 21st birthday. That night, my buddy Don Clark, whom I'd known since high school and who had been my plebe year roommate, and I had "liberty." As we made the rounds of the local *tavernas*, Don threw down the ritual coming-of-age challenge: I had to down one drink for every year of my age. Well, I was a typical red-blooded American male, so I did it. But Greek ouzo, as you may know, is pretty powerful stuff. And the result of my birthday overzealousness was that I volunteered to remain aboard ship the next night.

It was a fortuitous request.

That night, the *Essex* "flapped out." Responding to an emergency order, we pulled suddenly out of Piraeus, leaving the liberty party, including about a third of the ship's officers, ashore, and steamed toward the Middle East. President Eisenhower had ordered the Marines ashore in Lebanon.

Lebanon, in a foretaste of a situation that would recur 25 years later, was in the throes of a power struggle among its various Muslim and Christian denominations. Eisenhower had determined that the factional fighting was threatening to get out of hand, and that the Soviet Union appeared poised to exploit the turmoil by supporting one faction and thereby establish a foothold in the eastern Mediterranean. The prospect that the Soviets could gain a foothold on NATO's southern flank from which they could also spread their influence throughout the area and ultimately exert influence over the area's vital oil resources and key waterways, was anathema to the United States and the Western world.

Eisenhower lost no time in acting decisively. He opted to bypass diplomatic talks with Moscow and chose instead to provide a show of force that would leave no doubt as to our unwillingness to tolerate Soviet intervention in Lebanon. He sent in the Marines and publicly declared that the United States would use whatever means necessary to assure the sovereignty and territorial integrity of Lebanon. In diplomatic parlance, this meant that we would do whatever it took to keep the Russians out.

The deployment was thrilling. Because the ship was short of a full complement of officers, we midshipmen found ourselves performing real duties in a real crisis, standing watches in place of the officers who had been left behind, supporting the Marine landing on the coast.

I'll never forget coming up out of my stateroom the morning after we arrived off Lebanon to see the Marines on the hangar deck cordoning off and standing watch over the carrier's aircraft, which had been armed with nuclear weapons. It's not likely the American people knew how high the stakes in this instance were or how great the risks being engaged by their President. But it was undeniable that the Soviets understood, because in very little time, they and their clients backed down. Not a single shot was fired, nor one life lost in hostilities.

The lesson of that action is one I've carried with me ever since. President Eisenhower had defined the problem, defined the solution, made them credible to the American people, and acted with dispatch to resolve the matter decisively. It was a premiere leadership performance—a perfect integration of military power in support of diplomacy—and defined for me the model of firm action in a crisis. Yet it's dismaying to acknowledge how rarely it has been successfully applied by Eisenhower's successors in the years ever since.

—

Despite the usual obstacles of separation and youthful waywardness, my romance with Jonny Riley had not only continued but indeed intensified with time. We had been especially lucky during my plebe year. Plebes were not allowed to see women, except at ritual "tea dances" organized by the Academy once or twice a quarter on Sunday afternoons. But it happened that one of the members of our high school church group, Nancy Madden, was the daughter of a naval officer, Captain Robert Madden, who was coincidentally reassigned to the Academy my plebe year. As a result, Nancy was able to host Jonny on weekends. And I was able to launch my first covert operation. While the rest of my classmates suffered in a world without women, I would receive messages once a month passed by the mate of the deck: "Midshipman McFarlane: Report to Captain Madden's quarters," and race over to his Georgian house on Porter Road to spend the afternoon with Jonny.

A year after I entered the Academy, Jonny enrolled at Penn State. This school probably had at the time the best collegiate gymnastics team in the country, and was one of the Academy's chief rivals in that sport. As for me, after years of disappointment on the athletic front—I was a runt, and had never succeeded at the glamour sports of football or basketball—I had finally found an athletic niche for myself on the gymnastics team, specializing in the pommel horse. Our regular trips to Penn State for competitions provided Jonny and me with some welcome, happy—and free—opportunities to rendezvous.

Otherwise, because of the Academy's seven-mile limit, the burden of keeping a relationship going generally fell much more heavily on the girl. Girls, or drags as they were irreverently called, would have to travel up to Annapolis and find a room in a "drag house," as we called the accommodations provided by local matrons who opened their homes to visiting girlfriends. Sometimes the girls would stay four or five to a room, doubling or tripling up in beds.

Then, over the course of the weekend, they would more often than not end up footing the bill for most of the activities they shared with their dates—the Academy stipend to midshipmen was only $4 a month. Jonny and I liked to eat at the Little Campus Inn, because you could get crabcakes for $1.80—they were the cheapest thing on the menu—and then sometimes we'd get a couple of nickels in change that Jonny could blow on the slot machine.

Prior to the end of Jonny's first semester at Penn State, I asked her to wear my class crest. It was, in those days, the badge of going steady. To my dismay, she turned me down! She was a college girl, she said, and wanted to enjoy all the freedom that entailed. I was rather heartbroken for a time, but by the end of the year, Jonny told me she had decided to go to summer school so that she could accelerate and finish college at the same time I did. She did still care, after all.

On March 8, 1958, in my junior year, the Eastern gymnastics championships were held at Penn State. The competition was a tough one, but despite the presence of several very talented rivals, including an Olympic veteran, I won the third place medal for the horse. That night, Jonny and I drove out to Black Moshannon Lake for a look at the moonlight, then back to her dorm. In the parking lot there, I launched into a speech about how much I respected her, how many admirable qualities I thought she had, how good she was with children, how caring with people. When I looked over at her, her lips were inexplicably trembling and her eyes were filled with tears.

"Jonny," I asked solemnly, slightly alarmed, "will you be my wife?"

Jonny let out her breath in a great rush. "Yes," she cried in relief, "yes!" Later, laughing, she told me she thought I had been building up to a brush-off, about to break up with her and break her heart.

—

As a first classman at the Academy the next fall, I faced the decision of which service to enter. I had always assumed that I would go into the Navy and become a naval aviator, like my brother before me. In anticipation of that, I had even had my class ring inscribed to that effect the year before, and it carries the erroneous inscription to this day: "Robert C. McFarlane, U.S. Navy."

Unfortunately, a combination of genetics and possible overzealousness in my studies had weakened my eyesight, and when I took the physical in October, I failed to meet the vision requirements for an aviator. Forced to rethink my future, I concluded that I was less interested in pursuing a career that emphasized the technical aspects of the military, such as engineering, than I was in one that would make use of the leadership skills and capacity for command that I had developed at the Academy. I thought of myself as a people person. And the opportunities for working with people and exercising leadership, I saw, would be greatest in the Marine Corps. And so I indicated the Marines as my first preference, and considered myself supremely lucky when I was accepted into the corps.

June week, the week after exams and before graduation, seemed to come very quickly, and was an exhilarating capstone to what had sometimes seemed like four years of penal restraint. Looking back, of course, I see that those four years at the Academy were perhaps the most important in my life, for the discipline they instilled, and the analytical skills they allowed me to develop.

Three days after I graduated, Jonny received her degree in psychology from Penn State. The following day, June 7, 1959, we were married at Chevy Chase Presbyterian Church where we had met seven years before.

Our honeymoon destination was the Bahamas. We stayed at a wonderful old hotel in Nassau, the Royal Victoria, and spent a week basking in the sun, enjoying one of the happiest times of our lives. It was going to have to hold us for a while, because immediately afterward we embarked on a new and very different phase of life that was quite possibly the biggest demotion anyone could ever experience—going from first-class midshipman at the Naval Academy to second lieutenant in the Marine Corps.

———

I had thrived at the Naval Academy. It was a place where the idea of a meritocracy really meant something. There, if you worked harder, you'd go farther, simple as that. I had grown up in a disciplined household and approached life with that same attitude, so I had fit seamlessly into the Academy's structure and benefited from its philosophy.

But everything seemed to go haywire when I entered the Marines Basic School that July. For the next nine months, I suffered the most persistent period of failure in my entire life.

I just couldn't seem to get anything right, in the classroom or in the field. I thought I was absorbing both the written material and the field instruction, but on test day, whether in the classroom or on the obstacle course, I seemed to blow it every time. And I could never figure out why.

Separately, I got into trouble off campus as well. One Saturday, I drove up to Baltimore for the Navy-Notre Dame football game along with three Academy classmates. We took my car. Since I was driving, the others proceeded, during and after the game, to get severely inebriated. On the way back that night, even though I was stone cold sober, I took a wrong turn somewhere and spent an hour and a half wandering the backroads of Virginia. Just outside Dumfries, I fell asleep and drove smack into a telephone pole. Fortunately, no one was injured, and the local constabulary let me go after I had paid for the pole.

The Marines, however, were not so lenient.

"Marines," my company commander declared, "do not create civil disturbances." For the embarrassment I had inflicted on the Corps, I was sentenced to two weeks in hack, meaning that I had to leave Jonny at home and be restricted to bachelor officers' quarters for the duration.

I was despondent. I was convinced that this blemish on my record, combined with my mediocre academic and field performance, were indications that I had chosen badly in entering the Marines, and that I faced a future of failure and frustration.

This fear was only exacerbated when it came time for branch selection. In the Marines, the preferred image of the leatherneck is the infantryman, as opposed to the artilleryman, the tanker, the engineer, or the logistician.

Virtually all of our instructors had been infantry officers and their measure of the worth of any Marine was whether or not he—they didn't count "shes" in those days—was an infantry officer. So it wasn't surprising that I, together with all my classmates, took infantry as our first choice. But in April 1960, the Marine Corps headquarters informed me that I was to become an artillery officer.

I was devastated. To be consigned to this backwater while all of my peers were blessed with acceptance into the infantry was crushing. But if fate indeed has a hand in the course of our lives, this was surely an instance of its intervening. The artillery assignment ultimately turned out to be one of the best breaks I ever had. Whatever it was that had prevented my getting the hang of things in Basic School, that curse seemed dispelled when I arrived at Artillery School in Quantico, Va.

From the start, I learned quickly, adapted without difficulty, regained my footing and found myself once again on the ascendant path I had always previously trod. I moved from success to success, was assigned to ever more challenging positions, and soon came around to believing that I had made the right choice with the Marines after all.

It was a belief I held onto when the day finally came that Jonny and I had to be separated. The "hardship tour" to Okinawa was inevitable, and most of my peers looked forward to joining the real Fleet Marine Force. Jonny and I had been given five years' grace with domestic assignments, and I found it hard to leave her (especially as she was expecting a baby) and our three-year-old, Lauren, who had been born at Camp Lejeune in 1961.

But in April 1964 I went off to join the 3rd Marine Division, as directed, "wherever it may be." At Okinawa, I was given command of Battery F, or Fox Battery, Second Battalion, 12th Marines. We were a 105mm Howitzer battery that was to become known as McFarlane's Foxes.

On March 8, 1965, we became the first Marine artillery unit to land in Vietnam.

Chapter 8

'NAM

We were a generation steeped in optimism. Those of us who came of age in the 1950s grew up in an era of prosperity that generated unlimited confidence and conviction. Our belief system was simple: democracy and free enterprise would lead to progress for all, and the wealth and freedom we enjoyed could be replicated throughout the world if only we put our minds to it. All we needed was King Arthur to lead us in establishing the global Camelot. And just as we left college with missionary zeal, he appeared, announcing that "we shall pay any price, bear any burden, meet any hardship, support any friend, oppose any foe, to assure the survival and success of liberty."

John F. Kennedy's reign was short-lived, but the idealism he helped instill lingered. Why, we thought, couldn't we make possible for the people of Vietnam what we enjoyed here in the United States? Why couldn't the formula that had worked in Grand Rapids work as well in Dong Ha, Pleiku, Con Thien and Khe Sahn?

We couldn't have known then that our political leaders and the institutions they were to call upon to wage this crusade were not up to it. Our military was poorly schooled and, in the early days, poorly led, the Marshalls, Bradleys, and Nimitzes having given way to a mediocre cadre of conventional thinkers who devoted what time they spent in thought reflecting on the last great war and how to prevent its recurrence in Europe. Meanwhile, a new world was taking shape in the jungles of the Third World, its legions drawn by the simplistic appeal of Marxist dogma according to Mao, Ho, and Fidel.

As a lieutenant in the early 1960s at Fort Sill, Oklahoma, at the far end of the chain of command, I taught young officers antiquated artillery tactics that never took the least account of the reality of guerrilla warfare and how to deal with it. Nor did our curriculum reflect the fact that the new conflict we were entering involved a political dimension, and that victory required a political strategy that counted for far more than the military component.

For those who lived through it, the Vietnam War is undeniably the most searing experience they have undergone. And yet it's curious to remember how, in our blissful ignorance before the storm, we couldn't wait to get into the war. The Joint Chiefs were so self-confident, blithely assuring the President that the war effort might take 50,000 men and six months' time, but that "we could handle it." In reality, they had no more idea than a jackrabbit what it would take to prosecute this conflict.

For good or ill, however, the military was my profession. I knew that somehow I had to function and succeed in this war.

———

By the time the call to arms came in March 1965, after the Vietcong attack at Pleiku and seven months after passage of the Gulf of Tonkin Resolution, I had had a lot of time to think about the idea of going to war. I don't deny my first reaction was one of both fear and self-doubt, concern about whether or not I was up to the challenge ahead, and up to the effective command of troops under fire.

I was a captain, less than six years out of college. My wife and family were back in the States, in Bethesda, Maryland. Jonny had given birth to twins, Scott and Melissa, the previous September. I had never seen them. Now I wasn't certain that I ever would.

We thought we knew what we would be fighting for. Our mission was to contain the spread of communism. The ultimate threat we faced was ideological, the idea that freedom was gradually being subverted by communist forces, and that this process would one day reach the United States, if not directly, then by cutting off our access to critical commodities and markets. The domino principle, seemed sound and realistic.

My unit, the 9th Marine Amphibious Brigade, was deployed in the China Sea when President Johnson ordered us ashore. For all the loftiness of our supposed purpose, and almost mocking the fear and adrenaline that coursed through our veins the night preceding our scheduled landing, the first moments of our first war experience were hardly uplifting. They were a bungled, Keystone Kops-like attempt at landing the artillery battery over the beach despite clear evidence that tidal conditions would prevent it. Our engineers had identified a sandbar that, at low tide, would preclude our driving onto the beach without first hitting a deep, broad lagoon. For all the long day of our landing, we had encountered no resistance. As evening approached, the tide went out, and it came time for the artillery battery to disembark. I recommended to the battalion commander that we simply sail up to the pier, which had been secured hours before, and allow the battery to drive directly off onto dry land. He sent the recommendation up to the bridge. Before long the order from Brigadier General F. J. Karch came back down, short and sweet: Washington has said that we will land on the beach in traditional Marine Corps fashion, and those are your orders, Captain.

My appeals were unavailing. At last I resigned myself to the inevitable and ordered the battery into landing craft. As expected, we arrived at the sandbar and couldn't get over it. We opened the front gate, and I drove off—down into 60 feet of water.

Furious, I swam back to the craft and ordered the other craft in the vicinity to change course and go down to the pier regardless of what might happen to me. Then I made my way to shore.

We were able to see my Jeep at the bottom of the lagoon because the headlights were on. A dozen other vehicles from other units had gone down as well. We spent the first week on shore taking apart and overhauling all the engines and brakes damaged by the salt water. It was utter madness. All this wasted time and effort because of the stupidity of insisting that we present a specific image. Instead, what we presented was a farcial image of people who didn't know what they were doing.

Our mission, on that first tour, was to protect the airstrip at Danang. We commenced to dig in around the airfield and prepare for fire. But apart from a few isolated probes of our lines over the next few days, the area was fairly quiet, and the only casualties we suffered were to friendly fire.

The pace of Vietcong activities in other areas, however, was being used in Washington to justify a deepening of our commitment to the conflict. Within a short time, battalion after battalion, and then several divisions, were being called in, on the pretext of first defending Danang, and then all the battalions already ashore. And soon enough the ball was rolling with a speed that perhaps no one had anticipated, so that by the time I returned to Vietnam for my second tour, in the fall of 1967, our commitment to the war involved 500,000 troops.

—

I only spent a month at Danang in 1965; my one-year tour of duty with the Third Division ended and I shipped back to the States.

Soon after, I was selected for a graduate fellowship for study in Europe. There I spent an idyllic two years as an Olmsted Scholar at the Graduate Institute of International Studies in Geneva, Switzerland. The Olmsted program was created by General George Olmsted, a wealthy West Point graduate who after serving on General Eisenhower's staff in Europe during and after W.W. II was charged with several reconstruction tasks that required him to work closely with governments throughout western Europe. In this role he came to realize how little understanding there was within the U.S. military of the traditions, language, legal and political influences, economies, and cultural biases of these countries.

Looking to the need to forge an effective alliance among them, Olmsted decided to establish a cadre of officers in each service from among those expected to achieve Flag or General officer rank. He believed that the goal could best be achieved by educating these officers broadly at Universities in various regions of the world and that they—and ultimately our country—would benefit both from the scholarship and socio-politico learning that would occur. His only requirement was that the studies be conducted in a foreign language.

The program seems to have vindicated its purpose; one scholar has achieved Cabinet rank, another was Chief of Naval Operations, dozens have become Generals or Admirals and virtually all have served with distinction in foreign assignments. Recently, Jonny and I were delighted to receive word that our son Scott had been selected as the first second-generation Olmsted Scholar.

The two years in Geneva were immensely fulfilling, intellectually and by every other measure. Jonny and the children were with me. We lived in a contemporary villa in the nearby village of Founex, surrounded by a dazzling view of Lake Geneva and the distant Alps from our front windows and the Jura mountains of France behind.

I steeped myself in the study of history, geopolitics, diplomacy, language, and international law and culture at the feet of experts and wise men such as Paul Guggenheim, Pierre Lalive, Wilhelm Roepke and Louis Halle. Professor Roepke had worked with Konrad Adenauer to design and manage the postwar German recovery—the German miracle—and remained one of the most stimulating figures I've ever been privileged to hear. Louis Halle was one of the band of brothers at the State Department in the postwar period along with Paul Nitze, Dean Acheson, and George Kennan who together fashioned the foundation institutions and policies—NATO, the Marshall Plan, the doctrine of containment—which enabled our country to keep the peace and win the cold war. The Director of the Institute, Jacques Freymond, had been a general in the Swiss Army during World War II and later head of the International Red Cross. He was a serious student of strategy and a masterful professor on the works of Clausewitz, Jomini, Douhet and Mahan. Geneva, as the site of so many international negotiations—at the time, the Kennedy Round of trade talks, and numerous disarmament sessions—brought the governing elite of the world to our doorstep and we were privileged to hear as our lecturers the premier statesmen of the world. My classmates came from throughout the world—both East and West—and enabled me to learn as much outside the classroom as within. It was a thrilling time of huge intellectual absorption and writing and I was fortunate to complete a Masters in Strategic Studies as well as the resident work for a doctorate. It was also about as far from Vietnam as I could have gotten.

Our work in that country was far from finished. When the scholarship program came to a close, I moved my family back to Washington, and requested reassignment to Vietnam. I hadn't paid my full dues there yet. I arrived in Vietnam in September 1967 for a one year tour.

It was to be the fiercest year of the war.

—

There is no way to explain how much you can come to love someone who may die before you finish a conversation with him. There is no way for those who haven't experienced it to appreciate how you come to feel about someone who has saved your life and could again. You come to know what that person thinks and feels and how he manages to stay sane and to carry on. The men I knew in Vietnam clung to a multitude of anchors. Some believed they owed what they were doing to the grateful Vietnamese peasants who crowded around them every day. Some held to the faith they had absorbed as children in Sunday school. Some acted out of the fear of not doing their duty. Many acted out of love for their buddies. Most, in the end, did what they did because there was no choice.

As for me, the Kennedy notion—and he died before it ever became more than that—that America at its pinnacle might possess sufficient knowledge and resources to make possible for others the individual and political freedom and bounty of a free market economy we enjoy in the United States, was part of what sustained me. In addition I spent enough time talking to dirt-poor Vietnamese who had thought through the difference between the kind of life we foreshadowed versus that offered by their North Vietnamese kinsmen— and came out siding with us—to gain a sense of vindication. But what a price to pay. How awful is the violent death of a loved one. In that year, I watched too many of them die ever to be the same again.

I spent my second tour along the DMZ as fire support coordinator for the 9th Marine Regiment. For the first six months, I was responsible for planning and integrating the B-52 bombers, artillery, and naval gunfire in dozens of battles along the Zone. By this time, the generals in Saigon had decided that the best tactic for our infantry was to remain in fixed positions, and to draw the enemy into attacking so that our superior firepower could be used over time to win a war of attrition.

It was a misguided premise. The North Vietnamese and Vietcong could maneuver around our fortified positions to attack exposed villages with impunity while concurrently wearing down our forces with mortars, artillery, and sniper fire. Each day's kill ratios, which usually tilted our way, masked a central vulnerability on our side. Our losses were being graphically absorbed in every living room back home. Whatever the ratio might be, the American people kept seeing death without victory or any prospect of it. The kill ratios on our best day couldn't change that fact. Out in the boondocks, the troops, for their part, were demoralized at the prospect of spending a year in one spot—as virtual sitting ducks.

Sometimes I would go out to visit the infantry companies along the Zone to see and feel what they were living. There, the war was with you all the time. My forward observers and their riflemen— kids fresh off the plane—would face incoming fire within 24 hours of their arrival. They spent their days huddled in foxholes, soaked to the bone in monsoon rains, trying to keep their maps dry and an eye out for the enemy while they ate cold C-rations. They were getting shot at most of the time. They grew up quickly, if they lasted.

On September 25, in a gentle rain, the Huey set us down at

"Yankee Station," a flat spot on the south side of Con Thien, one of our outposts about ten clicks (kilometers) west of the coast, where the North Vietnamese Army couldn't see us. We made our way to the command post. On the way, we climbed past young Marines trying to reinforce ammo box bunkers whose collapse could bury alive three men at a time. As they slipped and fell and tried again, their grim faces showed the fear that comes from knowing they could be doing this for a year, and that things would never get better.

Within minutes, the incoming started—mortars, artillery including both 130s from up around the finger lakes and the heavier 152s from just north of the Zone. In the battalion command post, reports began to quickly come in of destroyed bunkers, mounting killed and wounded, and the need for medevac birds. The rain was coming too hard now; no chopper could get through in this.

Our own artillery cranked up and tried in vain to silence the NVA. But they were using Russian guns that had more range than ours. It was a bitter irony to think that we were members of a military that was about to send astronauts to the moon, but somehow couldn't throw a 100-pound projectile 19 miles.

From the chaos of the command post, I went out in the rain to visit the forward observers and their enlisted radio operators and riflemen. They were scared to death but trying not to show it. At the first Observation Post, the lieutenant had been hit by the first incoming mortars. I helped the corpsman drag him down the hill to the aid station and lift his body into the green body bag.

At the second OP, I crawled into the hole with the three-man team and immediately realized that I was taking up space that kept them from crouching lower. Before I could move to the next hole, the radio operator—a private, I later learned, from West Monroe, Louisiana—jumped out and rolled to the next trench, drawing sniper fire in the process. At almost the same time, the mortars started again.

Mortars are the worst. You don't always hear them coming, and when they hit, the shrapnel is devastating in all directions for a distance of 20 yards or so. Most of an artillery blast, by contrast, coming in on an incline, is absorbed into the ground.

There would be a lull of a few seconds between each round of mortars. Each time, they were a little closer. As we crouched lower in the hole, I felt that every cubic centimeter of the space was crammed beyond further compression.

Then a single round came in no more than 10 feet away. The FO, a young lieutenant, had stood up in the foxhole, exposing himself from the waist up, as he looked north for the source of the incoming. He gave out a choking sound. His helmet and binoculars were blown away and he had taken a four-inch piece of shrapnel in the face. "Get a corpsman!" I shouted, and rolled out of the hole, pulling his body with me. We slid a few feet down the ridge, and I stopped and straightened him out so that his head was higher than his feet. I held him in my arms, urging him to hang on. His mouth moved. "God bless Mother and...Mother and Daddy...and Ruth...oh God."

Within a minute, he was dead.

When someone dies in the war movies, there is usually a quiet moment before the action picks up again. But life is not the movies. Within an instant, as I hugged him to my chest, a sniper's bullet tore into the lieutenant's head. In panic, I arched my back and forced the two of us off the edge of the trail. Lying there for a few seconds in the wet torrent of rain and blood, I was as frightened as I have ever been in my life.

The corpsman crawled up. He looked at the lieutenant and shook his head. The lieutenant had only been there a couple of weeks, he said. They would have to wait until the rain cleared to medevac his body out.

—

There were many men whom I knew personally who died in the Vietnam War. There were times when, as an artilleryman, I felt almost unworthy for not being exposed to as much danger and risk as the men in the infantry units. We took our share of rounds from the enemy, but there was no question that, being five kilometers back from the enemy, we were far less vulnerable than the men up front.

Jack Phillips had been a classmate at the Academy, a close friend. He was tall, 6' 2", a Steven Seagal look-alike who had been a Marine before coming to Annapolis. For four years he had marched to class with me, sat next to me, talked about his girlfriends and how great it was going to be to get back to the Marine Corps. In October 1967, he took over an infantry company in the 2nd Battalion, 4th Marines, east of Con Thien. Within a week of his assuming command, they were hit by an attack. Jack took a rocket-propelled grenade right to the chest. It killed him instantly.

I was coordinating the artillery in that firefight, trying to help stem the tide. The news came over the radio right after it happened. The six—the company commander—was dead. Jack. I felt a piece of my own life had been suddenly torn away.

Pat O'Leary was a man I had known at Camp Lejeune, my first assignment in the Marines. In 'Nam, he was an aerial observer, one of the men who flew up and down in Piper Cubs, looking for the enemy and calling in artillery fire. He took a 50-caliber round in the gut up in the air one day, and died before he got back on the ground. I can't describe the impact that literally convulsed me every time I learned that someone who had stood next to me a day before had been blown away.

There were more of the young men I came to know in country, the young kids from middle America who had snapped to and saluted and gone off to war, trusting in the wisdom of our leaders, uniformed and civilian, believing their assurances that there was going to be a constructive end to this.

Instead, they paid the highest price, the most terrible price, for the folly of those very leaders.

By the time I returned to Vietnam for the second tour, our purpose for being there was blurred at best, incomprehensible at worst. Over the course of two years, Washington had sent out increasingly mixed signals on the rationale of our military involvement in Southeast Asia. On any given day, Americans might be told that our purpose was to make self-determination possible for the Vietnamese, or that it was to defend a fledgling democracy in South Vietnam, or that it was to contain communism or to hold back the Chinese threat.

What was clear was that because of political restrictions, we were not using our superior firepower to win the war in the north, and that, in ever-increasing numbers, the American people did not support the war.

Fortunately for the troops on the ground—at least along the DMZ—the answer to the question of why we were there was both rational and real. It was apparent from each day's encounters along the DMZ with Vietnamese peasants, children, and village leaders that they were profoundly grateful for our presence there, that they understood, even if people back home didn't, that there was a difference between what was offered in the north and what their leaders—however corrupt—offered them in the south. They had weighed both devils, the devil from the north and the devil from the south, and determined that the devil from the south was their better option. The human reaction gave us heart, from the millions of young Vietnamese men willing to fight to the death for their country, to the gratitude in the eyes of a peasant mother whose child you had treated for an infection at a "county fair," to the words of a village chief who could clearly tell you that he knew what freedom was, and that it was not what would come with the North Vietnamese. These things and the notion, back in some remote crevice of the mind, that long ago someone had done the same for us, kept us going. We owed it to the Vietnamese and our children and many, many others, from Yorktown to Belleau Wood to Inchon to Con Thien.

Yet ultimately, the lack of clarity in our purpose as enunciated by Washington, and the absence of an effective strategy for achieving a clear purpose, wore everything and everyone down. Our military strategy, of course, had been misguided from the start, led by Defense Secretary Robert McNamara's judgment that we didn't need to run the political risk of attacking North Vietnam, but instead could apply our superior technology in the south to win a war of attrition.

It was clear to all that the Vietcong-North Vietnamese advantage lay in their superior ability to maneuver, not in firepower, which was our long suit. McNamara, however, believed we could neutralize their superior maneuverability with technology. One story suffices to expose the depravity of this notion.

In the spring and summer of 1967, the Secretary of Defense decided that we would build an electronic "fence" across the DMZ separating North and South Vietnam, extending from the Gulf of Tonkin inland to the Laotian border, some 30 miles away. Its effectiveness was to derive from thousands of sensors—radar, sonic listening devices, motion detectors and other electronic black boxes which collectively would identify enemy movement and facilitate rapid targeting by nearby American forces. First, however, tens of thousands of acres of jungle would have to be defoliated. I'll never forget the smoldering rage with which the uniformed military at division headquarters and all along the DMZ greeted this ludicrous idea. They were furious at the waste of resources, particularly lumber, that could have been used instead to build bunkers to protect the troops against Vietnamese artillery. But pandering military back in Washington went along with the scheme. The fence was erected, but not by the military. It was installed by white-coated technicians from defense contracting plants in the States who were quite emphatic that there not be any military involvement. They were so adamant about the military staying out of their affairs that they did not even tell us where they were putting the sensors.

Not long after I arrived back in country in September of that year, I was visiting a battalion command post one morning just as the previous night's reconnaissance patrols were coming back in to report. These patrols, which consisted of a half-dozen enlisted troops led by a corporal or sergeant, would go into the DMZ to look for signs of enemy infiltration routes or other intelligence to inform our tactics.

On this morning, the young corporal who had led one of the patrols couldn't wait to give his report and seemed to be bursting with enthusiasm. Finally called upon, he blurted: "Skipper, we didn't find any VC last night, but we did find a lot of their comm wire and dozens of mines." And he announced proudly: "Which we blew the hell out of!"

The "mines," of course, were the shiny new sensors McNamara had ordered installed to detect the enemy.

—

Too late, I believe, our political and military leaders did learn how to wage the conflict. Politically, we pulled up our socks regarding the threat from China and the Soviet Union and recognized that they would not intervene if we took the war to the north. Militarily, we recognized that the North Vietnamese would always have the advantage in maneuver and that our advantage lay in strategic bombing, but to be effective, that firepower had to be delivered on strategic targets in North Vietnam. This wisdom did not settle on the leaders in Washington until at least 1972, by which time both the civilian and military authorities had lost most of their credibility with the American people.

Yet for all that I believe the effort was justified, I also believe that it should not have been expended absent strong and unequivocal support from the people at home. Human beings are so precious, and it is so important that no human life ever be wasted.

The press has to share in some of the blame. Much of the press coverage of the Vietnam War was unenlightened and overly partisan. What was needed was a press that understood the nature of the conflict and what it would take militarily and politically to win it and could better evaluate the situation on the ground. To be fair, the press was in part jaded by the lies and falsehoods that were fed to them by the military briefers in Saigon. But this did not justify the ignorance with which they covered key events in the war, notably the Tet offensive—an enormous defeat for the north. The fact was, few reporters ever came anywhere near the action. In my two tours in Vietnam, the only person approaching a reporter I saw was the columnist Joseph Alsop, who came up and spent an evening with me in 1968 in a bunker along the DMZ, attacking a bottle of Scotch.

Nevertheless, the central most important reason for our failure in Vietnam was that our President was unable to define the problem— why we should care—for the American people, define the political and military strategy for solving that problem, and develop popular support for that solution. Our loss resulted from inadequate knowledge about the nature of this struggle and what it would take to win it, as well as the inability to communicate effectively with the American people. One of the chief lessons I took from the Vietnam War was that an important part of any administration's responsibility is communicating through the press what it is trying to do, especially if the issue is one involving a commitment of forces and risking of lives.

Ultimately, I think our part in the war was vindicated, both by the Vietnamese boat people and by its effect throughout the rest of Southeast Asia—Thailand, Malaysia, Singapore, Indonesia—countries that had faced the risk of insurgencies and, in the case of Indonesia, outright Communist-inspired coup attempts. We bought ten years' time for these nations, enabling them to consolidate their economies and begin to be able to stand on their own and resist collectively whatever threats came their way.

But the chief lesson of the Vietnam War was the lesson of realism, realism about our socio-political fabric here at home. However right our purpose may have been in Vietnam, after it was over, I had no illusions about our ability to undertake, or the wisdom of undertaking, this kind of thing again without the thoroughgoing support and understanding of the American people and the Congress.

As much as I believed in the positive judgments of the

Vietnamese people toward our being there, the truth was that at the end of the day we caused a great many of them to lose their lives. If we hadn't gone there and waged a war, and all of the country had been brought under communist control, fewer would have died, although all would have lived under far worse circumstances. Still, for me, the lesson was: If you get to a point where the United States is asking people to risk their lives, and you see that you are not going to win, you owe it to those people to tell them so, and let them choose to cut their losses if that's what they want.

———

I left Vietnam for the second time in September 1968, yet I still wasn't finished with it.

We pulled out our line units in 1972, but the final denouement of that tragic story did not come until three years later, when the helicopters evacuated hundreds of American citizens and sympathetic South Vietnamese from the roof of the U.S. embassy in Saigon as the North Vietnamese closed in. It seemed an ignominious end to a long ordeal, but in fact it was an action full of bravery and mettle.

In late April 1975, I was military assistant to Henry Kissinger on the national security staff at the White House. The situation in Vietnam was tense. A C5 transport plane had crashed in the process of bringing some American military personnel out of Saigon, sparking fears in the U.S. Then, within 24 hours, the North Vietnamese swooped in toward Saigon.

Graham Martin, our ambassador, a strong, gutsy guy who had resisted pulling out until the last possible moment, finally called the White House and conceded the game was up. It was time to pull our people out, he said.

To his credit, Martin recognized the enormous vulnerability of so many Vietnamese who had worked with the Americans, not only those in the embassy, but those who had acted as cutouts or who had provided services to us, or people out in the provinces who had been cooperative. He wanted to save as many of them as he could.

The concern within the White House, understandably, was that no Americans should be overlooked or left behind. They were the priority. President Ford's guidance, accordingly, was that we could evacuate as many Vietnamese as was consistent with the complete evacuation of the Americans.

As fate would have it, I was put in charge of handling the communications with the embassy. The radio was set up right in my office in the White House. Kissinger directed that I get a head count from Graham so that we could get a sense of how long the evacuation would take so he could inform the President. We calculated that we had about a four- to six-hour window before the Vietcong tightened its noose.

I can no longer remember the precise numbers, but Graham gave me an initial headcount of several hundred that included both Americans and Vietnamese, and we started the sorties. After the first section of two helicopters had departed, Graham reported back. The first section had taken out several dozen, and now we had so many hundred left. And he gave me a number that was more than we had started with.

I knew what he was doing. I told him I understood his desire to evacuate as many Vietnamese as possible, but I warned him that this couldn't be an open-ended proposition. He agreed, but asked for some slack and promised that when things got to a crisis he'd let us know.

Since I sympathized, I went along. I didn't report anything to Henry. When he came by every now and then to ask how things were going, I would noncommittally respond, "All right." But after a couple of hours, Henry caught on. He asked how many had come out, and when I gave him the numbers of how many had been evacuated and how many remained, they added up to much more than the original headcount. I admitted that Graham was padding things a bit and bringing out more Vietnamese.

"Goddammit," Henry grumbled. "You tell him we get the Americans out first."

But Graham stubbornly, and masterfully, proceeded with his loaves and fishes gambit. He would evacuate 40 and add 50, and as time passed, Henry became more and more agitated. After about four hours, we still had 200 people in the embassy, and Henry snapped, "You tell Graham Martin to get his ass on the 'copter right away, it's a presidential order."

But Graham persisted for another couple of hours, until at last the mortar rounds began falling right near the embassy. Finally he conceded that he had done all he could do, and he got on the bird himself. Henry walked past my office just then, and I looked up and said, "Graham Martin just lifted off."

And Henry, with his quick, acerbic wit, growled with obvious relief, "Was it in a helicopter?"

In the end, we pulled out something over 1,200 people. Even in the last defeat of the war, Americans turned in some heroic performances. Yet the bitter pill had to be swallowed. We had lost the war, the first war America had lost in our history. It was a loss that tasted of gall and wormwood, and the best that could be said of it was that at least it marked the end of 10 years of division and self-hatred in American society. The war had scarred and shaken us, but it was over.

Over—yet, like all great traumas, never entirely done with.

Chapter 9

REGARDING HENRY:
THE NIXON-FORD YEARS

On February 21, 1972, President Richard Nixon arrived in the People's Republic of China to begin a historic visit, a visit signaling the renewal of political dialogue between Washington and Peking after more than 20 years of silence and official enmity. The trip was hailed as a diplomatic triumph, the brilliant result of two years of intense secret negotiations conducted by Henry Kissinger, who was both Nixon's Secretary of State and National Security Adviser.

A scant year or two earlier, no one in the U.S. Congress or public would have thought Nixon's trip possible or even necessarily desirable. There is no question that the China opening was one of the most brilliant strategic initiatives of the Nixon presidency, executed through masterful diplomacy on the part of Henry Kissinger. Yet it is ironic—and significant—to consider that had the existence of the China diplomacy come to light as it was being conducted, it undoubtedly would have produced an outcry from the American people and met with summary termination at the hands of Congress. Chinese bullets, after all, were killing American soldiers in Vietnam, and the Chinese Communist authorities had not long before unleashed a bloody Cultural Revolution, exterminating hundreds of thousands of their own people—not the kind of human rights performance our Congress would have been willing to overlook.

Nixon, however, weighing the balance of power *vis-à-vis* the U.S.S.R., as well as the strategic error of continuing to ignore one-fifth of the world's population, took a cold-eyed, calculated risk, and opted to engage in an exercise of *Realpolitik*—and succeeded. The judgment of history has been properly generous. The analysis of a problem, the definition of a solution, and the courage to take prudent risks to lead and manage the strategy through to a successful conclusion represents the ultimate vindication of the "special trust" the American people repose in their political and military leaders. The wisdom to see the right course and the courage to see it through, notwithstanding certain criticism if something goes wrong, is what leaders are paid to do. Americans don't expect their elected and appointed officials to come to Washington and do nothing. They endow them with "special trust and confidence" to act in their behalf, boldly and with determination. The reciprocal trust from the official to the individual American is not to act frivolously, dishonestly, or for personal gain. Thus it was tragic irony that the trust President Nixon vindicated to execute the China opening was so badly eroded for successive generations by his breaches of trust in the Watergate scandal.

I joined Henry Kissinger's staff in 1973, a year after the China opening was announced. The work of cementing the relationship was ongoing and was a major focus of the small staff in Kissinger's immediate office. Early in the effort to launch the opening, Kissinger had made it clear to the Chinese that our two countries could work to mutual advantage in sharing information and facilities that would advance the interests of each side with respect to the Soviet Union. Extremely sensitive exchanges of information had begun by mutual agreement in late 1971.

On our side, Winston Lord and Jon Howe from the NSC staff, working closely with Dick Helms and later Bill Colby, directors of the CIA, would prepare detailed briefings for the Chinese on our assessment of Soviet military dispositions and readiness. This involved not only strategic nuclear forces, but also conventional army, navy, and air forces positioned on the Chinese border and in ocean areas. In addition, the U.S. would brief the Chinese on the extensive Soviet military aid program to dozens of countries and guerrilla movements around the world, including Vietnam.

When in July 1973 I joined the staff, I helped prepare the material for an upcoming exchange in the autumn of that year. Jon Howe, the military assistant to Kissinger whom I had been hired to replace, was still on the staff at the time and was the designated briefer to the Chinese.

After Nixon's resignation a year later, Henry was eager that President Gerald Ford demonstrate his readiness to carry forward Nixon's activism in foreign affairs. Toward that end, Kissinger—still in his joint role of National Security Adviser and Secretary of State—arranged a summit meeting to be held in November in

Vladivostok with Soviet President Leonid Brezhnev. Ford and Kissinger believed it might be feasible to set the basic parameters of a SALT II agreement, something that might be more readily accomplished in a meeting between the two heads of state than in the grinding deliberations of day-to-day negotiations in Geneva and elsewhere.

Following the Vladivostok summit, Henry and I continued on to China. I carried along an armload of notebooks filled with information to be briefed to the Chinese. For three solid days then, and again a year later, I sat in a private room in the Great Hall of the People, opposite a senior official from the Chinese defense ministry, and, with great deliberation, went over literally hundreds of pages of data.

The gains from these exchanges were of enormous benefit to both sides. In a *quid pro quo* for the data, the Chinese gave us access to invaluable sites for intelligence gathering on the Soviet Union that were not available anywhere else in the world. Perhaps as importantly, the exchanges undoubtedly created enormous ambiguity in the minds of the Soviet leaders in the Kremlin as to what precisely was developing on their southern flank.

We had no doubt that the Soviets knew of the intelligence exchanges; we even assumed that the Chinese were letting Moscow know about them indirectly, since it would enhance their own deterrent to do so. The impact in Moscow had to be great; the Soviet Union could not take for granted that China would remain a benign presence to the south, and it now saw that China's capabilities were being enhanced by the American intelligence gathering system and—prospectively—even military cooperation. It had to fear facing not one rival military giant, but two. The contingent commitment of resources to deal with two such giants had to be enormous, and undoubtedly contributed ultimately to the collapse of the Soviet system and our victory in the cold war.

Once again, had Congress known about these exchanges, there is no doubt it would have immediately curtailed or ended them, and in that process vitiated the enormous potential of the relationship with China. Kissinger took a risk and clearly withheld information from the Congress. Yet in doing so, he undeniably nurtured a relationship of profound importance to our security. The Nixon-Kissinger strategy to outflank the Soviet Union by engaging the country on its

southern border was a historic stroke of geopolitical wisdom, and
one with extremely valuable returns for all Americans.

———

Before I went to work for Henry Kissinger, I had read every book
and article that he had ever written. His work is without peer:
exhaustive in its scholarship, rigorous in its analysis, elevated in its
language, visionary in its thinking. He is a giant intellect, and the
preeminent strategist of his generation.

Coming to know him involved much work, but also chance.

At the end of my second tour in Vietnam I was assigned to the
Marine Corps headquarters in Washington D.C. The next three
years, I was the Marine Corps action officer, first for Latin America,
then the Middle East and finally Western Europe and NATO. In that
role, I worked with the representatives of the other services in developing military contingency plans for conducting operations ranging
from the rescue of civilians to full scale invasions, to protect U.S.
interests around the world.

Following that assignment, I applied for a White House
Fellowship. This program was established in 1964 by President
Lyndon Johnson to bring promising mid-level professionals into
government for one year, to work with a Cabinet officer and observe
high-level decision-making at close range. The concept behind the
program was to prepare rising professionals who appear destined for
future leadership to better understand governance so as to be better
able to work with it in their own professions, be they investment
banking, manufacturing, education, the arts or the military.

From thousands of applicants each year, a panel of distinguished
Americans chooses a dozen or so as Fellows. In its 30-year history,
the program seems to have chosen well and served its purpose. Its
alumni include General Colin Powell; Gary Carruthers, the former
governor of New Mexico; Henry Cisneros, the current Secretary of
Housing and Urban Development; several current and former members
of Congress; judges; and accomplished artists and writers.

As a White House Fellow in 1971-72, I had worked in an office
next door to Kissinger in the West Wing. Kissinger was the National
Security Adviser—and I would see him often in the halls. He knew
who I was, but I was just a junior staffer, and Henry's manner always
called to mind the line about the Lowells speaking only to the

Cabots and the Cabots speaking only to God. I suppose Henry might have said that God spoke only to him, and he would share it with President Nixon.

He was an inconoclast, unapproachable, demanding, imperious. When the interview I had requested for a position on his staff came through in 1973, I worried about making the grade with him. He didn't go out of his way to ease my qualms.

The interview took place at San Clemente during a Nixon trip to his California home in June 1973. I had to spend a nervous half hour waiting before I was finally called into Kissinger's office on the edge of the Pacific. He looked me over noncommittally. He said he had looked at my record. Then he declared, quite deliberately, in his gruff German accent, that in his judgment, no one could ever replace Jon Howe.

Howe was, I knew, an extremely talented naval officer who had earned his master's and doctorate from the Fletcher School of Law and Diplomacy at Tufts University in a record two years' time, and had been Kissinger's military assistant for four years. He would go on to serve in a number of staff and command positions and ultimately rise to four-star rank as commander of NATO forces for the southern region of Europe. His reputation was certainly one to live up to.

Despite this inauspicious beginning, I was chosen for the job and was soon working 12- to 15-hour days for one of the most mercurial and difficult bosses it has ever been my pleasure or peril to know.

Kissinger set extremely high standards. He worked extraordinarily hard himself, and expected those around him to follow suit. He thought nothing of driving his staff to extreme efforts in producing policy papers or analyses or reports and occasionally rode people to the point of exhaustion. He was given to verbal abuse of his subordinates and rarely acknowledged the tremendous efforts his colleagues and staffers put in for him.

In my job, I was responsible for assuring that all the paperwork that came to Henry's office was thorough, well-coordinated with other White House offices and substantively sound. It was fascinating work that involved a great deal of learning at the hand of a master, and I loved it.

At the same time, I found certain aspects unsettling. Not only was Kissinger demanding and dogmatic, a man who did not tolerate rational argument with temperance or any measure of good grace, he was also distrustful, hypocritical, routinely dishonest and abusive to his friends. He is an extremely vain man, apparently without solid spiritual anchors, who was as absorbed with how he would be perceived by future generations as he was with his genuine commitment to sound policy. But he went at his job with a Spenglerian view of humankind, and believed that his role was to exploit the vulnerabilities of others as each situation demanded, by fair means or foul, to accomplish what he thought was right.

Fair play was to him just a rhetorical metaphor, and life and especially international politics were a very Darwinian process. Get the most you can with the least expenditure of capital and always play your cards close to your vest seemed to be his *modus operandi,* and he truly couldn't fathom, even disdained, people who operated out of a greater sense of honesty and forthrightness than he. I remember an incident during the congressional investigation of the organization and functioning of the CIA in 1976. Committees headed by Congressman Otis Pike and Senator Frank Church were requesting files from both the CIA and the White House relating to covert activities. Henry, true to form, was anxious to keep as much back as possible, to keep the flow of papers to the Hill very tightly controlled.

One day, as the tedious work of examining all the NSC and Presidential files dragged on, Henry came into the office. Brent went in to give him a piece of news: Bill Colby, the Director of the CIA, had okayed sending Congress a category of file for which the committees had not even asked. It was a preemptive move on Colby's part to keep a problem from arising later. But Henry, who was capable of throwing pencils and other projectiles when angered, went into a rage.

"Goddam Colby!" he stormed in his office. "They charge him with shoplifting; he confesses to murder."

Above all, Kissinger had intellectual disdain for nearly everyone around him, including the press, the Congress, and the President. Even Nixon he saw as a foil, a man who could be manipulated, usefully, to advance his own view of how our foreign relationships ought to be engaged or exploited.

Working for such a complex, conspiratorial man, I found it hard, at times, to maintain my moral compass. During the worst days of Watergate, I knew that he was capable of undermining Al Haig in a conversation with Nixon one moment, then hanging up and calling

Haig to disparage Nixon in turn. He would make commitments to senators or congressmen, then call the President to rip apart the position to which he had just committed.

It was a four-year course in political hardball. Often I asked myself, "Do I believe in what his purposes are, and do I believe that he can achieve them without severe damage to our institutions?" In the end, I did believe it. Ultimately, what he sought to, and frequently did, achieve transcended the dishonesty and cynicism of his methods. It was a classic case of the ends justifying the means.

———

I came to Kissinger's staff as his military assistant with 12 years experience in strategic planning and military operations. I had developed a true passion for foreign affairs that had been broadened during the two years I had spent in Europe on the Olmsted scholarship, and matured in the three years I spent on the staff of General Frank Tharin, the Marine representative to the Joint Chiefs of Staff, after my return from Vietnam. I had enjoyed the 18 months as a White House Fellow, working with Bill Timmons in legislative affairs, absorbing what had changed in the executive-legislative relationship since my father's day. But coming to the National Security Council felt wholly natural. I knew that this was the area to which I wanted to devote my career and my future.

The opportunities for learning in Henry's shop were boundless. Four months after I joined his staff, he was named Secretary of State and, in an unprecedented arrangement, served for the next two years both in that post and as National Security Adviser. During that time, I absorbed a huge body of knowledge in my role as repository of every piece of diplomatic traffic that came in from Moscow, Beijing, Jerusalem, Langley, and Capitol Hill. I saw how this information was forged, through analysis, into effective strategy for integrating U.S. political, economic and military power in times of both war and peace. I participated in the basics of crisis management, as practiced, for instance, in the Yom Kippur war, and of long-term policy planning, *vis-a-vis* the Soviet Union and China, and in Europe.

It was a period of learning and practice in national security bureaucratics: how to get the best from the Pentagon and the State Department, how to orchestrate studies that would evoke maximum imagination and knowledge out of the career professionals in the

CIA, Treasury, Defense, State, and the Joint Chiefs of Staff, by means of the incentives of bureaucratic leadership that allow the cream to rise to the top and perform.

This was the period of our disengagement from Vietnam, of Henry's famous shuttle diplomacy in the Middle East, of expanding relations with China. It was also the period of Watergate.

—

In mid-1974, I had been on the White House staff for more than two years. As the House Judiciary Committee and the Watergate committee continued their hearings, it seemed ever more certain that articles of impeachment would be moved, and that, concurrently, the Supreme Court would require that the White House tapes be turned over. Yet it was curious to me that no one in the White House believed that these things would happen.

Whenever I found myself on the fringes of conversations between Kissinger and Haig, who had by now taken H. R. Haldeman's place as Chief of Staff, and the lawyers, everyone would voice certainty that nothing would happen, citing all sorts of implausible reasons why.

Around that time, the President encouraged the idea of a foreign trip to divert attention from Watergate and focus it on the foreign agenda, thus recalling in the public's mind his strength in that arena. I did the Russian portion of the advance work for the trip, which would take Nixon to the Middle East and the Soviet Union. The trip was a relative success, but it hardly stopped the drumbeat of revelations on Watergate.

Not long after the President returned in July, we went out to San Clemente. I went along as staff support for Kissinger and his deputy, Brent Scowcroft. I would have lunch out on the terrace each day, as did Henry, Scowcroft, and Al Haig. It was remarkable to see the absolute confidence on the part of Haig and the President that the House Judiciary Committee would never move articles of impeachment, nor the Supreme Court require the turnover of the tapes.

Within two days of the last of these conversations, both those events came to pass. And the White House greeted them with genuine disbelief.

It was an object lesson for me on the perils of isolation and the necessity of keeping touch with reality. Certainly it seemed to me that the senior staff were seriously self-deluded and entirely out of touch with mainstream America and the voice of that mainstream as expressed by the members of the House Judiciary Committee.

If anyone did see the handwriting on the wall, it was Brent Scowcroft. An Air Force lieutenant general who was Kissinger's deputy, Brent began early in 1974 to meet for an hour or so a week with Vice President Gerald Ford. In each of these meetings, he would present the Vice President one of a series of 30 or 40 papers he had tasked the staff to prepare on the top national security issues of the day, in order to bring Ford up to speed on what he would presumptively face if he became President. It was clear Brent thought that was what was going to happen.

It was a terribly depressing time. Clearly the concept of "special trust" would be badly damaged in the public mind. In truth, for all of my lifetime, the practice of Presidents had been to act autonomously, to play hardball, to be cynical and Machiavellian. But for the first time, this was being exposed, and the result would henceforth be far greater scrutiny of executive action by the Congress and in the press, and far greater restriction of it. After investigating these events, the tendency of the Congress would not be to find the concept of "special trust" valid, though abused by a few. Instead, they would seek to legislate restrictions on the authority of the President and presidential advisers. Over time, I feared, these restrictions in latitude would so hamper initiative as to attract a lower quality public servant who would be more likely to abuse power, thereby inviting even further legislative restraint. Ultimately, this cycle of abuse and restraint could virtually paralyze governance.

Those of us in the national security arena found it especially difficult to reconcile what was going on in the Watergate scandal with the reality of our own operation. The fact was that we belonged to a disciplined organization that achieved solid, positive results; we felt we were part of a machine that worked. Everyone on the staff must have faced a moment of truth in trying to rationalize respect for the organization we served with competing concern for the climate that pervaded the White House, a climate of deceptions and wiretaps and enemies' lists.

Once again, I found I was asking myself the question: "How can I stay on in a place that is awash in cynics, liars, and people who have violated the public trust?" And once again, I found the answer in the product; I believed, completely and firmly, in the foreign policy we were making. This is not to say, however, that the climate in which I was functioning was healthy. Participating in meetings where gossip, criticism and hypocrisy were the order of the day exacted a heavy toll.

And yet, I had had enough exposure to the files of previous administrations to realize that this was pretty much the pattern of governance in the United States and in the White Houses of both parties. Lyndon Johnson had distorted the Gulf of Tonkin events and embroiled us in a chain of deceptions that wound up costing tens of thousands of Americans their lives. His Defense Secretary, Robert McNamara, aided and abetted him, blatantly lying in his portrayal of those events and many others in the conduct of the Vietnam War.

The day Richard Nixon left the White House, I sat in my small office in the basement of the West Wing. I had been given leave to attend the farewell gathering the President had convened in the East Room, where he gave his rambling good-bye speech to the tearful faithful who had soldiered with him through the thick and the thin of the past six years. But I chose not to go.

I sat at my desk, filled with a profound sadness, and stared blankly out at West Executive Avenue. My sadness was not so much for Nixon—more of that came later. I felt sorrow for the country at this national embarrassment. The boil could have been lanced if the truth had been told. But lying had been selected as the preferred route, and now the worst had happened.

I had grown up with a supreme confidence in the inexorability of predictable changes in governance in the United States, in contrast to the frequent public squalor and turmoil of European politics. Now that confidence was shattered. It was the bleakest of days.

Alone in my office, I laid my head on my desk and wept.

———

From the beginning, the presidency of Gerald R. Ford was a balm to the country. A 14-term congressman from Michigan and the Republican minority leader in the House of Representatives, Ford had been tapped by Nixon for the Vice Presidency in October 1973, after Spiro Agnew resigned in the wake of a no-contest plea to corruption charges.

Jerry Ford was widely liked on the Hill, and had many friends on both sides of the aisle. Most people in Washington recognized that in the wake of the Watergate trauma, Ford's would be precisely the type of personality needed to make up for the absence of character in the White House. His depth of knowledge and interest in foreign affairs certainly did not match that of Nixon, but he was a figure who evoked both respect and sympathy, a man of steadiness, moderation and honesty who would exert a stabilizing influence on a shaken administration and nation.

As a foreign policy specialist, I particularly appreciated his recognition of the unworkability of congressional micro-management of the conduct of foreign policy. As Minority Leader, he had consistently taken a strong position in support of executive dominance in foreign affairs. As President, he assumed an even stronger stance. On the War Powers Resolution, he was tougher than any President before or since. The resolution, giving Congress a virtual veto over the length of time and circumstances under which U.S. armed forces could be deployed for hostilities, had passed Congress over President Nixon's veto in October 1973. However, Ford, to his credit, never reported strictly under the resolution. He made reports to Congress on foreign policy undertakings, but was always careful to draw a distinction: he would make sure that War Powers reporting requirements were observed, without ever acknowledging the constitutionality of the law.

Ford was, above all, a thoroughly decent man, one with no Machiavellian instincts whatsoever. In the parlance of the present, he was a genuine case of "what you see is what you get."

His personal likability even had an effect on my crusty Democrat father. Dad came to visit me in Washington in 1976, when he was nearly 82 years of age. He had been not been happy with my going to work for then-President Richard Nixon; I remember as a child that it was dangerous even to speak the word "Republican" in my home. It would provoke my father into a stormy rage and a denunciation of all Republicans, whom he saw as degenerate and intrinsically evil creatures.

Growing up I had had no doubt of the Manichean division of the American political system—the Democratic Party was good, the Republican Party bad. Although I began to discern a rather less rigid demarcation as I achieved the age of majority, I had accepted the precepts of my father's tutelage and given the benefit of the doubt and my vote to Democratic candidates from John Kennedy to Hubert Humphrey. But after I returned to Washington from my second tour in Vietnam, and began to pay heed to the themes being developed by Republicans and Democrats on foreign policy, I identified more closely with the GOP than with the party of my forebears.

The center of gravity in the Democratic Party had shifted leftward, and the non-interventionist trend was ascendant. When George McGovern became the Democratic candidate for President, I could not seriously consider supporting a man with such a superficial grasp of America's global interests and what was required, in terms of both strategy and resources, to advance them. My judgment about our political leadership has come down on the Republican side of the ticket ever since, for essentially the same reason: namely, that the Republican candidates have each had a superior grasp of the basic requirements of defending our national security interests.

Concurrently, however, I have always believed it to be important that, to the extent possible, our political leaders try to act internationally with as strong a bipartisan underpinning as possible. And there are and always have been very sensible advocates for sound national security policies within both parties. People such as Scoop Jackson, John Stennis, Sam Nunn, Les Aspin and others have with few exceptions been reliable advocates of a strong national security policy.

My father, as he grew older, evolved into a "Scoop Jackson Democrat," strong on defense and strong on social policy. Nevertheless, he still considered himself a diehard Democrat when I brought him into the White House one day in 1976 to meet my boss, the President.

Ford was very gracious during that brief meeting, listening carefully as my father expounded on the fundamental tenets of his political philosophy, and agreeing with the importance of each one. My father was charmed. Hours after the meeting, he was still talking about how much he had liked the President. And after he returned home to Texas, he withdrew his support from a number of local Democratic candidates, and even sent me a contribution to Ford's reelection campaign!

He was proud of the fact that I worked for Ford, and that I had reached a position to influence government policy. Unfortunately, he didn't live to see the achievements of the Reagan years. He died in 1980, at the age of 85.

———

President Ford's mettle as a world leader was tested repeatedly in the course of his brief, two and a half-year tenure in the White House. From the start, the situation he inherited was fraught with uncertainty and the potential for crisis. In the wake of Nixon's resignation, and our final, demoralizing exit from Vietnam, the international image of the United States was at a historic low point, and concerns about our reliability as an ally reached beyond Asia. Ford, as an appointed president, did not have a mandate from the American people, and yet America and the free world were desperately in need of leadership.

On the morning of May 12, 1975, a U.S. merchant vessel, the *SS Mayaguez*, was attacked and seized by Cambodian naval patrol boats approximately 60 miles southwest of the Cambodian port of Kompong Som. The news reached Washington through the U.S. embassy in Djakarta. Brent Scowcroft informed the President of the development at about 7:30 a.m. but at the State Department, Kissinger didn't learn of it until 8 a.m. He seized upon it at once.

Ever-mindful of the U.S. humiliation in Vietnam, Kissinger believed that prompt and decisive action was necessary to avoid the appearance of the United States as a helpless giant, unable to defend its own interests against a nuisance power. The President agreed.

The administration began at once to consider options for recovering the ship. In the course of the deliberations, word was received that the crew had been taken off the *Mayaguez* and transferred either to the mainland or to a tiny nearby island, Koh Tang. This news raised the level of concern several degrees, as it called to mind the case of the *USS Pueblo*, a naval intelligence vessel that had been seized off the coast of Korea in 1968. In that incident, the United States had lost both the ship and the crew, who were held prisoner in North Korea for 11 months.

This time, the United States swung into action. Messages protesting the seizure and insisting on the return of the ship and crew were sent to the Cambodians via the Peoples Republic of China. The President ordered a Marine amphibious unit into the area, and ordered a carrier battle group steaming toward Australia to turn around and head back toward the Southeast Asian peninsula to provide support.

On May 15, after two days of air surveillance, an attack was launched on Koh Tang Island, where the crew was believed to be. Concurrently, bombing strikes were carried out against military facilities at Kompong Som. The Marines came under heavy fire immediately as they landed on the beach, and in the first hour and a half of fighting lost 15 men. Soon after, a boarding party of Marines was dispatched to the ship by helicopter. They landed and took control with no casualties.

The President and Cabinet officers were in the middle of a state dinner for Dutch Prime Minister Joop M. den Uyl as the operation got underway. I was monitoring the operations for the White House. As I got updates from the Pentagon and the National Military Command Center, I would send notes to Scowcroft in the state dining room informing him of how the operation was unfolding. After several hours of fighting, sailors on the destroyer *USS Wilson* spied a Thai fishing boat approaching the ship. In it were a number of men waving articles of clothing tied to long bamboo poles. It was the crew of the *Mayaguez*. They had been released by the Cambodians after our air and ground attacks made clear our resolve.

The state dinner ended and President Ford returned to the Oval Office with Kissinger, Scowcroft and chief of Staff Donald Rumsfeld. I was called to the Oval Office to brief. I reported that the battle on Koh Tang had been fierce and that we had lost 15 men. The crew of the *Mayaguez*, I said, had been released and safely recovered.

The President was saddened by the losses we had incurred, but relieved and pleased that the operation had succeeded, and prepared to order the Marines to withdraw from Koh Tang. As I finished my brief, the telephone rang. Secretary of Defense James Schlesinger was on the line from the Pentagon.

By the time of the *Mayaguez* incident, Ford and Schlesinger were already on poor terms. Their relationship had gotten off on the wrong foot back when President Nixon resigned. Ford had bristled at press accounts saying that Schlesinger had put U.S. forces on alert; it was a usurpation, Ford believed, of his own presidential authority. That bad start had only degenerated over time. Ford considered the pipe-smoking, scholarly Defense Secretary ponderous and patronizing; on more than one occasion, Schlesinger had made it evident that he didn't think the new President was quite up to his job.

Now Schlesinger was calling to report with some solemnity that the *Mayaguez* crew had possibly been sighted at sea on a boat. The Secretary was obviously out of touch with his own command center. Ford, who already knew from me that the crew was in fact safe in U.S. hands, gave no indication of this to Schlesinger, but thanked him and hung up.

Then he let out a loud guffaw. "Schlesinger didn't have a clue as to what was going on," he said, laughing. "He didn't even know the crew had already been recovered."

Kissinger, Scowcroft and Rumsfeld joined in his merriment. All three broke into loud laughter. At that moment, David Hume Kennerly, the White House photographer, snapped a picture. Later, press secretary Ron Nessen, looking for a quote to put under the picture, asked me what the President had said when he heard the crew had been recovered. I told him truthfully that he had reacted with relief and thanked God that they were all safe.

The next day, the photograph appeared on the front page of *The New York Times*, the caption indicating it was a shot of the President and his aides reacting to the news that the *Mayaguez* crew had been released. Everyone certainly looks happy in the photo, Kissinger with a big grin on his face, Scowcroft, Rumsfeld and the President with their mouths open in laughter. In fact, you might say they look a little happier than would be commensurate with the completion of a risky mission in which a number of American lives were lost. But there was no reason to let on that there was anything else to account for their glee.

Despite some partisan grumbling from Congress and some concern over the cost in casualties, Ford's handling of the *Mayaguez* incident was generally hailed as a solid example of sound crisis management and boosted the President's popularity and standing both at home and abroad. It was a successful beginning to a restoration of American credibility and resolve.

Ford was a man of both courage and conviction, and the way in which he handled foreign policy and decision-making in general restored a dignity to the presidency for which he deserves enormous credit. Two examples serve to illustrate this fact.

In the spring of 1976, when Ford was gearing up to run for re-election, the situation in Rhodesia (now Zimbabwe) was heating up.

The country was experiencing the convulsion of a transition from a white single party to a pluralistic government. The United States was in a position to play a mediating role, and the President was considering sending Kissinger to Africa for that purpose. At a White House meeting with his advisers and Republican leaders, just prior to the Texas primary, Ford listened thoughtfully as nearly everyone, to a person, urged him not to intervene. They believed it would anger conservatives and cost him the primary. Kissinger's was the only voice in favor of becoming involved.

Ford heard everyone out, puffing calmly on his pipe. When they had finished, he leaned forward in his chair and said that he appreciated the advice and respected the judgment of every man in the room. "But we've got to do this," he said, "because it's the right thing to do."

He sent Kissinger to Rhodesia and lost the Texas primary.

A few months later, on August 18, came another crisis. Two U.S. army officers supervising the pruning of a poplar tree in the Korean Demilitarized Zone were brutally murdered by North Korean soldiers. The outcry at home over the vicious and unprovoked assault was loud and furious.

Ford was about to depart for the Republican convention in Kansas City. He was facing a stiff challenge from the right for the Presidential nomination by former California governor Ronald Reagan. In the face of the crisis that had just occurred, there was some pressure on Ford to vet his conservative bona fides and launch a heavy military response, including using B-52s against the North Koreans.

Ford, to his credit, recognized that the incident, while serious, did not warrant a response that could provoke extended hostilities, and chose to follow the course proposed by General Richard G. Stilwell, Commander in Chief of United Nations forces. Stilwell recommended that the United States reaffirm its rights in the DMZ by sending in troops to cut down the offending tree while supported by a show of force staged by units in Korea and additional forces deployed to the area offshore.

Once again, the strategy worked. The North Koreans backed down, issued an apology of sorts for the murders, and life in the DMZ returned to "normal." As for Ford, he won the Republican nomination.

But he lost the election.

It was a genuinely sad outcome for those of us who worked with him. He had appeared to be gaining momentum in the closing months of the campaign. Then came San Francisco.

Ford and his Democratic rival, former Georgia governor Jimmy Carter, were nearly finished with the final debate of the campaign, on October 6 in San Francisco. On foreign policy, Ford was clearly the winner, displaying superior knowledge and understanding of every issue that was put on the table by the panel of journalists. Then someone asked a question about Poland, and the President made what was to become known as the most serious gaffe of the campaign. Ford said that there was no Soviet domination of Poland.

From the full context of his answer, it was clear what Ford had meant to say. He had meant, as he later said, that the Polish people were not dominated in spirit by the Soviet Union, that they remained resistant in heart and mind to the order that had been imposed on them by Moscow after World War II.

If Ford had come out quickly to make this explanation, the whole matter could still have been diffused. But Jerry Ford was occasionally subject to starchiness when people criticized his statements, and he couldn't bring himself to acknowledge that what he thought he had said, and what the perception was, diverged.

Immediately afterward, Brent Scowcroft and Dick Cheney, Ford's Chief of Staff, tried to neutralize the misunderstanding with the press, but the reporters weren't buying. The next morning, we were scheduled to fly down to the University of Southern California for an appearance. On the plane, I wrote out a quick comment on the debate for the President to issue, to the effect that the obvious intent of his remarks had been that the Polish people are indomitable and someday would prevail.

Ford would have none of it. He kept saying, "Everybody knows that." And Brent and Dick said, "But they don't know it, Mr. President." Still he would not agree.

At last, about 48 hours after the debate, he issued a statement. It was too late. The newspapers had already had a field day. Ford had been portrayed as a geopolitical naif who did not even recognize the realities of the bipolar world. How could he be trusted to continue to govern, to act as leader of the western world? The truth, which became clear during Jimmy Carter's term as President, was that Jerry Ford knew a lot more about Soviet dominance than Carter did.

After five years in civilian service, following Ford's defeat I was reassigned into military uniform and fulltime duty with the Marine Corps. As I left the White House, President Ford awarded me the Distinguished Service Medal, the country's highest peacetime military decoration, primarily for my work in China. I was the first lieutenant colonel to receive it.

The hiatus from the military had been challenging and fulfilling for me, but it was not viewed with such a sanguine eye by my superiors back at headquarters. In their judgment, I had been away too long from my real job—serving the Corps. It is fair to say that there isn't a great demand in the Marine Corps for officers trained in strategic studies. I respect that. The Marines focus on their mission—to take and hold the beach—not on forging national policy.

I spent a year and a half at the National War College writing a book—*Crisis Resolution*—and getting to know my family again. Then it came time to ship out to Okinawa for a final tour.

Okinawa is a post to which Marines are discouraged from bringing their families. This was not a hard-and-fast rule, but disregarding it was decidedly frowned upon, and the Marine who ignored it could expect to pay a price. But I felt I had already been away from my family enough during my five years at the White House and determined to have them with me in Japan. It meant we had to find our own lodgings and life would be lived on a shoestring, but Jonny and I were prepared to put up with that hardship in order to be together.

Matters quickly got off to an unsatisfactory start with the commanding general. Soon after arrival, I reported in to Lieutenant General Dolf Schwenk. It was a Saturday. He was in his office, dressed in golf shorts, practicing his putting on the rug. He barely looked up when I came in.

"You're McFarlane," he said.

"Yes, sir," I said.

"You brought your family," he said.

"Yes, sir," I said.

"Well," he said, and swung the putter, "no battalion for you."

That was all. It struck me as an exceedingly mean-spirited, stupid way to lead, and was the first event that began to persuade me that with this turn of mind, this capacity for professional mismanagement, this Marine Corps was not where I could best serve the country.

I left as quickly as I could and went down to the 12th Marine Regiment headquarters. The new commander there was Bob Gibson, an intelligent man, a 1954 Academy graduate, and a good, solid artilleryman. But he, in turn, gave me some stinging news. He had only two battalions, he said, and he had to give them to men who were going to get passed over for promotion because they needed command to qualify. "You're going to get promoted, so I don't need to worry about you," he said.

I was flabbergasted. I had never heard a more contorted, backward, irresponsible line of reasoning in my life. What did it say about Gibson that he wanted his troops led by inferior officers? Actually, he had probably received his orders from General Schwenk. In any event, it was a clear signal to me that my career in the military was winding down.

I spent the year in Okinawa as operations officer of the regiment and made the most of it. I came up with an inventive new concept for running the first live-fire, combined air and ground maneuver operation in the history of the division in Korea. For more than 30 years, the Marines had trained their infantry in one place and their pilots in another, the two never working together as a team. Putting them together made an enormous difference in their effectiveness.

As I neared the 20-year mark in the spring of 1979, I queried my monitor back in Washington for what I might expect to do next. I assumed my assignment would be related to strategic studies, but I was wrong. I had "done" strategic studies, the monitor said. Now I had to go and learn to be a communicator, or supply person, or a personnel officer; I had to absorb new skills to prepare myself to be a general.

It was inconceivable to me that the Marine Corps, this corps of professionals, which I loved, should have invested 13 years in my effort to become a competent professional in strategic studies, only to turn around now and say, "We're never going to use that again." But this is what they were saying.

It was the last straw for me. Twelve thousand miles from the job market, I began to think about a new career. I wangled a trip stateside by winning the Naval Institute's Alfred Thayer Mahan Award for Literary Achievement, enabling me to fly to Dallas for the awards ceremony. I had written to my old friends Tom Korologos and John Lehman, with whom I had worked at the White House in the office of legislative affairs. They both recommended that I get in touch with Texas Senator John Tower about a position. Tower was the ranking minority member of the Senate Armed Services Committee and was looking for a staff aide.

From Dallas, I flew to Washington and contacted his office, only to be told that he had just gone to Texas! Scraping together my pennies, I flew back to Texas and finally caught up with Tower in Austin. We hit it off and he hired me on the spot.

I retired from the Marine Corps on June 30, 1979, and returned to civilian life for good. For the next 18 months, I worked on Capitol Hill, immersed in defense budgets and the SALT II treaty. I worked with exceptional people—Tower himself, of course, and my three fellow staff members, Rhett Dawson, Alton Keel and Ron Lehman. All of us, as it turned out, were destined to achieve cabinet or near-cabinet rank in the Reagan and Bush administrations. In the Senate, we made up a band of brothers who, with the enthusiastic support of not only Tower, but also two of the Democratic members of the committee—Scoop Jackson of Washington and Georgia's Sam Nunn—sought to send a signal to Jimmy Carter about the declining state of America's defenses and the effect it had and would continue to have on our security interests overseas.

It is noteworthy that in 1980, the Senate succeeded in adding roughly seven percent to what President Carter had proposed as his defense budget, an extraordinary achievement given that the normal course is for the Congress to cut the President's proposed defense appropriations. It's also remarkable to note how small the committee staff was in those days: all the excellent work we accomplished, concerning billions of dollars and exposure of critical flaws in the SALT II treaty, was done with a total of ten people from both parties. Today, committee staff members on the Hill number in the thousands.

As the 1980 Republican National Convention approached, Senator Tower tapped me to work with John Lehman to draft the foreign policy and defense planks for the platform. Platforms have become a curious phenomenon. Through the 19th century, they served as doctrinal manifestos on which each party based its campaign and which were ultimately translated into policy by cabinet officers after the election. But since the 1950s, they have served more as vehicles for intraparty argument, with little relevance to the conduct of government, with one or two exceptions, after the election is over.

In 1980, the party's anticipated nominee was Ronald Reagan, the staunchly anti-communist, conservative, former Hollywood actor and governor of California who had succeeded in a steady four-year drive to place himself at the top of the Republican ticket, and in mowing down a string of formidable rivals, including George Bush, Alexander Haig and John Connally, along the way. Led by Reagan's fervent assertion of America's superpower status and responsibilities, the party was relatively unified on the importance of a strong defense, the unacceptability of the SALT II Treaty, and the importance of supporting Israel. The more contentious issues were on the domestic side. But the platform gave me a visible role at the convention, and it changed the direction of my life.

After leaving the Marines, I had intended to spend a year or so on the Senate committee with Tower and then go into private life, most likely into international business. In any event, I intended to start a new career. But after working on the platform committee, at hearings with luminaries from my past such as Kissinger, Haig, and others, I became a natural candidate for a presidential appointment to State, Defense or the White House if Reagan won.

On November 4, 1980, Ronald Reagan was elected the 40th President of the United States, ushering in a new Republican administration after four years of Democratic rule that had been marked by a sharp decline both in America's domestic economy and strength, and in our image as a resolute and reliable world leader to be reckoned with. At home, inflation was soaring into the double digits and the economy was in a shambles. Overseas, the United States had repeatedly been humiliated during the Carter years, with the seizure of 52 American hostages in Iran and the Soviet invasion of Afghanistan. Reagan vowed to restore our economic strength at home and respect for our leadership abroad.

To help him in this mission, he designated Alexander Haig his Secretary of State. I had remained in touch with Haig even after leaving the White House. Following his nomination, he asked me to help him in the confirmation process. After he had moved into his new office, I soon got a call. Al Haig was asking me to accept an appointment as Counselor to the Department of State. I could hardly believe my good fortune. As far as I was concerned (and I still believe this to this day), I was being offered the best job in government.

Chapter 10

ON THE SHIP OF STATE

When Ronald Reagan arrived in the White House in January 1981, he was blessed with the fortuitous opportunity for greater accomplishment in foreign affairs than any other President in the post-war period. He had a strong mandate from the American people for a more activist foreign policy, a rare willingness on the public's part to spend the money to underwrite such a policy, and an adversary, the Soviet Union, whose economy was nearing the limit of its ability to sustain the burden of a huge defense establishment and still meet minimal social demands.

At the same time, however, he faced a domestic situation of near-chaos. President Carter's legacy of skyrocketing inflation, interest rates and unemployment cast a pall over the political landscape. Our economic decline was having a damaging effect overseas among our allies, who had developed serious doubts about America's ability to solve problems—even its own. It was reasonable that Reagan should devote his first year in office to domestic matters. From the outset, it was clear that the first year, and perhaps the entire first term, would be oriented chiefly toward translating Reagan's philosophy toward government—downsizing, eliminating intrusive regulation and lowering taxes—into action.

Reagan's only stated prominent foreign policy goal for the first year was to restore the strength of America's military foundation. Yet in order to exploit the opportunity presented to him by the strong American support for restoring our position of leadership, it was vital that the drive for renewed military strength be launched concurrently with the revitalization of the economy, recognizing that it would take several years for a resurgence to materialize and for the Kremlin to absorb that this turn in U.S. fortunes was not a momentary phenomenon but the bow wave of a fundamental and enduring tide of renewal. Such a drive, simultaneously, required a disciplined process for developing policy on which the President could rely to generate sound analysis and sensible options. In the first year of the

Reagan administration, however, we were never able to put this essential policy process into operation.

In mid-January, Al Haig directed me and Dick Kennedy, another old hand from the Kissinger years at the NSC who had been appointed as Undersecretary of State for Management, to prepare a directive for the President to issue shortly after Inauguration Day that would put in place an interdepartmental framework for bringing together career experts and new appointees in a coherent arrangement to develop options for his consideration and ultimate decision. We drew up a document that replicated essentially the same system used by Kissinger during his days as Secretary of State, which I had implemented so many times as Chief of Staff for the NSC. Simply put, the system provided for the State Department to chair interdepartmental groups for developing foreign policy in the various regions of the world, and for the Defense Department to chair interdepartmental groups oriented toward developing defense policy.

After approving the draft, Haig coordinated it with Defense Secretary-designate Caspar Weinberger and made appropriate changes to accommodate his interests. He did the same with Bill Casey at the CIA. In effect, Haig was doing nothing more than translating the mandate he had received from Reagan during a meeting at Blair House on January 6. This, however, was not how the document was viewed by the President's senior staff.

In the White House, responsibilities for managing the executive branch were to be divided among three principals—Ed Meese, who was named Counselor to the President, Jim Baker, the Chief of Staff, and Mike Deaver, Deputy Chief of Staff. This "troika" had enormous reach; anything that passed into or out of the Oval Office was subject to their triplicate control.

Meese, a conservative and close, longtime California friend and adviser to Reagan, was initially, among these three, first among equals, and saw his role as the coordinator of all policy, foreign and domestic. Haig delivered the procedural document to him on Inauguration Day, January 20, fully confident that we would soon have a system to launch a variety of studies for the President on foreign policy issues.

Meese accepted the document and promptly shelved it. As a result, a full year was lost in launching a disciplined policy process. In retrospect, I see Meese's action as a genuine desire to assure that a White House filter prevented policy inconsistent with the President's philosophy from being put in place. But I've also heard it said in the years since, by Mike Deaver and others, that Meese was simply suspicious of Haig's motives. Haig, after all, had been a candidate for President himself in 1980. Meese feared that the new Secretary of State would allow personal ambition to enter into his policy calculations over the next four years, that he would use his position to go beyond making or analyzing policy to deciding it and taking credit for it publicly.

Whatever his motives, Meese's action had the effect of rendering the administration's foreign policy and national security machinery effectively useless for Reagan's entire first year in office. It was a lamentable lack of understanding on Meese's part of the need for a system. The ship of state is a deliberate, slow-moving leviathan and the ability to change course and turn it in a new direction requires great bureaucratic, political and diplomatic skills. Leadership in new directions does not happen simply by fiat. Changing the minds of tens of thousands of bureaucrats who have been working for one President and have become committed to his course requires persuasion and time. It requires the new President to provide incentives and reasons for his civil servants to engage with him and feel a part of his new plan.

Ed Meese was among many in not recognizing this. Early in the administration, I went to the President's National Security Adviser, Richard Allen, to discuss the problems I foresaw and to describe to him the value in having an interdepartmental system to provide the President with policy options. I also noted several pressing issues that called for fairly urgent analysis through such a system.

Allen listened to me noncommittally. When I finished, he responded with an answer that still astonishes me whenever I think of it. "I don't think we need to do a lot of elaborate planning," he said in effect. "As events happen overseas, we'll react to them with good judgment and timely decisions."

What an amazing expression of ignorance regarding the nature of international politics! Sadly, it seems to be an approach shared by the administration of President Bill Clinton. I traveled to the funeral of former President Richard Nixon aboard Air Force One with Clinton and members of his party and listened to the conversation around the table in the forward section with interest. It quickly became clear that the new administration had no plans for tackling foreign policy beyond reacting to global events. Their approach obviously was to look at each day's headlines in *The New York Times* and *Washington Post* and say, "Well, what are we going to do about what's happening in the world today?"

History tells us that no President can expect to achieve more than one or two significant foreign policy goals in a four-year period. To achieve a goal of any magnitude—peace in the Middle East, for instance—requires a strategy that brings together the political and economic resources of the country. It also requires coordination with allies, a vigorous lobbying effort with the Congress, and a sustained campaign to engender public support through Presidential speeches, travel and advocacy by cabinet officers and dozens of subordinate officials. All in all, literally thousands of events and activities must come together to produce a significant change in the course of our foreign policy. Victories of any scale cannot be achieved by reacting to events "with good judgment and timely decisions."

Allen, I knew, was totally loyal to Ronald Reagan—but acting from a lack of experience and understanding of governance, combined with a fundamentally narrow perspective. The unfortunate upshot of his ineptitude, however, was that neither the document I had drawn up nor any other decision-making framework was put in place during the first year of the Reagan presidency, a situation that led to policy being made *ad hoc,* often by the last person who spoke to the President, and seldom written down.

This theater of chaos, with no clear process for developing foreign policy, led to a kind of guerrilla warfare within the administration. Absent any interdepartmental system for developing coherent plans, each cabinet officer tried to put his personal agenda in front of the President. So it was that in August 1981, without any analysis of our interests in Central America, Bill Casey came forward with a proposal for a covert action program to train the freedom fighters in Nicaragua. The Director of Central Intelligence is not supposed to play a policy role. His job is to provide objective analysis of the situation in various parts of the world. But, *faute de mieux,* there Casey was, with the only game in town. We at the State Department didn't even receive the briefing paper on Casey's proposal until the very day it was to be presented to the President at the NSPG.

One of my duties as Counselor was to work with the appropriate Assistant Secretary to screen covert action proposals. But by the time Tom Enders, the Assistant Secretary for Inter-American Affairs, and I received Casey's proposal, there was almost no time to consider it. Haig immediately liked it and wanted us to sign off on it before the NSC meeting. He was not interested in hearing our argument that a covert action program alone should not have been the center of our policy toward the Sandinista regime in Nicaragua. Covert action never works as a core policy. For one thing, because it is secret, you can't sell it or engender public support for it. You can't even talk about it. For another, it always provides too little in the way of resources to make a significant difference. Covert action is properly designed as a marginal program; from the first, when the National Security Act was passed in 1947, Congress limited these programs generally to no more than about $50 million. In Nicaragua, where the Soviet Union was spending $200 million, and later $400 million a year, Casey's $27 million program was a mere drop in the bucket. If we had gotten a positive, comprehensive policy toward Central America and Nicaragua out front in 1981, we might well have avoided many of our later problems with that region.

———

Faced with the reality that we had no system in place for bringing government experts together, Haig set about establishing foreign policy options for the President as best he could. He had attracted a first-rate team of professionals to the State Department and elevated a number of especially qualified career foreign service officers. Walt Stoessel and Larry Eagleburger, both career professionals, had worked with Al in years past and fit in extremely well as the number three officer in the department and the Assistant Secretary for European and Soviet Affairs, respectively. Tom Enders was a professional who had proven highly effective in the field as *charge'* during the last days of the Vietnam War and the fall of Cambodia and was also a first-rate economist. Nick Veliotes, another professional, was put in charge of the Middle East bureau, while Chet Crocker, a distinguished professor from Georgetown University and acknowledged expert on Africa, was placed at the head of the Africa bureau.

Two other key jobs—head of the policy planning staff and director of political-military affairs—were reserved for outsiders, Paul

Wolfowitz and Rick Burt. Paul, the son of an eminent mathematician at Cornell, was one of the most thoughtful and best-read appointees of the Reagan or Bush years. He has an extraordinary grasp of how leaders from other cultures view their own interests, and consistently displayed uncommon imagination as to how we might both play upon their vulnerabilities and exploit their strengths. Rick, a Cornell and Fletcher graduate, came to government from a few years at the London International Institute of Strategic Studies and later *The New York Times*, where he reported on national security affairs.

With some exceptions, Haig tended to look to the regional bureaus and to the career foreign service to manage day-to-day affairs and prevent him from being blindsided by surprises. For new ideas and policy initiatives, however, he tended to look to Burt and Wolfowitz. At the beginning, this did not sit well with the career professionals. After several instances when their memoranda to the Secretary were short circuited, delayed and bureaucratized, Burt and Wolfowitz came to me seeking help in getting their thoughts into Haig's office. I was more than glad to help, since I believed that their imagination and the experience of the career foreign service were equally essential to serve both the Secretary and the President properly.

My own job, as I've said, was the best one in government. As a position without portfolio, it offered its holder the chance to have an impact on the wide breadth of foreign policy issues. Historically, the position of Counselor of the State Department had been shaped to suit the preferences of each Secretary. When George Kennan was Counselor of the department, his focus was the Soviet Union and the conduct of the cold war. Later, Helmut Sonnenfeldt focused on essentially the same portfolio for Henry Kissinger. Haig wanted me to perform two functions. The first was to act as policy adviser on key regional and functional issues—notably the Middle East, Latin America and arms control with the Soviet Union. The second was to serve as his representative and channel for sensitive communications between himself and foreign ministers and prime ministers in a dozen countries he considered to be the most important on our agenda at the time, primarily in the Middle East.

As an undersecretary level position, I had an office on the seventh floor of the department, where the Secretary's suite is located. Once Haig offered me the job, I called the White House and asked Wilma

Hall to come and serve as my secretary, organizer, surrogate mother and critic. Wilma was a highly professional career White House secretary. She started with MacGeorge Bundy in the Kennedy administration and has worked for every National Security Adviser since. She and Brent Scowcroft and another secretary named Ann Bradley and I had formed close friendships when we were all working together in the Nixon and Ford administrations. After Brent and I left the White House in 1977, Wilma and Ann stayed on to work for Zbigniew Brzezinski, but we all continued to have lunch once a month. Wilma was a good friend, so I was doubly pleased when she agreed to join me at the State Department. I welcomed the challenges of the job with great confidence in my skills but also a sober sense of obligation to vindicate the trust being placed in me.

In early 1981, there was no dearth of foreign issues on which the administration needed to focus its attention. Over the previous five years, the Soviet Union had extended its reach and influence into several countries in Africa and South Asia—Angola, Ethiopia, South Yemen, and most recently Afghanistan—and Moscow had recently made major commitments to support insurgent movements in Central America. There was a need to advance the peace process in the Middle East begun in the Camp David accords, and to help negotiate the return of the Sinai Desert to Egypt and ultimately seek to advance the autonomy negotiations between Israel and the Palestinians. Elsewhere, we needed to try to consolidate our relations with China, which had been elevated to formal diplomatic relations during the Carter administration. There was the growing problem of international terrorism, sponsored by states such as Libya and Iran and promoted by autonomous groups operating primarily from the Middle East with growing evidence of indirect Soviet support. Finally, the administration faced the imminent threat of crisis in Poland, where the heroic pressure being mounted by the Solidarity movement posed the risk of precipitating a Soviet invasion.

With all these pressing questions on the horizon, Haig's first choice for a policy initiative came as a big surprise. At an early meeting, he announced peremptorily: "I want to go after Cuba, Bud. I want you to get everyone together and give me a plan for doing it."

It wasn't what any of us had expected to hear. It was as though Haig had come into office thinking, "Where can we make a quick win?" and judged that place to be Cuba. With the Soviet Union preoccupied with Poland and Afghanistan, he apparently believed that with boldness and sufficient resources we could close Castro down. Further, he believed that doing so was the key to preventing a tide of Soviet-supported subversion from sweeping through Central America and ultimately to South America. I couldn't deny the long-term threat but the idea didn't seem workable to me.

For one thing, I believed it would take at least a third of the Navy, substantial casualties, and a long time to do the job. Secondly, the American people and the Congress would have to understand the nature of the problem and recognize its importance in order to make the kind of campaign Haig envisioned sustainable. I didn't believe such support could be developed, certainly not without a major public information campaign. Thirdly, I was not convinced that this was the most important matter we could tackle in foreign affairs. And finally, I doubted that the President would want a distraction of this enormity competing for resources on the Hill at a time when he was trying to put a major domestic legislative program in place. I marshaled my arguments against it.

But Haig persisted. Once he had tasked me to put together a Cuban strategy, he badgered me for the results weekly. "Where's the plan for going to the source?" he would ask.

After several weeks of work with counterparts from Defense, the CIA and the Joint Chiefs, all of which produced unsatisfactory answers, he became exercised over the delay. By the middle of March, the possibility of Soviet intervention in Poland had become acute once more. Haig told me to look at the possibility of going after Cuba as a reaction to a Soviet move into Poland.

Reluctantly, I called in Paul Wolfowitz and Rick Burt. After a lengthy discussion in which we analyzed the situation from every angle, we worked up a paper evaluating the likely response of the Soviet Union and our allies to direct U.S. action against Cuba "intended to 'cut Fidel down to size.'" We delivered it to Haig's office at the close of business one afternoon in mid-March.

The bottom line, we wrote, was that if the U.S. acted quickly, decisively and successfully, any political problems among the allies could be contained. Similarly, the Soviet response would be manageable and the impact on U.S. forces elsewhere would be limited. However, we wrote, we wanted to raise two important questions.

"In an earlier memorandum in which we outlined a strategy for

My father and stepmother,
Inez Bishop McFarlane,
on their wedding day,
June 2, 1945.

My mother, Alma Carl McFarlane,
and I shortly before her sudden
death, 1938.

1937 Christmas card: my sisters Betty and Barbara, my mother, me at
five months old in her lap, my father, my sister Mary and my brother Bill.

At twelve, proudly wearing my medal for five years' perfect attendance at church, 1950.

With "Betty" at the local stable near Inez' house, Paris, Texas, 1946.

Congressman William D. McFarlane (D-TX) campaigning in Texas with President Franklin D. Roosevelt, 1938.

As company commander at the Naval Academy with my staff:
Ed Gross, Bill Garrity, me, Lee Bickley, Jack Langford,
Bob Drozd (my roommate), 1959.

Jonny and I on our wedding day, June 7, 1959.

Jonny with Lauren and the twins, Melissa and Scott, born while
I was in Vietnam, 1964.

As a White House Fellow with President Richard M. Nixon, 1971.
The White House

Celebrating the release of the *SS Mayaguez* in the Oval Office with
Deputy National Security Adviser Brent Scowcroft, Secretary of State
Henry Kissinger, White House Chief of Staff Donald Rumsfeld and
President Gerald R. Ford, May 1975. *The White House*

Being promoted to
Lieutenant Colonel by
President Ford aided by
Jonny, July 1975.
The White House

Introducing my father, a lifelong Democrat,
to President Ford, 1976. *The White House*

In the Oval Office, President Reagan calls Prime Minister Menachem Begin regarding the Israeli bombing of Beirut, with Secretary of State George Shultz, Counselor Ed Meese, Chief of Staff James Baker and Deputy Chief of Staff Michael Deaver, August, 1982. *The White House*

The President, Jonny and I at a dinner honoring the Scowcroft Commission. I was about to be named as the President's Envoy to the Middle East, July 14, 1983.
The White House

Visiting the Marines assigned to the 24th Marine Amphibious Unit in Beirut with Colonel Tim Geraghty (right), September 30, 1983.

George Shultz and I brief the President in the middle of the night on the bombing of the Marine barracks in Beirut, October 23, 1983, Augusta, Georgia. *The White House*

Meeting with Pope John Paul II in Anchorage, Alaska.
The Papal and Presidential entourages crossed paths as we returned
from China, May 2, 1984. *The White House*

A surprise birthday party for me in the Situation Room of the White
House: Jonny, Vice Admiral John Poindexter, Jim Baker, Situation
Room Communicator Bill Clark and the President, July 1984.
The White House

An Oval Office briefing regarding Central America, with CIA Director William Casey, Ambassador at Large Vernon Walters, George Shultz, Jim Baker, Vice President Bush, and President Reagan, March, 1984.

The White House

Briefing the President and Bipartisan Congressional Leadership before the Shultz-Gromyko meeting in Geneva, January 4, 1985.

The White House

At Camp David discussing Mikhail Gorbachev's visit to London before
the upcoming visit of Prime Minister Margaret Thatcher to Washington,
with Ambassador Charles Price, George Shultz and President Reagan,
December 22, 1984. *The White House*

With President
Reagan at the
Annenberg
estate. New
Years Eve,
1984.
The White House

After the President's Daily Brief (held in the White House family quarters as
the President recuperated from cancer surgery) discussing the Iran initiative
and preparing to meet with a Chinese delegation, with Chief of Staff Don
Regan, George Shultz and Vice President Bush, July 23, 1985. *The White House*

Aboard Air Force Two
with Vice President George Bush, August 1985. *The White House*

An Oval Office discussion with President Reagan and Egyptian
President Hosni Mubarak, September, 1985. *The White House*

Greeting British Prime
Minister Margaret
Thatcher with Rozanne
Ridgway at the United
Nations General
Assembly, October 1985.
The White House

Discussing the upcoming meetings en route to the Geneva Summit
aboard Air Force One with George Shultz, President Reagan, and
Don Regan, November 16, 1985. *The White House*

Working at the plenary session on the second day of the Geneva Summit
with George Shultz, President Reagan, Don Regan, Soviet Foreign
Minister Eduard Shevardnadze, Soviet President Mikhail Gorbachev,
and First Deputy Foreign Minister G.M. Korniyenko,
November 20, 1985. *Ronald Reagan Presidential Library*

With President Reagan at my farewell ceremony, December, 1985.
The White House

On my return from Tehran I briefed the President, Don Regan and
Vice President Bush and recommended that the initiative be closed down,
May 29, 1986. *Ronald Reagan Presidential Library*

Bud
Don't give up your day-time work !!
Love to all on your birthday   G. Bush

"Performing" with The Capitol Steps at my surprise 50th birthday party,
July 12, 1987. Vice President Bush, right corner.

The US-Japan Leadership Council "Class Photo," Ojai, CA, 1990. I
founded this group—comprised of two former Presidents, four former
Prime Ministers and a dozen US and Japanese CEOs and political
leaders—to focus on the resolution of problems in US-Japan relations.

Timothy O. Teague

Melissa and I
exchange a solemn
moment just before
her wedding,
July 6, 1991.
Ron Hall

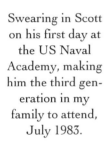 

Swearing in Scott
on his first day at
the US Naval
Academy, making
him the third gen-
eration in my
family to attend,
July 1983.

Our daughter Laurie made
us so proud, graduating
magna cum laude with a
Juris Doctor and a
Master of Science in Social
Administration from Case
Western Reserve Law
School, May 1991.

Skiing at Snowmass, Colorado with the whole family: Jonny, Laurie and her husband Steve, me, Melissa and her husband Eamon, and Scott, 1992.

Sharing a light-hearted moment with our
wonderful granddaughter Cara, 1994.

interdicting men and materiel coming out of Cuba, we emphasized the importance of achieving quick, decisive results," we wrote. "We doubt whether this could be accomplished. Not only would it take several weeks to marshal the necessary forces, but, more important, the interdiction campaign itself promises to be a protracted enterprise, particularly if Cuba responds to initial attacks by reducing or even temporarily curtailing the tangible manifestations of its export of revolution. If this assessment is correct, and if one accepts the judgment that it may be impossible to sustain such an engagement either at home or within the alliance for an extended period, then it is clear the entire undertaking requires further analysis."

"Instead," we wrote, "it is our view that the long-term interests of the United States and the West would be best served by using a Soviet intervention in Poland to forge new attitudes at home and abroad about defense spending and countering Soviet advances, to launch a few new initiatives in this direction. Action against Cuba should therefore be delayed until this new anti-Soviet attitude is consolidated and until we begin to benefit from some of the initiatives engendered by it. We would then be in a much improved position not only to cut Cuba down to size but to cope with Cuban and Soviet responses in other locales."

The next morning, Haig came into the staff meeting steely-jawed and looking obviously displeased. It didn't take long to find out what was bothering him. As he took his seat at the head of the table, I could see he held our paper in his right hand. He slammed it down in front of me, and in firm, stentorian tones, announced: "This stinks. I want to see you in my office after this meeting."

When we had finished, I went into his suite. He was still steaming. He came across the room, took a moment to look out the window and compose himself, and turned to me.

"Bud," he said, "you're the only one in this building I can look to to use some imagination and come up with creative ideas for how we can use the power of this country to turn the tide. We've got four years to make a difference. Six weeks ago I asked you to get busy and find a way to go to the source in Cuba. What you've given me is bureaucratic pap.

"I want you to go back to the boards, get General Paul Gorman, the CIA, and anybody else you need, but give me something I can take to the President so that he can show a substantial gain during his first year in office. I want something solid, not some cookie-pushing piece of junk!"

I went back to my office and brooded over his words for a couple of hours. Try as I would to accept Haig's reasoning, I couldn't bring myself to believe that blockading Cuba was the best first foreign policy move for the new administration.

I went to my special assistant for Latin America, Ford Cooper, to talk the issue over. Ford had served throughout his career in Central and South America and had an excellent feel for what was needed to deal with the root causes of social unrest and political instability. Both there and elsewhere in the world, the intractable problem had been engendering sustained economic growth. The region's long history of military dictatorships and feudal autocracies had stymied the best efforts of the Kennedy administration's Alliance for Progress and similar measures attempted by his successors.

Cooper and I ended up, however, reaffirming the idea that rather than "going to the source," as Haig wished to do in Cuba, we would be better off dealing with the extremities and attempting once more to fashion a comprehensive program to try to build models of economic and political stability in one or two countries. I knew it could well cost me but I asked Ford to assemble the representatives from Treasury, State, Defense, CIA and the Joint Chiefs, with whom I had been working, to put together another outline of such a plan.

That plan paralleled in its content what ultimately became the solid centerpiece of the Reagan administration's second-year policy—the Caribbean Basin Initiative. It was based on integrating a triune of U.S. policy instruments—trade, aid and investment—for the island nations of the Caribbean, and represented the sort of positive approach to solving Central and Latin American issues that most of the Latin America experts agreed made the best sense. Ultimately, it formed the core of what was recommended by a bipartisan commission to study our policy toward Central America in 1983.

So in the end, despite the blood on the floor, and despite Haig's passionate attitude on the Cuban question, calmer heads prevailed. Most specifically, of course, Ronald Reagan's calmer head prevailed. Reagan may not have outlined a foreign policy agenda to anyone else in his administration, but he evidently knew what it was that he did not care to do. Haig took his ideas about Cuba to the President himself, who shelved the proposal. We would stick instead, the

President said, to the understandings on Cuba's status that had been agreed upon after the Cuban missile crisis.

———

Al Haig was a military man's military man: thoroughly organized, extremely disciplined, used to working in a highly structured system. From the first at State, he established a disciplined staff, a clear chain of command, and made evident what he expected of everyone. He assumed that everyone else throughout the Cabinet and in the White House was proceeding to do the same. When it became obvious that this was not the case, he found it difficult to cope. The chaotic functioning of the Reagan administration alarmed him.

At the same time, the continuing suspicions of the President's aides about Haig's ambition created a tense relationship between Foggy Bottom and the White House. This already delicate state of affairs was only exacerbated by the unfortunate events of March 30, 1981.

After a speech to a labor audience, the President, departing the Washington Hilton, was shot and seriously wounded by a young man named John W. Hinckley, whose mad act was a pathetic effort to attract the attention of the young movie actress Jodie Foster. As Reagan was rushed to George Washington University Hospital, the news spread throughout the city and fear for the President's life mingled with concern about interim leadership in the White House.

I was in my State Department office when I heard the news. Soon after, Al Haig rushed to join other Cabinet officers at the White House, where top aides were gathering in the Situation Room, the basement communications and crisis center. A number of us assembled before the television set in Haig's office to follow the news about the President's status. In the White House press room, Assistant Press Secretary Larry Speakes was doing his best to deal with a situation without having many facts at his disposal. His own boss, presidential Press Secretary Jim Brady, had sustained a near-fatal head wound and was fighting for his life.

Speakes was questioned about whether U.S. armed forces had been placed on alert, and replied that he didn't know. Shortly thereafter, Haig suddenly burst into the press room and took over the podium. There was no need for alert measures at this time, he declared. Then, since Vice President George Bush was in transit from Texas to Washington, Haig went on to announce: "As of now, I am in control here."

To those of us watching from the State Department, it didn't seem to be an extraordinary announcement. We well knew what was behind Haig's thinking. A small part of national security planning involves a doomsday scenario in which the Soviet Union attacks at a time of U.S. vulnerability. While throughout my lifetime there has always been a relatively high level of confidence that the Soviets in fact would not attack, those responsible for the U.S. government have always understood that the only conditions under which they might are those where our ability to make decisions seemed doubtful. The President's sudden incapacity certainly qualified for those conditions. What Haig was doing was acting quickly to persuade the Soviets that there hadn't been any loss in our continuity of governance.

All of us—Paul Wolfowitz, Rick Burt, Larry Eagleburger, myself—thought that what our boss had done and said was a fairly normal reaction. But it turned out we were alone in our thinking .

With one statement, Haig managed to infuriate a whole coterie of administration movers and shakers. He already had an openly antagonistic relationship with Defense Secretary Cap Weinberger. Now, Weinberger was peeved that Haig had incorrectly cited the military chain of command, erroneously placing the Secretary of State in it. On military matters, decision-making and control over our forces has for years devolved from the President to the Vice President (acting for the President) to the Secretary of Defense. This chain of command is distinct from the constitutional line of succession, which in the event of a President's death flows from the President to the Vice President, the Speaker of the House, the President *pro tempore* of the Senate, and then to the Secretary of State.

It was an unfortunate misstatement on Haig's part. But his enemies in the White House, Meese and Deaver, needed no further proof of what they saw as his vaunting and dangerous ambition. As far as they were concerned, Haig had written his own political epitaph.

Over the next 16 months, Haig's standing and performance would deteriorate as he sought with ever-increasing passion and frustration to make his case to the unheedful White House. Over time, his alarm at White House indifference to him and ignorance of foreign affairs would lead him to become almost a caricature of himself and thereby to lose even more credibility in a self-perpetuating cycle of decline.

It was unfortunate. I have always admired Haig and liked working for him. He was a hardworking taskmaster who expected others to work hard as well. He gave you as much as you could handle, gave you credit when credit was due and chewed you out when it wasn't. I never saw him do anything that was dishonest or even deceptive. He was someone who deserved respect and earned it.

Most of all, he was a true patriot and a thoroughly sound analyst of U.S. interests and how they should be protected. Like Kissinger, he was a realist who espoused the advancement of concrete U.S. interests rather than some abstract moralistic crusade. His undoing was a loss, to the administration and the nation.

Reagan's near-assassination was also an eye-opening experience for those of us in his administration who had not been true Reaganites when we came to it. The President's bearing and conduct throughout the crisis impressed all the Washington types like me who hadn't really known Ronald Reagan. The strength of character, resiliency, and sense of humor he displayed ("I hope you guys are all Republicans," he said to the doctors who were preparing to operate on him) rallied our respect for him. I had been proud to be working for the presidency before; now I was honored to be working for this particular President.

———

Among the tasks of my job as State Department Counselor was to serve as a line of communication to moderate pro-U.S. heads of state and governments in the Middle East. The message I was to bring to them in a series of private meetings in that first year was this: in America's view, the moderate states of the Middle East faced three categories of threat—from the Soviet Union, from various neighbors, and internally. In addition, the continuing dispute between Israel and her Arab neighbors posed the persistent risk of sparking renewed warfare and of a wider conflict that ultimately could engulf the entire region and involve Soviet intervention as well.

To deal with this agenda, the United States would be prepared to work to enhance the security of our friends in the region against the Soviet threat through a program of military assistance and sales, training, joint exercises and economic assistance where appropriate, as in Egypt, Israel, Jordan, Pakistan and one or two others. Concurrently, the United States intended to lend its good offices to advancing the peace process between Israel, Egypt and her other

Arab neighbors.

As important as the substance was the change in style Haig wanted
to adopt. He wanted the leaders of each of these nations in the
region to know that they had a willing ear in the Secretary of State,
and that they should feel free at all times to exercise the channel represented by my visit, to bring to his attention matters on their minds
that we might have missed in Washington.

My travels in this regard took me to Saudi Arabia, where I met
with then-Crown Prince Fahd; to Egypt for meetings with President
Anwar Sadat; to Oman for meetings with Sultan Qaboos and his foreign minister Qais Zawawi; to Pakistan for meetings with President
Zia; to Jordan, for meetings with King Hussein; and to Israel, India
and Qatar. Haig deserves credit for putting in place this series of
relationships, which proved extremely valuable in avoiding and preventing a number of problems and solving others over the next few
years. Although these trips were designed to open a high-level channel to each head of state, I was careful always to involve the Middle
East bureau in the department and our ambassadors in the field, both to
benefit from their knowledge and to avoid circumventing established
protocol.

The task did require a measure of judgment. Having heard of the
Secretary's wish to develop these sensitive channels of communication in the Middle East, Mike Ledeen, a consultant who had been
brought aboard by Haig, promoted the idea that an analogous channel of communications ought to be established in Central America.
The Secretary should start, Ledeen suggested, by having a meeting
with Panamanian strongman and chief of military intelligence,
Manuel Noriega.

More than ten years earlier, as a Latin American desk officer for
the Marine Corps, I had gotten "the book" on Noriega, which
inclined me against this idea. But to make sure that I hadn't missed
something in the intervening years, I called Admiral Bobby Inman,
the deputy director of the CIA, for his advice. Inman is normally a
very reserved person. On this occasion, however, he became down-
right animated. He fairly shouted into the phone: "Noriega is every
kind of rascal known to mankind! I strongly recommend that Al
Haig not come within a thousand miles of him!"

It was how I advised Haig. For my own part, I can only wish that
I had recalled this earlier incident when, four years later, Ledeen rec-

ommended that I meet with "an Iranian genius" named Manucher
Ghorbanifar.

———

In 1981, it seemed important to me that the Reagan administration put down its marker on the survival and security of Israel as a
vital American interest. This seemed, first of all, intrinsically the
right thing to do. For more than 2,000 years, fascists of a dozen
nationalities have been trying to exterminate the Jews. If there is to
be hope for humankind, it must start with our common acceptance
that genocide is wrong.

It was equally important that in our own interests we create a
more stable and enduring basis for our relationships in the Middle
East. As long as hatred and bitterness characterized the relationship
between Israel, Syria and other Arab states, the United States would
face the risk of a war that could ultimately lead to both Soviet intervention and our own.

I believed that we could take an important step in the direction of
building Israeli confidence in the reliability of the United States as a
guarantor of Israeli security by elevating Israel to the status of ally.
This would put her on a level equal to the United Kingdom, France,
Germany and other states to whom we have security commitments
enshrined in treaties and carrying the force of law. I wasn't the first to
have this idea; something less ambitious had been considered at the
Pentagon prior to the Reagan administration by Paul Wolfowitz and his
deputy James Roche. We all believed that ultimately we should aspire
to engage with Israel on all the same sorts of measures as we pursued
with the U.K. or Korea. We envisioned bilateral consultations at the
highest levels, as well as bilateral military sales, programs and a trading relationship that would advance the interests of both parties.

All of us involved in developing this concept recognized that
establishing a relationship of "alliance" did not mean that both parties would always see their interests as congruent. Indeed, they
would often diverge. Being an ally does, however, mean that on
those occasions where either party intends to take an initiative which
will affect the interests of the other side, it will at least take the interests of the other party into account and if possible consult, in an
effort to minimize any damage.

Soon after arriving at the State Department, I began to discuss the possibilities for elevating the U.S.-Israeli relationship with my approximate counterpart in the Israeli Foreign Ministry, Director General David Kimche. David and I met several times in 1981, either in Washington or Tel Aviv, and once in Geneva, to flesh out the parameters of this new relationship, which we called "strategic cooperation."

Both of us believed the program would offer mutual gains to the United States and Israel. David recognized that our interests in the Middle East were threatened by the potential of Soviet invasion, either of Iran or Iraq, thus putting the oil resources of the region at risk. He proposed that the United States consider pre-positioning military equipment and supplies that would be needed to support the heavy armored units that would react to such an eventual crisis. He proposed that Israel give the 6th Fleet access to the naval ship repair facilities at Haifa, and increased R&R port calls for U.S. vessels. On our side of the ledger, in addition to sales of military hardware and substantial U.S. military and economic aid to Israel, we discussed the possibility of applying Israel's experience and talent in the areas of water resource development and police and security training in third world areas, particularly Central America, under contracts from the Agency for International Development. We also promised to use our diplomatic influence to encourage various Muslim countries in Africa to restore relations with Israel.

Both David and I knew we had two major problems with selling this idea to our respective governments, however. In Washington, I knew I would face opposition from the Pentagon to enhancing U.S. relations with Israel. Since the early 1970s, the Pentagon, both uniformed and civilian personnel, had tended to view U.S. relations with Israel and the Arab states as a zero sum game, prohibiting us from working with both at the same time. Because they saw our strategic interests as centered in access to the region's oil, which is all located in Arab states, the military believed our interests were best served by strong relationships with those states. Now, with the pro-Arab Caspar Weinberger at the helm of Defense, that position had solidified.

The other obstacle lay in Israel. There, the problem was one of arrogance and stupidity on the part of the Minister of Defense, Ariel Sharon. Sharon was a legendary figure in Israeli history, a courageous combat leader throughout his career in the army. In the Yom Kippur

War in October 1973, he took his division through fierce combat, breaching Egyptian lines, crossing the Suez Canal and, but for the intervention of Prime Minister Golda Meir, would have bulldozed his way into Cairo, in the process destroying Anwar Sadat and the hopes for a peace agreement that Sadat was uniquely positioned to conclude.

Sharon is truly one of only a few men I have ever encountered who is completely without fear. He is also a passionate Zionist absolutely committed not only to the survival of Israel but to the enlargement of the state—the creation of Eretz Israel—which would encompass parts of Lebanon, Syria and Jordan.

It never seems to have occurred to Sharon that such goals were unachievable by Israel acting alone, and that they could never win the support of the United States. But Sharon is a man who has succeeded by creating facts on the ground and worrying about the consequences later. In 1981, he saw talk of strategic cooperation with the United States as an instrument to be exploited, not a concept for broadening mutual trust. Israel's Prime Minister then was Menachem Begin, likewise a devoted Zionist, who saw himself as the legatee of Ze'ev Jabotinsky, his spiritual mentor in Zionism, founder of the Herut party and executor of the mandate to advance at least the idea of Eretz Israel.

In spite of these obstacles, Kimche and I managed to advance the strategic cooperation idea successfully. By November 1982, I was able to get the President to approve it in writing and to get it translated into a formal memorandum of understanding between the Pentagon and the Israeli defense ministry, which would form a joint political-military group to serve as the instrument for developing a broader agenda of cooperation.

Unfortunately, the ink was scarcely dry on this MOU before Begin decided to extend Israeli law to Syrian territory captured on the Golan Heights in the six-day war of 1967. It was a blatant violation of the concept Kimche and I had asserted had to exist for the new relationship to be viable. It inflamed opinion throughout the Middle East bureau and finally led to the President's decision to suspend the MOU. Later, in 1983, it was reinstated, but it never reached its full potential, owing primarily to the exploitiveness of the Begin government and the animus toward Israel harbored by Defense Secretary Caspar Weinberger.

It's fair to say that the Begin government entered into the strategic cooperation agreement in bad faith. They saw it not as serving Israel's long-term strategic interest, which was its intent, but merely as a cover providing them greater access to U.S. economic and military support. Throughout the Begin years, the Israelis were to abuse it recurrently, falsifying their intentions toward Lebanon and misleading us at every turn.

———

Shortly after New Year's, 1982, Dick Allen resigned as National Security Adviser to President Reagan. For weeks, Allen had been the subject of daily press stories concerning his acceptance of gifts and gratuities from Japanese sources and some irregularities discovered on his financial disclosure forms.

The pressure from the media provided an excuse for the White House to push Allen out, but in fact the troika had already come to the conclusion that a change was in order at the top of the NSC to bring about an end to the foreign policy drift that infected the administration. With Allen out of the way, they cast about for a new National Security Adviser.

In October 1981, as the Allen story began to develop in the media, it seemed clear to me that it was an obvious cynical stratagem by the "troika" to get rid of him. Believing their strategy would lead to Allen's resignation, I sent a memo to Al Haig urging that Haig recommend to the President that Allen's successor be Al's classmate at West Point and former National Security Adviser to President Ford, Brent Scowcroft.

Ultimately, the troika decided that it was important that the new man be someone who could work with Al Haig, but someone whom they also knew. They turned to Bill Clark.

Judge William P. Clark was an old California friend and supporter of Reagan's—he had been Chief of Staff for Reagan during his years as governor. Later, Reagan appointed him to the California Supreme Court. At State, Clark had been Haig's deputy, the number two man in the department. He knew little about foreign policy and said so. His Senate confirmation hearing had made him mildly famous, because his candor was so refreshing. Instead of pretending that he was a wizard at foreign policy, he admitted that he learned most of what he knew about the world by reading *Newsweek*.

Pondering the new White House position, with which he was

totally unfamiliar, Clark realized that he would need someone at his side who knew how the NSC functioned and how it should be organized. He told me later that he thought of me right away. He said that when he told Haig about his new post, Haig was completely encouraging and told him to take along anybody he wished. A day or two later, Clark went back and said, "I want to take Bud McFarlane."

"My God, you can't do that!" Haig answered. "He's my right arm."

But Clark did take me. I was on a rare ski vacation with the family in Vail when the call came.

A couple of weeks later, my assistant Wilma Hall and I moved back to the west basement of the White House, to the National Security Adviser's offices. We were back where we had started. Back home again.

PART THREE

In The Reagan
White House

Chapter 11

MAKING THINGS WORK

It was year two of the Reagan administration, and the men gathered for lunch in the Cabinet room were concerned about appearances. The first year had been devoted successfully to domestic concerns and the economy. Now attention was needed on foreign policy.

The popular judgment on Ronald Reagan's approach to foreign affairs was not favorable: it was being said that he had none. The first year had been one of drift, of reacting to events—generally with success, as luck would have it—instead of planning and directing them wherever possible.

"We have to do something. We're perceived as not having a foreign policy," someone said as the President came in to join us. A murmur of agreement went around the table. I was sitting in the back row of chairs, behind Judge Clark, the President's new National Security Adviser. I was annoyed at the naysaying coming from the principals at the table. Mike Deaver, Jim Baker, Ed Meese, Larry Speakes, communications director Dave Gergen, Office of Management and Budget Director David Stockman—to a man, they were all projecting gloom over a field of endeavor to which none of them had given much thought. Nor were any of them aware of the work that had been going on at State to put in place the broad outlines of policy.

I seized the moment. "But you do have a foreign policy, Mr. President," I spoke up. The attention in the room shifted to me in a solid wave.

I took a deep breath. "It has five components," I began. "The first is to strengthen our economic base so as to provide the resources essential to underwriting our foreign aid program and to restore the defense foundation of your policy. And to show that America is once more capable of solving problems.

"Number two is to restore our defenses so as to deter attack, renew confidence among allies and underwrite our diplomacy. This will also provide key leverage with which to engage the Soviet

Union during the second term.

"Number three is to restore the strength of alliances with key allies in Europe and the Far East by setting forth a sound global policy and bringing them into closer consultation.

"Number four is to advance the peace process in the Middle East by mediating between Israel and her Arab neighbors the execution of the Camp David accords.

"And number five is to foster accelerated growth in developing countries through a north-south dialogue that would be keyed less toward foreign aid and more toward a combination of trade, aid and investment."

I finished and waited uncertainly for a reaction. For a long moment there was only silence.

"I'll be damned," Mike Deaver said at last. "I think we just got a foreign policy."

———

The foreign policy machinery of the Reagan administration really didn't get rolling in orderly fashion until that second year. It was amazing how little it took. Bill Clark, after all, was Reagan's close friend; he didn't have to look to Ed Meese first for approval of his actions. So the first thing Clark did when he took up his new post in January 1982 was to pick up the same piece of paper Al Haig had carried in to the President a year before—the framework for decision making—and take it into the Oval Office for the President to sign.

With that authority and formal process in place, we were able to launch a series of interdepartmental studies aimed at developing Presidential policy options in the various regions of the world, as well as a single overarching national security study designed to define U.S. global interests and threats to those interests that crossed regional boundaries, such as nuclear proliferation, terrorism, and Soviet efforts to subvert friendly governments from Cambodia to Nicaragua. That was known as National Security Study Directive 1, and it set the agenda for what U.S. national security strategy would be in the 1980s.

Apart from long-term planning, I was also concerned about crisis handling and the need to prepare for and prevent crises before they happened. So I established the Crisis Pre-Planning Group. Already in place was something called the Special Situations Group, a crisis management group chaired by the Vice President and including the Secretaries of State and Defense, and the heads of the CIA and the Joint Chiefs. It was a good body as far as it went, but it seemed to me that this group of elephants at the cabinet level should have been able to do more than react once a crisis occurred.

The purpose of the CPPG, which I initially chaired, and which consisted of deputy level Cabinet officers and their subordinates, was to anticipate crises and propose steps to prevent them. At the outset, it was given a four-item agenda to tackle immediately: 1) an Iranian succession to Khomeini, which was a matter that had been on my mind for some time; 2) an Israeli strike into Lebanon; 3) civil war in Poland; and 4) a North Korean incursion into South Korea. As it turned out, this was an extraordinarily prescient look at the world, both at that moment and in the light of events that subsequently unfolded.

The CPPG turned out to be one of the most productive organizational schemes ever established in the 1980s—or since for that matter. It spawned a number of notable successes. One of the most marked involved our great nemesis, the Ayatollah Khomeini. In the early 1980s, the Ayatollah was given to periodic rantings and threats involving Western access to the oil resources of the Persian Gulf. He would threaten to cut off access to the gulf for Western, especially American, vessels, and, in his melodramatic words, to turn the Gulf into a sea of blood.

These outbursts caused fretting and anxiety among our European allies, and invariably sent the stock markets into alarming fluctuations. In 1983, while still Deputy National Security Adviser, I had charged the CPPG to do a contingency study on the consequences of a cutoff of oil from the Persian Gulf. The results were intriguing. The group found that even if Iran managed to block the Gulf, the worldwide supply of oil was more than sufficient to make up the shortfall. Furthermore, although the Iranians might cause some short-term problems, our own military could overcome Iranian forces and restore production within six months.

I presented the results of the study to President Reagan, Cap Weinberger and George Shultz myself. They were pleased with the news. Reagan suggested that we share it with our allies, and emissaries were dispatched to the European capitals and Tokyo to brief on the study's findings. The outcome? In May 1984, just before the economic summit of industrialized nations was to meet in London, the Ayatollah unleashed another burst of rhetoric about making the Gulf run red with Western blood. And the heads of government then assembled—Margaret Thatcher, Francois Mitterrand, Bettino Craxi and the rest—greeted the headlines with a collective yawn. The stock markets never wavered. It was one of the best examples of crisis prevention on record.

The basic entities charged with producing the foreign policy studies the NSC launched were the Interdepartmental Group and the Senior Interdepartmental Group. One of the most important IGs dealt with arms control and in 1982, it quickly became paralyzed. A constant and long-running argument developed between the chair, Assistant Secretary of State for Political-Military Affairs Rick Burt, and his defense counterpart, Richard Perle. These were two strong-willed men with equally strong egos, and, as they were equal in rank, either one could stop the action simply by not showing up at meetings or by using a dozen other bureaucratic stalls.

Their differences were ideological and doctrinal, and reflected the differing approaches of State and the Pentagon to arms control questions. Perle, a conservative ideologue, believed in a confrontational strategy toward the Soviet Union and was against concessions of any kind. In his view, there could be no convergence between the American and Soviet systems; the challenge before us was to compete. He believed arms control was something of a delusion; it was a myth to think that U.S. security could be improved by means of agreements over numbers and types of weapons that would inevitably be violated by the Soviets. Burt, on the other hand, hewed to the State Department philosophy that engagement was both desirable and necessary, and that confrontation was politically infeasible. And over these differences, they constantly butted heads. Even if policy did finally move out of their group up to the next level, it got no further. For then Weinberger would weigh in, stopping any movement before it got started.

At last, realizing this was far too important an issue to allow to languish for very long, I took the reins into my own hands. I moved the group into the White House and took over the chairmanship myself. Over the next 12 to 18 months, the Situation Room, where we met, was the site of some of the hardest, and most productive, work I've ever done. This group may have represented more experience, brainpower, and passion than any corresponding body in post-war history. It included such giants as Paul Nitze, the author of the containment strategy developed 30 years before; veteran SALT negotiator General Ed Rowny; Ambassador Max Kampelman, who had done a masterful job as head of our delegation to the CSCE (Conference on Security and Cooperation in Europe); Burt, Perle, CIA experts, senior officers from the Joint Chiefs of Staff and three very solid staffers from my own shop, Colonel (now Major General) Bob Linhard, USAF; Sven Kraemer, a 16-year veteran of the NSC staff, and Steve Steiner, a professional foreign service officer.

The agenda we dealt with covered a range of matters, from the START (Strategic Arms Treaty) and INF (Intermediate-Range Nuclear Forces) treaties to review of Soviet non-compliance with past agreements. Every night for weeks at a time, I would receive a two-inch stack of paper to digest for the next day's meeting, and then for days we would go over in great, and often arcane, detail questions such as whether or not the phased array radar at Krasnoyarsk was a violation of SALT II.

It was tedious, backbreaking work, but at the end of the day—and I think all the men who sat around that table with me would agree— it produced some of the most constructive work any of us ever did, and that ever came out of the Reagan administration. I firmly believe that the first reductions in nuclear weapons in history would not have occurred but for the work of these men.

Another challenge arose out of our effort to counter the nuclear freeze movement, which began to gain momentum nationwide in the spring of 1982. The movement, whose constituency was heavily religious, drawn largely from the Roman Catholic Church but also from a number of Protestant denominations, proposed that the number of nuclear weapons be frozen at then-existing levels. Nor did it insist that this freeze take place concurrently in East and West; a unilateral freeze on our part would have sufficed for its purposes.

The freeze movement was comprised of well-meaning people, but their idea was superficial and, in the last analysis, dangerous. Yet its appeal on the Hill was undeniable. It wouldn't have been enough for the White House to simply dismiss the movement or ignore it; we had to be able to engage it, get our side of the story out, and help people understand why a freeze was not the best solution to arresting the growth of nuclear stockpiles.

In response to the movement, therefore, I formed the Arms Control Information Working Group. Its purpose was to bring together political-military experts such as Perle and Burt and the public affairs people from the White House and Cabinet to determine how to package and disseminate our policy. With excellent staff work by Sven Kraemer and Steve Steiner, we developed the guidelines, wrote the policy in digestible form, and then set out the counter arguments, in Q&A fashion, to all the central criticisms of our policy.

Then, using the briefing book that resulted, we fanned out to bring the administration's position to the public. We based the strategy on ambitious goals I set: 85 appearances in the next 30 days in the 12 major media markets of the United States by a Deputy Assistant Secretary or higher to explain this policy. Each appearance was to encompass four settings: an editorial board, a drive-time radio show, a civic-oriented group, and an academic setting. And for the next month, Perle, Burt, all the deputy assistant secretaries from the Pentagon, State and Arms Control and Disarmament Agency, and I would get called upon whenever we traveled somewhere, or visited troops, or the like, to stop, give speeches, hold briefings or give interviews somewhere.

And over the course of 30 days, we found that in fact we had effectively begun to counter the freeze movement. We did it by depth of persuasion. It was not dirty tricks. It was engagement, giving the public the information it needed to understand our point of view. And it worked.

It worked so well in fact, that soon afterward, Bob Sims, the NSC press spokesman, came to me and said we needed to apply the same strategy more broadly, to the range of national security issues. Dave Gergen thought it an extremely useful idea, and Charlie Wick, a good friend of Reagan's who was a tireless entrepreneur and enthusiastic showman as the head of the USIA, loved it. He loved to come to White House meetings, and this was a chance to do that and to get some visibility for his agency. He and his deputy, Gil Robinson, did a very solid job.

———

In June 1982, while President Reagan was in Europe for the G-7 economic summit in Versailles, two events coincided to create a situation of some havoc within his administration. On June 6, Israel invaded Lebanon. And out on the road, a serious fracture developed in the relationship between Reagan and his Secretary of State, Al Haig.

I was back in Washington working with the Vice President on the crisis management team when the Israelis launched their drive into Lebanon, so I only have secondhand accounts of the events that drove a final wedge between Reagan and Haig. Some said the problem arose from Reagan's pique over Haig's continuous seeking of the limelight after news of the invasion broke, combined with a number of perceived slights toward Mrs. Reagan. Haig stepped out front publicly several times on the Lebanese crisis in a manner that seemed to pre-empt the President's authority. On at least one occasion, he issued instructions to our Middle East envoy, Phil Habib, on how to proceed with negotiations without getting approval from the President first. Haig's version places the blame with the White House staff, which failed to recognize the seriousness of events in the Middle East and interfered gratuitously with Haig's ability to advise the President on developments in a timely fashion.

In truth, the situation was complicated by the fact that the presidential party was on the road, which meant there was a lag in communication between events unfolding in the Middle East, Washington, and the presidential party in Europe. The Vice President's Special Situations Group—which included State, Defense and CIA—was making recommendations for U.S. responses to Israeli actions and the White House was sending them to the President's party, where a decision on the U.S. course of action was made and conveyed back to the White House within a matter of an hour. Simultaneously, however, the State Department was sending its own report of the meeting to the Secretary of State, who would then talk to the President only after the decision had already been made. This led to a recurring confusion in the flow of instructions and amendments to instructions, which worsened as personal sensitivities were added to substance. Yet all the time, ironically, the State, Defense and NSC staffs were all essentially in agreement.

At any rate, by the time the trip came to an end and the President returned to Washington, relations with Haig had become extremely raw. The White House staff, notably Jim Baker and Mike Deaver, returned from Europe with a white-knuckled animus toward

Al Haig. Deaver was especially harsh in portraying Haig as heady, self-aggrandizing and vainglorious, and since Mike's office was right next door to the President's, he had ample opportunity to influence Reagan's thinking. Mike, however, didn't have the scope to consider whether Haig's larger worth in his ability to conceive sound policy outweighed these essentially personal disagreements. Baker did, but he may well have seen the worsening of the fight as a means to facilitate the exit of a potential competitor on the political scene in the years ahead. It didn't help Haig, either, that these two men, who had never held him in terribly high regard, were now joined by Bill Clark, who had heretofore hoped to be able to salvage a working relationship between Haig and Reagan.

Clark came to me after the presidential party got back to Washington. "This situation with Al is very serious," he said. "It's always been very prickly and abrasive, but on this trip it was the worst I've ever seen. The President has just about reached the end of his rope."

Clark thought Haig's apparent discourtesy toward Mrs. Reagan involving trivial matters of protocol was what had really stoked the President's ire. Ronald and Nancy Reagan were truly as close as they appeared to be in the public eye; their public shows of affection were no act. The President doted on Mrs. Reagan and was unable to endure sustained agitation on her part. He had an old-fashioned, genuinely chivalrous view of his responsibility to protect his wife. It hadn't been judicious of Al Haig to get on the wrong side of Nancy Reagan.

"I'm very worried," Clark told me. "I'm afraid this relationship just may not work. What can we do?"

It was a difficult situation for me, because I was torn. I had known Al Haig for a long time; he had been my sponsor and had urged my appointment at State and later to the White House. More broadly, he had been a lifelong public servant, and a good one, a man with whose views I basically agreed. At the same time, I realized that if the chemistry was wrong, the President ought to make a change, because he had to be comfortable dealing with his Secretary of State, or nothing would ever be accomplished. That's what I told Clark.

"Neither the President nor Haig deserves this death of a thousand cuts that seems to be where we're headed here," I said, and the Judge nodded in agreement.

We took the discussion no further that day, but a day or two later,

Clark asked me whom we ought to propose to the President as a replacement.

I thought of two people immediately: Henry Kissinger and George Shultz. I didn't know whether it was realistic that we could actually get Kissinger, and even if we could, I knew he would be resisted by the President's friends, and probably the President, too, as oriented toward very different policies. But Shultz was a distinct possibility. He struck me as a strong choice. As the head of Labor, the Office of Management and Budget, and the Treasury during the Nixon years, he had demonstrated his ability to function as a cabinet officer and to work with a President. His intellect was demonstrably superior. He had been the head of the University of Chicago Business School and president of the Bechtel Group, one of the largest private corporations in the world. That latter job, as well as to some extent his time at Treasury, had given him some experience in international diplomacy. He was an adopted Californian, and had known Reagan during his years as governor. And finally, he had never seemed to be a person who sought the limelight or would ever be a competitor for visibility with the President. It was a quality that, in this administration, couldn't be discounted. Shultz seemed the ideal combination of brains and managerial talent in a benign package.

Clark agreed. He instructed me to find out where Shultz was and how we could get hold of him quickly if need be.

Meanwhile, the President was preparing his own showdown with Al Haig. In addition to his genuine anger over Haig's behavior, Reagan believed that he had been patronized in his policy role and that the time had come for him to make clear his ultimate responsibility for the conduct of U.S. foreign policy. In my judgment, it was this gut conclusion, that he needed to put his mark indelibly on decision-making in foreign policy, that governed Reagan's actions over the next two weeks and led inevitably to Haig's resignation. The policy issue that served as the vehicle for this essentially personal confrontation happened to be Poland, but it could have been any policy issue.

In Reagan's mind, the issue was taking charge.

Throughout 1981, due to growing pressure from the Solidarity labor union movement on the Polish government of General Wojciech Jaruzelski, the Soviet Union began to see the potential for

serious damage to its interests throughout Eastern Europe if analogous movements were to arise in Hungary, Czechoslovakia or elsewhere. At the same time, Moscow's relations with Western Europe,
which believed it was deriving significant benefits from the détente
established by Nixon in the mid-1970s, were reasonably good.
Moscow consequently had to find a way to clamp down on events in
Poland without inciting West European anger.

The Soviets' solution was to pressure Jaruzelski into imposing
martial law, which he did on December 13, 1981. Soon thereafter,
the United States unilaterally imposed a package of economic sanctions. These included suspending Aeroflot service between the United
States and the Soviet Union, closing the Soviet purchasing commission in the U.S., suspending the issuance of licenses for high-tech-
nology exports from the U.S. to the U.S.S.R., halting the export of
oil and gas equipment to the U.S.S.R., suspending talks on the
renewal of several bilateral agreements, including the long term
grain agreement, and stepping up Voice of America broadcasts to the
U.S.S.R..

The goal was to pressure Moscow to allow the Poles to lift martial law, and to make clear that the Soviet Union would pay a heavy
price if it continued its repressive actions *vis-a-vis* Poland. At the
same time, we wanted to accomplish these objectives in a way that
would win allied support without creating a schism between the U.S.
and Western Europe, and that would demonstrate to the American
people that we were living up to our moral responsibilities in trying
to stand behind the Polish people.

The allies were generally supportive of the measures. NATO
issued a statement criticizing the Jaruzelski regime. On January 23,
the foreign ministers of the European Community agreed to raise
interest rates for any credits extended to the Soviet Union. But on
the same day, the first crack in the dike appeared: the French signed
a long term contract to purchase Soviet gas.

As 1982 wore on, Polish-related matters calmed down, although
the United States and the West Europeans kept pushing in diplomatic
channels for the lifting of martial law. As no change in Warsaw
occurred, however, we had to consider what additional measures might
be taken. From Washington's point of view, two stood out as conceivable. One was to permanently block a planned second Soviet gas
pipeline to Western Europe, a project that represented a potential of

several billion dollars annually in hard currency revenues to Moscow. The other was to cut off the long term U.S.-Soviet grain agreement.

To achieve the former, we considered prohibiting European subsidiaries and licensees of American companies from selling equipment for use in the pipeline to the Soviets. This raised an outcry from the Europeans, who saw it as an unwarranted intrusion on their sovereign authority to regulate the behavior of businesses on their soil. It didn't help that they stood to lose substantial revenues from the lost business. They found it particularly galling that we would reach such a decision, asking them to bear the burden of economic loss, while we apparently saw no contradiction in continuing to sell U.S. grain to Moscow. I pointed out this obvious contradiction in a memo to Clark and the President. But I was admittedly a peripheral player in the President's thinking, which in the end was far more influenced by his wish to take control than by the merits or demerits of the matter.

The President and his party had not been back from Europe long when the issue came to a head in mid-June. The Secretary of State was opposed to our extending sanctions to U.S. subsidiaries in Europe involved in exporting oil and gas equipment to Moscow. He argued that this extraterritorial application of U.S. law would cause irreparable harm to our relations with all our European allies.

The President called an NSC meeting to let the interested Cabinet officers air their arguments. Reagan listened courteously to everything that was said in the meeting. The Commerce Department sided with Haig, while Weinberger disagreed. But it hardly mattered what anyone said. The President's mind was clearly made up. He asked no questions of anyone, and as soon as the last officer finished speaking, he said "Thank you," and adjourned the meeting.

The next morning, at the national security brief, Judge Clark and I presented the President with two memoranda on the matter for him to choose between. One favored Haig's position of not applying U.S. law overseas; the second favored the U.S. sanctions.

As Clark ran through the situation for him one more time, Reagan appeared almost impatient for him to finish. When Clark wrapped up, the President leaned forward and said intently: "Tell me Al's option again."

"That's option one," Clark said, and almost before he had the words out of his mouth, Reagan snapped: "Good, I want option two."

I have no doubt Reagan believed in the principle he was applying, but there was no question in my mind that its application was chiefly a matter of establishing Reagan's control over foreign policy and putting his Secretary of State in his place. There was no question that Haig was upset by the announcement of the decision. It was several more days before he resigned, but the die had been cast. Unfortunately for him, Haig did not read the situation clearly. The State Department and the White House continued to war over the handling of the crisis in Lebanon. Dustup followed dustup, especially between Haig and Clark. Haig openly scorned Clark's lack of knowledge of foreign affairs and how they should be handled, and bristled at suggestions that he was overstepping his own authority. But with every succeeding row he only aggravated his own tenuous position.

Over at the State Department, Haig brooded and smoldered over the unqualified criticism he saw continuously directed at him from the White House. Backed up by his aides, including Larry Eagleburger, Walt Stoessel, and Jerry Bremmer, the department's executive secretary, he determined to take the matter in hand and act to clear the air with the President. However, in all his brooding he underestimated Reagan's parallel passions, while overestimating the value the President would place on avoiding turmoil and the public costs of firing his Secretary of State.

When Haig came to the White House on June 25 for the showdown, he was prepared to hand in his resignation, but he did not truly believe that it would be accepted. He believed that the effect of his gesture would be to clear the air and be sobering to the President, who would react by giving him a renewed mandate and stronger authority over the conduct of foreign affairs.

It was a grievous misreading of reality.

As Haig left for the White House, his executive assistant, Woody Goldberg, telephoned me. Woody, a career military man, had worked closely with me at State, and he and Haig and I had always worked as soulmates.

The secretary was on his way, Woody told me, and had his letter of resignation with him.

"He doesn't want to, but he's prepared to offer it," Woody said. "I can only hope the President will understand the value of Haig's service to the country and not accept it, but give him a stronger mandate."

"Woody," I said grimly, "I think you're misreading the situation over here. If Haig offers his resignation, the President will accept it."

"Oh, my God," Woody said.

It was all over in about 30 minutes. Haig offered his resignation. The President accepted it.

That same day, Clark told me to get hold of George Shultz for the President. I placed a call to him in London, where he was on a business trip for Bechtel. In the Oval Office, Reagan got on the phone with him. Shultz agreed on the spot to become Secretary of State.

—

Tension among neighbors has been an enduring reality of the Middle East. In the first half of 1982, however, tensions had been rising more rapidly than usual.

Despite intelligence reports indicating that an Israeli move into Lebanon was a distinct possibility, the State Department had adopted a policy of essentially whistling past the graveyard. It downplayed the risks of war, discounting reports such as that carried back to Washington in December 1981 by Doug Feith, an NSC staffer responsible for Mid-East affairs, indicating that the ultimate aim of Prime Minister Begin and Defense Minister Sharon was to wipe out the PLO, and that they intended to do so at the earliest opportunity. Sharon wanted to establish an Eretz Israel with boundaries that encompassed all of the West Bank and much of southern Lebanon and the Golan Heights. This tendency to downplay clear evidence of growing tensions was a reflection of the general culture in a department whose professionals regard themselves as the custodians of peace. To them war represents a failure to keep the peace; consequently, they have a tendency to resist the idea that war is coming. They believe that whatever is happening, however stormy and ominous it may appear, is subject to resolution by diplomacy.

In the case of Lebanon, the State Department placed all its faith in the diplomacy of its special Middle East envoy, Phil Habib, and his assistant, Morris Draper, who were on the ground assuring Washington that they had an explicit commitment from Begin that Israel would not attack unless it were attacked first with substantial force from Lebanon.

Israel had peacefully returned the Sinai to Egypt in April 1982. That same month, however, a round of Palestinian attacks against

Israel from Lebanon, and swift Israeli reprisals, should have awakened everyone to the reality that the prospects for a diplomatic solution to the Lebanon crisis were remote at best. From Israel's perspective, the PLO menace was not simply a matter of recurrent terrorist attacks; Israel saw the PLO as a strategic military and political dagger pointed at the very heart of Israel and threatening her existence.

On June 3, 1982, Arab terrorists attempted to assassinate Israel's ambassador to the United Kingdom, Shlomo Argov. At the White House, the atmosphere grew tense as we awaited the inevitable Israeli reprisal against the PLO. For a few days, nothing happened, and some hope swelled that Israel would show restraint. But it was soon dashed. On June 5, Israel launched retaliatory air strikes against PLO targets, and on the morning of June 6, Israeli ground forces advanced into Lebanon.

Syria, intent on protecting its own position in Lebanon, soon joined in the war against the Israeli Defense Forces. Throughout the ensuing three weeks of hostilities, the Israeli government repeatedly lied to Washington about its intentions. On the ground, Phil Habib moved from Tel Aviv to Damascus to Riyadh seeking to negotiate a cease-fire and a diplomatic solution to the conflict. At almost every turn, the Israelis would assure him they intended to pursue one course of action, only to do the opposite as soon as he was out of earshot. After the initial incursion, they promised to go no farther than 40 km into Lebanese territory, but Habib was no sooner out of the building than they made a further thrust, ultimately reaching the outskirts of Beirut itself.

It was the worst case of bad faith on the part of Israel that the U.S. administration had ever experienced. Over the course of its 40-year existence, Israel had dealt with the U.S. in good faith even in the worst of times. But the Likud government of Begin and Sharon was showing us a new face. We would have understood their strategic purpose in pushing the PLO out of southern Lebanon to free their northern territories from attack, had they shared it with us; this was a legitimate security interest and deserved our support. But we could not have agreed to their broader desire to annihilate the PLO. As bad as we thought that PLO leader Yasser Arafat was, the alternative would have been an even more radical Palestinian group led by fanatics such as Abu Moussa or Abu Nidal.

After nearly four weeks of fighting, frantic negotiations and some sharp diplomatic exchanges, a cease-fire was at last arranged. When the smoke cleared, it was revealed that Israeli forces had achieved a stunning military victory. They controlled access and egress to the capital city of Beirut and a large swath of territory running eastward to the Bekaa Valley. All of the Syrian SA6 surface-to-air missiles in the Bekaa had been destroyed, along with much of Syria's artillery and front line infantry. In the air, the Israelis destroyed 82 Syrian aircraft, virtually Syria's entire inventory of first-line fighters, without suffering a single loss on their own side. This wipeout was so dramatic that it reverberated roundly even in Moscow, the supplier of the downed Syrian Mig fighters. Nothing could have demonstrated more spectacularly the superiority of U.S.-made military hardware. The Soviets were so embarrassed by the defeat that they tried to blame the losses on the incompetence of the Syrian fighter pilots. And, in truth, the excellence of the Israeli fighter pilots was undoubtedly an equally important factor in the outcome of the air war.

After the war, Syria was for all intents and purposes militarily crushed. In the region, Habib set out on an intensive round of negotiations to work out a PLO evacuation and the withdrawal of Syrian and Israeli forces from Lebanon. Back in Washington, the new Secretary of State, George Shultz, appointed a team to draw up a plan for the President to regain the initiative and advance the peace process in the Middle East. I was asked to join this team, which was headed by Paul Wolfowitz and included Nick Veliotes, head of the Middle East bureau at State; Rick Burt; Geoff Kemp, head of Middle East affairs at the NSC, and his number two man, Howard Teicher.

Working throughout the summer, we produced what became President Reagan's September 1 initiative, a framework for establishing stability between Israel and her Arab neighbors. Explicitly foreclosing the idea of a Palestinian state, it called upon Jordan to negotiate on behalf of the Palestinians toward an outcome foreshadowed by the Camp David accords—an interim period of autonomy ultimately followed by a Palestinian confederation with Jordan.

In retrospect, the initiative was doomed to fail before Reagan ever even delivered the speech outlining it on September 1, 1982. On the one hand, it was based in large part on a secret understanding between Nick Veliotes and King Hussein of Jordan that the King would be willing to step forward and represent the Palestinians. Yet shortly after Reagan's speech, the Arab League met in Rabat,

Morocco, and refused to confer upon Hussein the mandate to negotiate on behalf of the Palestinians, thus foreclosing his ability to commit himself to the outlined process.

On the other hand, Menachem Begin wanted no part of any plan that would undercut his own determination to destroy the PLO for good. His strategy—devised and promoted by Arik Sharon—was to redraw the basis for Israel's security by expanding her borders to take in the West Bank and southern Lebanon. It was important to him not to be distracted by the American President nattering about some peace process which he saw as at variance with this grand design. Like Arik Sharon, Begin saw the ultimate guarantor of Israel's security as being not the United States, but nuclear power. That, he believed, would be sufficient to safeguard the new geography of the Israeli state. Begin rejected Reagan's initiative out of hand. But it also set him to thinking about the need to divert American attention away from forging accommodation between Israel and Jordan that would inevitably involve Israel's giving up at least part of the West Bank.

Over the summer, even after the ceasefire to the war had been put in place and as negotiations over a withdrawal were being conducted, the Israelis had kept up their pressure on the PLO to evacuate Lebanon. On August 10, Israeli F-4s had unleashed a 14-hour attack on West Beirut, which in the early 1980s was a Palestinian stronghold, the place where Palestinian fighters in the thousands lived, trained, and stored arms and materiel. The August 10 attack was designed to clean out as many as possible in one fell swoop. I remember watching the news reports of the attack that night on television. The pictures were spectacularly vivid and, absent any historical context of the Middle East conflict, thoroughly devastating. You could see the F-4s diving down, raining bombs on the buildings, flames shooting into the air, napalm all over the place, and women carrying babies and dragging little children running and screaming and falling in the streets. It was horrific.

The next morning, it was a grim Reagan who greeted us as we filed into the Oval Office for his national security brief. What he had seen the night before on television, he said, was an inhuman attack on innocents that he could never condone. As we sat there, he surprised us by picking up the telephone and placing a call to Menachem Begin.

Over the next few minutes, he excoriated the Israeli Prime Minister for the air attacks, and warned him, in terms as severe as I had ever heard him use, that unless the attacks ceased immediately, the United States would have to reassess its relationship with Israel. "Our entire relationship is at stake!" he said. Begin barely got a chance to put a word in edgewise.

I have no doubt Reagan was urged to make this unusual call by Mike Deaver, who while very anti-Begin to begin with, would have seen it as essential for Reagan not to appear insensitive in the face of the Israeli brutality that had been shown to the world on television the night before. However, Mike probably didn't have to urge too hard. Reagan was not at all anti-Israeli himself, but he was a humanist who could not tolerate violence when he believed he could prevent it, and when he believed there was an alternative way of solving a problem. For my own part, while I understood the historical context of conflict and violence in the Middle East, I, too, believed the Israelis had gone beyond the pale in this instance. They had engaged in overkill as a part of their grand strategy of enlarging their borders. I was beginning, in fact, to feel on somewhat shaky ground, and personally vulnerable, since I had been the person espousing the notion of elevating Israel to the level of ally and promoting the program of strategic partnership. My assertions had been based on the belief that Israel would engage in such a relationship in good faith, take our interests into account, and share with us their larger vision. Instead, we were being exploited by a prime minister and minister of defense who seemed to believe that Israel's vital interest had to be secured without taking the President of the United States into account, and that whatever they needed from the United States could be secured through the exercise of their influence on the U.S. Congress.

Five days after the bombing of West Beirut, the PLO finally agreed to terms for a peaceful withdrawal of its fighters from Lebanon. On August 21, the pullout began. To prevent any Israeli interference and to protect Palestinians living in Lebanese refugee camps, Phil Habib had negotiated the introduction of a multinational force of 800 U.S. Marines, 400 French and 800 Italian soldiers to oversee the evacuation.

On September 10, with all the Palestinian fighters gone, Secretary of Defense Cap Weinberger issued a fateful—and treacherous—

order. In negotiating the PLO withdrawal, Phil Habib had agreed that, after the fighters were gone, having left their families and loved ones behind, the multinational force would stay on for up to 30 days to guard against possible Israeli attacks, until the Lebanese Armed Forces could move in to take over the security of Palestinian refugees. Yet as soon as the last fighter had left Beirut, Weinberger, without consultation or notification, ordered the Marines back aboard ship. The French and Italian forces soon followed suit. The Beirut newspapers noted the Marines' departure with somber and ironic headlines—"Last In, First Out."

There then unfolded a series of events that would both undo Begin's grand strategy for Israel, and spur our own commitment to a protracted and ultimately tragic military presence in the Middle East.

On September 14, Bashir Gemayel, the newly-elected President of Lebanon, was assassinated by terrorists. Bashir was the charismatic and respected younger son of Pierre Gemayel, the elder statesman of the Lebanese Phalange, the Maronite Christian community, and Lebanon's great hope for advancing a reconciliation among its disparate warring religious factions. Israel had established a dialogue with Bashir, believing that he would be able to create a stable political framework within Lebanon, rid the south of its anti-Israeli elements, and establish a peaceful *modus vivendi* with Israel. His murder was a serious blow to Israeli hopes.

The election of his older brother, Amin, to the presidency, dashed them further. Amin was little more than a playboy who possessed none of the leadership qualities necessary for governing a stable country, much less one so riven by factional strife as was Lebanon in 1982. He had no vision of the desirability of political compromise among the Sunni, Shia, and Druze factions. Nor did he see the wisdom in recarving the economic pie to provide improved welfare for these communities. Above all, he lacked Bashir's courage in standing up both to his father and to the various strong-willed leaders inside Lebanon and in Syria.

Bashir's assassination was reported as having been executed by Palestinian terrorists. In fact, there is ample evidence to believe that it was committed at Syrian instigation but made to appear as though the attack and the attackers had been Palestinian.

Two days later, what had been feared by so many when the Palestinian fighters were withdrawn happened. On September 16, as Israeli occupying forces stood passively by, Phalange militia entered two Palestinian refugee camps and proceeded to slaughter more than 600 unarmed women, children, elderly and disabled in retribution for the death of Bashir Gemayel. It was a massacre that provoked outrage from every Western capital, and a strong burst of anti-Israeli feeling on the part of Ronald Reagan.

Reagan came to the office having heard the news on the morning television shows, but he wanted the full report. I gave him our account of the massacre at Sabra and Shatilla. A look of uncomprehending despair spread over his face.

"Why? How?" he gasped. "What could move people to do something like this?"

Reagan unfortunately had no historical framework for dealing with what he was seeing, having never read accounts of what had tragically been very nearly a routine of massacres and counter-massacres among communal factions throughout the history of Lebanon. Yet even though I had referred to the fact that there had been equivalently gross atrocities in the Middle East for centuries, I stressed that he could not be indifferent to this slaughter, and that we had a responsibility to make amends for it in any way possible. For what made this tragedy especially anguishing was Weinberger's irresponsible removal of our Marine protection from these hapless innocents.

Weinberger, with his pro-Arab convictions, had no doubt acted out of concern that the Marines could be identified as tilting toward Israel, and that they could become involved, even if only coincidentally, in violence against Arabs that would damage our position *vis-a-vis* the Arab states. But the Arabs had in fact reacted with alarm to the withdrawal of the Marines, and pleaded with us not to leave the Palestinians in such a vulnerable position. For Weinberger to have precipitated the betrayal of Phil Habib's pledge to the Palestinians without so much as a phone call to the Secretary of State or the President was criminally irresponsible.

Later the same day, a conference call was convened on a secure line among Ed Meese, Bill Clark, Shultz, Weinberger, Bill Casey and Jack Vessey. With the exception of Weinberger, all the participants expressed guilt at the massacres and a sense that the United States should offer to do something to help ease the situation in Beirut. Shultz recommended offering another MNF. Meese, Casey and Clark agreed. Weinberger and Vessey opposed. Clark reported the results of the discussion to the President. Reagan told him to offer an MNF to the Lebanese.

The Lebanese promptly accepted, and on September 29, the 32nd Marine Amphibious Unit returned to Beirut.

———

Sending the troops back in was acceptable as far as it went, but the fact of the matter was that it should not have been done without a strategy that integrated this military power with diplomacy to secure the withdrawal of foreign forces from Lebanon and to re-establish effective Lebanese sovereignty over the country. The Marines were sent in out of guilt and compassion, purely as moral support, without clarity or analysis beyond that level.

At this stage of the game, Syria was on its knees. It was the moment to take heed of W.C. Fields' admonition: "Never kick a man unless he's down." There was a need to act quickly to force the Syrian troops out of Lebanon before they had time to rearm and dig in their heels.

Positioned as it is between Israel and Syria, Lebanon in 1982 seemed likely to remain, as it had been for so long, a potential battle-ground for these two powers, a site for conflicts that could conceivably involve the Soviet Union and the United States. It was clearly in our interests to get all the foreign forces out of the country and to move our own forces in, to provide security as we worked toward establishing a stable Lebanese government and building up an integrated Lebanese military capable of preserving the security of Lebanon's borders with its neighbors.

I argued very forcefully for this approach as we dispatched the Marines to Beirut in the fall of 1982. But my arguments, and those of others who thought as I did, were overruled or ignored. Cap Weinberger, for one, didn't want to get into an argument with the Syrians. Like Phil Habib on the ground, he was receiving assurances from Saudi Arabia that they would see to it that the Syrians would withdraw from Lebanon when the Israelis withdrew—an unbelievable prospect, as far as I was concerned. But George Shultz bought into the same argument. As a result, the United States was seduced into a protracted negotiation with Israel regarding the terms of its withdrawal from Lebanon, forgetting the peace process, ignoring the implausibility of the Gemayel government enforcing such an agreement and demonstrating a grave lack of analytical depth in the career foreign service. This performance would irretrievably shake President Reagan's confidence in the Middle East Bureau.

As a result, a fragile but golden opportunity was lost. It is ironic that wars provide unusual chances for enhancing political stability. All parties to a war, bloodied by loss, emerge with incentives for compromise. An outside party who understands that reality and possesses the skill to integrate its military and political power can achieve great gains if it moves with confidence and dispatch. Henry Kissinger had done this in 1974 and 1975 after the Yom Kippur War, and we could have done it in 1982 with even a modicum of cooperation between the Departments of State and Defense.

But it was not to be.

Chapter 12

STAR WARS

In August 1982, newly-confirmed Secretary of State George Shultz convened the first of what would become a series of periodic policy roundtables with government and civilian analysts and experts to discuss issues of significance to the administration. At this first meeting, the issue on our agenda was the foreign policy issue of greatest significance to the Reagan administration, the same issue that had preoccupied and dominated the foreign policy of every postwar American administration: U.S.-Soviet relations. How were we to deal with the other superpower across the seas? How could we bring our resources to bear in a strategy that would spur concrete changes in Soviet behavior with respect to arms control negotiations, in its efforts at subversion of foreign governments, and ultimately in the very nature of the Soviet system itself?

The participants at Shultz's first roundtable were divided over the question of how the United States should compete with the Soviet Union in the global arena. Two opposing camps had formed as the discussions progressed. On one side sat the advocates of détente, those who believed there was no evidence that the Soviet Union was in danger of imminent, or even ultimate, collapse. The best policy, in their view, was to accept that Marxism, with all its flaws and weaknesses, was an inexorable machine that would continue to roll indefinitely across the pages of history, and to concentrate on dealing with its external manifestations and endeavoring to limit its expansion beyond its borders. Deal with the tentacles, not the brain, this group believed.

On the other side were those I would call the "challengers," those who believed that the U.S. should confront the Soviet Union on an ideological level and focus its strategy on the fundamental flaws of Marxism as a dysfunctional, wrong-headed idea that was doomed to failure and could be hurried along the path to implosion by extreme internal stress stimulated by the United States.

The most thoughtful voice among the challengers was that of

Henry S. "Harry" Rowen. Harry, who had served 20 years in the CIA and the Rand Corporation, was a highly respected Russian scholar and Soviet analyst well known to everyone in the national security community both inside and outside the government. And on the day of the Soviet roundtable, I heard Harry make a prediction that no other living person, as far as I knew, had ever made. The key to dealing with Moscow, Harry said, was to place as much stress on the Soviet economy as possible. Within 10 years, he foresaw, the burden of defense spending would outstrip the ability of the Soviet economy to continue producing and to compete with the West and would require fundamental, thoroughgoing change in the Soviet system. The result would be to end communism as we knew it.

There was no great rallying around Harry that day, but his remarks made a strong and indelible impression upon me. Whether or not Harry was right, I was convinced that we would never have a better chance to find out than we did at that moment in American history, a moment that saw the rare convergence of American willingness to adopt a more assertive foreign policy with the readiness to spend the money necessary to conduct it.

From the first, others in the administration and I had been spending a great deal of time thinking about U.S.-Soviet relations and what sort of mark this administration should endeavor to make on this most intractable of foreign policy problems. It was a particularly urgent problem as Ronald Reagan took over the White House, for at that time, it was true that to most outward appearances, the balance of power had tipped in favor of the Soviet Union.

In early 1981, the view of the United States from inside the Kremlin had to have been a gratifying one. To the communist leaders who had been locked in a cold war struggle with the United States for 35 years, we no doubt looked to be staggering toward the final decline and fall they had been predicting for all that time.

Over the previous decade, the United States had lost a war, and with it the support of the American people for involvement in risky ventures overseas. Our military readiness had declined to the point that almost half our army divisions were not combat-ready, and more than one-third of our ships could not go to sea for want of adequate crews. Our economy was in a shambles, and people both at home and abroad had begun to wonder whether the United States could solve its own problems, much less anyone else's. Relations with our allies were at a low point. Allied leaders such as Helmut Schmidt in West Germany and Giscard d'Estaing in France were heading off to Moscow to hedge their bets with the Soviet Union without so much as waving in our direction as they left.

By contrast, Moscow had used the last 10 to 15 years to establish a dominant role in country after country around the globe. In the space of a mere five years, the Soviets had moved, using Cuban surrogates, into Angola; then, employing their own generals, they had swept into Ethiopia, South Yemen and Afghanistan, and were fueling promising communist movements in Nicaragua and Cambodia. In 1981, they were operating in 27 African countries with 50,000 advisers in place.

As our star was apparently fading, to the outside world theirs seemed to be vigorously on the rise.

In the postwar period, United States policy toward the other superpower had swung between two poles: stolid confrontation characterized by an arms buildup but no purposeful dialogue to reduce tensions on the one hand, and on the other, accommodation, the naive belief that the Soviet Union had no imperialist ambitions, that it was possible to manage peacefully a convergence between our two systems by engaging with the "doves" in the Kremlin.

The latter school had been thoroughly discredited by several spasms of Soviet behavior over the decades. In the mid-1960s, for example, at a time when our policy was to seek to engage the so-called dovish Soviets, it was the view of Defense Secretary Robert McNamara that if we limited our number of land-based nuclear missiles to just over 1,000, the Soviet Union would do the same, creating a condition of balance and stability. The 1,000-missile level became declared U.S. public policy in 1965, and since then, the United States has added no new launchers. This policy, however, was hardly embraced by Moscow as McNamara had anticipated. The Soviets reached 1,000 missiles in 1968, and kept right on going. They continued to build until, by 1975, they had built one-third more land-based missiles than we. Their count reached 1,380 missiles, which they subsequently proceeded to MIRV, adapting the missiles to take multiple warheads, ultimately supplying them with 6,400 warheads. By contrast, the United States had just under 2,200 ICBM warheads.

This sort of development made it clear that the Soviets were not agrarian reformers interested only in a balance of power. They were interested in dominance, a goal made manifest by their support of insurgent movements abroad as well as the extravagant nuclear advantage they constructed.

Those who espoused the romantic view of the Russians were not yet ready to give up, however. Shortly after Jimmy Carter became President in 1977, he made another explicit statement of unilateral disarmament: he announced the cancellation of the B-1 bomber.

Carter must have hoped that the Soviets would make a reciprocal gesture and perhaps cancel their Backfire bomber program. Not surprisingly, they did not do so. They went right ahead and built a stable of Backfires and proceeded with the next generation of bombers as well.

Unilateral restraint, clearly, did not work. The Soviet Union had demonstrated amply and repeatedly that without an incentive to give up any phase of its defense program, it would proceed with the most massive and costliest military buildup in the history of the world and use it to expand its empire overseas. I remembered what Secretary of Defense Harold Brown had said when testifying before the Senate Armed Services Committee in 1979: "When we build, they build. When we stop, they build." It was imperative for the United States, when dealing with the Soviet Union, to operate from a position of strength, to give Moscow a reason to come to the table and engage in real bargaining that would yield significant results.

While working on the Republican platform during the summer of 1980, I had developed a six-point program that I hoped would be adopted to guide us through the first term. Its core elements were:

1) To restore the domestic economic foundation. Without a strong economy, there would be no resources for strengthening national security. We had to prove to our allies that we could solve our own problems and were worthy leaders, while demonstrating to the Soviet Union that we were not, as they believed, in decline.

2) To rebuild the military foundation of our defenses. The United States had not built a new strategic missile since the late 1960s. Our newest bomber, the B-52, had been designed more than 20 years earlier. (The average age of Soviet systems in 1980 was five years.) During the 1970s, Soviet expenditures had surpassed ours by $200 billion.

3) To establish a new basis for engaging with the Soviet Union based upon the twin pillars of reciprocity and restraint. This rhetoric

was translated into concrete policies on trade, regional disagreements, arms control, human rights and the bilateral agenda in a defining document, NSDD 75 (National Security Defense Directive), that was issued in early 1983.

4) To reorient arms control toward achieving actual reductions, rather than simply controlling the pace of growth. In May 1982, at START talks in Geneva, the Reagan administration proposed reducing the level of ballistic missile nuclear warheads—the most dangerous weapons due to their short flight time and, in the case of ICBMs, their high degree of accuracy—by one third from their existing levels, and cutting the number of launchers by one half, while simultaneously insisting on effective verification procedures, rendered essential by numerous past instances of Soviet cheating.

5) To adopt a new approach to stimulating growth in developing countries. The new policy would emphasize private investment over outright aid. Its best expression was the Caribbean Basin Initiative, launched in early 1982, which integrated the three components of trade, aid and investment in a balanced program of self-help.

6) To step up peacemaking efforts, particularly in South Africa and the Middle East.

This new approach to the world, which was dubbed President Reagan's "framework for peace," was presented publicly for the first time in a speech that I wrote for National Security Adviser Bill Clark to deliver in San Diego in October 1982.

With the foundation laid, the next step was to draft the administration's explicit policy toward the Soviet Union itself. In the spring of 1982, now at the White House with Judge Clark, I directed the launching of a major study for precisely that purpose. Leading the effort was Richard Pipes Ph.D., a distinguished scholar and Harvard professor who was one of the country's leading experts on the Soviet Union and head of the NSC's Soviet affairs office. The team assembled for this study labored for nearly eight months, finally emerging in December with a directive that was signed by Ronald Reagan in January 1983 and declassified for inclusion in this book (See Appendix). It was the explicit statement of Reagan administration foreign policy toward the Soviet Union, and the basis of what came to be known as the "Reagan Doctrine."

The President's signing of NSDD 75 signaled his administration's clean break with the Soviet policy of the past. Specifically, it repudiated the policy of détente, which had been put in place by President Nixon in the 1970s and had served as the basis of the Carter administration's policy toward Moscow. Détente's underlying premise had held that the Soviet Union was of sufficient power and economic wealth to enable it to endure indefinitely and that it would seek to expand for the foreseeable future. Détente implied that the best the West could hope for was to negotiate a *modus vivendi* with the communist superpower and check its pace of expansion. Concurrently, détente involved engaging in trade with Moscow in an attempt at co-opting its economic interests in order to lower the risk of confrontation or hostilities. Yet over the years, it had become evident that there were limits to the gains that could be expected from this policy. There was no expectation of being able to persuade the Russians to reduce the level of nuclear weapons; when a half-hearted attempt to encourage the Soviets in this direction was made by President Carter's Secretary of State, Cyrus Vance, in April 1977, the Soviets dismissed it out of hand. And by the end of the 1970s, recurrent Soviet breaches of the SALT I treaty and of their 1972 pledge not to expand their influence at the expense of the United States had rendered détente void of content. To be fair, the gains and limits of détente have to be seen in context. From 1968 forward the public antipathy toward the Vietnam war, and military spending generally, imposed clear limits on American leverage in dealing with the Soviets. The administrations of Presidents Nixon and Ford simply did not have the money, and therefore the defense programs, to try to leverage the Soviets toward restraint in their nuclear buildup. President Reagan did.

The grand design that emerged from NSDD 75 based future U.S. policy on three principles: realism, a recognition that the United States and Soviet Union were based on divergent political and ideological systems and that we would always disagree; strength, as the only incentive to the Soviets to negotiate arms reductions; and dialogue, as a vital adjunct to our military buildup and our efforts to nudge the Soviets toward change and toward establishing a stable framework for relations.

—

In precise terms, NSDD 75 declared that "U.S. policy toward the Soviet Union will consist of three elements: external resistance to

Soviet imperialism; internal pressure on the U.S.S.R. to weaken the sources of Soviet imperialism; and negotiations to eliminate, on the basis of strict reciprocity, outstanding disagreements."

The directive called for modernization of our military forces, nuclear and conventional, as a warning to Moscow. "Soviet calculations of possible war outcomes under any contingency must always result in outcomes so unfavorable to the U.S.S.R. that there would be no incentive for Soviet leaders to initiate an attack."

Economic policy, meanwhile, was to be designed to avoid in any way subsidizing the Soviet economy or facilitating the Soviet military buildup, while allowing the possibility of extreme measures in the case of egregious behavior by the Soviets or extending positive benefits as a reward for improved behavior.

The fundamental commitment of the Reagan doctrine was to engage in a vigorous competition. The United States would compete actively with the U.S.S.R. on all fronts—political, economic and military. On the political front, we moved to compete by selling democracy and free enterprise around the globe in our own propaganda drive, employing the Voice of America, Radio Free Europe and Radio Liberty. At USIA, Charlie Wick developed a system called Worldnet, a television broadcast in which U.S. policymakers in Washington would sit for interviews that would be transmitted overseas to our embassies everywhere and made accessible to the foreign public.

Economically, we strove to compete with the Soviet Union as vigorously as possible and impose burdens that would weaken the system internally. This was what led us into the argument with our West European allies over the Soviet gas pipeline, an argument in which we ultimately prevailed. In November 1982, the sanctions that had been imposed against Western European subsidiaries of American companies that sold materials or services to the U.S.S.R. for the pipeline were lifted after an agreement was reached with our allies on the principles that were to govern East-West economic relations. This agreement consisted of four provisions: 1) the West would no longer provide credit to the Soviet Union at reduced rates of interest; 2) the West agreed to withdraw support for the Soviet pipeline; 3) the West would work to improve the functioning of COCOM (Coordinating Committee), the body formed to review and establish standards for technology transfer to the eastern bloc; and 4) the West would work to develop alternative energy sources and supplies. The conclusion of this agreement was a major victory for the administration, and George Shultz deserves credit for the skilled diplomacy he displayed in dealing with our European allies, who had been profoundly upset with Reagan's extraterritorial application of U.S. laws that would impact their economies while refusing at the same time to impose a grain embargo that would have pinched American farmers.

Militarily, we committed not only to rebuilding our own defenses, but to endeavoring to roll back some of the imperialist gains Moscow had made between 1975 and 1980 and to supporting freedom fighters such as the mujaheddin in Afghanistan and the contras in Nicaragua in their efforts to overthrow the communist-backed regimes in their countries.

From the perspective of the present, it is clear that the Reagan doctrine succeeded dramatically in its fundamental purpose of placing economic stresses on the Soviet Union and exacting costs for Soviet behavior that would contribute to inevitable and decisive internal change in the communist system, and ultimately to the irreversible collapse of that system as a whole. It was a forceful and assertive strategy that worked, in the way that Harry Rowen had predicted on that summer day in August—although even he had anticipated a somewhat longer timetable than the process actually required.

This is not to say, however, that the doctrine's implementation was perfectly smooth and accomplished without hitches. In fact, in late 1982 and early 1983, I was worried that the doctrine could founder before it was fully implemented. The military pillar was in danger of collapsing.

—

The Reagan administration had thrown its weight behind the MX missile, dubbed the "Peacekeeper," as the American answer to the Soviet buildup of intercontinental ballistic missiles in the late 1970s that had outstripped our own nuclear capacity and shifted the strategic balance of power to Moscow. Although earlier Presidents had worked on developing the MX, starting with President Ford in 1975, we were determined to promote it as a centerpiece of the Reagan doctrine's emphasis on restoring our own military strength, a prerequisite to confronting and negotiating with the Soviet Union.

The 10-warhead MX, however, was a natural target for liberals and nuclear freeze proponents who deplored the very idea of a military modernization program. As was to be expected, these opponents raised a hue and cry over the missile that reverberated loudly on Capitol Hill.

The congressional battle over the MX centered around the method of deployment. We needed to find a way to deploy the MX that was at once survivable, politically tolerable, and affordable. The Carter administration, after exhaustive study, had promoted a deployment configuration known as MPS (multiple protective shelters), a scheme based on overstressing the Soviet missile capability by providing more target silos than the Soviets had warheads to handle. During the 1980 campaign, Reagan and his advisers had challenged the Carter proposal as unworkable and promised to submit a better one. So far, however, the Pentagon had failed to do so.

By early December 1982, two years into the administration, the Congress had roundly rejected two deployment proposals from the Pentagon and was on the verge of quashing the third and most recent, known as "closely spaced basing," or densepack. Densepack was based on the notion that if you placed all your missiles in close proximity, the entire incoming attacking force would be destroyed by the first explosion. This was a theoretically interesting principle of fratricide, but it proved to be unpersuasive to Congress, where resistance to the MX was stiff.

It was not eased any by the man whose task it was to sell the military program to the senators and representatives on the Hill. Cap Weinberger's contemptuous attitude toward the Congress made his dealings with that body fractious and troublesome at all times. For its part, the Congress had no confidence in Weinberger as a spokesman for defense issues; on the Hill, he was considered lacking in knowledge of the details of defense matters and incapable of explaining how the programs he presented to the Congress for appropriation were connected to a strategy for keeping the peace.

On December 7, 1982, the House voted to deny funds for the MX. The Senate soon followed suit, and the Pentagon was instructed to go back to the drawing board to come up with yet another basing option for congressional consideration. Soon thereafter, I heard from two senators who offered their views on the reasons for this third administration defeat on the MX.

"Your problem," Senator Sam Nunn of Georgia told me, "is your witness, Bud." In Nunn's opinion, the entire basis for Senate and House opposition to the MX was their lack of confidence in Weinberger. He was not considered credible on defense issues, Nunn said, and his protestations of thoroughness in looking at alternative modes of deployment for the MX were transparently false. Neither house had much confidence that a new MX study to be done over the next three months would offer anything different. Many who favored the missile were disposed to vote against it sooner rather than wait until the next year, because, Nunn said, "if Cap is allowed to proceed as he has, it will surely fail."

Senator Bill Cohen, a Republican from Maine, concurred. "You know, Bud," he said to me, "you had better put together a bipartisan team of respected analysts to study this issue for you in the next two months, because if the new plan is sent up here in March by Cap Weinberger, it will definitely fail." The Chairman of the Armed Services Committee, Senator John Tower, said essentially the same thing.

Not long after this, we launched a bipartisan commission headed, at my suggestion, by Brent Scowcroft, to look into further basing options and analyze how we should proceed to assure stable nuclear deterrence.

In the meantime, I had begun to think about the future of our military program along somewhat divergent lines. The MX defeat prompted me to step back from the course we had been pursuing and consider whether there might not be another approach.

Throughout the nuclear era, the goal of our nuclear strategy has been to convince the Soviets that, whatever the situation, it would make no sense for them to initiate a strategic nuclear exchange, as a consequence of the survivability and retaliatory capacity of U.S. forces. The popular term for this strategy is "deterrence." It is an offensive strategy in the sense that it threatens the enemy with intolerable devastation of his forces and/or territory, as opposed to a defensive strategy, under which we would seek to prevent his attack from reaching our territory or that of our allies.

Throughout the 1950s and 1960s, this strategy succeeded in keeping the probabilities of nuclear conflict relatively low. Experts then and now have asserted that the reason for the success of our strategy was in part because the Soviet Union had accepted the irrationality of nuclear conflict and the implausibility of finding a military strategy that could produce a logical nuclear war scenario leading to any meaningful gain. These assertions have always seemed irresponsible to me. At a minimum, they are unsupported by the facts expressed in written Soviet doctrine, which envisions the conduct of nuclear war with both equanimity and analytical detail. A more likely reason for the effectiveness of deterrence for the first thirty years after World War II was the simple reality of the great imbalance between the forces of the two sides. Quantitative Soviet inferiority and the ability of many of our forces to survive a Soviet attack guaranteed such a powerful American response as to foreclose to the Kremlin any reasonable notion of gain. During this 30-year period, each side had developed and deployed forces in three domains: ballistic missiles deployed on land (ICBMs), and at sea (SLBMs), were able to reach the opposing side's territory in a matter of 25 to 30 minutes, and bombers carrying nuclear bombs and, more recently, cruise missiles, which took 12 to 14 hours to reach their targets.

Our reliance through the years on the ability to threaten credibly a devastating offensive counterattack—the concept of deterrence—as opposed to defending against an incoming missile attack, has been the subject of periodic debate. The SALT I agreements of 1972 capped this debate for a time. In those agreements, the two sides agreed to the concept of limiting offensive launchers and to forgoing significant defense of those forces or of populations. At the time, this decision reflected the U.S. hope that perhaps the Soviet Union would accept as doctrine that an approximate balance of forces and mutual vulnerability could provide for stable mutual deterrence. It also reflected the practical reality that the state-of-the-art in defensive technologies foreclosed the possibility of effective defense, at least on a cost-effective basis—that is, if one side fielded units of defense, the other side could add the unit of offense necessary to overwhelm it more cheaply.

At this stage, I was thinking less in military than in economic terms about our basis for competition with the Kremlin. And in those terms, it was evident to me that the manner in which we had been competing, essentially trying to maintain a rough mirror-image force to that of the Soviets, played distinctly to their advantage. The fact was that the Soviets could build missile after missile, tank after tank, without any concern for congressional restraint. They had no

Congress. To my thinking, this factor alone required that we focus our investments on areas where we clearly had a competitive advantage and could exploit our qualitative superiority. That advantage lay in high technology. This is what the United States does best.

The challenge was to find a way to exploit our comparative advantage in high technology in a way that solved the basic military problem we were facing—an emergent Soviet capability to launch a successful first strike; that is, to destroy all of our ICBM force in one fell swoop leaving us without a plausible means of striking back. That problem is most easily understood in straightforward numerical terms. The Soviets had roughly 6400 highly accurate ICBM warheads to our 2200 (which were deployed on approximately 1000 missiles, or targets). For deterrence to be stable, we had to find a way to deal with that lopsided imbalance. There were only three ways to do that; either they reduced unilaterally (something they would never even consider), or we increased unilaterally (something the Congress would never let us do), or we found a new, credible way to deal with the 4200 warhead advantage they possessed.

Anti-ballistic missile systems had first been considered in the late 1960s. I recalled the debates that had raged around them at the time, and understood, from the perspective of 15 years' passage, why such defensive systems had been rejected. Their central vulnerability lay in our inability to deal with the anticipated level of attack and destroy it with confidence. Neither the speed of computation nor the guidance technology then available had been sufficient to offer a high measure of confidence that we could defend successfully against a Soviet missile attack.

By 1982, though, we had made substantial advances in a number of the areas upon which defensive systems rely. Notably, advances in computers had provided enormously increased speed of computation. Likewise, significant advances in high energy physics had led to the development of a family of systems known as directed energy weapons, including lasers and particle beams, which held promise of being able to destroy missiles in flight.

Knowing of these substantial technological gains, I thought it was time to reconsider the feasibility of developing a strategic defensive system. I went to John Poindexter, who was Judge Clark's military assistant at the time. During the long struggle with the MX basing options, John had once remarked to me that we ought to take another look at the strategic defense option. Now, I asked him to do just that, and to get me an update on the current state of the art in defensive systems.

For his answers, John in turn went to Admiral James Watkins, then Chief of Naval Operations. Within just a few weeks of my request, John had returned with a report that Watkins had not only been encouraging, but was highly optimistic that improvements in computation speed and directed energy systems could give us a foundation for moving gradually away from an offensive to a defensive strategy within our lifetimes. To his credit, Jim was more motivated by moral considerations than military ones, although his knowledge of physics and the state of the art was rock solid.

This was good news. As good as it was, however, the fact remained that in Washington, finding the right solution is only half the problem. The other half involves working successfully through the bureaucratic process of getting the idea adopted in-house first, and then selling it to the Congress and the American people and the allies.

The first step of that process was to bring the military itself on board. After John's report to me, I asked him to arrange a session for me with Watkins. The three of us had lunch at Watkins' home in the Washington Navy Yard in early January 1983. Jim laid out in greater detail the basis for his optimism regarding strategic defense. Technology had moved forward by leaps and bounds since the 1960s, he said. Where then the discussion had always centered around a ground-based system that would shoot upward to hit incoming missiles, now it was possible to consider a space-based system, consisting of platforms floating in space, equipped with missile-destroying lasers and microwaves that would shield us from attack. I came away from that lunch heartened and believing we had a pretty solid basis for confidence, in technological terms at least.

However, there were many other, non-scientific problems to deal with. Chief among these was the Allied reaction. For nearly 40 years, our security relationship with NATO had rested on the foundation of deterrence afforded by the offensive potential of U.S. strategic nuclear weapons. It would require no small effort of persuasion to convince the allies that our adoption of a defensive strategy would not sever the cord that had bound the United States to its European partners so well for so long. It could all too easily look to the Europeans as though the United States were adopting a *pax*

Americana and erecting a virtual Astrodome over our own territory. Worse, the adoption of this new strategy might alarm Europeans and Americans in the street into believing that the real purpose was to give the U.S. a first-strike capability. Heretofore, everyone had assumed that peace essentially derived from our mutual vulnerability, known as mutual assured destruction, or MAD. What kept the peace was a balance of terror. Now it might be said that if Reagan were going to put up a defensive shield, the Soviets might be induced to strike first to destroy us before the new protective system were ever deployed.

Further, although the technology sounded promising, there was still a certain risk that such an elaborate system might not work. And lastly, there was the matter of cost. An advanced system of the sort Watkins had envisioned surely would run to tens of billions of dollars. Yet if ever the American public were going to be disposed to spend such amounts of money on defense, the time was now.

I asked Jim Watkins to determine whether his counterparts in the Army, Air Force and Marines agreed on the wisdom of a serious effort to investigate an effective strategic defense. He reported back very quickly that the Joint Chiefs were indeed in full agreement with the idea.

It was time to take the proposal to the President.

It was clear that getting Ronald Reagan on board was not going to be much of a problem. Before he became President, Reagan had visited the North American Air Defense Command in Colorado Springs, Colorado, for a briefing on the U.S. deterrent strategy, which described our ability to ride out a Soviet attack and strike back successfully to inflict severe damage on the Soviets. Reagan, I knew, had been appalled by the grotesqueness of this entire concept and concerned by the realization that we had no defense against nuclear attack. Now, as President, he had a strong and persistent sense of responsibility to protect Americans against attack. He had mentioned it on occasion, whenever we would be discussing some military program or other—Tridents, or nuclear submarines, or ICBMs. "You know," he would say, "I just wish we could deliver on these things and protect Americans from this scourge of nuclear annihilation." He was convinced that we were in fact heading toward Armageddon, the final battle between good and evil. "I'm telling you, it's coming," he would say. "Go read your Scripture."

Nonetheless, in two years in office, his Secretary of Defense had done nothing to reorient U.S. strategy. During two years of enhanced defense budgets, he had merely continued the relatively low-level research programs that had been in place under President Jimmy Carter.

The President's next regular meeting with the Joint Chiefs of Staff was scheduled for February 11, 1983. Working together, John Poindexter, Jim Watkins and I arranged for the Chiefs to signal their support for a strategic defense at that meeting.

As it happened, Judge Clark was out of the country on that day, attending the Wehrkunde Conference in Munich. The Chiefs arrived and took their places in the Cabinet Room across the table from the President. I sat on his right.

The Chiefs' briefing was centered around an update of the strategic modernization program. After an introduction by General Jack Vessey, each of the Chiefs took ten minutes to summarize the status of and projections for his service's defense programs. They discussed the costs and problems of the various MX basing options under consideration, including placing the MXs in Minuteman silos, an option that was most likely to be the recommendation of the Scowcroft commission. When it came time for Admiral Watkins to speak, however, he stressed how much had changed in the area of defensive technologies and stated his belief that a significant investment was warranted to explore whether, within five to ten years, defensive systems could give us the ability to deal with an attack. That was my cue. I intervened, deliberately underscoring the significance of what Watkins had said and the possibility he offered of moving away from the post-war strategy of deterrence.

"Mr. President," I said, "I believe that Jim is suggesting that new technologies may offer the possibility of enabling us to deal with a Soviet missile attack by defensive means."

The President had been listening attentively to what Watkins and I had to say. "I understand; that's what I've been hoping," he responded.

Then he proceeded with a very canny querying of all the other service chiefs, endeavoring to record and assure himself of their complete corporate support. In turn, the five Chiefs—Vessey, the Navy's Watkins, the Army's John Wickham, the Air Force's Charlie Gabriel and the Marines' Bob Barrow—voiced their support for the idea that the time had come to increase our investment in defensive systems. They recommended a special new initiative to increase research and development funding for studying defenses such as high-energy lasers and particle beams that could lead to non-nuclear ballistic missile defenses before the turn of the century.

Reagan concluded the meeting with a request to the Chiefs to report to him promptly on what steps should be taken to launch such an initiative. Within 48 hours of the meeting's adjournment, Jack Vessey called Bill Clark, who had returned from the Wehrkunde Conference. "Did I hear what I think I heard at that meeting?" Vessey asked.

"You sure did," Clark replied. The President, he told Vessey, was dead serious about wanting the Chiefs to tell him what kind of program they recommended. Three weeks later, in early March, the Chiefs submitted a written proposal calling for a significant expansion of U.S. research into defensive technologies.

It was all the President needed. He was ready to announce the strategic defense initiative publicly and launch his dream of building a system to protect Americans from nuclear war.

I didn't agree that he should move so quickly. I was concerned not only about the central vulnerabilities of the idea; I also believed that the political content of it was so powerful that Reagan could use it as an instrument to forge bipartisan support, not only for this policy, but for others as well. I hoped, although I hadn't quite convinced myself, that if he took House Speaker Tip O'Neill and three or four other congressional leaders into his confidence, they would be so swayed by the political power of the idea that they would back it whether they truly believed it was practicable or not.

I tried to use this line of reasoning on the President, but I got nowhere. He understood my point, but he wasn't buying it. "Bud, I'm just afraid that one or more of them would take the easy way out," he said. "They'd go public and grandstand with criticism. I don't want to risk that." In fact, he said, he worried about the same sort of thing from within the administration, although no more than half a dozen people, outside the military, even knew about the initiative. "I want you to keep this tightly under wraps," Reagan told me. "Do the work in your own staff and write the speech and let's get ready to give it."

I was still concerned, genuinely so. At a minimum, I thought we ought to coordinate the announcement with our key allies. And I didn't want to undercut the work of the Scowcroft commission, which wasn't due to make its recommendations on our nuclear strategy until early April.

Within the next couple of days, I laid out the risks to the President again. He authorized me to brief Brent Scowcroft, and to prepare some messages that would be sent to key allied leaders on the day of the speech. "But don't breathe a word to another soul right now," he said. Then he said that he wanted to insert the announcement of the strategic defense into his speech in support of the defense budget, which he was scheduled to deliver on March 23, only a week away. "Pull it all together and put it into my speech," he said.

I thought, "Uh-oh." Now I had more than the allies to be worried about. I had been invited to an Aspen Institute Conference in Courchevel, France, for the upcoming week and had promised to take Jonny and the children along for some skiing and long-awaited family togetherness. For months the prospect of skiing the unparalleled Trois Vallées had filled our home-to-college conversations, and excitement was running sky-high. I dreaded the call I knew I was going to have to make.

Jonny was not in the least sympathetic. The plans were made, the tickets bought, the kids were already enroute home for spring break toting suitcases full of ski gear, and she wasn't going to let me off the hook. "They're going to be devastated," she declared. "You'd better figure something out, quick."

I hung up meekly and pondered the possibilities. At last I placed a call to John Lehman, an old friend who was now Secretary of the Navy. "I'm in trouble," I said. "Is there any chance I could get into the Navy guest house down in Key West?"

Ten minutes later, he called me back. "It's yours," he said.

I phoned People's Express, made some reservations, and called Jonny back. "It's swimsuits, not ski suits," I said. "And I can join you on Friday."

I held my breath through the long silence that followed. Then, always the trooper, she came through. "It's a deal," she said, and I breathed a long sigh of relief.

Then Ray Pollock, Dick Boverie, John Poindexter and I got down to work, drafting the text of the announcement. The President's speech writing staff was instructed to write a defense speech as originally planned, but was warned that a significant insert would be delivered immediately before the President delivered the speech. This did not go over very well in the speech writer's shop, where, with good reason, great pride of authorship prevailed. The day of the speech, Dave Gergen was down in my office every ten minutes demanding, "Where's the insert? Where's the insert?"

Nervousness was the order of the day. I had come to respect Reagan's ability to persuade, and knew that any congressional reaction would be heavily influenced by the popular reaction to Reagan's speech. Victory builds its own constituency; if the speech evoked popular resonance, Congress would quickly come on board. I was a little worried about the scientific community, because criticism from that quarter could legitimize congressional criticism. But we had striven to preclude just that eventuality. In preparation for the speech, Jay Keyworth, the President's science adviser, and I had worked together to identify those scientists who would find this new strategy, this investment strategy, attractive. We had invited 30 scientists, including such prominent names as Edward Teller, Hans Bethe, Robert Jastrow, and Johnny Foster to come to the White House on the night of the speech to be briefed beforehand so that they would be able to comment immediately afterward.

But I was very worried about the allied reaction. George Shultz, who received a copy of the speech 24 hours in advance, was equally worried. His political-military assistant secretary, Rick Burt, seeing the implications of the initiative for the allies, had hit the ceiling when Shultz informed him of it. I told them we had prepared cables to send to the heads of state, and that I had argued to send them in advance. But the President had vetoed that idea, insisting that the cables were not to go out until an hour before the speech, at which time everyone in Europe would be in bed.

On the day of the speech, Cap Weinberger and Richard Perle were in Lisbon for a NATO meeting. We sent a message informing them that Reagan would be delivering the speech that night and advancing them a text of the address. Cap wanted to brief the allies immediately. In fact, Richard Perle called me several hours before the speech to deliver an impassioned plea on behalf of the allies and their right to know about this sea change in U.S. nuclear policy and the importance of coordination. I found it hard to keep from laughing at Richard's advocacy in behalf of the Allies. Neither before nor since had Richard Perle ever cared a whit about the allies and coordination. "Strong leadership creates its own consensus," had been his credo. His call was nothing but a manifestation of professional pique; Cap and he, though witting of the President's support for the defense idea, were upset to be in Europe and out of the action, watching a military initiative being launched in which they had played no role, and which they had to admit was "not invented here."

In any event, I told Cap and Richard that while I agreed that the allies should be briefed, the President had put his foot down again. "Nope, no way," he had said. "I'm going to be the one who breaks the news on this."

And that night, as the world watched, he did.

"Let me share with you a vision of the future which offers hope," Reagan intoned in his velvety, comforting voice. "It is that we embark on a program to counter the awesome Soviet missile threat with measures that are defensive. . . .

"What if free people could live secure in the knowledge that their security did not rest upon the threat of instant U.S. retaliation to deter a Soviet attack, that we could intercept and destroy strategic ballistic missiles before they reached our own soil or that of our allies?

". . . Tonight, consistent with our obligations under the ABM Treaty and recognizing the need for closer consultation with our allies, I'm taking an important first step. I am directing a comprehensive and intensive effort to define a long-term research and development program to begin to achieve our ultimate goal of eliminating the threat posed by strategic nuclear missiles. This could pave the way for arms control measures to eliminate the weapons themselves. We seek neither military superiority nor political advantage. Our only purpose—one all people share—is to search for ways to reduce the danger of nuclear war."

The simplicity of the idea combined with Ronald Reagan's inimitable delivery carried the day. Immediately after the speech, media reports mockingly dubbed the Strategic Defense Initiative "Star Wars," and some stories strove to portray the President once again as the reckless cowboy who had denounced the Soviet Union as the "evil empire" and now wished to spend billions to fight a fantasy war in space.

But, although the "Star Wars" moniker stuck—it was a pretty

clever one, after all—most of the criticisms of SDI faded quickly. The key to this undoubtedly was the muted congressional reaction to the initiative. The Democrats never mounted a sustained opposition, chiefly because opposition meant that a senator or congressman would have to cast him or herself in the role of champion of nuclear weapons, whereas Ronald Reagan had declared his commitment to protecting all Americans from nuclear weapons. It was one thing for the congressional leaders to come to the leadership meetings at the White House on Tuesdays and say, as some did, "This is nuts." It was another to go out on the White House lawn and stand before the television cameras and say that to 200 million Americans who liked the idea of being protected against nuclear attack with a defensive instead of an offensive system.

In post-SDI briefings, I worked assiduously to persuade the Congress to back the initiative. I already enjoyed a close rapport with the key Republicans and had developed a good rapport with Democrats such as Les Aspin, Al Gore, Vic Fazio and others in the course of the tough fights we had experienced over the MX missile. Now I went to them and, hewing very closely to the President's line, urged them to give him their support, to vote funding for SDI, to proceed with the research and development and thereby give the Soviets the incentive to negotiate a reduction in nuclear weapons. We agreed not to refer to it publicly as a bargaining chip—the President never would have conceded that, he really meant to build this shield—but that was its primary value at the time, a means of imposing a fearsome financial burden on the Soviets and leveraging their behavior at the bargaining table.

And this is precisely the effect that SDI had. Predictably, we had some turbulent initial strife with the allies over the program and its meaning for them. Margaret Thatcher, especially, was on the ramparts for a year or more about SDI and the risks it posed of de-linking the Allies from the United States; she wouldn't let us hear the end of it. But in the end, the program proved to be everything we had hoped and anticipated it would be.

In the post-cold war world, I've talked to Russians who confirm this personally. In 1983, Roald Sagdeev was a respected member of the Soviet Academy of Science while working at the USA-Canada Institute; he is now married to Susan Eisenhower and teaching at the University of Maryland. In conversations, he has told me that SDI had a dramatic effect on Kremlin thinking. Countering it would have required a substantial increase in Soviet expenditures for strategic forces at a time when the overall budget was stretched to the limit. Andrei Kokoshin, formerly a colleague of Sagdeev's at the Institute and now Russia's deputy defense minister, as well as Vladimir Lukhin, formerly chief of the foreign relations committee of the Supreme Soviet and later Ambassador to the United States, have said the same. At a meeting of the Carnegie Endowment for International Peace in Washington in 1992, in response to my question, Lukhin said: "It's clear that SDI accelerated our catastrophe by at least five years."

A vital lesson that the experience of SDI taught was the need for secrecy in launching any fundamental reorientation of policy. There's little doubt in my mind, after the fact, that Ronald Reagan was right. The premature disclosure of our planning for SDI would have evoked such a storm of criticism as to assure its abortion. Certainly there were risks in maintaining secrecy, and in the light of history they were clearly prudent ones, but the fact is that the concept was successfully presented and executed and produced truly historic results.

In the Reagan doctrine, in all its manifestations—from rolling back Soviet gains from Afghanistan to Angola, to imposing costs and preventing an accretion of Soviet wealth by curtailing their hard-currency earnings through energy sales to Europe, to stressing the Soviet economy with SDI—President Ronald Reagan launched the most comprehensive national security strategy since the end of World War II.

And, when the Berlin Wall came down in November 1989, we all saw the tangible proof of its historic success.

—

I flew down to Key West the morning after the speech. The weather was glorious, the family was delighted to see me, and we all had a wonderful time.

Chapter 13

THE EMERGING
NEW WORLD ORDER

I had not thought of Hafez al-Assad—the ruthless Syrian President who harbored terrorists and pulled strings in the Middle East with the wanton but calculating will of a mad puppeteer—as a mystic. I knew he was a man capable of acts as bloody as the recent annihilation of 10,000 of his own people in the village of Hama for little more than modest dissent. I knew he had promoted the murder of Lebanese President Bashir Gemayel in order to prevent a Lebanese accommodation with Israel, and that he was thus indirectly responsible for the slaughter of 600 Palestinian innocents in Lebanon. I knew he was cunning and calculating, intelligent and audacious, and that these qualities had served to keep him in office as ruler of one of the Middle East's most important states for 13 years.

What I knew of Assad did not comport with the man before me. It was July 1983, and I had come from London and Riyadh where I had met with Arab leaders who hoped I would become the new American envoy to the Middle East. I had been sitting in Assad's office in the Presidential Palace in Damascus for more than an hour, listening to a monologue that was unlike anything I had expected to hear. How insignificant was man's life on earth, Assad was saying. How little the relationships among nation-states mattered in the great scheme of time and the cosmos. He looked upon the short period of his own life as a blessing that could be devoted to nothing but pondering the purpose of being. His mission, his mandate from God, was simply to strive to understand God's purpose and to translate it into action and reality. Tell that to the people of Hama, I thought.

Assad regarded me with a steady gaze, his dark eyes glinting and a disarmingly engaging smile on his face. He sat erect, both feet flat on the floor. On the wall behind him hung a large painting of turbaned men on plunging, rearing horses raising curved swords over bloodied figures lying in assorted poses of agony on the ground.

Saladin's victory over the Crusaders. The Arab defeat of the Christians. I shifted a little in my seat.

Assad leaned forward slightly. "Tell me," he said in Arabic as his interpreter translated. "How do you account for the Bermuda Triangle?"

My mind raced, trying to identify a strategy in this perplexing choice of subject and the Syrian leader's enigmatic manner. I had thought, listening to his existential ruminations on the meaning of life, that perhaps his goal was to present an image of patience and of a sense of responsibility for his country and his people. But the Bermuda Triangle? I had to pinch myself. Apparently, Assad's intention was little else than remaining unpredictable and unreadable, in an effort to keep me off balance. If he were engaged in nothing more than an elaborate exercise of groundwork-laying for the real negotiations to follow, I was perfectly willing and able to play along. I decided to relax and enjoy the situation.

I only knew what I had read about the Bermuda Triangle (not having ever spent much time thinking about it), and I described the primary theories that seek to explain this phenomenon of ships and aircraft disappearing without a trace in the waters off Cape Hatteras, N.C., between the island of Bermuda and the U.S. mainland.

Yes, Assad nodded, he had heard of those three or four theories as well. "But they are not satisfactory," he said. "I believe there is something more extraterrestrial to account for this."

And we launched into a lengthy discussion of the Bermuda Triangle. Then, in the third hour of our talk, Assad abruptly switched to the subject of his experience in negotiating with the United States. Now we were getting closer. I had, after all, flown to Damascus with the express purpose of determining whether Syria, which had refused in May 1983 to deal any further with our Mideast envoy, Phil Habib, would be willing to resume a dialogue with the United States through a different representative.

Over the years, some negotiators, Assad noted, had engaged in good faith, while others had not. Never mentioning Phil Habib by name, he began to sing florid praises of Henry Kissinger, emphasizing that Kissinger's diplomatic success in Syria had derived from his respect for Syria's history and his understanding of her legitimate role in the world. Kissinger, he said, had delved into the real Syria, visiting museums, going to the *suq* (marketplace), visiting an

Aramaic village outside Damascus, absorbing the richness of Syrian culture and history as a basis for deciding what constituted a legitimate Syrian interest. For more than an hour, he waxed nostalgic about his meetings with Kissinger, which he ticked off in calendar order as if reading from a diary, recalling something specific about each one—the fourth visit, and the fifth, and the ninth, and the fourteenth, and on through the thirty-one occasions on which he and Kissinger had met.

I knew that if we were going to be successful, we were in for a long negotiation with Hafez al-Assad.

At last he paused. He hoped, he said, that he and I could engage with each other on the same basis of mutual respect that he had shared with Kissinger.

Taking my cue, I began at last to speak. I opened with an overview of President Reagan's thinking on U.S. security interests in global, regional and finally bilateral terms. I thought that a discussion of our view of the nature of stability between the United States, China, Europe and the Soviet Union, and of the dimensions of competition among those states, would appeal to Assad's sense of his own strategic grasp and reach. But I focused most of my remarks on the situation in the Middle East, on the United States' commitment to Israel's security and the enduring quality of that commitment, and on our presumption that all states could understand the importance of fidelity to friends.

However, I stressed, we looked to develop a harmonious relationship with Syria as well, and had indeed enjoyed such a relationship periodically. Then I summarized what had taken place over the past year between Israel, Lebanon and Syria and gave him President Reagan's view of what it would take to restore stability among those three states. I told him our goals: withdrawal of all foreign forces from Lebanon, the restoration of the government of Lebanon, and the establishment of that government's effective control throughout its sovereign territory.

The meeting drew to a close. There had never been any starchiness between us, and the twinkle had never left Assad's eye. Yes, he was willing to talk, he said. Indeed, he looked forward to it, and hoped that I would return soon.

Six and a half hours after I had arrived at the Presidential Palace, I finally took my leave.

A year after the war in Lebanon, the situation inside that country had reached a stalemate. Precisely as I had predicted, Israeli and Syrian forces both remained inside Lebanese territory. Acting in bad faith once more, the Israeli government of Menachem Begin had seduced and sidetracked George Shultz and the U.S. State Department into a protracted negotiation over the conditions of Israeli withdrawal. Shultz had negotiated an agreement between Israel and Lebanon, which was finally concluded and signed on May 17, 1983. The agreement provided for the withdrawal of Israeli defense forces from Lebanon, made arrangements in southern Lebanon to guarantee the security of Israel's northern territories and established a foundation for relations between Israel and Lebanon. And it was a dead letter the day it was signed.

The Syrians had opposed the agreement from the first, and pressured the Lebanese government of Amin Gemayel not to sign what they viewed as a betrayal of the Arab cause. Moreover, the Syrians had made ample use of the eight-month delay the Israelis had created with the negotiations over the agreement. They had rearmed and were flexing their muscle with confidence once again. The Saudis, for their part, had shown and continued to show no signs of willingness to urge the Syrians to withdraw from Lebanon. The Saudi promises to exert influence over Syria had been Phil Habib's ace in the hole in the elaborate poker game he was playing for peace in the Middle East. But it had been an illusion from the first.

Meanwhile, no effort had been made to create a reconfiguration of the power structure inside Lebanon itself. Amin Gemayel, far less politically skilled than his assassinated brother, Bashir, had demonstrated no inclination to work for a reconciliation between his own Maronite Christian community and the disenfranchised Shia, Sunni and Druze Muslims of Lebanon. To be fair, Phil Habib had not pushed him to do so.

Our own interests and presence in Lebanon, represented by the 2500 Marines of the 32nd Amphibious Brigade who were providing security for Lebanon in a multinational force with French and Italian soldiers, had received a bloody warning blow. On April 18, a terrorist car bomb blew up the American Embassy in Beirut, killing 63 people, including 17 Americans.

We had wasted eight months dithering in Lebanon, and nothing had changed. Now, we faced the prospect that nothing would.

Phil Habib's ability to bring the State Department along on his misguided path had lain in his giant reputation as a skilled diplomat who had played a key role as a staffer to Henry Kissinger at the negotiation of the Paris Peace Accords during the Vietnam War, and later as Ambassador to South Korea and Assistant Secretary of State for East Asian Affairs. The success of his diplomatic career in Asia lent him enormous credibility.

When it came to the Middle East, however, all Phil really knew was what he had learned growing up in a Lebanese-American family in Brooklyn. He had no depth in the Middle East. He had no experience dealing with Arabs or Israelis, nor had he ever been a man with strategic breadth, able to analyze American interests regionally, not just in Lebanon. As a consequence, he misread everything that happened after the war. He misread the Israelis, believing they genuinely wanted simply to consolidate a peaceful relationship with a second Arab neighbor (Egypt being the first). He misread the Saudis and what they said about supporting a Syrian withdrawal. And, most egregiously, he misunderstood the vital importance of effecting a reconciliation among the internal Lebanese factions.

But repeatedly, he returned from his talks in the Middle East with upbeat reports. And he knew just how to appeal to Ronald Reagan. Phil was an affable, jocular fellow, good at telling funny stories. He'd come into the Oval Office and spin a yarn and tell a joke and the President would be charmed and say, "Gee, I like that guy." But in the meantime, Habib had fed him a pointless line.

After the May 17 agreement was signed, Habib returned to Washington in July and announced his resignation. By then the Syrians considered him *persona non grata,* and he could no longer effectively discharge his duties as Middle East envoy.

The fact of the matter was, the Syrians had not wanted to talk to Phil Habib for eight months, since he had brought them messages from Israel regarding the conduct of the war that had repeatedly been proven false by subsequent Israeli actions. The Israelis were at fault, but the Syrians believed in killing the messenger. It was undoubtedly the reason why Habib had been so willing to rely on the Saudis to get the Syrians out of Lebanon: he couldn't negotiate their withdrawal himself. Unfortunately, this is only another reason to fault his diplomacy. At a time when Syria was so vulnerable to external pressure, Habib should have stepped aside, if he knew he was not useful in Damascus, and given us a chance to get someone else in there to talk to Assad.

The question now became who would replace him. At this point, I had been in government service for almost thirty years, years of strenuous days and long, exhausting 90-hour weeks, getting home at 9 or 10 o'clock at night, seven days a week. I was beginning to feel some physical wear. And, too, the sacrifice Jonny and the family had made over that time had been enormous, although they never gave me anything less than complete and unstinting support.

Nonetheless, I had begun to think, early that summer of 1983, about leaving the government for the private sector. Frustrations within the national security community, the tensions between the State and Defense departments and between George Shultz and Cap Weinberger personally, were persistent and possibly growing, rather than diminishing.

Six months earlier, my colleague Frank Carlucci, who had been Cap's Deputy at the Pentagon, had left the administration after a long career of superior service and joined the Sears corporation, where he had started a new global division called Sears World Trade. As part of this new division, Frank had had the idea of establishing a think tank to focus on analysis of overseas markets and trading opportunities and the like. I was surprised but pleased when Frank contacted me and asked me to consider joining him to become the President of this think tank, the International Planning and Analysis Center.

The idea was undeniably appealing. It would mean more time with Jonny, as well as a more financially secure future. We had been fortunate; there would only be one year when we would have two children in college at the same time, but we had eight years of college commitment, and it was certainly a financial stress. So I agreed to go and talk to Frank.

A day or two after that meeting, I went in to see Bill Clark. "I'm thinking about leaving," I told him, and laid out the reasons for my feelings.

Clark shook his head when I finished. Was there some way he could keep me in government, he asked? Would I possibly consider becoming Ambassador to Israel?

I was surprised at this, but found the thought challenging, and told Clark I would think about it. I even went so far as to discuss the job with Jonny, who agreed that it would surely be interesting. Yet before it ever became a serious consideration, Phil Habib quit and Clark asked me to take over as the Middle East envoy.

The idea of mediating in the Middle East appealed to me. The challenge was indisputably daunting, but very likely that's what made the prospect so attractive. Moreover, I had always been fascinated by Lebanon; the kind of complex, complicated problem it represented was exceptionally attractive to me.

I told Clark, however, that the first step was to determine whether the Syrians would be willing to talk to any American at all. The Saudi ambassador, Prince Bandar, offered to set up a meeting for this purpose. I urged Clark to ask George Shultz about the mission we planned. I had always insisted that the Secretary of State be involved in any diplomatic initiatives the administration undertook. I knew too well that the whole history of White House-State Department bickering turned on suspicions that the White House was intruding upon the Secretary's turf, either to usurp or undermine his diplomacy. I was concerned that no such breach occur on this occasion.

Judge Clark assured me that he would inform Shultz of my trip to Damascus. Yet Shultz has always maintained that he was kept completely in the dark, and indeed upon my return showed considerable anger and pique about the entire mission.

In any event, on July 12, Bandar and I boarded his plane, an elaborate Gulfstream III for a flight to London, where I met with Wadi Haddad, the National Security Adviser to President Amin Gemayel. Then we flew on to Riyadh, where King Fahd pledged his full support to trying to persuade Syria to withdraw and to U.S. goals of reconstituting a new political balance in Lebanon. Then, in the middle of the night, I got back into Bandar's plane and flew to Damascus for the meeting with Assad.

I returned to Riyadh the next evening and reported Assad's willingness to resume talks. Fahd was obviously greatly pleased with this news. In a magnanimous gesture, he directed that I be flown back to Washington on his royal aircraft. I was the sole passenger on the King's plane, all alone on a Boeing 707—the entire aft section of which consisted of a bedroom, completely outfitted with an enormous bed, extensive closets and a bath with a Jacuzzi and solid gold fixtures. Forward of the bedroom was a large sitting room with four or five armchairs and a movie screen that folded up to reveal a conference room with a table big enough to perform surgery on. I settled with a good book into what seemed like a quarter-acre bed.

——

I was appointed President Reagan's Personal Representative in the Middle East on July 22, 1983. Shultz asked that I work for the State Department and report through him to the President, an arrangement I readily endorsed. At the same time, Judge Clark asked that I be allowed to retain the title of deputy National Security Adviser. He believed that the White House imprimatur would lend me special credibility in the Middle East; he also hoped that this would only be a temporary assignment and that before long I would be able to return to my former job.

I spent the next week putting together the team that would travel with me. It included Richard Fairbanks, an Ambassador at Large for the State Department; Christopher Ross, an Arab specialist with State who is currently ambassador to Syria; and Geoff Kemp, Howard Teicher and Commander Phil Dur of the NSC staff. The support staff included my secretary, Wilma Hall, Florence Gantt and one or two others.

We left for Beirut on August 1. In the days leading up to our departure, and on the 18-hour plane flight, I had thought through the situation confronting us and how to establish priorities. The balance sheet of our accomplishments in Lebanon was exceedingly spare. Of the three original tasks we had set—securing the withdrawal of foreign forces, redrawing the political map and adjusting the distribution of power in Lebanon, and building an effective Lebanese army—only the last had been tackled with any success. A solid start had been made toward organizing and training the new Lebanese Armed Forces. Their unfortunate acronym, LAF, was always a poignant reminder to me of the contradictions inherent in its very existence. The truth was that this army could not amount to anything if there were no political agreement among all the factions that it represented. Only when those factions came together would this be the national army. Until then, it was only an agglomeration of various factional militias.

It was apparent to me that my first priority had to be to persuade President Gemayel of the urgency of the need for reconciliation. He had to make a public commitment to reconciliation, and shoulder the responsibility of acknowledging the unfairness of Lebanon's existing distribution of political power. He had to demonstrate his willingness to make concessions to assure that each religious faction's demographic strength would be proportionately represented in the government, and that each group would receive its due share of economic benefits. With all this in mind, I prepared intensively for my first meeting with him.

And yet, I should have spotted a clue as to what awaited me in an event that took place before we even met.

—

Arriving in Beirut, I was greeted by our ambassador, Robert Dillon, and our party was taken to his residence, which was to be our base of operations. The ambassador's residence is located about five or six kilometers east of Beirut, on higher ground, and sits down the hill from the Lebanese defense ministry. On the afternoon of my arrival, President Gemayel had presided over a ceremony at the defense ministry. Upon its conclusion, he had led his key staff members in a parade down the street that passed the ambassador's residence. I went outside to watch.

There he was—Amin Gemayel, the President of Lebanon—in a white suit, marching at the head of a small column of seven or eight men, a rumpled-looking, Runyonesque lot. And he was loving it. He was leading a parade, strutting down the street, and he was enjoying himself the way a 12-year-old would. Months later, I thought back to this scene and realized that "being the President," not governing, was how Amin Gemayel viewed his role.

We met the next day. I presented my view of what was necessary to restore Lebanon's stability and emphatically stated my opinion that the keystone to any prospect of peace and the renewal of his sovereign control over the country was his commitment to yield power to rival factions.

Gemayel's reaction was defiant. Lebanon was at the mercy of foreign forces, he said. The country had only three choices. "We can take the Israeli option, the Syrian option, or the American option. I've chosen the American option, even though it poses risks for me. Now it is up to the United States to deliver on its pledges."

I was astonished. Here was the President of a country showing no aspiration whatsoever to establish a government worthy of the name and to govern. Instead, he was ready to yield that responsibility to the United States. Rather than acknowledge the political imbalance between his own Maronite Christian party and its Muslim competitors, he was stating flatly that there could be no compromise. I contemplated him gravely. What he was really saying, this 40-year-old lawyer who had never shown any inclination to politics before his brother died, was, "I am the Christian son of Pierre Gemayel and I don't have the courage to change the *status quo* favored by my father."

I went back to the residence greatly sobered. I sat down with Bob Dillon and Dick Fairbanks and asked Bob to give me his own sense of what he thought could realistically be achieved with Amin Gemayel. The more he talked, the more depressed I became. "Amin is a fop," he said, "a pretty boy without political vision, with no history of any relationships with counterparts in the Sunni, Shia or Druze communities, and who enjoys no respect in any of these factions. He's a man with none of the courage of his brother Bashir." Bob did not believe that Amin would ever agree to engage seriously with any of the other Lebanese parties.

The outlook was poor, but you play the hand you're dealt. I decided that U.S. policy, however it had previously been explained by Phil Habib, required political reconciliation among the Lebanese factions, and that unless Amin could bring himself to work toward that, he would risk an inevitable decrease in U.S. support. I told him again, in no uncertain terms, that I would not cease pressing for that internal reform.

Externally, I intended to travel to neighboring capitals in an effort to secure the orderly withdrawal of Syrian and Israeli forces on a timetable consistent with the ability of the Lebanese armed forces to move into the vacuum they left behind and maintain security. For the next thirty days, dividing the responsibility between us, Dick Fairbanks and I visited Damascus, Tel Aviv, Jerusalem, Riyadh, Cairo, and Amman, Jordan, to press these two objectives.

Among the Arabs, our efforts were devoted chiefly to moral suasion with Assad—unhappily to very little effect—while we sought to curtail the support he received from his Arab colleagues in Egypt, Saudi Arabia and Jordan. Each head of government would pay lip service to our requests and promise to do his best, but it was clear that none of them would risk reprisals from Hafez al-Assad by taking unilateral measures to isolate him. On more than one occasion, after the formal meetings, key Arab advisers would take me aside and say something like, "Bud, the United States has wasted eight months out here. Hafez al-Assad respects power, and unless you are prepared to use it against him, he will not yield. None of the Arab states are going to deliver anything of consequence to put pressure on Syria." So much for almost a year of diplomacy—all in vain.

That Syria was the troublemaker was the core of the problem. I knew the Arabs were right when they said that Assad would only take us seriously if we were prepared to use force. For such force to be legitimate and effective, I believed we first needed to establish clearly in Assad's mind what our purposes were, and our determination to support the restoration of Lebanese sovereignty over Lebanese territory, using all means necessary to achieve that end.

I made it clear to Amin Gemayel that I believed President Reagan would stand behind this proposition if he, Gemayel, carried his end of the bargain and publicly declared his commitment to political reconciliation in Lebanon. After hammering away at him for two weeks on this score, he finally began to take what I was saying seriously. Even then, it wasn't until September 1 that I was able to persuade him to deliver a national speech in which he committed himself publicly to the goal of national reconciliation. It was a historic first for a Christian President of Lebanon—but at the last moment, Gemayel, true to form, still watered down the language, delivering something less than a full endorsement of the idea.

I was having even less success with the Syrian withdrawal. Early in my sessions with Assad, it became clear that he felt no pressure to make any concessions, and that I had no leverage to coerce them. Even the prospect of U.S. assistance in promoting an Israeli pullout was not a convincing instrument. After a year of struggle and combat losses, the Israeli body politic was becoming less and less supportive of the war and had begun to call for the withdrawal of Israeli troops. From Assad's point of view, if the Israeli withdrawal was inevitable, there was no need for him to give anything up to achieve it. Indeed, he could seize the opportunity of an Israeli withdrawal to solidify his own position inside Lebanon.

Toward that end, as August drew to a close, Syrian-instigated firefights had begun to break out in and around Beirut. From strongholds along the Matn, the mountains overlooking Beirut, Syrian artillery rained mortar fire down on the city and on the MNF, sitting immobile at the airport and on the beach. Two Marines were killed. Assad was determined to undermine our Lebanese policy and prevent a national reconciliation of any sort. He was not going to surrender his influence over the Muslim factions in Lebanon. And his prospects of success were dramatically increased when the Israelis, responding to pressure from home and ignoring U.S. pleas—now ironically turned on their head—not to withdraw until the Lebanese Army was ready to take their place, announced that their troops would begin to pull out of Lebanon on September 4.

On September 1, I was called home to report to the President, who was receiving growing pressure from the Congress to show some results. I also needed to determine what sort of backup support I could count on to accomplish anything of value. On that score, I was prepared for a tussle. From telephone conversations with Washington over the last month, and from the observations I had made over the previous year while at the White House, I was aware of Pentagon resistance to any use of force on the grounds that it could potentially damage our relations with the Arab world. There was another element that played a role, however. Over the last year, it had become clear that there was an overarching coolness in the relationship between Cap Weinberger and George Shultz, a coolness that was usually, but not always, masked by a claim of policy difference.

Weinberger had not gotten along with Al Haig, either. In both cases, there was a dimension of genuine policy disagreement. It was Cap's judgment that military force should not be used against Arabs. He had no confidence in either Haig's or Shultz's diplomatic strategy, and was therefore unwilling to back it up militarily. This was a reflection of his basic lack of historical knowledge as to how force had been used in support of diplomacy through the centuries. He need only have studied President Eisenhower's resolution of an analogous Lebanon crisis 25 years before.

In Cap's relationship with Shultz, though, there was an undeniable undercurrent of jealousy. For many years, Weinberger had operated in Shultz's shadow. He had been his deputy at the Office of Management and Budget under Nixon; at the Bechtel Group, Shultz had been president, Weinberger general counsel. Now, Cap found himself head of a Cabinet department that was still, in a hierarchical sense, subordinate to that headed by Shultz. Whatever the true wellspring of his hostility to George, the plain truth was that he was always ready to pick a fight, challenge Shultz's position, or oppose State Department strategy at the drop of a hat.

In this situation, Cap also felt vindicated in his position by his conviction that he understood Reagan—the Reagan doctrine, Reagan's views and Reagan's philosophy—better than Shultz, because he was closer to Reagan than was Shultz.

For any Lebanese strategy to be successful, however, it had to be founded on an effective political-military strategy upon which all parties in Washington agreed. The President, the Secretary of State and the Secretary of Defense all had to be committed to the goals of reconciliation and political change. They all had to understand that the threat to these goals was twofold: Gemayel's weakness combined with Syrian interference, and Syria's ability to manipulate the Druze and the Shia. And now, for the first time, there was a new wild card, the Iranian-sponsored radical Hezbollah, or Party of God, which had been introduced into Lebanon with Syrian acquiescence.

Back in Washington, I laid out my game plan to the President and the other members of the National Security Planning Group. Bill Clark was adamant in his support of my strategy and the importance that it be backed up with military power if necessary. He and I, joined by George Shultz, argued for an expanded MNF presence and mission. But Weinberger, predictably, was as adamantly opposed, and he was joined in his position by General Vessey. The division was deep, and the President made no decisions about military force at the time. He did not change the rules of engagement for the Marine forces in Lebanon: they were not to move outside the Beirut area, and they were not to fire unless fired upon. Conducting "aggressive self-defense" was as much latitude as the President was going to give them.

I headed back to Beirut. Five days after my return, on September 9, President Reagan decided to send the battleship *New Jersey,* with its 16-inch guns, to Lebanon. Bill Clark had exerted all his powers of persuasion to convince the President that this much, at least, was necessary. Yet as glad as I was to get the news that the ship was coming—a platform of heavy guns, after all, can be very visibly imposing—I was still worried that this firepower was not being made available as part of a coherent strategy. I felt I had the President's solid backing for my efforts to push Gemayel toward reconciliation, but I had little confidence that any of my diplomacy would ever be backed up by the responsive use of force.

Syria had apparently reached the same conclusion, for it was still testing our resolve with attacks on the Lebanese forces around the city. In the year since their formation, the Lebanese Armed Forces had done a good job, with the help of superior U.S. training teams, in equipping and training a little over three infantry brigades. In addition to their competence in fire and maneuver, these units, at all levels, from enlisted men to officers, represented all of Lebanon's confessions. They were truly an integrated force. But by September 7, the Lebanese army was surrounded and running out of ammunition.

On the night of September 10, the LAF's Eighth Brigade, now positioned for a last stand on the high ground east of Beirut at a village named Suq al-Gharb, came under attack from Syrian-sponsored surrogates, including Iranian Revolutionary Guards, PLO fighters and some leftist Lebanese militias. As the pitched battle raged on the ridge line, mortar and artillery fire began to fall on the ambassador's residence. A mortar dropped in the courtyard, and the swimming pool was sprayed with shrapnel. My team and I mustered in the residence, in a shelter that was not much more than a large closet. I felt it was the moment of truth for our entire Lebanese strategy.

The President of Lebanon had gone public with his commitment to compromise and reconciliation with all factions. He had stated his willingness to meet with them and engage in good faith. An integrated Lebanese army had deployed to assure the security of Druze, Shia and Christian forces without discrimination. If that army were allowed to be defeated by Syrian-backed forces in its first engagement, our entire strategy and the confidence of Lebanese leaders in proceeding down the path we had chosen would be shattered.

The next day, casualty figures brought to me and the team at the ambassador's residence showed that the Lebanese forces had suffered seven dead and forty-three wounded, with more missing. Brigadier General Carl Stiner, the Joint Chiefs' representative in Lebanon, and I conferred. We were both concerned that another attack could destroy the LAF and wipe out our Lebanon policy for good.

At General Stiner's urging, I sent a flash cable to Washington. "There is a serious threat of a decisive military defeat which could involve the fall of the Government of Lebanon within twenty-four hours," I began. "Last night's battle was waged within five kilometers of the Presidential Palace. For those at the State Department, this would correlate to the enemy attacking from Capitol Hill. This is an action message. A second attack against the same Lebanese Armed Forces unit is expected this evening. Ammunition and morale are low and raise the serious possibility that the enemy brigade . . . will break through and penetrate the Beirut perimeter. In short, tonight we could be in enemy lines."

It was time for the Marines to fire back. I urged the administration to modify the rules of engagement to allow our forces to fire in support of the Lebanese Army and in defense of the Americans in Beirut.

Another attack came, as expected, that evening. Mortars fell around the residence. In a moment of lull, I crossed the 20 yards to the communications wing and called Judge Clark in Washington. "Our basic strategy is on the line here," I told him, summarizing what I had said in my cable. "I know this is going to be difficult to sell. But even if Cap will not endorse my conclusions regarding the political process we've set in motion here, which Assad is trying to destroy, you do face the undeniable reality that Americans are also under fire and the existing rules of engagement provide authority for returning fire if you're being fired upon."

The Judge clearly understood what I was trying to tell him. The President's decision to modify the rules of engagement was handed down at an emergency NSPG meeting in Washington that same day.

Clark directed the JCS to implement the decision immediately, but the military vested ultimate authority for deciding when to fire in Colonel Tim Geraghty, the commander of the 24th Marine Amphibious Unit in Beirut. Tim, wary about getting his Marines drawn into combat and officially surrendering their "peacekeeping" role, waited a week before finally giving the order. On September 19, the *USS Virginia,* a cruiser with five-inch guns, and three other Navy vessels began to shell the ridge line above Beirut. The attacking forces withdrew.

The next day, I drove up to the scene of the battle along the ridge line. I talked to the brigade commander and walked throughout the position, visiting casualties and talking to the troops and small unit commanders as well. I wanted to know the truth. I wanted to know who they were. I wanted to know who the attackers were, whether they were people who ought to have been supporting the LAF, or whether they truly were Syrian-inspired elements. I wanted to know if they were Druze, as many reports had indicated. If this were true, it would have been a political disaster.

Two things emerged very clearly and reassuringly. Among the Lebanese Armed Forces, the commanders included a Shia major and a couple of Druze captains, and some wounded of each confession. This was in fact the integrated force we had striven for. As for the attacking force, I got reports of confirmed Farsi conversations, the presence of Iranian advisers and trainers, as well as confirmed Syrian radio transmissions and undeniable artillery and mortar fire coming from confirmed Syrian positions in the Matn. The assault obviously had been Syrian-sponsored and inspired.

As I walked around among the wounded and the soldiers tending them, I had the inescapable impression that they felt pretty good about having stemmed the tide together as Lebanese—not as Druze or Sunnis or Christians. They had all fought together and won. Assad had tested them, and they had stood up to the test. It was analogous to the Tet offensive in the Vietnam War. Just as the North Vietnamese had decided to challenge the Americans and the local national government and failed, so, too, had Syrian-backed elements tried and failed.

A similar, though far less favorable, analogy had to be made with regard to the press reporting of Suq al-Gharb and Tet. Press reporting of the Tet offensive, heavily influenced by North Vietnamese propaganda, had erroneously indicated that the United States had suffered a serious defeat. In the same way, Syrian propaganda surrounding Suq al-Gharb was successful in distorting the results and spreading the impression that American forces had taken sides with the Lebanese Christians against the Muslim factions. Though countered by Druze and Shia soldiers, the false account gained sway and still stands to this day. Even responsible journalists like Tom Friedman of *The New York Times* have wrongly portrayed the U.S. role in the attack on Suq al-Gharb as the result of a misguided decision to take sides with the Maronite Christian forces.

Nevertheless, the situation after the battle was promising. I felt that if I could get Gemayel to take some concrete steps, we had a shot at making some progress. I continued to lean on him, but in the meantime, Assad was showing he wasn't going to take defeat easily. The Syrians kept up intermittent shelling of Beirut, the residence and the Marine position. I continued to meet with Assad, never for less than four and a half hours, and always in an atmosphere of formality and absence of rancor. Yet after two or three such meetings, I could see that Syria was willing and able to test our resiliency for weeks and months and perhaps even years. I was going to have to give Assad some evidence of our resolve.

On September 23, I traveled to Damascus again. As our meeting concluded and I rose to leave, I looked at Assad. "By the way," I said. "The President has ordered the battleship *New Jersey* to Mediterranean waters. I expect it to arrive tomorrow."

It was a final gambit. I had pretty well reached the end of my rope with Assad. We had bolstered the Lebanese forces, we had bloodied his own forces, I had gotten Gemayel to commit to a reconciliation. But if anything, all this seemed only to goad Assad into continued defiance. In the past few days I had negotiated to the limit of my own skills, brought in as much firepower as I could muster from Washington and the U.S. Navy and Marines to back it up and provided the parties with sensible incentives to stop fighting. Unless they did, however, the government of Lebanon might soon unravel and thereby set in motion a bloodbath as each of the religious factions in turn took revenge. On September 25, two days after I returned from the meeting with Assad, the mortars began to fall again around the ambassador's residence about 6 o'clock in the evening. As the incoming rounds crashed around the compound, I paced the floor inside. I needed help. After a few moments of reflection, I picked up the phone. Jonny emerged from the shelter. "Who are you calling?" she asked.

"Jim," I replied, knowing that she would understand it was Dr. James Macdonell, our pastor as Saint Mark Presbyterian Church back home in the suburbs of Washington. It was just after 11 a.m. and the second service had already begun, but Roger Powell, the Sunday school teacher who answered the call, said he would run and get Jim. Before long, Jim was on the phone.

"Jim, I really need your help," I said. "We've got a shot at a ceasefire here in Lebanon that will go one way or the other within 24 hours. Could I ask you to pray for it and to ask the congregation to join in?"

The telephone connection was poor, but I heard the voice on the other end say "Sure, Bud. We're with you. Hang in there."

I hung up. Outside, the firing thundered on, but I began to experience a curious peace of mind. I must have looked a little funny because Jonny came up to me and asked what was wrong.

"Nothing," I answered. "Let's go for a swim. I think it's going to be all right." We swept the shrapnel from the side of the pool and dove in.

The next morning I awoke to the news that the Syrian and Lebanese presidents had agreed to a ceasefire.

—

The cease-fire was a watershed. In the wake of it, Gemayel agreed to convene a conference of reconciliation at the end of the year in Geneva. We left Beirut in October on a high note, feeling that we had carried the day and that the situation in the Middle East was at least temporarily stabilized.

Back in Washington, however, change was afoot.

One day in late September, I had flown to Rome to meet with Judge Clark at his request. I remember thinking he sounded odd when he called, and when I arrived at Ambassador Max Rabb's residence, I could tell Clark was both exhausted and depressed. We sat beside the swimming pool and talked for two hours.

Things were very bad at the White House, he said. Working with the Baker-Deaver crowd, as he called them, was becoming impossible. What was most troubling, he said, was that Deaver was poisoning the well for him with the First Lady, and his relationship with Nancy Reagan, which had always been warm and cordial, was now severely strained.

"I don't know what's happened between Mike and me," Clark said sadly. "I hired the guy when I was Chief of Staff for the governor 10 years ago." Yet now, he said, he felt consistently undermined by Deaver and Baker, who would interfere in national security decisions and perform end-runs around him, going in to the President after decisions had been made and persuading him to reinterpret or even reverse his position.

"I've tried and tried to straighten this out with Mike, but I just don't seem to be able to do it," he said. "I'm about at the point of concluding that, out of loyalty to the President, the situation might improve if I left and went somewhere else, maybe back to California."

I tried my best to cheer him up and dissuade him from this line of thinking. "You mustn't leave," I said, and I felt that very strongly. Whatever he may have been lacking in knowledge of foreign issues was compensated for by his relationship to the President, and especially to Weinberger. He was a very close friend of Cap's and they shared a strong mutual respect, grounded in the confidence each had in the other's loyalty to Ronald Reagan. They both, in fact, fancied themselves keepers of the Reagan Holy Grail and defenders of Ronald Reagan against all comers. It was an invaluable relationship in light of the Shultz-Weinberger animosity, and gave Clark a vital ability to maintain harmony.

I had been aware, before leaving Washington, that Mike Deaver believed that the President's image as a superficial, hardline cowboy and his confrontational attitude toward the Soviet Union had to be softened. I had not been aware that to promote that change he had adopted the strategy of undermining Clark. Apparently Deaver felt that the Judge was encouraging President Reagan to maintain an image that would be damaging to him politically, and therefore Clark had to go. On the surface, however, Deaver was portraying Clark simply as not up to the job of National Security Adviser, not informed enough in a position that required someone of greater depth. Moreover, he was insinuating these things to Nancy Reagan, knowing that whatever she said to the President was certain to be heard. And Nancy apparently bought his line and turned against her old friend.

That had taken the situation beyond worry on Clark's part, to hurt. He was a sensitive person. Now, the job to which he was devoting so much time and energy was not only no longer fun—it hadn't been that for a long time—it was painful. I was distressed for him. He was a thoroughly decent person, the most loyal friend Reagan had in his government. I liked him, liked working for him. We had been a good working team: I did the substance, and he made sure that the President devoted enough time to the issues and kept the peace between his warring elders. The Judge was utterly reliable and straightforward; what he told you in private was the same as his public stance. He was not too proud to defer to experts on issues he knew little about, while at the same time actively promoting the President's principles, which he understood better than anybody. And now here he was, another victim of the sort of meanness and White House guerrilla tactics I had witnessed so often in the Nixon

White House. In my view this man didn't deserve it.

At the end of our two-hour talk, I knew I had not really dissuaded him from thinking about leaving the White House. I wasn't surprised when he urged me to think about coming back to Washington from Beirut as soon as I could. But I was surprised by what he said next.

"If I leave," he said as we parted, "I think you should take my place."

Chapter 14

TAKING CHARGE

I became President Reagan's National Security Adviser on the 1,000th day of his presidency. He made the announcement to the White House Press Corps on October 17, 1983, at 1 p.m. There was no ceremony. It was a matter of plunging right in.

Nevertheless, it was a moment of great pride for me. I had reached the pinnacle of a long public service career, a position of special trust and authority that represented the culmination of all my efforts and aspirations.

It was hard to believe that I had survived the Darwinian process to reach this point.

Judge Clark's parting words after our meeting in Rome had reverberated in my mind for some days afterward. I was gratified by his trust in me, but after brief reflection I had concluded that the likelihood of my being selected as his successor was slim. There were far too many people, I told myself, with longer and stronger personal relationships with Ronald Reagan.

Back from Beirut, back at my old Deputy National Security Adviser desk, I found that the pace of events in the White House was as frantic and frenetic as ever. And a potentially explosive issue was developing in the Caribbean.

On October 13, a military coup overthrew the government on the small island of Grenada. The prime minister, Maurice Bishop, was placed under house arrest. Grenada was a place most Americans had never even heard of, but the events unfolding there were ominous. Bishop was a Marxist and a protégé of Fidel Castro who had been in the process of building a new 10,000-foot runway at the airport on the island with the help of Cuban workers. The purpose of an airport of such dimensions on such a tiny island was suspect; clearly it was not designed simply for tourist traffic. Despite his friendliness with the Cubans, however, Bishop apparently was not radical enough for the military leaders who overturned his government. The prospect of a second Cuba at our doorstep, with all that implied for the export of revolution to countries in South America, was a serious challenge from Moscow. We were going to have to act.

The crisis pre-planning group for the region, which included Ollie North and Constantine Menges from the NSC staff, as well as Tony Motley, the Assistant Secretary of State for Latin America, and others, convened immediately to evaluate the Grenada situation. I tasked an analysis of our options, both political and military. I also instructed that we determine whether the other Caribbean states, including Dominica, Barbados, St. Kitts and Nevis, Antigua and others might be inclined to coordinate a call for assistance from the United States that would legitimize our involvement in the events occurring in their region.

Judge Clark came to me in the middle of all this activity. He was leaving the White House, he announced. The President had asked him to become Secretary of the Interior and, although he had hoped to be able to leave government and return to private life in California, he felt he had to honor the President's request. Had I thought about his earlier suggestion? he asked. I was still his choice to succeed him.

Again, I was surprised, and flattered, that he was still thinking along those lines. I said that yes, I had thought about it, and if he was indeed serious about nominating me, I would talk to Jonny about it and get back to him.

That night, Jonny and I discussed the pros and cons of my becoming National Security Adviser. It had been a long haul in government, for Jonny perhaps even more so than for me, what with all the stresses she had had to endure while I was at the office or away from home. In 1964, she had given birth to twins and had to care for them and a three-year old for another eight months alone until I returned from my first tour in Vietnam. Two years later I was gone to war for another year. She had essentially raised the children single-handedly. The sacrifice she had made over the last 10 to 12 years had been tremendous. Could I in all conscience ask her to make any more? Before Clark had spoken to me, I had again been considering leaving the government in order to provide a better future for us in the private sector. Yet here I was, once more considering another step up on the public service ladder, into a position that was one of immense opportunity to make a significant difference in our country's security, but also one that would demand more than the normal pound of flesh. I went over all this with Jonny, she listening to me soberly as I ran through my checklist of pluses and minuses.

The idea that I would be chosen still seemed implausible to me, I said finally. "But you know," I admitted, "if it were offered, I'd like to do it. I've trained all my life toward this goal of shaping effective policy, and I believe I could do a good job."

Jonny didn't hesitate. "You couldn't not do it," she said firmly. "It's the right job for you." As always, she was full of understanding and generosity.

An NSPG meeting on Grenada was scheduled for the next day. The Judge usually went upstairs to get the President for those meetings and escorted him back down to the Situation Room, where everybody would be waiting. He did the same that day, but this trip, as I found out later, was a little different from the usual. As they were coming back down the narrow stairway that led from the west lobby to the basement of the West Wing, the President said casually to Clark, "By the way, I've decided to nominate Jim Baker to succeed you."

Clark, as he told me later, was thunderstruck. He felt that Jim Baker's views were simply not in synch with the President's more conservative philosophy, and having him in the position of National Security Adviser would undermine the doctrine of firmness that Reagan had come to Washington to put in place. But he composed himself, and before they entered the situation room, managed to ask the President not to go forward with the appointment until the two of them had had a chance to discuss it. Reagan, according to Clark, stopped and looked at him in surprise and asked him if he did not agree with the choice of Baker. Clark admitted he thought it would be a mistake, and once again asked for an opportunity to discuss it. Reagan, though surprised, agreed to hold off on the announcement that he had planned to make at the very meeting they were about to enter.

Following the NSPG meeting, Clark called Ed Meese, Cap Weinberger, George Shultz and Bill Casey into his office next door to mine. My only knowledge of what was discussed at that meeting comes from Clark. After about 20 minutes, when all the other participants had filed out of his room, Clark came into my office and sank onto the small couch against the wall. He told me about the President's deflected intentions regarding Baker. Meese, Weinberger, Shultz and Casey had all emphatically agreed that Baker would be a harmful choice for National Security Adviser and that a consensus had been reached in my favor.

"We think you're the best choice, Bud," he said.

I thanked him for the trust and told him that if the President were to ask me to be his National Security Adviser, I would accept.

"Good," Clark said, jumping to his feet. "I may not win on this, but I'm going to give it all I've got."

Forty-five minutes later, he was back to say that the President was amenable to the idea and would consider it over the weekend. "But you'd better start to get ready," he said, "because I think it's going to happen."

On Monday, during the national security brief, the President told Clark he had decided in my favor, and the announcement was made that same day.

Jim Baker took the decision in stride. Our cordial relationship never wavered. Dick Darman, Baker's top aide, who would have been in line to become his deputy at the NSC, sent me a friendly note. The President couldn't have made a better choice, he wrote. Look forward to working with you.

———

My tenure as National Security Adviser started off briskly.

Certainly the agenda I inherited from Judge Clark was filled with a normal but daunting group of volatile foreign policy issues. Controversial Pershing and cruise missile deployments were scheduled for a month later in Europe, and the Soviets were threatening to walk out of Geneva talks on INF; our arms control positions for START talks needed further developing; we needed to determine what sort of costs to impose on Libyan leader Moammar Gadhafi for his invasion of Chad; Grenada was simmering; the Middle East had started to bubble again; we needed to work on convening Gemayel's reconciliation conference. My work was definitely cut out for me.

I thought I would be able to get my bearings and get a head start on the workload over the weekend of October 21-23. The President was scheduled to go to Augusta, Georgia, at the invitation of Senator Nick Brady (R-N.J.) to play golf with Brady, Don Regan and George Shultz at the Augusta National Golf Course. On Friday afternoon, we flew down to Georgia for what we all anticipated would be a quiet weekend. I felt confident in my new position, secure in my abilities as well as my readiness to respond to any contingency. At most, I thought, I would be monitoring events in Grenada. Matters there had taken a turn for the worse when Maurice Bishop, shortly after having been freed by some supporters, was murdered by soldiers acting on orders of the junta that had taken power. I had talked with Vice President Bush before leaving. As head of the Special Situations Group, he would be dealing with the situation and communicating with the Organization of East Caribbean States regarding their attitudes toward the Grenadan coup and their possible wishes that the United States intervene militarily.

On Friday night, we had a pleasant dinner at the clubhouse. The President, Shultz, Regan and Brady had all brought their wives; I wished that Jonny could have been there, too. Afterwards, the President and Nancy retired to the Eisenhower cottage, the house where President Eisenhower had always stayed whenever he came down to Augusta to play golf, and the rest of us turned in to our assigned lodgings.

Shortly after 3 a.m., the telephone at my bedside rang. George Bush was on the line. Dominican Prime Minister Eugenia Charles, acting on behalf of the OECS, had requested that the United States intervene to prevent the consolidation of Marxist power on Grenada on the grounds that this would constitute a threat to the security of Grenada's neighboring states. It was the call we had expected.

"The operative issue is how do we respond," Bush said. If we were going to act, there was at that moment a MAU just off the coast of North Carolina, heading for the Mediterranean, that could be redirected southward. The change in course was not likely to be noticed by the press, Bush said.

I thanked him for the information and said I would brief the President and get back to him.

I called George Shultz and relayed Bush's message. "I'll wake up the President," I said. I got out of bed, threw on some clothes, and headed over to the Eisenhower Cottage, where Shultz joined me.

The President greeted us in his robe and pajamas. I went over the situation for him, from the beginning of the crisis to Prime Minister Charles's call and the status of the MAU in the Atlantic.

"The United States is seen as responsible for providing leadership in defense of Western interests wherever they may be threatened," I said. "For us to be asked to help and to refuse would have a very damaging effect on the credibility of the United States and your own commitment to the defense of freedom and democracy."

The President never hesitated. "You're dead right," he said. "There's no way we could say no to this request."

I asked him whether the Vice President could begin to task the contingent military planning for a landing, along with the intelligence gathering and all of the preliminaries that would have to precede an invasion, and he agreed that we should get it all underway. I suggested that he talk to Bush himself, so we made the connection right there in his sitting room and he got on the phone with George. "OK, George," he said, "tell Mrs. Charles that we recognize the problem, we'll be glad to respond, and we'll stay in close touch with her while we get busy planning." That said, we all went back to bed.

The next day, while the President was out playing golf, a minor incident occurred. As his foursome was teeing off on the 16th hole, an armed man somehow broke through the heavy security at the country club, made his way to the pro shop, and, seizing five hostages, including two White House aides, demanded to speak with President Reagan. Secret Service agents quickly sequestered the President, who insisted on trying, unsuccessfully, to call the gunman on a radio phone. The man was ultimately persuaded to surrender without incident.

After all that stir, we had an uneventful dinner and turned in early. I was sleeping soundly when, again, the phone shrilled to life. It was 2 a.m. This time, it was the watch officer in the Situation Room calling, and the news he had to impart was horrifying. A suicide bomber had driven a truck loaded with explosives into the Marine barracks in Lebanon. The casualties were high, approaching 100, and climbing.

I felt as though I had been stabbed in the heart. In the two and a half months I'd spent in Beirut, I had come to know many of the Marines stationed there, the fine young men who had been sent to Lebanon out of a sense of moral responsibility, but without the proper mandate and flexibility, who had been made to stay in one place like sitting ducks. Now they had become Syria's latest victims. For I knew, as soon as I heard this gruesome news, that the Syrians weren't finished; they were going to find a way to defeat our Middle East strategy. I had very little intelligence on the identity of the bomber, but I sensed that if he were not Syrian, then he was at least backed by Syria. Soon enough, I would learn I was right.

With a heavy heart, I awakened Shultz and the President for the second night in a row. The President's face turned ashen when I told him the news; he looked like a man, a 72-year-old man, who had just received a blow to the chest. All the air seemed to go out of him. "How could this happen?" he asked disbelievingly. "How bad is it? Who did it?"

John Poindexter, who had been appointed my deputy, and to whom I had already spoken, had passed on the only intelligence we had so far that seemed related to the suicide bomber. One of our sources in Beirut had reported seeing a party of people run from the Iranian embassy, get into trucks and drive off right after the explosions occurred. What connection this might have had to the blast was as yet unclear, I told Reagan, but we would do our best to find out.

The President's sadness began to turn to anger. "Let's go back to Washington," he said. I said I would arrange a departure for first light. At 7:30 a.m., we boarded Air Force One for the return flight to Washington.

———

To say that the next several days were intense, frenzied, exhausting, stressful, solemn and significant is still to miss their true impact. Barely a week into the job, I was experiencing the proverbial trial by fire.

Two major foreign policy matters required resolution simultaneously. Let me describe Grenada first.

Our intelligence on Grenada was very poor. There had never been any reason to have a CIA station on such a sleepy little island; now we had to work from scratch to gather any data. When we gathered Sunday afternoon at 4 p.m. for an emergency NSPG meeting, Bill Casey didn't have much he could tell us. A couple of Navy Seal teams had been sent in to reconnoiter but had not yet reported back. The CIA was sending a communicator to Barbados to establish ground communications. The best estimate, Casey said, was that there were a couple of hundred Cubans on the island, chiefly the airport workers, who probably had some military training as members of the Cuban reserve, meaning there could be resistance when we went in. Our objective was to secure the airstrip, the island's Governor General, a man named Schoon, and the 800 or so

American students at St. George's University Medical School on Grenada. The plan of the operation was for the Marines to come over the beach in an amphibious landing on the east coast of the island, while the Army Airborne units from Fort Bragg, N.C., would air-drop and seize the airstrip and the port on the southwest side.

On Monday, we received word that the Navy Seal teams dispatched to Grenada had encountered hostile fire, and two Seals had been killed. It was an ominous signal. In the White House, concern about the mission began to grow; we faced the possibility that our lack of knowledge about the beach and the level of resistance we might face could end up aborting the operation. The military, however, insisted that they were ready.

The invasion was scheduled to be preceded by additional reconnaissance missions commencing at 9 p.m. on Monday evening. As the teams set off on their mission, the President met at the White House with members of the congressional leadership. In the oval drawing room of the family quarters, on the second floor of the White House, he received House Speaker Tip O'Neill, Majority Leader Jim Wright, Minority Leader Bob Michel, Senate Majority Leader Howard Baker and Minority Leader Bob Byrd. Determined to protect the secrecy of the mission, he had warned all these men not to disclose their whereabouts to anyone, not even their wives.

After my introduction and remarks from Cap Weinberger and Jack Vessey, Reagan laid out his view of the stakes in Grenada and our plans for invasion, and asked the congressmen's and senators' endorsement. American citizens were at risk, he said, and a military operation was necessary to rescue them. But in addition, failure to act now, he stressed, would mean the prospect of a permanent, Soviet-sponsored Cuban presence on the island, a presence that could expand and threaten our interests in South America and, ultimately, in any larger conflict, given Grenada's location along the sea lanes through the Panama Canal and the Atlantic.

The reaction from the congressional delegation was disappointing. The invasion was premature, Tip O'Neill insisted. The use of force against an as-yet unestablished threat would put American lives unnecessarily at risk. Politically, he warned in severe tones, "You're going to take a lot of heat over this. Americans don't want their kids put at risk for something that's none of our business." Wright agreed that the situation wasn't clear enough yet to warrant military action. Bob Michel deferred mildly to the President's judgment, but Howard Baker, at least, threw his full support behind us. There would be criticism, he agreed, but we were doing the right thing.

Before the meeting was over, President Reagan was called out to the telephone. Prime Minister Margaret Thatcher was returning his earlier call from London. And she was livid. Earlier press speculation about our intent to invade had led her to ask our Ambassador, Charlie Price, about our plans. After checking, he had told her no invasion was planned. On that assurance she had stated publicly her confidence that it wouldn't happen. Now, her special relationship would be exposed as apparently having limits at best. She was clearly not happy at having been kept in the dark. Grenada was a member of the British Commonwealth, she reminded Reagan. What was the United States doing launching a military operation there? Why hadn't she been informed? Indeed, why had she been misinformed, assured by press statements from the White House and the ambassador in London that no force was going to be used against the island? She demanded a halt to our plans at once. It was rather incredible to hear such criticisms coming from the woman who had invaded the Falklands, with our support, and one who was normally supportive of all our efforts against communism and Marxism. Despite her arguments that the invasion would hurt Reagan politically in Europe, I'm convinced that she was chiefly piqued at not having been informed earlier, and at how this would play to her disadvantage in Parliament.

Reagan listened patiently to her outburst, occasionally holding the receiver a couple of inches from his ear. When she had finished, he said he hoped that we could still look to her for understanding and support and that we would keep her informed, and hung up.

The Marines and Army Rangers landed on Grenada at about 5:30 in the morning. In spite of greater resistance than they had expected, they managed to move quickly to secure the airport, port, the Governor General's house and the medical school. The greater part of the fighting was over by noon, and though there were pockets of resistance throughout the rest of the day, the mission was essentially wrapped up by nightfall.

The costs of invasion were high—19 American soldiers killed and more than 100 wounded. But by all other measures, the Grenada invasion was an unqualified, and worthy, success. In the immediate aftermath, the usual suspects—the press and the

Democratic opposition—did not want to grant us that. The media was especially sour because we had kept the mission secret right up until the time it was launched and initial reporting portrayed the United States as a military Goliath moving to crush a weak little island barely twice the size of Washington, D.C. Tip O'Neill, for one, called our foreign policy "frightening." But soon enough, we discovered the truth about that little island, and minds began to change.

The "couple of hundred" Cuban "workers" believed to be on Grenada turned out to be more than 1,000 well-trained and equipped Cuban soldiers. The new airfield, with its 10,000-foot runway, included a barracks that was stacked floor to ceiling with weapons and ammunition. In the Cuban embassy, we discovered literally hundreds of documents that proved that the Soviet plan to create a second Soviet-backed base in the Caribbean was well under way. These documents and some of the weapons were later displayed at Andrews Air Force Base outside Washington, and helped to make clear that we had not been reacting to a false alarm.

Right after the invasion, Dominican Prime Minister Eugenia Charles, the woman who had conveyed the OECS message asking for U.S. intervention in Grenada, and Prime Minister Tom Adams of Barbados both agreed to come to Washington to meet with people on the Hill. Their visit helped a great deal in allaying criticism of the invasion.

But what really turned the tide of opinion was the arrival back home of the American students. As the first student stepped off the airplane onto the tarmac at the air base in Charleston, S.C., he fell to his knees and kissed the ground. What more dramatic and spontaneous gesture of relief and gratitude could anyone have made? Watching it on the television news at the White House—and despite Ollie North's claims, neither he nor I were anywhere near the President when this happened—I knew that all our potential problems with criticism of the invasion had just been wiped away.

Well, not all of them. Margaret Thatcher still had not forgiven us for ignoring her on Grenada. Reagan called her after the invasion to smooth her ruffled feathers, but she still directed another blast our way. Western democracies, she declared in a public statement on October 30, do not use force against small countries.

I'll be damned, I thought when I heard that. I couldn't understand her behavior. It was especially upsetting to hear this kind of rhetoric from a friend at a time when we were experiencing our own national anguish over the Beirut bombing. Reagan, too, was upset at her comments, but since he valued his relationship with her highly, he didn't want to sully it by sending her a nasty message. I had no such compunctions. As another aspect of the special relationship, the White House maintains a CABO, or direct cable line, between the President and British prime minister, controlled by the National Security Adviser in Washington and his British counterpart in London. At the time, that person was a man named Sir Robert Armstrong.

At the morning brief the day after Mrs. Thatcher's remarks, I asked the President if he would mind if I sent Sir Robert a little note. "No, by all means," Reagan replied gratefully. And that day I dispatched a starchy cable, not hesitating to contrast our behavior during the Falklands crisis with the British lack of support for us in Grenada.

It seemed to do the trick. We heard no more from London about Grenada.

—

Although the Grenada episode ended happily, whatever sense of buoyancy we might have derived from such a success under normal circumstances was completely negated in this instance by the Marine disaster in Beirut.

As the rubble of the barracks was cleared over the days following the explosion, the body count kept rising steadily. In the end, 241 Marines perished in the bombing. It was a devastating tragedy. A pall settled over the White House. All of us were numbed by shock and horror that wouldn't recede.

We knew we had to react. Reagan, after all, had always promised that this government would provide "swift and effective retribution" against terrorists. Now he held to that line.

"This is an obvious attempt to run us out of Lebanon," the President declared bluntly at the NSPG meeting convened on Sunday, October 23. "The first thing I want to do is to find out who did it and go after them with everything we've got." That same day, Reagan issued a written directive (NSDD 109) calling on the Director of Central Intelligence to prepare an urgent summary from all sources to identify the elements that had planned, perpetrated, supported or otherwise facilitated the attack on the Marine barracks. The Department of Defense was directed to submit options for overt military retaliation against identifiable sources of terrorist activity against our forces. Five days later, he issued NSDD 111, expanding the rules of engagement that had governed Marine reaction at Suq al Gharb to cover other strategic arteries leading to Beirut.

Both these directives were resisted by the Pentagon and the Joint Chiefs of Staff. Weinberger and the military chiefs had never been happy about our Marine presence in Lebanon, and the bombing of the barracks seemed to vindicate their position in their minds. To them, the Middle East was a zero sum game, and raising the stakes at this stage would inevitably mean killing Arabs, something they all, especially Weinberger, wished at all costs to avoid. Even in light of this, the Joint Chiefs' reaction to NSDD 111 was quite extraordinary. In essence, the JCS refused to implement the President's decision. Besides affecting the safety of the U.S. soldiers in the MNF, they argued, a modification of the Rules of Engagement "could adversely impact the ongoing Lebanese national reconciliation talks in Geneva."

The reconciliation conference to which Amin Gemayel had agreed in August had in fact convened in Geneva on October 31, but such a political argument by the JCS was astonishing. In fact, it constituted insubordination. It was not the role of the military chiefs of staff to advance political arguments against military orders. Furthermore, for them to feel no obligation to find and destroy those who had killed 241 of their own was appalling to me.

What the President did not want to do, above all, was to pull out of Lebanon immediately, to be seen as running away as a result of the tragedy that had taken place. To the contrary, the barracks bombing seemed to strengthen his resolve to stay. At the same time, however, I believe that as a result of the bombing, Cap Weinberger adopted an absolute commitment to getting us out of Lebanon as soon as possible. And in it, he was no doubt backed by the Joint Chiefs, who didn't want to lose any more troops, and didn't want to take a proper military role in support of the diplomacy the President had approved for the Middle East.

After the Joint Chiefs sent back their response to the NSDDs, I met with Weinberger in an effort to harmonize the political and military dimensions of the situation, but without much success. Not only was Weinberger against the State Department's Middle East policy, he was against George Shultz personally, and that made winning him over virtually impossible.

On Thursday, October 27, the President and Mrs. Reagan traveled to Camp Lejeune, N.C., to attend a memorial service for the Marines who had been killed in Beirut. The ceremony was held behind the headquarters of the Second Marine Division, to which the dead men had belonged. It was a drizzly, rainy day and we stood under a sea of umbrellas. I was shattered and unable to maintain my composure during the service. The President, clearly heartbroken himself, carried off his role with grace and humility. He offered condolences to the families and to the Second Division commander, Major General Al Gray, a Vietnam hero who was obviously himself devastated over the loss of all these men.

I've seldom been to a more moving ceremony. The loss of human life always had a profound effect on Reagan, and this was no exception. He felt a personal attachment to the men he had lost. Even battle commanders often try to avoid becoming absorbed in the deaths of their troops, so that they remain able to function, but Reagan, as Commander in Chief, would be literally heartsick with genuine grief whenever he lost one of his troops.

That same night, President Reagan delivered a speech to the country from the Oval Office to explain the events in both Grenada and Lebanon. The speech had been in the works for several days, since we had returned from Augusta. In it, Reagan dismissed press criticisms of lax Marine security measures in Lebanon that pinned the blame for the barracks bombing on the negligence of the Marine commanders on the ground. "I am Commander in Chief," Reagan said. "I take full responsibility."

I had urged this course on him from the first. To me, as a former Marine, it was the natural, instinctive course. Taking responsibility is what a commander does. He does not allow his subordinates to be scapegoated for things that have gone wrong on his watch. In truth Reagan, having never held real command, did not have this instinct. But to his credit, he didn't hesitate when, with Mike Deaver's backing, I urged him to take responsibility for the bombing of the barracks. "You're right," he said at once. "I'm responsible and I'll say so."

And so he did. With that one step, he defused a building storm of criticism and rallied the country to his side. It is only unfortunate that three years later, during the Iran-contra crisis, he did not have similar advice, and could not find within himself the resolve to act in a similar manner.

The CIA had tracked the source of the bombing to a Shia Muslim commando unit known as the Husayni Suicide Forces, led by Abu Haydar Musawi, a radical Shia Muslim who had broken away from the mainline Amal organization in 1982 and formed the radical Islamic Amal. This group was put under the command of the Iranian Revolutionary Guards in June 1983. If the Iranians didn't plan and launch the attack, they were nonetheless witting conspirators in it. And the Iranians were allied with Syria. French observers in Beirut had watched the evacuation of an Iranian embassy office in West Beirut 10 minutes after the explosion occurred. In addition, Majid Kamal, an Iranian intelligence official who had guided the terrorist activities of pro-Iranian groups, was in Beirut at the time of the bombing. Seven intercepted Iranian messages since September showed Iranian officials in Tehran and Damascus urging their Lebanese colleagues to attack French and American targets. (The French were in Iran's bad graces for having sold Super-Etendards aircraft to Iraq.) Specifically, the Iranian ambassador in Damascus stated on September 22 that he had instructed Abu Haydar Musawi to "undertake an extraordinary attack against the U.S. Marines."

The Iranian Revolutionary Guards were billeted in the Bekaa Valley in a building known as the Al Shams Hotel, in Baalbek and in the nearby Sheikh Abdullah Barracks. The plans for an air strike against this barracks got underway in coordination with the French. Since they had also been attacked in Beirut, my military aide, Commander (now Rear Admiral) Phil Dur, who had worked closely with the French Navy while commanding the *USS Comte de Grasse,* recommended that they be included in the reprisal raid, and I concurred. On November 14, I convened an NSPG meeting to address this matter. The President gave his approval for a retaliatory strike to be conducted on November 16. It was a direct, unambiguous decision.

On the afternoon of November 15, Admiral Jerry Tuttle, commander of the Sixth Fleet, reported through the European command that he was ready to strike and asked for authority to conduct the attack at first light the following day. But he never received it.

Shortly after I arrived at the White House at 6 a.m. on the morning of the 16th, Cap Weinberger called.

"Bud," he said, "I had a request [to strike], but I denied it."

I was dumbfounded. "I don't understand, Cap," I said. "What went wrong?"

Weinberger launched into a long series of obfuscations about mis-understandings with the French and all the things that could have gone wrong with an attack. "I just don't think it was the right thing to do," he said.

It was outrageous. Weinberger had directly violated a presidential order. Whatever his feelings about our role in Lebanon, whatever his disagreements with our policy, the fact was that a presidential decision had been made and an order given and that should have been that. In a private corporation, someone who defied authority as Weinberger just had would have been fired on the spot. But Weinberger knew Ronald Reagan better than most of us, and that knowledge of his old friend had probably given him the confidence to behave as he had.

I said, as firmly as I could, "The President isn't going to be able to understand this, Cap. You were there. You saw how strongly he felt about this."

"I'll be glad to talk to him," Weinberger replied without turning a hair. "But I thought it was the wrong thing to do." I went in to the national security brief and told the President what had happened.

"I don't understand," Reagan said. "Why didn't they do it ?"

"There is no excuse for it, Mr. President," I said. "You approved this operation, and Cap decided not to carry it out. The credibility of the United States in Damascus just went to zero. There's no justification. The Secretary of Defense was wrong, and you ought to make clear to him how you feel about it."

"Gosh, that's really disappointing," Reagan replied evasively. "That's terrible. We should have blown the daylights out of them. I just don't understand."

He went on in that vein for some minutes, but it was more for my benefit that anything else. It was clear he wasn't going to call Cap. It was more than he could bring himself to do, to embarrass an old friend. But in the end, this inability on Reagan's part to act decisively on matters that involved his friends was destructive to our Middle East policy, and damaging to other foreign policy initiatives as well.

As far as I know, he never did take Weinberger to task for his insubordinate behavior. Weinberger, for his part, had won a decisive battle in his now all-out effort to pull us out of Lebanon.

―――

A month after the failed strike, the United States made one last effort to prove to the world that we were not a paper tiger in the Middle East. On December 3, Syrian forces fired SA-7 missiles at U.S. F-14s conducting a reconnaissance mission over Lebanon. The Joint Chiefs, in accordance with the expanded rules of engagement, which Reagan had finalized in another decision directive handed down on December 2, recommended air strikes against Syrian SAM batteries in retaliation.

The plans were made quickly, the President approved, and the attacks were launched just before first light on December 4. The operation was a failure. The Navy had prepared perfectly so as to launch and execute the attack before Syrian Air Defense batteries could react. Incredibly, however, after the planes had launched, the European Command in Stuttgart, Germany, placed a hold on the mission—with the aircraft meanwhile being "painted" by awakening Syrian gunners.

Two of our aircraft were shot down, one at sea, one over land. The pilot of the aircraft that crashed into the sea was rescued. The pilot of the other plane, Lieutenant Mark Lange, died after parachuting out, while his crewman, Lieutenant Robert Goodman, survived but was taken prisoner by the Syrians.

It was an embarrassing demonstration of American military ineptitude—at least in our command structure. The sense of deflation was palpable. I knew it was time to step back and take a hard, rigorous look at the realities of our very ability to forge viable strategy in the Middle East—so determined was Secretary Weinberger's resistance to any use of force at all.

There were three loci of that strategy, and in each one we appeared to be failing. In Lebanon itself, the Syrians had to be concluding that they were going to win the war. We had been unable or unwilling to respond to their consistent and persistent attacks. That they were the ultimate force behind the barracks bombing was not in doubt in anyone's mind. It was what President Francois Mitterrand of France had told Reagan when they spoke by telephone after the explosion. In late November, the Vatican had expressed the same opinion.

In Geneva, we were getting nowhere with the reconciliation conference. There, Syria was providing instructions to the Druze, whose leader, Walid Jumblatt, a weak figure whose father had been assassinated by the Syrians, was vulnerable to Assad's control and was holding out against any agreement with Gemayel.

And in Washington, the situation was bureaucratically frozen. The President, George Shultz and I were of one mind, Secretary of Defense and General Vessey of another. The result was that we had no coordinated, responsive political-military strategy toward the Middle East. I had tried to get the President to intervene with real emphasis but much as he agreed with me in principle, he was unwilling to put his foot down firmly to insist that his orders be carried out. Shultz and Weinberger simply weren't going to pull together in harness on this issue. Meanwhile, the people at risk were our Marines on the ground and their French and Italian colleagues.

At Christmas, the President headed out to Palm Springs for the holiday vacation. I sent John Poindexter with him and stayed behind to review the bidding. It was clear we were at a moment of truth. The next year was an election year. I had been through enough election years to know that as they unfold, a political overlay begins to influence foreign policy. And any foreign policy that put lives at risk was not going to make it through the political filter of an election year.

It was time to bow to the inevitable. Although we hung on for another month, in early February 1984, with the guns of the *New Jersey* firing in a belated show of power, the U.S. Marines retreated from Lebanon.

It was one of the worst defeats of the Reagan administration.

Chapter 15

TO THE FUTURE

Ronald Reagan headed into the campaign for re-election in 1984 with all the important indicators pointing decisively in his favor. The domestic economy was perking along and visibly on the upswing. After four years of solid military appropriations, we were well on the way to restoring our defense foundation. Our allied relationships were proving solid and resilient. In effect, all the predictions the Soviets had sounded at the end of the Carter years about the decline of the West were being exposed as hollow and unfounded.

By contrast, the Soviets themselves—after losing more heads of state in two years than in the previous 25—seemed to be stumbling. In very little time, the good fortune that had brought them so much success and bolstered their expansion since the mid-1970s appeared to be deserting them. Two blunders in late 1983 especially tarnished their international image. One was the mistaken shootdown in September of a Korean passenger airliner, KAL 007, as it inadvertently passed over Soviet airspace. The attack resulted in the death of 269 civilians and raised a shocked outcry from around the world. The Soviets tried desperately to cover up the error with claims that the plane was on a secret spy mission, but try as they did they could not avoid an international black eye. The second incident that revealed them, even to their Western sympathizers, as less than devoted to the cause of international peace, was their abrupt decision to walk out of the INF talks in Geneva after the deployment of U.S. Pershing and cruise missiles in West Germany and Great Britain went ahead as scheduled in the fall of 1983. Although the deployment itself may have caused some generalized anxiety in Western Europe, the Soviet walkout was even more significant; it proved that the Soviet attitude toward arms control negotiations was not constructive. As far as arms control talks went, the Soviets were suddenly and definitively cast in the role of fear-mongers and spoilers. After all, their medium-range SS-20 missiles had long been in place. By deploying on our side, we were only trying to even the balance, a prospect the Kremlin apparently could not accept.

Viewed in this light, our own foreign policy problems of the last year seemed less onerous than before. It was true that our Lebanon policy had failed, but from the perspective of the American public, the vital thing was that our troops were out of danger and back home. Similarly, President Reagan upheld his promise that all American troops in Grenada would be home by Christmas.

At the outset of 1984, therefore, the outlook was bright. Personally, I was excited about the opportunities we faced to make the second term more productive and more successful than the first. My sense of the precious convergence of public willingness to spend money and to be more assertive overseas was even stronger than it had been three years before. I was determined that a second-term Reagan administration would not squander the opportunity and would make use of this rare convergence to the best ends.

That meant translating this precious commodity with which we had been endowed into something of lasting value, something that went beyond peace in our time, beyond simply minding the store, to a positive legacy that the Reagan presidency could bestow upon subsequent generations. By the time I became National Security Adviser, we had gotten the Strategic Defense Initiative off the ground, we had launched a number of sound policies, we were holding our own in various regions of the world and were within reach of rolling back Soviet gains in two places.

I'd been frustrated over the last two years by Judge Clark's reluctance to launch a second term planning effort for the administration. I had been sending him periodic memos urging the setting of priorities in coordination with the Secretaries of State, Defense and the Treasury (one was written in October 1982 and another in July 1983), but more often than not, these memos had stopped at Judge Clark's desk and never reached the President. In late 1983, I queried Shultz, Weinberger, and Don Regan, then still the Treasury Secretary, for their advice on matters to be tackled in the second term. All three sent back disappointing, perfunctory answers, saying in effect little more than that they believed their respective departments would accomplish everything they wanted them to.

I was highly mindful of the planning void of 1981 and what it had cost us. Such a void was not going to be permitted to develop on my watch. I knew that in order to accomplish anything of value, you have to put a huge amount of time into planning. I also knew that planning is something that most people don't like to do.

But I had become accustomed to planning in the military. And so, as 1984 got underway, I set in motion all the planning that would make it possible for us to make concrete accomplishments in the next four years of Ronald Reagan's administration. George Shultz signed on to my concept reluctantly. In the spring of that year, we forwarded our only joint memo to the President recommending a series of studies, to be conducted by experts both inside and outside of government, of twelve issues of strategic interest to the United States, to identify the top two priority foreign policy items on which the Reagan administration should concentrate in the second term.

As Shultz's State Department was to undertake the analyses inside the government, I charged my deputy, Don Fortier, with finding and bringing together the finest minds outside government to conduct independent studies for me. The roster of participants we assembled for this purpose truly reads like a who's who of foreign affairs analysts and brilliant academic minds. It included people like Sam Huntington, the distinguished Harvard scholar and one of the top specialists in the world on NATO, Europe and the Soviet Union; the highly respected social critic, Irving Kristol; Jim Billington, another Soviet specialist who is now Librarian of Congress; Adam Ulam, a noted Soviet scholar; Dick Solomon, a well-known China hand, and many, many others.

I watched their work get underway with enthusiasm and the confident anticipation that by November I would have a solid set of papers to present to the President, trenchant analyses from which he, as the final arbiter, would be able to select the two tasks he wished to set for his second term, the two goals he hoped to achieve, the two solid accomplishments he would leave behind as Ronald Reagan's legacy to the American people, and the world.

It's in the nature of politics and politicking that foreign affairs generally take a back seat to domestic issues in the course of a re-election year. In 1984, this natural de-emphasizing of foreign policy coincided with a rather fortuitous lull on the international scene. No great overseas crises loomed in that year to challenge Ronald Reagan in his role as leader of the free world, to test his skills as a decision-maker, or to threaten his commitment to world peace and stability. The withdrawal from Lebanon put the Middle East, ever-simmering but in no imminent danger of explosion, on the back burner. The Soviet walkout in Geneva at least temporarily diminished the Soviets' stature on the world stage and gave us breathing room to plan aggressively for renewed contacts, on new terms, in 1985.

Whenever a potential storm did seem to be gathering, it was quickly dispelled. Thus, the Ayatollah Khomeini's bluster in the spring of 1984 about restricting access to the Straits of Hormuz and preventing international vessels from entering the Persian Gulf was deflected by the excellent work of the crisis pre-planning group which I had established. Under the extraordinary leadership of Bill Martin (later Deputy Secretary of Energy), it quickly determined that Khomeini did not have the military wherewithal to block the Gulf for an extended period, and that world reserves of oil were more than sufficient to tide the West over until the Gulf was accessible once again. This information, shared with our allies in Europe and Japan, effectively took the teeth out of Khomeini's threats and silenced him on the matter once and for all.

One area that still gave me concern was Central America. Despite Ronald Reagan's strong feelings about the Soviet-backed Sandinista regime in Nicaragua, and obvious Soviet efforts to undermine the government of neighboring El Salvador, we still had not, in all the time I had been at the White House, put together a comprehensive policy toward Central and South America. That void was made very clear by the congressional debate that centered on U.S. support for the Nicaraguan contras and reached a crescendo in the spring of 1984.

Latin America, we can see today, was one of the real success stories of the 1980s. That decade, the decade dominated by the Ronald Reagan presidency, witnessed a dramatic tide toward pluralism in all of Central and South America. In 1980, sixty percent of the states in that region were authoritarian; by 1990, ninety percent were democratic and pluralistic. During Reagan's first term, democratic elections were held in every Central American country except Nicaragua.

To sustain that progress, however, economic stimulus is the vital ingredient. Life has to get better in order for political stability to take hold. "Better," in this case, covers all the social indicators—housing, health care, education, infrastructure. In the past, the jump start for these improvements had traditionally come in the form of foreign aid grants. Our experience in the United States in the post-war period, however, had been that much of the money passed directly to author-itarian rulers had ended up in Swiss bank accounts, earning a lot of interest but otherwise not working very hard, or at least not in the way it was supposed to be working.

In the Reagan years, as a result, we decided that we would rely more on the private sector to provide an infusion of capital to needy states. There's no denying that you get better accountability over investments by working with teams of private entrepreneurs—from both the U.S. and the host country—who have an interest in making a profit. In addition, we would continue to fund some economic assistance for projects unlikely to attract private investors, as well as military assistance for security purposes. Yet while we had put together a successful package of trade, aid and investment in some parts of the world, notably the Caribbean basin, by the end of 1982, we still had no comprehensive policy of this nature toward Latin America.

In Central America in the 1980s, in the meantime, a new situation had come into being. The Soviet Union, through its Cuban interme-diary, had stepped up efforts to subvert the governments in Nicaragua and El Salvador. In Nicaragua, indeed, by backing the Sandinista rebels, Moscow had succeeded in ousting the government of Anastasio Somoza in 1979 and establishing a Marxist-oriented regime in Managua. That regime, in turn, willingly played surrogate in the battle for the soul of Nicaragua's neighbor, El Salvador, and openly backed Marxist guerrillas seeking to overturn the U.S.-backed government there.

The response of the Reagan administration to this set of circum-stances was twofold: in El Salvador, we stepped up the number of advisers we had in the field and sought additional higher levels of military aid; in Nicaragua, we promoted the creation of a cell of freedom fighters that we hoped would grow over time into an effec-tive democratic movement. Both these initiatives, however, were largely the work of Bill Casey and his CIA, which had stepped into the void left by the State Department in formulating workable policy for the region.

As it had in the Middle East and on the issue of the nuclear freeze movement and other U.S.-Soviet-related matters, the State Department was dropping the ball in Central America. It was not exercising its role in chairing the interdepartmental group charged with developing regional policy for Latin America. State's bureau for Inter-American Affairs, headed first by Tom Enders and later by Tony Motley, simply would not call meetings or, having called them, was unable to prevent them from degenerating into disagreements with the Defense Department. State did not have the bureaucratic courage to elevate the issue to the next higher level so as to get it off dead-center.

Part of this problem was ineptitude, and part was Motley's fear of appearing unable to forge policy at his level and having instead to kick it upstairs. In part, too, he feared that if he did send the problem on to the deputy secretary level, he might lose the argument. Stalemate, in his view, was preferable to defeat. It was typical bureaucratic gamesmanship, but its result was paralysis, and a distressing and harmful void in policy.

While State and Defense bickered, Congress had time to focus on the most concrete element of policy the United States did have in place—administration and CIA support of the contras. The Democrats on the Hill began to focus the spotlight on contra operations, and soon some very powerful voices were being raised in opposition to it. Chief among them was that of House Speaker Tip O'Neill, who in fact had a greater than usual interest in this particular part of the world. O'Neill's Boston-based district was home of a convent of Maryknoll nuns, who sent many of their number to work among the poor in Nicaragua. On behalf of their colleagues in Nicaragua, this order espoused the doctrine of liberation theology, then popular with the Catholic Church throughout Central and South America. In truth, liberation theology is little more than Leninist doctrine wrapped in the cloth of the Church and packaged under the label of egalitarianism. But its appeal to the poverty-stricken masses in Central America and elsewhere was strong, and its emotional appeal to the clergy in that region was undeniable and difficult to combat. When a Vatican representative visited the White House in 1983, President Reagan appealed to him for help in countering the influence of liberation theology in Central America. While agreeing that the doctrine was dangerous and, in its emphasis on Marxist-Leninist tenets, inconsistent with the actual doctrine espoused by the Roman Catholic Church, the papal representative professed to be at a loss as to how to persuade the priests and religious of the region to abandon it.

Meanwhile, the Maryknoll sisters had managed to exert substantial influence on the Speaker of the House and, by extension, on many Democratic members of Congress. In addition, the intelligence committees, charged with overseeing CIA operations, became concerned about CIA objectives in the jungles of Nicaragua and El Salvador. Congressman Edward Boland, the Massachusetts Democrat who chaired the House Intelligence Committee, was particularly opposed to the contra activities, which in his view appeared aimed at nothing less than an overthrow of the Sandinista regime, a government which the United States officially recognized. In 1982, he had pressed for and won passage of a legislative amendment that permitted continued CIA support of the contras, but not "for the purpose of overthrowing the Government of Nicaragua." This is what became known as the Boland amendment, specifically Boland I, and by the end of 1982, it had put at risk our entire package of both nonmilitary economic aid and military aid to Central America.

The administration's problem clearly rested in our failure to get our message out and to seek public support for our Central America policy. Senator Henry "Scoop" Jackson, the Washington Democrat who had led the charge for our Central America appropriations in 1982 and 1983 and was a man I had worked with while at the Armed Services Committee and greatly respected, told me as much. The administration was right on the issue, he said, but we were falling down on making our case publicly. But without a coherent and comprehensive policy, we could have no public affairs campaign and no public appeal.

In July 1983, therefore, in light of State Department inaction, I took matters into the White House and formed a bipartisan commission on Central America to study the region and make recommendations for policy improvements and approaches that could be presented to Congress in defense of requested appropriations. This was an approach I had used before to overcome the persistent State-Defense rivalry that so often crippled Reagan administration foreign policy making. In December of 1982, for instance, I had had to form the Scowcroft commission to overcome Cap Weinberger's inability to develop and promote our defense policy successfully, which had led to repeated defeats on the MX missile basing system.

Even though the State Department had failed to take the lead on Central America, it still took me four or five months to convince George Shultz of the need for a bipartisan commission on the region. However, he did finally agree to go along with the idea, and the

President issued a directive calling for the formation of an outside commission to define our interests and role in Central America. Henry Kissinger agreed to chair it, and we assembled an impressive group of members, including Lane Kirkland of the AFL-CIO, U.N. Ambassador Jeane Kirkpatrick, University of Southern California scholar James Q. Wilson, Henry Cisneros, then the mayor of San Antonio, and other notable personalities of Hispanic background from politics and academia. I assigned Ollie North and Jackie Tillman to the commission's staff.

The commission reported in early February of 1984. Its findings backed our assertions that U.S. national security interests were threatened by Soviet-backed, Cuban-conducted subversion of the governments of Nicaragua and El Salvador and recommended continuing aid to the rebels in Nicaragua and to the government in El Salvador. But, the commission's report went on to say, it was simultaneously necessary to address the fundamental conditions that created the climate, which in turn bred acceptance of such subversive activities. That climate was one of economic deprivation, which must be tackled through foreign aid, not only in the form of grants, but a combination of stimuli including trade, aid and investment. The report recommended $1 billion in new economic and military aid for Central America for fiscal 1985.

The commission fulfilled its mandate in grand manner; in August of 1984, Congress did indeed approve $1.2 billion in aid to Central America, a huge windfall that could be put into economic programs in the region, which soon began to bear fruit.

In the meantime, however, the domestic war over the contras had not ended. In early April 1984, Congress had once again risen up in arms when it learned that the contras had been mining harbors in Nicaragua to discourage Soviet shipments of oil and supplies to the Sandinista government. The decision to provide the contras with funding to mine the harbors at Corinto and El Bluff had been considered by the principals of the National Security Planning Group in accordance with the normal covert action review process in January 1984, and the President had signed a Finding. The intelligence committees, however, created an uproar, insisting they had not been briefed on the Finding. Both the House and the Senate voted resolutions of condemnation that passed by lopsided majorities.

More than concern over the tactic, however, the Congress was acting out of a sense of *amour propre,* believing that it had not been properly consulted and briefed on the matter; and "properly" is a charitable addition. Casey had told me that he had briefed the two committees as the law requires, that he had gone to the Hill and informed them in closed session of the plan. Shortly after the issue erupted, I spoke at the Naval Academy Foreign Affairs Conference in Annapolis and was questioned by a journalist in the audience about the briefing. In response, I said "I am informed that the Director of Central Intelligence carried out a proper briefing." The next day, Senator Pat Moynihan, the ranking Democrat on the Senate Select Intelligence Committee at the time, got up on the Senate floor and denounced this as untrue. He placed a furious call to me as well, and insisted that Casey had not briefed the committee.

It was admittedly not the first time this had happened. Bill Casey was notoriously contemptuous of Congress and really had no interest in telling it anything more than he had to in order to keep from being locked up. Later I heard from others that when he went up for the briefing, he first went through a long agenda that did not include the mining of the harbors. At the end, as interest on the committee was waning and members were beginning to assume that the briefing was over, Casey tossed out a low-pitched aside, something like "By the way, we're going to be doing some mining of the harbors down there." Only one or two members actually even heard him say this. The timing of his delivery, I have no doubt, was hardly accidental on Casey's part. And there was the matter of his mumbling. Casey spoke in an infamous incomprehensible mumble that was the subject of jokes all over Washington. Even the President got in on the act. When I would inform him that Casey would be coming in to brief or update, he took to quipping, "Who's going to interpret?" Sometimes, we would sit through sessions in the Oval Office where Casey would sit at the President's side, mumble his way through a long monologue with the President listening intently and nodding while the rest of us in the room stared at each other in utter incomprehension. Afterwards, when the President had sent Casey off with authorization to do whatever on earth it was that he had been describing, Jim Baker would say to me, shaking his head, "God knows what he just approved."

Through this combination of factors, Casey no doubt was able to convince at least himself that he had mentioned the mining in committee and received no adverse reaction. But it didn't lessen congressional ire over the episode. In fact, it is the incident that cost us continued support for contra funding. Casey formally apologized to the Senate, but it was too late. The Congress had been ignored, and it was going to show its disdain for people who didn't respect it. The contra funds, which had been capped at $24 million a year before, were running out fast and probably would be depleted by the end of June. Now, Congress would refuse to appropriate any additional monies.

It was this state of affairs, facing off against Ronald Reagan's deep personal commitment to supporting the freedom fighters in Nicaragua, that led to my appeal to Saudi Arabia—entirely legal at the time—for assistance in backing the contras. It also led, unbeknownst to me, to Ollie North's aggressive pursuit of illegal activities to boost the contra cause, activities I never would have permitted had I been witting of them. Despite the setback in our Nicaragua policy, I still believed that situation was salvageable, and began to urge the contras to reorient themselves both as a political organization and as a military organization capable of winning victories in the field. This strategy ultimately proved successful. And, when Congress appropriated the $1.2 billion in Central American aid in August, I felt hope that, if we improved the presentation of our case, we could continue the contra struggle with renewed support in 1985.

Looking back on our Central America policy, I believe the evidence shows that on the whole, despite some blunders and wholly irrespective of North's unnecessary, unauthorized and illegal activities, it was successful. In 1987, in his own memoirs, Tip O'Neill worried that in 10 years the United States would be invading Nicaragua. Instead, in less than half that time, Nicaragua went the way of all its neighbors and established a fledgling, albeit troubled, democracy—all the trouble, incidentally, stemming from the continuing role of corrupt and inept Sandinista elements in the Managua government. Elsewhere, Central America today is marked by positive growth rates and a rejection of authoritarianism that shows no signs of reversal.

When all is said and done, life in Central America since the Reagan administration looks better than it ever did before.

As the election year unfolded, Ronald Reagan traveled to China, where he addressed a broad agenda and also delivered a candid criticism of the government's human rights record. He went to the shores of Normandy, where, on the 40th anniversary of D-Day, he delivered a stirring speech commemorating the glorious sacrifice of the "boys of Pointe du Hoc." In keeping with the permanent requirement that the administration be at all times prepared for nuclear attack, I accompanied the President wherever he went, but I was for the most part in the background of activities; my role in the campaign consisted chiefly of contributing facts and rhetoric to the foreign policy themes the President wished to stress.

Traditionally, however, since the days of Jerry Ford, the opposing candidate in a Presidential election has been entitled to a briefing on national security affairs during the campaign. In September, I traveled to Minneapolis-St. Paul to brief the Democratic candidate, Walter Mondale, and spent a couple of hours going over foreign affairs issues of the day. Afterward, I was told that Senator Moynihan, who was present as an adviser to Mondale, remarked to the candidate and others that my presentation had been the best overview of foreign policy he had ever heard.

Apparently, the briefings Mondale received in other areas weren't quite as successful, because he made the lamentable and fatal mistake of volunteering that if elected, he would raise taxes. He had an uphill battle against the immensely popular Reagan as it was, but that commitment simply sealed his fate. On November 6, Ronald Reagan carried 49 of 50 states—Mondale's home state of Minnesota was the lone holdout—and was re-elected to the presidency in the biggest landslide in American electoral history.

With the election behind us, and the President's mandate revealed to be the most impressive any modern chief executive had ever been granted, I was eager and anxious to get started on all the work there was to do in the second term. Before that could happen, though, I felt there were some problems President Reagan needed to iron out first.

The President had been in California for the election, and on the following Sunday we headed back to Washington. On Air Force One, he and I sat down together for a long session, one-on-one. I told him about my planning for the second term, and the detailed issue analyses that were being prepared for his consideration, from which I hoped he would select the two issues on which we would focus for the next four years. There was, however, something more urgent I wanted him to address.

I paused and looked at him with obvious foreboding. "I must tell you, Mr. President," I said, "that I fear that nothing can get accomplished if you don't recognize that you face paralysis within your administration owing to the largely personal animus that exists between Cap and George."

I told him I believed he would find that the process would work more smoothly if he built his team around one or the other of these two men, but that together, they were like oil and water. If he insisted on keeping them both, I said, "then you're going to have discord, and you're going to have to be the arbiter and be much more active."

These were thoughts I had been having for a long time, and it was time to air them. The need for constant mediation between Shultz and Weinberger was exhausting, pointless, unworthy and immensely frustrating, and although I felt that I handled it well, I felt it was important to make this pitch to the President and that he either change the configuration or become more actively involved and in control of his own administration. Over the course of 1984, the recalcitrance between State and Defense had been most trying in the area of arms control. I don't know how many dozens and dozens of meetings with Richard Perle and Rick Burt I had chaired trying to overcome heated argument and deep-seated hostility to produce a verification report to the Congress that would represent sound policy and be respected by both departments. The effort had succeeded, but now I wanted to see if the President would be willing to help me out in future.

I weighed my next words very carefully. "Perhaps there is someone you can think of who would be a more effective National Security Adviser than I with regard to this specific problem of the intractability of these two people," I said. "If so, then by all means you should appoint him, and I would be willing to step aside."

Reagan regarded me with a look that commingled fondness and alarm. He shook his head. Then he said what, in my heart, I knew he would.

"Bud, I know there's always been this thing between Cap and George. I don't know why, but it's there. I wish they could get along with each other better. But at my age and their age, people don't change very much.

"And they are both my friends. I don't want to fire either one of them. I know that means you're going to have to work harder. But you do it right, Bud. In all my time in public life, I don't know if I've ever found a person as indispensable as you. I don't know what I'd do without you."

He would only accept my resignation, he insisted, if I came to him with a personal reason of overriding importance for wishing to leave his employ.

Listening to him, my emotions moved from gratification to dismay and back again. His comments about my value to him were terribly generous and I was grateful for his trust; at the same time, he had only confirmed that we were headed for another four years of guerrilla warfare in the policymaking process.

When we arrived in Washington, I told Shultz about the discussion. George and I had discussed the problem he had with Cap on a couple of occasions, and he professed himself perplexed by Weinberger's apparently deep-seated hostility and jealousy of his role. He immediately agreed to broach the subject with Reagan himself. At my instigation, Shultz regularly came to the White House twice a week for private meetings with the President. At the next one of these meetings, he picked up the thread of the discussion I had had with Reagan on Air Force One. Working with Cap was nearly impossible, he said. The President's program would be better served if he built his national security team around either him or Cap, instead of having the two of them continue to struggle to get along. He did not directly offer to resign, but said he would defer if the President felt his ideas would be better served by Weinberger.

But the President would have none of it. He did not want to let go of either of his old friends. "I need you both, and I want you both to try to work together better," he said. Shultz, knowing better but respectful of Reagan's wishes, grimly agreed to try.

Having been unsuccessful in obtaining Reagan's cooperation on the personnel front, I turned my attention to the substance of the second term. The studies I had ordered up in the spring had been turned in, and they were uniformly excellent and impressive. To my chagrin, Shultz had fallen down on his end and not really put any significant time or effort into the second-term agenda; at the last minute, he tasked his policy planning chief, Peter Rodman, to do a hurried analysis of what seemed to be the most important application of U.S.

leadership in the next four years and came up not with a selection of priorities, but a straightforward recommendation of U.S.-Soviet relations and the Middle East as the areas on which the second term should focus.

Nonetheless, I was pleased with the work my people had done. As the President headed out to California once again for the Thanksgiving holidays, I had the 12 studies bound into a notebook and carried it out with me, planning to give it to Reagan to digest over his vacation. The first day, as I perused it in my suite at the Biltmore Hotel in Santa Barbara, I felt physically elated. This was such good work, I thought. I sensed we stood on the threshold of what could be the most fulfilling moment of U.S. foreign policy in the post-war period.

The next day, I called the President and asked to come by the ranch to drop off the notebook. I drove up into the hills and the Secret Service let me in through the gate to Rancho del Cielo. The President came out to the patio, and I handed him the notebook with my cover memo, which described his rare opportunity to make history and leave behind a substantial legacy, and asked him to select the most important issues for us to focus on.

I drove away still feeling energized. I couldn't wait for the President to react. But several days went by, and I heard nothing. One day, I was invited to the ranch to have lunch with the President and Mrs. Reagan and their son Ron and his wife, Dorrie. I thought perhaps the President would say something then, but he didn't. It wasn't until we were on Air Force One headed back to Washington that he finally responded.

He called me up to his compartment in the forward section of the plane. He was standing up, with Nancy behind him, and he was holding the notebook in his hand. I could tell he didn't intend to have a long meeting with me. No sooner had I entered the compartment than he handed me the book, grinning broadly.

"Gee, I've looked this over, Bud, and I think these are just terrific ideas," he said enthusiastically. "Let's do them all!"

My heart sank. And yet, at bottom, I hadn't expected anything different. That was how Reagan was. He was the ultimate heroic figure who believed in the shining city on the hill and the capacity of the man on horseback to accomplish all things. It was not in his frame of reference to think that you might leave anything undone once you were aware of it. To him, the idea was all. He didn't appreciate that the better part of policymaking consisted in selling that idea, and that this was hard, complicated work.

I thanked him, took the notebook, and headed back to my seat. I tried to rest as the plane headed eastward over the many states that had so resoundingly voiced their approval of Ronald Reagan and his leadership just a short time ago. But I was agitated and anxious to get back to my desk. I knew that, whatever we decided to tackle and managed to accomplish in the coming years, much of the work was going to fall to me.

Chapter 16

A TURNING POINT IN HISTORY

Ronald Reagan's 1984 landslide victory was a wake-up call that rang loud and shrill inside the enshrouding stone walls of the Kremlin. The Soviet leadership was jolted into awareness of the truth that in four years of endless maneuvering, burdensome defense spending, intense propaganda, intimidation and psychological warfare, they had failed to face down, frighten or flush out the man they had always portrayed as the reckless cowboy of the West. November 6 had come and gone, Reagan was still ensconced in the White House, and Moscow was going to have to deal with him and all that he stood for—rolling back their gains in Afghanistan and elsewhere; challenging their human rights abuses; arms reduction and the dreaded Strategic Defense Initiative—for the next four years.

On November 17, 1984, the President received a letter from Soviet Premier Konstantin Chernenko stating that the Soviet Union was prepared to reconvene talks on reducing the level of nuclear arms and avoiding the militarization of outer space. Our strategy had worked; a year after they had walked out of the Geneva INF negotiations in a huff, the Soviets were coming back to the bargaining table.

On November 22, Thanksgiving Day, I issued a statement in Santa Barbara announcing the news. "The United States and the Soviet Union have agreed to enter into new negotiations with the objective of reaching mutually acceptable agreements on the whole range of questions concerning nuclear and outer space arms. In order to reach a common understanding as to the subject and objectives of such negotiations, Secretary of State George P. Shultz and Foreign Minister Andrei Gromyko will meet in Geneva on January 7-8."

For those of us in the foreign policy arena, it was a time of great anticipation and enthusiasm. Since becoming National Security Adviser a year earlier, I had focused intently on all our arms control positions—on ICBMs, submarine-launched missiles, cruise missiles, and bombers—and had worked to determine what positions would give us the best chance of achieving results. During the year-long

hiatus in negotiations, we had managed to receive another appropriation that had kept SDI a healthy program. By January 1985, I
believed, we were very likely to be in the strongest position the
United States had enjoyed in the post-war period in terms of the
robustness of our defense programs and the political power of a
President who had just received an overwhelming mandate from the
American people.

It was a position we had worked very hard to achieve. And,
despite our dramatic announcement of Soviet willingness to reconvene talks, which seemed to derive entirely from the President's
re-election, we had worked quite hard to make that happen as well.

———

Despite the huge investments that had been made in rebuilding
our defenses and some evidence that after two harsh years our economy was turning around, in early 1983 the Soviet Union was still
unwilling to engage seriously with us on genuine arms control and
arms reductions. They were not yet convinced of our recovery, nor
of Reagan's resolve to stay the course and resist Soviet expansionism around the globe. In Washington, nevertheless, a consensus,
spurred by Bill Clark, George Shultz and me, was building within
the administration that dialogue was a necessary component of U.S.-
Soviet relations. It did no good to have our two countries, enemies
as we were, staring at each other over the abyss without speaking.
Making the effort to resolve some of the rivalries between us, especially those centering around nuclear arms, in a peaceful fashion
appeared to us to be a logical course of action.

In February of that year, the President authorized the Secretary of
State to open private conversations with the Soviet ambassador,
Anatoly Dobrynin, aimed at trying to establish a framework for the
U.S.-Soviet relationship. The framework included four areas: human
rights, arms control, bilateral relations (trade, cultural exchanges, various areas of cooperation ranging from earthquake research to medical
research), and regional disagreements. I established a high-level working group to develop policy for these talks and to backstop their conduct. The group consisted of Larry Eagleburger, Fred Ikle, Paul
Gorman, Bill Casey and Dan Murphy.

On June 15, 1983, following the summit of industrialized nations
in Williamsburg, Virginia, the President convened a meeting in the

White House Treaty Room, upstairs in the residence, to evaluate the results of the ten Shultz-Dobrynin meetings that had been held so far. Shultz reported his belief that two years of high defense budgets and the improved cohesion among the allies that had been reflected at Williamsburg (at which the longstanding frictions over the Soviet pipeline had at last been laid to rest) had begun to restore our credibility with the Soviets.

I agreed that we had made substantial progress, but I thought that it was premature to expect that the Soviets could yet bring themselves to engage seriously, and that we would need one or two more years of high defense budgets and economic recovery before we could expect to get significant results from any talks with Moscow. The President, who had an oddly indifferent air toward the discussion going on around him that day, seemed to agree with me.

After the President's speech announcing the development of the Strategic Defense Initiative, however, the Soviet attitude toward Washington seemed to undergo a dramatic metamorphosis. Between April and October of 1983, the KGB made several attempts to establish an "informal" channel of communications with the U.S. government. Tentative feelers, indicating special interest in making progress on INF, were made by Soviet and Hungarian officials in Washington. In July 1983, Ronald Reagan wrote to Soviet General Secretary Yuri Andropov urging progress on arms control, but noting: "Historically, our predecessors have made better progress when communicating has been private and candid. If you wish to engage in such communication, you will find me ready."

The importance the Soviets placed on a private channel of communications was part and parcel of their secretive ways. Moscow had tried to make back-channel contacts with the White House as early as 1981, but their efforts were rebuffed on instructions from Al Haig at State. Later, a reliable channel to Andropov was established between Max Kampelman, the head of our delegation to the Conference on Security and Cooperation in Europe in Madrid, and his Soviet counterpart Sergei Kondrashev, but it was blown when Shultz and subordinates at State discussed it with Dobrynin and others in the Soviet foreign ministry. By definition, to be effective, a private channel must be private. On the Soviet side, it must not engage the jealousy of the Soviet foreign ministry. Max worried that this blunder may in fact have set back efforts to gain the release of

Soviet dissident Anatoly Shcharansky, whose imprisonment in the U.S.S.R. was an international human rights *cause célèbre* at the time.

This Soviet preference for doing business via a private channel was best described in a memo written by Jack Matlock, the Soviet expert on my NSC staff. Jack was a career foreign service professional who was an acknowledged scholar on the Soviet system and highly experienced in the ways of the Kremlin. His November 1983 memo was entitled "Can A Private Channel Be Useful?"

"If it is handled properly, I believe it can," Matlock wrote. "Principally because it permits more direct input into and feedback from the Soviet decision-making process than are possible in formal exchanges. This flows from the nature of Soviet bureaucratic politics and the psychological mindset of the Soviet leaders.

"...The Soviets are conditioned not to believe what is said publicly (their public statements are largely propagandistic, so they assume those of other countries are as well). They assume that we, like they, speak strictly in private when we are really serious. And they are most likely to believe statements they receive through intelligence channels. (They normally utilize KGB officers as their contacts, presumably because they have their own communication channels, which bypass the foreign ministry and the bureaucracy in general.)"

Matlock believed it was time for a private channel, "since we need informal communication most during periods of tension.... We lose nothing from talking privately (so long as we are reasonably careful about what we say). And refusal to do so only encourages a Soviet stonewall—and perhaps worse."

At the end of 1983, heading into 1984, I still believed it unlikely the Soviets could engage soon due to the twin defeats of the KAL shootdown and the impending INF deployments. Matlock, in another memo, agreed with me. Though it was their own fault and no one else's, the Soviets felt internationally humiliated by the KAL disaster and saw themselves as having suffered a serious foreign policy defeat. "When their prestige is so directly at stake as it is in this instance," Matlock wrote, "they are incapable of making rational moves, even in their own interest, if these seem to be retreat under foreign pressure." As for the deployments, he wrote, "the Soviets will have to display a truculent, stonewalling mood (or worse), at least for a few months. The odds, therefore, are very much against a summit or major progress in the arms reduction area for the next 6-9 months."

At the same time, we faced a tricky situation *vis-a-vis* the Soviets. After KAL, the Soviets were rightly seen as provocateurs, an image that was reinforced after their walkout from Geneva. But Western publics have a very low tolerance for threats and intimidation; in an election year, especially, Moscow could yet undermine our position by both threatening us on the one hand and promoting positive proposals such as reductions in conventional and chemical weapons on the other. A frightened public might find irresistible the temptation to make concessions merely for the sake of getting back to the bargaining table.

For more than a year, George Shultz, George Bush and I—and, for different reasons, Mike Deaver and Nancy Reagan—had been nurturing a change in President Reagan's attitude toward engaging with the Soviet Union. Reagan had come into office as a hardline confrontationist, a man who called the U.S.S.R. the "evil empire" and saw no reasonable or justifiable purpose in giving them any quarter, or in engaging in a dialogue with a country he considered our sworn enemy. But slowly, he came to accept his responsibility to look beyond achieving "peace in our time" to creating results that would last indefinitely—notably treaties codifying reductions in nuclear weapons. On December 13, 1983, he gave an interview to *Time* magazine in which he spoke of the possibility of engaging with Moscow. I wrote his talking points for the interview; across the top I wrote the message he was striving to impart: "Your commitment to solving problems with the Soviet Union."

That same month, I wrote a draft for what was to become Reagan's stock U.S.-Soviet relations speech in his second term. I've always called it the RS&D speech, for realism, strength and dialogue, the three girders of the new policy. Realism—a recognition that the United States and U.S.S.R. disagreed on virtually every organizing principle of political conduct toward our own people as well as toward other nation-states, and that these vastly different systems would never converge; strength—a commitment to rebuilding our national defense in recognition of Soviet respect for power, the only incentive that would make them willing to negotiate; and dialogue—the need, even across the chasm created by our differences, to talk. I polished up the speech and sent it over to Reagan at Camp David on December 18. On January 16, 1984, Reagan delivered this watershed speech from the Oval Office.

The response it elicited from Moscow was not encouraging. Twelve days later, the President received a scathing letter from Andropov that once against criticized the INF deployments in Europe and didn't give an inch on any of the other differences between Washington and Moscow that had deadlocked the Geneva negotiations. However, the President did pick up on a reference on the second page: "We were prepared to accept very deep reductions both of the strategic and the European nuclear weapons. With regard to the latter, even to the point of ridding Europe entirely of medium range and tactical nuclear weapons. The Soviet Union continues to be in favor of this." I got a handwritten note from the President attached to that portion of the letter: "He suggests that they want an elimination of nuclear weapons. In Europe, that is. Let's take him up on that."

We didn't get the chance. On February 9, 1984, Yuri Andropov died after barely 14 months in office. His successor, Konstantin Chernenko, was another elderly hardliner who appeared from the first days to be in generally ill health and not nearly as firmly in control of the Communist Party or the Politburo as Leonid Brezhnev or even Andropov had been.

Vice President Bush represented the United States at the funeral in Moscow. He had asked Reagan before going whether he should invite Chernenko to the United States in the spring, but Reagan said no. I had said that at this stage, it was important not to appear over-anxious, and the President agreed, in spite of the fact that a meeting with the Soviet General Secretary would have come off as a big coup during an election year.

On the same trip, Jack Matlock met with Vadim Zagladin and Stanislav Menshikov, two senior policy officials of the Soviet Union's USA-Canada Institute. "Now is a good time for a fresh start," Zagladin said to Matlock. It was a significant signal. The men briefly discussed conventional weapons and the issue of verification, and Zagladin replied that there might be fewer problems in that area than the U.S. anticipated. For his part, Matlock informed the two men that Brent Scowcroft would soon be making a private trip to Moscow with the Dartmouth Group, an arms control symposium that generally traveled to the U.S.S.R. once a year. Jack asked that Brent be received at the policy-making level for a frank, informal, non-binding exchange.

Soon after Andropov's death, Senators Bill Cohen and Joe Biden also visited Moscow. Upon their return, they reported to the White House and played back to us the Soviet line developed for congressional visitors, which was that the Soviets doubted our sincerity and urged that we give them a signal of some sort, such as ratifying the Threshold Test Ban and Peaceful Nuclear Explosions treaties. But also, significantly, they said that any U.S. proposals in arms control should be conveyed through private channels. The Soviets, they said, had dismissed Reagan's January speech, deeming it to be election-year rhetoric. They remained deeply suspicious of us.

The importance of a back channel and quiet diplomacy was clear. Otherwise, the Soviets would think anything we said was simply grandstanding for domestic consumption. Moreover, it was conceivable that Chernenko saw some benefit to his personal interests in engaging the United States in serious talks. The trick was to avoid unilateral concessions while getting him to focus on our agenda. The President decided to open a quiet dialogue through a letter and see how it developed. Meanwhile, we determined how best to proceed in the four areas the President had outlined as the topics of engagement with Moscow. On regional issues, we proceeded to institute private talks among experts on the Middle East, Latin America, Africa and Asia. In the area of human rights, we decided to continue to stress the prominent cases, such as Shcharansky, Andrei Sakharov and Yuri Orlov, as well as the general levels of Jewish emigration. In the bilateral area, we decided to push for talks to prevent another KAL incident, as well as to push for the opening of consulates in Kiev and New York. As for arms control, my advice to the President was contained in a memo I sent to him in early 1984: "We should not make concessions to bring them back to START and INF, nor should we create obstacles to their return. Resumption of talks will be accelerated if our allies are firm, major defense programs proceed, the walkout is not rewarded, and domestic pressures are controlled."

As to channels, we decided to keep up an active exchange of letters between Reagan and Chernenko, and to engage as well the Shultz-Dobrynin channel and one between our ambassador Arthur Hartman and Soviet Foreign Minister Andrei Gromyko.

This course was set at a meeting between the President and his senior advisers in the Treaty Room of the residence on March 2, 1984.

That same day, Chernenko gave his first speech as General Secretary, assaulting the United States for seeking "world domination" and citing in particular our "invasion of Lebanon, occupation of Grenada and the undeclared war on Nicaragua." His words were fiery, but his manner told the tale of his condition. He stumbled repeatedly and embarrassingly over his text.

Four days later, Reagan sent a letter to Chernenko, indicating that he believed "an improvement in United States-Soviet relations is feasible," and stressing "the importance of communicating with you directly and confidentially." On March 8, he wrote Brent Scowcroft, asking him to discuss with senior Soviet leaders "our current thinking on possible ways to improve the relationship and in particular to reduce the levels of nuclear arms. As you know, I attach the highest importance to making progress in this vital area."

It is important to recognize that the purpose of establishing a White House-Kremlin channel was to get results; historically, the Soviets had not taken traffic in normal diplomatic channels as authoritative. The channel was not to outflank or undermine the Secretary of State, who was party to all exchanges.

Reagan actually hoped to get Scowcroft in to speak to Chernenko himself. In New York, Jack Matlock met once again with Stanislav Menshikov at Harry's New York Bar and stressed the importance of the Scowcroft visit as a portent for establishing a better dialogue on arms control issues. Menshikov assured him that Moscow was interested in exploring ideas on START and INF privately and unofficially. All indicators were that the meeting would happen. The only thing needed was for George Shultz to call Ambassador Dobrynin and send a high-level signal that Scowcroft was a private emissary of the President and should be received for a meeting with the General Secretary.

Disappointingly, Shultz never made the call. Brent arrived in Moscow and informed the foreign ministry that he was carrying a message for Chernenko from Reagan, but no one seemed to know what he was talking about. Shultz had not wanted to let the diplomacy with the Soviet Union leave his own channel. It was a petty reaction, and because of it, an opportunity to advance our agenda with Chernenko was lost. Reagan was frustrated; to him, it was another example of his State Department missing the point.

In truth, however, Chernenko was so much in decline from the first day of his rule that there was virtually no energy in Soviet governance and no agility for new initiatives after the walkout in 1983. Most of 1984 consisted of a series of desultory exchanges between the White House and the Kremlin that scarcely moved matters forward. It was essentially a tactical year, but as such, it was important.

The issue that came to dominate the agenda for the spring and summer was the Soviet proposal to open "discussions that could lead to negotiations" on space arms. They referred very specifically to their desire to prevent the "militarization of space." It was a deliberate semantic choice, referring to the Strategic Defense Initiative, and one which we, of course, were not about to accept. Nevertheless, Moscow was undoubtedly taken aback when we came back on June 30, a day after their proposal, with a statement that we were prepared to meet in September to begin talks on the reduction of nuclear weapons. As we expected, Chernenko fired off a letter to Reagan saying that we had not answered their request for negotiations on preventing the militarization of outer space. In response, Reagan wrote back to urge an effort to make progress on arms control and reaffirming our willingness to meet in Vienna for talks without preconditions.

Clearly, we were demonstrating much more flexibility and ability to engage than were the Soviets. From that point on, Moscow appeared to make a deliberate decision to hunker down and wait out the next few months in the hope that Reagan would not be re-elected, and they could start over from a position of strength with a new President—a liberal one—in the White House. They even turned down the cold war temperature a degree by boycotting the Olympic Games in Los Angeles in July.

In September, Gromyko came to the White House and conferred with Ronald Reagan. Given that Gromyko was the man who had been the keeper of the Soviet foreign policy flame for nearly 40 years, a man obsessed with the relationship with Washington and convinced of his nation's and system's superiority, it was hardly expected to be a useful meeting. Indeed, Gromyko, already in his dotage, merely used the occasion to give Reagan the standard Soviet tongue-lashing about American imperialism. Adroitly, Reagan turned the lecture back at Gromyko, ticking off the countries where Moscow had overturned governments and backed Marxist rebels for the last 15 years. Yet while stressing the new U.S. approach of realism toward the Soviet Union, he also held the door open for dialogue: "You and I disagree profoundly on the best way to organize society and in our basic philosophy of life," Reagan said. "Neither of us is going to change his view, but there is no reason we cannot lead our countries into a more stable and cooperative relationship. Our people need it; the world expects it of us as the two superpowers who hold the fate of the world in our hands."

In early November 1984, on the heels of KAL and the INF deployments, the Soviet Union suffered another serious setback on the international scene. After lengthy negotiations, Cuba agreed to pull its troops out of Angola in return for South Africa's withdrawal of its troops from Namibia. Communism was beating a retreat from southern Africa, and the West had successfully rolled back one of Moscow's imperialist gains. Chet Crocker, the Assistant Secretary of State for Africa, deserves great credit for his tenacious diplomacy, which over eight years of efforts, led to the Cuban withdrawal and laid the foundation for political reform in South Africa. Chet Crocker ought to be a giant figure in the modern history of southern Africa. He is regrettably much undersung.

When the election results flowed in to Reagan campaign headquarters on the night of November 6, it was already early morning in Moscow. As the Kremlin leaders rose from their beds and headed for their offices that day, they knew that in Washington nothing had changed. In Moscow, however, everything was changing, slowly, almost invisibly, but with grim inevitability. The Soviet Union, in more senses than one, was heading for the dawn of a new day.

—

In December 1984, British Prime Minister Margaret Thatcher had a visit in London from a new young man on the Moscow scene, a 53-year-old Politburo member named Mikhail Gorbachev. Energetic, articulate, a snappy dresser, and more attuned to Western styles and attitudes than most official Russians of the day, Gorbachev made a favorable impression on the formidable Mrs. Thatcher, who declared after the meeting that he was "a man one could do business with."

This phrase was immediately snatched up and disseminated globally by the media, in contexts implying that Mrs. Thatcher was a gullible woman foolishly charmed by a smooth-talking communist whose intentions could not, as any hardheaded man would know, be honorable. In reality, nothing could have been further from the truth. Margaret Thatcher was not a woman whose head was about to be turned by a glib tongue and a good-looking suit. In fact, she pointedly said in her statement that "there is no doubt that [Gorbachev] is completely loyal to the Soviet system, but he is prepared to listen and have a genuine dialogue and make up his own mind." Moreover, in her letter to Reagan, she said, ". . . the overriding impression left was that the Russians are genuinely fearful of the immense cost of having to keep up with a further American technological advance and are therefore prepared to negotiate seriously on nuclear weapons if they believe that you are politically committed to reductions." Mrs. Thatcher told Reagan much the same in a meeting the two had shortly before Christmas. The Soviets were seriously worried about SDI.

That the spokesman for these impressions was Mikhail Gorbachev was more significant than any of us could have known at the time. Gorbachev was not just any member of the Politburo—he was one with a singularly important future. In a recent conversation, Roald Sagdeev, a leading member of the Soviet Academy of Sciences and a principal at the USA-Canada Institute, told me that following Andropov's death in 1984, Gorbachev had very nearly been elevated to the General Secretary's post, but had fallen just short of a majority. The post had gone to Chernenko to prevent further wrangling and delays that would have given the impression of disarray in the Kremlin; Gorbachev, however, was virtually promised the top post upon Chernenko's demise, which was considered not very far off even within the circle of the Politburo.

And indeed, on March 9, 1985, only 13 months after he came into office, Konstantin Chernenko died. Americans picking up their newspapers at breakfast the next day saw the image of yet another new Soviet General Secretary plastered across the front page— Mikhail Gorbachev.

Once again, George Bush flew to Moscow for the funeral. Meanwhile, at home, the appointment of the new General Secretary was giving rise to hopes and optimism that a change in U.S.-Soviet relations was in the offing. Gorbachev, as a member of a younger generation, three generations removed from the revolution, was believed to be more pragmatic than his aged predecessors and less encumbered with the baggage of Leninist orthodoxy. Although he was undeniably a committed communist, having risen through party ranks in time-honored tradition, he was intelligent, well-traveled and, the CIA believed, open to influence. Given these factors, combined with his remarks to Margaret Thatcher in December, Gorbachev's ascendance just two days before the resumption of arms control talks after a year and a half of silence was taken as a positive development.

Preparations for the talks had consumed most of my time from the day that the President had received Konstantin Chernenko's letter in November 1984, expressing Soviet willingness to return to the table. All of December, I had worked with the senior arms control group to engender a spirit of goodwill and enthusiasm for resumed talks. On December 20, I sent out a memo inviting Shultz, Weinberger, Ken Adelman, the director of the Arms Control and Disarmament Agency, Bill Casey and the JCS and others to comment on what ought to go into our position for the meeting with Gromyko on resuming Geneva talks. When I received their responses, I had the staff identify areas where compromise was possible, and headed out to Palm Springs with the President for Christmas. Before our first meeting there, I sent him the papers I had received from the others, along with a memo:

"We have reached the climax of our preparations for Geneva. As a footnote, looking back on other preparations during the Nixon and Ford administrations, this has been by far the smoothest. This . . . has been the consequence of your willingness to invest a substantial amount of time in listening to opposing viewpoints among your cabinet officers as they arose, and providing firm guidance on your thinking. This means that today, we have put behind us virtually all of the problems. It is true that a few remain, but I expect we can resolve these here in Palm Springs.

"As you know, we have two purposes. First, we want to get Soviet agreement to open formal talks within a month or so on the entire family of nuclear arms control issues; in short to establish the format or procedures under which we will do business in the coming months. Second, we want to begin a process of education and persuasion with regard to your view of how together we can agree on a road which will lead us toward less reliance on offensive systems and more on defensive systems. This latter goal represents a truly historic initiative. For a generation the world has lived under the surreal notion that we are better off being unable to defend ourselves under a balance of terror. Your concept of changing that has provoked enormous public interest and criticism. But there is no question that you have the moral high ground with the American people. In order to assure that we keep it that way, we have been preparing a "public affairs blitz" involving your speaking to the nation, and a widespread campaign involving dozens of spokesmen inside and outside of government who will carry the gospel into the 14 major media markets in the next three months. I intend to meet with the network news directors next week to state plainly that this issue is of such historic importance as to warrant a truly vigorous national debate, and that you have directed me to make available to them our full cooperation in presenting our rationale and technical concept. As a separate but related matter, you have thrown the left into an absolute tizzy. They are left in the position of advocating the most bloodthirsty strategy—Mutual Assured Destruction—as a means to keep the peace."

I explained also why we ought to avoid talking to the Soviets under a rubric which included our virtually non-nuclear SDI, but let them off the hook for their very sophisticated nuclear ABM program. Instead, I recommended that we propose talking about nuclear offensive and nuclear defensive arms.

In California, I had a long session with the President to go over this material and then moderated sessions with Reagan, Shultz and Weinberger. On the afternoon of New Year's Eve, we met at Sunnylands, the estate of Walter Annenberg, founder of *TV Guide* and a well-known philanthropist and friend of Reagan's. We sat in the library, and everyone was in casual attire. Cap, predictably, wanted the line held on one or two levels of force, but the arguments were not shrill, and within 24 hours we had all come to an agreement on the language to be approved by the President as the instructions Shultz would carry to Geneva to negotiate with the Soviets. They were issued in the form of NSDD 153 of January 1, 1985, in which President Reagan set forth a comprehensive elaboration of the post-war history of U.S. strategic doctrine and the Soviet response to it. It also laid out the fundamental rationale for SDI research and made the following foundational point: "... the overriding importance of SDI to the United States is that it offers the possibility of radically altering the dangerous trends [of ever-growing offensive arsenals] by moving to a better, more stable basis for deterrence, and by providing new and compelling incentives to the Soviet Union for seriously negotiating reductions in existing nuclear arsenals.

"The Soviet Union fully recognizes that the SDI program—and most especially that portion of the program [associated with space technologies]—offers the prospect of permitting the U.S. technologically to flank years of Soviet defensive investment and to shift the 'state of the art' in defenses into areas of comparative U.S. advantage."

On January 7, George Shultz and I traveled with a small party to Geneva, Switzerland. I was anxious and expectant. We had a reached a point where I felt our leverage was as great as it would ever be. I was confident that, after four years of increases, defense appropriations were going to start declining again. It was vital that we take full advantage of this optimal moment.

In the first plenary session, the issue, as I had anticipated, quickly became an argument over how defensive systems would be treated in any future negotiations. Specifically, the Soviets wished to have their defensive systems excluded. Their defensive systems consisted of ground-based nuclear interceptors—a missile on the ground that shot upward to hit a warhead in space. In their judgment, however, such traditional interceptors were not the problem; the problem was space arms, the militarization of the heavens, opening up an entirely new domain of warfare. In other words, SDI.

Shultz had carried most of the talks, which had been fairly routine with no surprises. But on this sticking point of the meaning of "space arms," I intervened. The Soviets were essentially attempting to exclude a huge category of their weapons systems—nuclear systems—from negotiations, while insisting on the inclusion of SDI, which was almost entirely non-nuclear.

"Let us be clear," I said. "Are you willing to accept that the issue is what weapons are designed to defeat offensive systems, regardless of how they're based?"

Gromyko's answer, in a nutshell, was "no."

"Well, then, we don't have a deal," I said. "That's out of the question."

We broke for a short while at that point, and George and I went out to consult. During the break, we received word from Washington about an unexpected change of personnel—White

House Chief of Staff Jim Baker and Treasury Secretary Don Regan had swapped jobs. We received the news with puzzlement, but I didn't give it any more than a passing thought at the time.

It was important to urge George to stand firm on the issue of defensive arms. "We can win on this," I said to him. "There's no way that they can justify keeping an entire panoply of ground-based interceptors out of these talks. They're nuclear weapons, first of all. These are not just interceptors; they have nuclear warheads on them, and the idea is to reduce the number of nuclear warheads. SDI is essentially non-nuclear; we've got the moral high ground on this."

George nodded in agreement. "OK," he said. We went back in and he presented our position to Gromyko. "We're willing to undertake negotiations for the reduction of nuclear and space arms, bearing in mind that 'space arms' encompasses space-based systems or ground-based systems."

There was some more haggling and to-ing and fro-ing on the subject, but in the end, the Soviet side finally agreed to our formulation. With agreement reached, we turned matters over to the drafters who would write up the formal terms and language of agreement for Shultz's and Gromyko's final signature the next day. Richard Perle from Defense and Roz Ridgway, the Assistant Secretary of State for European affairs, stayed up the better part of the night with their Soviet counterparts working over that draft, a tedious and demanding job that they performed with great skill. On January 8, we formally announced that the United States and the Soviet Union had agreed to reconvene promptly talks oriented toward the reduction of nuclear and space arms.

After the formal statement was issued, I was tasked to go and debrief some of our key allies on the meeting. The first stop was London, for a meeting with Prime Minister Thatcher.

From the outset, Margaret Thatcher had been concerned about the prospect of the Strategic Defense Initiative and the fear that it might bring about a strategic decoupling of the United States from its allies across the Atlantic, who lived several thousand miles closer to the Soviet Union and its nuclear missiles than we. She had been forthright about expressing her displeasure, and had done so persistently both immediately after SDI was launched in March 1983 and on several occasions since then. In December 1984, shortly before Christmas, she had paid President Reagan a visit at Camp David to brief him on her recent meeting with Gorbachev. Gorbachev was concerned about SDI, she reported. And so was she, and the other allies. She delivered a stern lecture to Reagan on European concerns about SDI and its potential to undermine 40 years of post-war NATO strategy. What she wanted from Reagan, she said, was a statement, something to reassure the allies.

Reagan admired Thatcher. He and she were ideological soulmates and had a strong relationship; it was important to him that she trust him, and remain his strong ally and good friend. To meet her needs, her assistant Charles Powell and I prepared a statement that identified SDI as a research program and promised that any deployment would be negotiated and terms agreed upon among the allies. The statement, which seemed to satisfy Mrs. Thatcher, was read to a press pool at Camp David. But afterward, the President pulled me aside. "Bud, you know, she's really missing the point on SDI," he said. "And she's doing us a lot of damage with all this sniping about it.

"Why don't you see if you can't find a way to get her to come off this position, or at least modify it a little bit?" the President urged.

Three weeks after our session at Camp David, I met with the Prime Minister in her office at No. 10 Downing Street. She listened with interest to my report on the talks with Gromyko, but no sooner had I finished than she embarked on the same sort of lecture against SDI that she had delivered to President Reagan at Camp David. First, there was the risk of splitting the United States from NATO, she said. Second, there was the risk of appearing to be seeking a first-strike capability, which would be destabilizing. Third, there was technological risk; there were no guarantees the system would work. And fourth, it would cost pots of money that the United States ought to be spending on other things.

She came up for air then, and I seized the moment. "Prime Minister," I said, "the President believes that there may be as much as $300 million a year in SDI research and development that ought to be subcontracted to British firms." We were willing to subcontract work to most of the allies as a means of providing them with some financial benefits and alleviating opposition to the Strategic Defense Initiative.

Mrs. Thatcher sat up and brightened a bit. She looked at me, she looked away. At last she looked back at me and said: "You know, there may be something to this after all!"

A month later, Prime Minister Thatcher visited the United States, addressed the United States Congress and voiced her support for President Ronald Reagan's Strategic Defense Initiative.

But she never fully let me off the hook. The G-7 economic summit was held in May in Bonn, West Germany, that year and on the day before the conferences got underway there was a reception for the delegates in a grand palace on the outskirts of Bonn. The minute I walked through the door, I saw the Prime Minister detach herself from the group she was with across the room and make a beeline straight for me. "Now, Bud," she began from several feet away, without even saying hello, "are you keeping SDI under appropriate restraint, adhering to the ABM treaty and so forth?"

"Yes, Prime Minister," I replied. "Things are on course." She nodded with satisfaction and walked off. No doubt about it, she was and is a formidable—and brilliant—political leader.

———

Immediately after Mikhail Gorbachev came to power in the Soviet Union, President Reagan invited him to a summit conference in the United States. The message was hand-carried to Moscow by Vice President George Bush on the occasion of Chernenko's funeral. Gorbachev responded a few weeks later in a letter leaving open the possibility of a summit—though not in Washington. But from the time this new leader took office and the new negotiations got under way in Geneva, a summit clearly was what everyone in Washington—and no doubt Moscow—had in mind.

For Reagan, things were going very well at this stage. The Geneva talks had opened on March 12. On March 28, the House of Representatives voted to approve Reagan's request for 21 additional MX missiles, a critical victory that was bound to have an effect on the Soviets in both Moscow and Geneva. It was a good time for the administration to signal its openness to a meeting with Gorbachev, and in early April we did so.

At that point, I began to send the President in-depth papers, one a week, about 10 pages in length, on various themes in Russian and Soviet history. They included subjects such as the role of the Communist Party, the role of the military, the role of the secret police, Gorbachev's personality, Soviet ties to Eastern Europe, the Soviet/Russian view of their place in the world, and their image of the United States. There were 25 such papers in all, prepared by

Jack Matlock with help from the CIA and the State Department. Reagan read the papers enthusiastically. A few days after I sent him the first one, he brought it in to a national security meeting. It was heavily marked up, and he said, "This is terrific. Don, did you read this?" he asked, turning to Don Regan. And then to George Shultz, "George, I want you to read this." He had me pass the papers around to the others because he was so impressed by them. He became a near-Russophile over the course of the next six months, studying each paper thoroughly and waiting eagerly for the next. President Reagan was clearly determined to be thoroughly prepared for his first meeting with a Soviet head of state. He worked hard, and by the time he reached Geneva, was thoroughly in command of his brief.

He was determined that such a meeting would take place, but we weren't about to let the Soviets think we were too anxious. After the Bonn economic summit, George Shultz and I went to Vienna for another meeting with the increasingly grumpy Gromyko, who undoubtedly saw his star in jeopardy with the rise of a new generation in Moscow. Our job in Vienna was to try to speed up matters relating to our four-part agenda of bilateral issues, regional issues, human rights and arms control. We were also to try to get a commitment for a summit, if possible, but without being the *demandeurs*. I had urged the President to have us take a low-key approach; it would put more pressure on the Soviets if we appeared indifferent to a summit. The President had agreed.

Gromyko was in an exceptionally contrary mood in Vienna. This was more than his usual intransigence; it suggested a preoccupation in Moscow with other matters. He adopted a hardline approach to all the items on our agenda and seemed unwilling to compromise in any significant area. Perhaps he was expecting us to react as our predecessors had, to search for a compromise and ultimately yield to the Soviet position. However, we didn't. At the end of the day, Gromyko was in a state of visible angst. He turned to Shultz and remarked that Shultz had made no mention of a summit meeting. Shultz shrugged and asked if Gromyko had anything to say on the subject. Gromyko, tight-lipped, said "No."

The next day was much the same. We worried our way through the 27 items on our agenda and Gromyko didn't give an inch. At the end of the day, he asked again whether we had anything to say about a meeting. Shultz shrugged again. At that, Gromyko came unstuck.

"Let's talk privately," he said, and he and George went into a private room where they spent about 15 minutes. Gromyko pressed again about discussing a summit, but Shultz responded that there was no point to that discussion when no progress had been made on the agenda. It had not been George's instinct to hold back on the issue, but he managed it exceptionally well.

Within weeks, Gorbachev agreed to meet Ronald Reagan in Geneva in November 1985 for the first U.S.-Soviet summit conference in six and a half years.

———

Although preparations for the summit were foremost on my mind as the summer of 1985 got underway, several events occurred that proved powerful distractions. On June 14, TWA flight 847 out of Athens, with 153 passengers and crew on board, 135 of them American, was hijacked by members of the Islamic Jihad, a radical Iranian-backed terrorist faction, and forced to fly to Beirut International Airport. In the White House, the tense drama that ensued absorbed our attention and demanded most of our energies for the next two weeks. The terrorists demanded the release of more than seven hundred Palestinian prisoners in Israel in exchange for the American hostages. Ironically, Israel had already been planning to release those very prisoners, but, properly, backed away from its intentions rather than be viewed as succumbing to terrorist pressure.

The hijacking was a vivid test of Ronald Reagan's anti-terrorist policy, which declared to the world the United States' refusal to make deals with terrorists and its determination to deal firmly with states that sponsored them. Many lives were at stake, and the world was watching nervously. The hijackers' murderous intentions and volatility were underscored by the cold-blooded killing of U.S. Navy diver Robert Dean Stethem, whose body was tossed onto the tarmac by the terrorists in a chilling display of indifference to human dignity.

After the plane had sat several days on the runway in Beirut, Shia Muslim leader Nabih Berri negotiated having the hostages turned over to his custody. I had met with Berri during my months in Beirut as the Middle East envoy, and knew him to be a very canny, self-interested figure, a kind of Nicely Nicely of West Beirut. He immediately saw the hostage situation as an opportunity to become a hero in the Arab world by obtaining the release of the Palestinian prisoners in Israel. When the hostages were turned over to him, I proposed to the President that I call Berri to relieve him of that notion. I made clear to him that the United States was not going to lean on Israel to release anybody, and that contrary to his expectations, he would be branded as the person responsible for the continued captivity of so many Palestinians—and Americans.

My call seemed to have some effect, in the sense that Berri began to defer to Hafez al-Assad in Damascus and to move away from his public stance of asserting his authority. Of course, that meant we were now dealing with Assad, which was not necessarily an improvement. We entered a week of intense exchanges between President Reagan and the Syrian leader, including one phone call, as well as discussions with the Israelis, who indicated they would release the prisoners as planned once the hostage crisis was resolved, but would not allow any linkage of the prisoners' release to the release of the hostages.

These exchanges, combined with a surprise call to Assad from Iranian Speaker of the House Hashemi Rafsanjani, encouraging the release of the hostages, finally led to a happy outcome. The hostages were let go unharmed. During the ensuing months, the Israeli government released its Palestinian prisoners back into Lebanon.

At the White House, some of us mulled the significance of the telephone call from Rafsanjani. What did this gesture mean? Was Rafsanjani already sensing that his country's theocratic crusade was a bad idea, and that to isolate himself from the West was economically misguided? Did he hope to change policy in Tehran, and was he sending some kind of signal to the United States of openness to change?

We had no answers to these questions, but they were on my mind. The status of Iran was an issue that had occupied me from my earliest days in the Reagan White House. The question of an Iranian succession following the death of the Ayatollah Khomeini was one of the first subjects I had wanted the crisis pre-planning group to look into when I formed it in 1982. In my first memo on the Middle East as National Security Adviser to President Reagan, I had written: "Our position on the Iran-Iraq war is also extremely sensitive. . . . I do not think we should undertake actions which could be seen as a clear tilt toward Iraq, unless Iraq is on the losing end of the fight. As hostile as the current government of Iran is, that country remains a strategically decisive one; we do not therefore want to burn all of our bridges, particularly to those elements which will be of interest to us in any post-Khomeini succession struggle."

These concerns made me receptive to the possibility of getting some answers about Iran, a possibility that was laid before me on July 3, when Israel's David Kimche walked into my office. It was just a few days after the end of the TWA crisis, but the beginning of the most fateful series of events of my life.

Early in August, I traveled to Vienna for meetings with Roelof "Pik" Botha, the South African Foreign Minister and former Ambassador to the United States, with whom I had worked ten years before. The meeting was arranged to discuss South African progress toward ending apartheid and bringing the black majority into a representative government. The promises Botha made to me there—of several liberalizing measures affecting the daily lives of blacks— were measures he believed in, but as it turned out, could not deliver on. The commitments he made in Vienna were later overturned by South African President P.W. Botha.

We spent most of the rest of August in Santa Barbara. Feeling we had been betrayed by South Africa and conscious of the need for a severe response, I worked on a proposal for preemptive sanctions, which I promoted forcefully with Reagan. He had always resisted the idea of sanctions, but I finally persuaded him that South Africa's recent show of bad faith had been the last straw in its defiance of world opprobrium and that Reagan's action was needed to forestall even stronger measures by the Congress.

Otherwise, the flow of news while we were in California was so slow that Presidential spokesman Larry Speakes was reduced to briefing the reporters every day on the President's intention to go out and cut some brush for exercise. His statements became so predictable that one day, when he said he would forgo a statement and take questions from the reporters, CBS's Bill Plante shot him the wiseguy query: "Larry, are you bringing in fresh brush for the President to cut today?"

I was busy working on our policy toward South Africa when I got a call from John Poindexter saying the Congress was demanding responses to news media charges that my NSC staff—that is, Ollie North—was violating the Boland Amendment in providing assistance to the contras in Nicaragua. It was the first major sign of

trouble in the second area of the impending crisis that would overwhelm me a year later.

———

I returned from Santa Barbara a little ahead of the Presidential
party so that Jonny and I could go down to New Market, Virginia, to
close on a log cabin we had bought there as a weekend retreat. We
enjoyed a few days of respite from work and the daily grind, but
soon enough I was back into it, with a vengeance.

In mid-August, we had been receiving signals from the Soviet
embassy that Moscow was dismayed at the slow pace of preparations for the summit; they complained that nothing seemed to be getting done. Sergei Rogov, a Soviet policy guru at the USA-Canada
Institute, indicated privately that Moscow was preparing to take a
position calling for deep cuts in offensive forces, less restrictive defi-
nitions for research and testing bans, and a more liberal verification
regime than the Soviets had heretofore accepted. In addition, the
Soviets were looking for a way to negotiate behind the scenes.
Rogov's report stated that the Soviets "feel that McFarlane has taken
charge of foreign policy and thus [the Soviets] are looking for the
sort of relationship they had in the past [in the early 1970s]."

We stepped up the pace of our work. I will always remember the
autumn of 1985 as the busiest period of my life. In the two and a
half months running up to the summit conference in Geneva, scheduled for November 19-21, I worked even harder than I had before,
harder, probably, than I ever had or would again. I met more than
100 times with the President, managed 11 meetings of the National
Security Council, and chaired at least 71 meetings with State and
Defense on arms control, human rights, bilateral issues, and regional
issues—the whole gamut of issues that would be discussed in
Geneva—to put together our agenda of positions.

My mission from September onward was to build support for
these positions among three constituencies: the allies in Europe, the
American people, and the Congress. To do that, I launched another
public affairs blitz. The President's role was to build support on the
open stage, in a series of speeches. Meanwhile, I worked behind the
scenes to lay the groundwork for him to build on: I held backgrounders for the press, one-on-one sessions with columnists, interviews with reporters. This was not merely a political gambit; it was

vital that the President arrive in Geneva with the clear power behind him to back up what he was saying with appropriations and concrete action. Americans needed to understand what was happening so they could support the agenda.

We held 13 bipartisan leadership meetings with Congress and a dozen other ad hoc congressional sessions during which I would brief members and take questions and spend endless hours explaining the President's agenda and trying to solidify bipartisan congressional support.

In late September, President Reagan met in Washington with the new Soviet foreign minister, Eduard Shevardnadze. Shevardnadze, part of the Gorbachev new guard, had replaced Andrei Gromyko on July 1. It was a change warmly welcomed in Washington. Because Gromyko had so thoroughly dominated Soviet foreign policy for so long, it was obvious that there would never be any opportunity to change it, or for Gorbachev to get any credit for Soviet foreign policy initiatives, as long as the fierce old hardliner was in charge. The Politburo seized on the pretext of the INF deployments and the Geneva walkout to kick Gromyko upstairs and put a new man in charge.

Shevardnadze struck me as a sentimental man, the virtual opposite of the calculating, Machiavellian Gromyko. He was a Georgian who had grown up in the party system and had been the authoritarian party boss of Georgia, but it almost seemed that he did not entirely have his heart in it. He seemed to have come to Washington to convey a message of desperate hope, the hope that we would understand the severity of economic decline in the Soviet Union and the dangerous disharmony in our communications that had occurred during the two government transitions his country had undergone in the last two years. His manner was very nearly pleading as he spoke to Reagan of the need for the United States to understand the Soviet Union's wish for peace. He acknowledged the disagreements in basic beliefs that Reagan had outlined, but he said with earnestness that he believed Washington and Moscow could work together, and had to do so "for the sake of our children."

It was the first time we had met a Soviet who seemed open to genuine change. The President was greatly buoyed, and came away from the meeting more optimistic than he had been, ready to put his heart into preparing for the summit.

Meanwhile, I traveled overseas to work with the allies. I briefed

Prime Minister Thatcher and President Mitterrand over the weekend of September 29 and 30 to make certain they were on board with our positions. Their commitment to our stand was proven a few days later, on October 3, when Gorbachev visited France and called for separate arms control talks between the Soviet Union and the West Europeans. Gratifyingly, Mitterrand rejected the proposal out of hand.

On October 12, Jack Matlock, in the private channel, had a candid discussion with Stanislav Menshikov, who told him that the Soviets were offering to come to terms in Geneva at a 50-percent cut in warheads, with a separate reduction for intermediate-range nuclear forces. We were getting somewhere.

President Reagan traveled to the United Nations on October 24 to address the General Assembly, where he delivered a speech citing five countries where communism was at war with the people, and further explaining the summit agenda to the public. He then held a positive meeting with the other G-7 leaders—Thatcher, Mitterrand, West Germany's Helmut Kohl, Bettino Craxi of Italy, Prime Minister Nakasone of Japan, and Canada's Brian Mulroney. All the leaders offered their support for our Geneva positions, and feelings of solidarity ran high. Reagan received a rousing send-off from the group that was underlined by Mrs. Thatcher's words: "You are our champion. There can be no question of separating the U.S. from its allies."

In mid-October, as the pace of activity quickened further, a group of terrorists seized a cruise ship in the Mediterranean and murdered an elderly, disabled passenger, Leon Klinghoffer. The hijacking of the *Achille Lauro* was resolved with the dramatic seizure of the terrorists after four U.S. Air Force fighter jets intercepted the airliner on which they sought to escape to Rome.

Strangely, Cap Weinberger opposed this use of force—even against terrorists caught in the act—for fear of the anti-U.S. reaction in Arab capitals.

On November 2, George Shultz and I flew to Moscow for advance meetings in preparation for the summit. Shultz and I were anxious to meet Gorbachev, who was getting so much positive billing in the West European press. And indeed, Gorbachev in person was quite impressive; he was a skilled performer of great energy. He seemed to want to present a contrasting image to that of his predecessors, to portray himself as a man with a strong intellectual grasp, who knew a great deal about the United States and was a canny negotiator. His style was certainly formidable—he pounded the table, leaned forward in earnestness, and maintained strong eye contact.

Unfortunately, what he had to say did not match his imposing presentation. In fact, it was very weak, especially his commentary on the United States. He spent about 45 minutes in the first session seeking to impress us with his knowledge of the United States. He was not intimidated by the strength of our economy, he said. Our false sense of security came from the propaganda put forth by our military-industrial complex, which was the foundation of our economy and the basis for our imperialist policy. By dint of its disproportionate influence, the military-industrial complex, Gorbachev said, had come to dominate our system, and without it the United States would suffer extreme unemployment and would collapse.

Shultz and I were taken aback by this wrongheaded monologue. It was not an impressive presentation to make to the man who had been president of the University of Chicago School of Business and another who was a 20-year veteran of the U.S. Marine Corps.

Shultz turned to me. "Bud," he said, "why don't you tell the General Secretary about the role of the military in our society." I began with a brief primer that included the fact that our military industry accounts for only about six percent of the U.S. gross national product.

At that, it was Gorbachev's turn to look taken aback. "That can't be right," he said.

I assured him it was, and also pointed out that our military is constitutionally controlled by the civilian leadership, and that it has never been involved in the governance of our country.

This seemed to make Gorbachev even more uncomfortable. He had to be concerned about the quality of the staffwork he was getting. But he skirted the issue and moved on to SDI. He went into a long critique of the initiative and its destabilizing potential. The Soviet Union could counter, he insisted, and would counter it, by building more and more offensive weapons systems. He spoke forcefully, but his manner grew agitated. He sat on the edge of his chair and shifted his arms on the table; he was without a doubt a man discussing something that genuinely worried him, a man looking at the potential expenditure of huge amounts of money to cope with SDI.

In the years since, we've learned that before Gorbachev came to power, and soon after the announcement of SDI, an intense debate had developed between the military and civilian leadership of the Soviet Union. The military, led by Marshal Ogarkov, had insisted that notwithstanding SDI, the coming battle between East and West would be a conventional battle, and had insisted on budget increases for conventional forces. The civilian leadership had argued for putting increased spending into countering SDI, the funds for which would have to be drained from conventional forces. Ogarkov lost that battle and was fired shortly after Gorbachev came into office. The need for money to deal with SDI was more compelling.

Gorbachev knew how pressed his economy was; his hope was to reduce arms to the level where no increase in defense expenditures would be necessary. But SDI was standing in the way. This was good for our side.

Shultz and I returned from Moscow on November 6, buoyed by the sense that, while Gorbachev had a lot to learn, he was eager to engage and had the incentive to try to ease the pressures on his own economy, and that, moreover, he had the political skill to accomplish that.

The time for the summit was drawing near. At my suggestion, President Reagan called former President Richard Nixon the week before we left for a discussion of how to proceed in Geneva. I had maintained a correspondence with President Nixon for a number of years and had recently written him laying out my hopes for an agreement for a 50-percent arms reduction at the summit. Nixon had replied with a four-page *tour de force* suggesting an approach to take in Moscow and suggesting that he write a letter to the President with the same advice—which he had done on November 14. Reagan had a high regard for the former President, and the telephone call was valuable in reinforcing Reagan in his positions and boosting his confidence.

———

We started out for Geneva on Saturday, November 16. Right off the bat, we had to deal with a gratuitous jibe from Cap Weinberger. From the time the summit had been announced, Weinberger and his Defense Department had worried about what the President might give up to the Soviet Union in Geneva. The Secretary would not be accompanying the President to the summit, and in the Pentagon fears ran rampant that the "McFarlane-Shultz cabal" might persuade the President to give away the store. But in the many Arms Control

Working Group sessions I had chaired in the previous month, I had been careful to hold the line against concessionary pressures from the State Department, something both Richard Perle and Fred Ikle had acknowledged. And in the meantime, we had been receiving intelligence reports and other indications that the Soviets were willing to commit to a 50-percent reduction in nuclear warheads—our position.

Still, on the day we left, there on the front page of *The New York Times* was a story reporting a letter Weinberger had sent to Reagan urging him to stand firm in Geneva. I had no doubt that Perle or even Weinberger himself had leaked the letter. To be fair, it probably had a useful effect on Gorbachev for him to know that the pressure in the United States was coming from the right, justifying Reagan's taking a hard line. But it angered Reagan. He thought the leak unnecessary, a signal that someone didn't think he could handle the account and that he needed a public goading to keep him in line. It represented lack of confidence in him and a breach of teamplay.

The day after we arrived in Geneva, Reagan took a walk around the site of the meetings in the Fleur d'Eau, a nineteenth-century chateau on the shores of Lake Geneva. Already the atmosphere was charged, full of anticipation. Reagan was in high spirits, crackling with energy; he had all his reading on the Soviet Union behind him, well-digested, and now he was itching to get started. He couldn't wait for the call: lights, camera, action. He was an actor, after all, and he was about to walk onto the most important sound stage of his life.

———

President Reagan and Secretary General Gorbachev opened the summit with a one-on-one meeting on the morning of November 19. Their private session lasted for 64 minutes. After some opening remarks, Gorbachev went straight to the jugular on SDI. For a full 45 minutes he went on passionately in an attempt to discourage Reagan from proceeding with the initiative. In the following plenary session, Gorbachev's concern about SDI was again made abundantly clear. Twice he raised the economic considerations surrounding the initiative. "Do you have money to burn?" he interrupted to demand at one point in the discussion. He remarked that his advisers had told him that a leading reason for U.S. interest in SDI was to have orders for our industry, which they estimated at $1 trillion.

"Why don't you believe that we won't attack you?" he asked.

"Why won't you believe that all I want is a shield?" Reagan countered.

"You are trying to catch the firebird with technology," Gorbachev said. "How can we go before the world and say we lost the chance for 50-percent reductions [in nuclear weapons] because we wouldn't stop research on space weapons?"

Reagan's response came easily.

"How can you defend missing a chance for 50-percent reductions because you were stubborn [about a] research [program]?" Reagan replied.

Throughout, Reagan stressed his belief in the importance of reducing nuclear weapons. He acknowledged the potential Soviet worry over our gaining a first-strike capability but said that we would open our labs so that they could assure themselves that we were not working toward that end. Reagan did not realize that our military and intelligence officials would never go along with the idea of open labs. The President also was dismissive of the fiscal implications. Because Gorbachev understood these to be real problems for Reagan, he had to conclude one of two things: either Reagan was being cynical with all his preaching about eliminating nuclear weapons, and his real intention was to bankrupt the Soviet system; or he was incredibly ignorant. Whatever Gorbachev concluded, the fact was he had to live with the reality of Ronald Reagan's total commitment to SDI, his extraordinary popularity and his ability to sustain an ever-growing SDI program.

An hour after the afternoon plenary session began, Reagan suddenly rose and invited Gorbachev to join him in some further private conversation in the chateau's small poolhouse beside the lake. Gorbachev readily agreed, and the two men set off on the short walk down a winding gravel path. On the way, they talked about Reagan's old movies. The President confessed to a little pique over a comment from Georgi Arbatov, head of Moscow's USA-Canada Institute, that Reagan had only made a few grade B movies. He had also made a few good ones, he said. Gorbachev mentioned that he had seen *King's Row* and enjoyed it very much.

The move to the poolhouse was meant to look spontaneous on Reagan's part, but in fact we had planned it the day before. I had suggested the idea of a second private conference to Jack Matlock, who had agreed that it would be the only way we would find out what Gorbachev's limits truly were. Mike Deaver had a fire built in the poolhouse before Reagan even extended his invitation.

The two men were alone in the poolhouse but for an interpreter for each side; the interpreters' notes served as the report of the meeting and the source of the descriptions and quotes presented here.

Once they were settled, Reagan gave Gorbachev a copy of the draft compromise I had given him earlier. Gorbachev looked it over and said that he agreed to the first section on 50-percent reductions in ballistic missile warheads, but only if SDI were foreclosed. He liked much of the second part on reducing INF systems, but it omitted the British and French systems and air-launched cruise missiles. In the third part, on space systems, he could not tell what we had in mind in terms of research. Lab research was one thing, but what about the construction of prototypes or samples or their testing?

The President acknowledged that it would be necessary to construct test vehicles and to test them; otherwise we would only have lab theories, which were insufficient. He believed that this problem could be covered by an "agreement" that the results of research and testing would be shared by all. It was an idea the President had promoted for two years, and which former President Nixon had encouraged.

Gorbachev then made an emotional appeal. "If the two sides are indeed searching for a way to halt the arms race and to begin to deal seriously with disarmament, then what would be the purpose of deploying a weapon that is as yet unknown and unpredictable?" he said. "It must be clearly understood that verification of such weapons would be totally unreliable because of their maneuverability and mobility, even if they were classified as defensive.

"People would not be in a position to determine what it was that would be placed into space and would surely regard it as an additional threat, thereby creating crisis situations. If the goal is to get rid of nuclear weapons, why start an arms race in another sphere?"

To which Reagan replied: "These are not weapons that kill people or destroy cities. These are weapons that destroy nuclear missiles.

"If there were an agreement that there would be no need for nuclear missiles, then one might agree that there would also be no need for defenses against them," Reagan said. "SDI is still years away from reality. Why then should we sit here in the meanwhile with mountains of weapons on each side?"

Gorbachev was not yet fully convinced. He understood the human sentiments Reagan was expressing, he said, but he had to face reality. If SDI were actually implemented, he said, "then layer after layer of offensive weapons, Soviet as well as U.S. weapons, would appear in outer space and only God himself would know what they were. In this connection, I would note that God provides information only very selectively and rarely."

The session lasted for an hour and five minutes. What was significant was Reagan's saying, for the first time, that if nuclear arms were reduced below a certain level, there wouldn't be a need for SDI. Gorbachev was certainly shrewd enough to pick up on the fact that the answer to his dilemma lay in deep reductions on the Soviet side.

To the rest of us, waiting in the chateau, the time seemed long. At one point, Dave Fisher, the President's personal assistant, called me and George Shultz aside and asked if he ought to go down to the poolhouse and break the session up. "They've been in there a long time," he said. George Shultz looked at him in disbelief. "Are you crazy?" he said. "That's the good news."

And it was. George and I met the President outside under the carport as he returned from the poolhouse. He stood there for a minute in his overcoat and scarf, looking like the cat who ate the canary. It had gone well, he said. He had asked Gorbachev to come to the United States, and the General Secretary had agreed. And he thought Gorbachev was finally accepting the idea that the U.S. was not going to back down on SDI.

That night, the Soviets hosted a dinner for the official delegation. Only about six people from our side were present: the President and Mrs. Reagan, Shultz, myself, Chief of Staff Don Regan and Arthur Hartmann, our Ambassador to Moscow. I was seated next to Raisa Gorbachev, the General Secretary's attractive wife. Mrs. Gorbachev, who was from a vastly different mold than her predecessors, was a well-educated woman and a voluble propagandist for her society. She was very proud of women's access to professions in the Soviet Union and the general breadth of opportunity she believed the U.S.S.R. fostered for them. She and I got into a spirited discussion of the subject. I acknowledged the legitimate framework of equality of opportunity for women in Soviet society, but I thought she was putting quite a gloss on Soviet society as a whole. We have excellent medicine, she was saying, wonderful science, premier universities.

"When do you think there will be a woman General Secretary?" I asked innocently. Raisa stiffened when the interpreter translated the question. Then, rather coldly, she replied, "We don't need woman General Secretary."

Trying to move quickly off an apparently touchy subject, I began to tell her how my wife and I had lived not far from Geneva many years before. We had come to appreciate so many things about Switzerland, I told her, including the wonderful Swiss chocolate. Again, she appeared to bridle.

"We have excellent chocolate in the Soviet Union," she said, as though I had been impugning the quality of Russian bonbons.

"I'm sure you do, that's right. No question," I replied quickly. I couldn't seem to find any neutral ground with her, and I was relieved when the dinner came to an end.

I headed back to the villa where I was staying. Before I had had time to go upstairs, a black limo pulled up, a messenger hopped out and handed me a box—of Russian chocolates!

Raisa appeared to be as astute a politician as her husband.

—

The second day was a grinding one of negotiations on bilateral and regional issues and human rights. Both sides seemed to know that things were going to turn out all right, but everyone had to posture a bit for points, and there was no real excitement in the air.

That night, our side hosted a reciprocal dinner for the Soviets. Afterward, we discussed the prospects of reaching our goals and the instructions we should give our overnight drafters, but all of it essentially was an unfounded case of summit nerves. In the strategic context, we can see today that Gorbachev was a great deal more vulnerable than we were. We had come to Geneva with a huge amount of power behind us, while he was suffering from a very weak economy. Still, none of us really thought in those terms then. We were still thinking in terms of the traditional Soviet stance of unyielding confrontation.

In the end, we issued the instructions that Shultz and I had developed as the bottom line; the drafters were to insist on a commitment by both sides to a goal of reducing nuclear weapons by 50 percent. I went over to the Intercontinental Hotel to boost the troops who were grinding out the communiqué. Again, Richard Perle and Roz

Ridgway did the lion's share of the work. They were up until three in the morning, but along with their Soviet counterparts, they worked out an agreement that said exactly what we wanted.

The next day, Ronald Reagan and Mikhail Gorbachev signed the agreement.

It was truly a historic outcome. No administration in post-war history had ever before been able to get the Soviets even to talk about reducing nuclear weapons; now they had agreed to do it. The sense of euphoria in the delegation was palpable.

As I headed out with Jonny on a trip to debrief key allies and consolidate allied support, I reflected on this achievement, which I had helped make possible. It was an accomplishment to be proud of. Over the past two years, I felt, I had fulfilled my career in ways I wouldn't have imagined possible when I graduated from the Naval Academy more than 20 years before. Ronald Reagan's approval rating at the end of 1985 was soaring.

It was, I thought, a good time to leave government.

Chapter 17

A Time To Go

I loved the job I had, but there was no denying that it was not fun, as measured in each day's bureaucratic battles. A *New York Times Magazine* cover story on me in May had pinpointed a large part of the problem—the rivalry between the Secretaries of State and Defense. While such rivalry is natural and exists to an extent in every administration, in the Reagan administration, the rivalry between State and Defense was extreme, endemic and ultimately corrosive.

The problems between George Shultz and Cap Weinberger had not improved over time. If anything, despite my efforts and those of their subordinates at creating harmony, they persisted. We had put in place any number of mechanisms to try to handle the hostility between these two cabinet officers. One was the "Family Group," so called because we met for lunch in the family dining room of the White House residence. It had been an idea Shultz proposed in November 1984, after both he and I had tried to get President Reagan to resolve the struggle between these two cabinet officers. Once or twice a month, Shultz, Weinberger, Bill Casey and I would have lunch with no aides present or notes taken to talk over sensitive issues and our disagreements in a private setting in the hope of expediting policy and decisionmaking, if not reaching consensus on it. Our goal was to make decisionmaking work faster, if not more smoothly. But in the end, probably the best that can be said for the family group was that it prevented matters from deteriorating.

The other forum was the Wednesday morning staff meeting, where Shultz, Weinberger and I and our immediate staffs would meet at either State or Defense for breakfast. This meeting had started with Al Haig and continued under Shultz, taking in Bill Clark and subsequently me. On one occasion, not long after Shultz had taken office in late 1982, we had a particularly contentious agenda for the breakfast. Shultz raised an issue gingerly, but no sooner had he spoken than Weinberger launched into one of his infamous monologues, which often lasted five minutes or longer, denouncing the idea in question. As he rolled on, Shultz suddenly rose from the table and started to walk out of the room. At the door, he turned to Weinberger and said, "You know, it's pointless to try to do business with you, Cap. You don't analyze things. You take stances. If you're going to govern, you have to listen and analyze to figure out the right thing to do. But you don't ever do that, Cap."

The room was perfectly silent. We all seemed to be holding our breath. It wasn't like Shultz to make a scene. But Weinberger never yielded an inch. He simply resumed talking, and after a few minutes, Shultz was persuaded to sit back down and the issue was papered over. After a few such episodes, it became clear that Weinberger was acting not out of reasoned policy differences, but instinctively; he was not giving anti-policy speeches, he was giving anti-Shultz speeches.

After dealing with this for three years, I was hard-pressed to know what more could be done to alleviate the situation, short of Cap's becoming Secretary of State, which in the last analysis is what he wanted. Weinberger lusted to replace Shultz, no doubt believing that as the President's conservative conscience, he was the man best suited to formulating and running foreign policy. He had betrayed his desires in this regard on several occasions:

• In January 1982, Weinberger had sent a memorandum to Judge Clark on the subject of the West Siberian Pipeline Project. "The Europeans are finally awakening to the dangers this project poses for the West's energy security and the financial bonanza it represents for Moscow," the memo read. "We need to move quickly before the lessons of Poland fade from memory. The interagency process, chaired by the State Department, has thus far failed to come up with the necessary package of alternatives. I suggest that your staff take the lead in developing such a package, using detailees from Commerce, Defense, State and the intelligence agencies. Defense would be willing to provide space and clerical support on a temporary basis."

The Soviet pipeline project was a policy area that had nothing to do with defense. Yet Weinberger was not only accusing the State Department of dismal failure in handling that policy, he was also suggesting that the locus of new policy formulation should be the Pentagon. It was a transparent power grab that laid bare much of Weinberger's thinking. Clark declined Weinberger's offer.

• In October 1983, Weinberger sent a letter to President Reagan expressing his views on the subject of Polish debt and fishing rights, with suggestions as to how Treasury Secretary Don Regan should deal with these issues at a forthcoming Paris Club meeting. It was a gratuitous weighing in on subjects well beyond Cap's purview.

• Finally, in September 1984, Cap sent the President a long memo discussing how the administration should conduct Middle East policy. It treated what we ought to be doing in each Arab country and then urged early meetings with each state to try to begin to promote the President's September 1, 1982 initiative. It was the sort of memo you expected to get from the administration's chief diplomat, not the man in charge of military affairs.

It's true that Weinberger was miscast as Secretary of Defense, a position for which he had no background or qualification. His stewardship was marked by recurrent failure with Congress, to which he was unable to explain U.S. strategy and how the money he proposed to spend on weapons procurement fit in to that broader strategy. To his credit, he was a very tenacious, devoted, zealous person, one who never moved off a position having once adopted it. This quality had no doubt served him well in the courtroom. But it meant he was not open to suasion or new ideas or new facts. Once he had adopted a position, the only way anyone could change it was to take it to President Reagan. This cost us on more than one occasion, most notably during the FY'84 budget debate. The President had sent Congress a defense budget representing 10 percent real growth. It was a substantial boost, and not likely to be passed intact. But I worked with John Tower and Sam Nunn and others to put together a deal that would net us 7.5 percent real growth. Pleased with this, I took it to Cap. And Cap said he wouldn't agree to it.

"The minute you start making deals," he said, "they'll nibble you to death. If you don't dig in your heels and fight, you're just going to get wasted. No deals. No compromise. No way." That year, we ended up with 3 percent growth in defense. Cap's intransigence cost us $12 billion.

The Secretary of Defense has two basic responsibilities: first, to propose sound military strategy to the President; second, to manage with care the expenditure of a huge budget. Judgments on both counts don't rest on my opinion. On the first, after two years of Pentagon failure to develop sensible nuclear strategy, it became necessary to appoint the Scowcroft Commission to come to the rescue. On the second, two years after recurrent episodes of $700 toilet seats and worse, President Reagan appointed the Packard Commission to overhaul Pentagon internal management.

My own relations with Weinberger had been cordial and stable, if not warm, through most of 1983 and 1984. But as the President's second term began, Cap became increasingly hostile. He challenged my advice to the President on U.S.-Soviet relations and arms control, where his approach was much more hardline than mine or Shultz's. He came to believe—wrongly—that I was not presenting his views fairly to the President.

George Shultz and I did not always agree, either, although I admit that in conflicts with Cap I probably sided with George about 60 percent of the time. Shultz's pragmatic approach was more in tune with the President. This is not to say that Shultz and I didn't have our flareups. We had disagreed on Middle East and Lebanon policy throughout 1982 and 1983; when I agreed with Weinberger that we should pull the Marines out of Beirut in February 1984, George was outraged. He called me from the Caribbean to demand an explanation. "What are you trying to do?" he sputtered.

"I'm trying to serve the country and the President," I said. "I don't believe that, as matters stand, we're going to be able to forge effective policy with you and Cap as much in disagreement as you are. And I'm not going to leave the Marines vulnerable to the vicissitudes of Cabinet warfare in Washington."

As it happened, we *had* managed to forge effective policy together, in many areas, notably U.S.-Soviet relations. But in 1985, another element was added to our already volatile mix.

———

I had not known Don Regan before he swapped jobs with Jim Baker in January 1985 to come to the White House as Ronald Reagan's Chief of Staff. Regan had been a preeminent Wall Street banker and chairman of the board of Merrill Lynch before accepting an appointment from President Reagan to become Secretary of the Treasury, a post in which he had served with distinction for four years.

I did not expect that this exchange was going to generate conflict. I had always reported directly to the President on some matters, and I assumed that this procedure would continue to be honored by

Regan. And I had never had personality problems with colleagues and co-workers in the past during 30 years in various bureaucracies.

Soon after Regan assumed his White House post, I got a call in the middle of the night from the Situation Room. A U.S. Army Major, Arthur D. Nicholson Jr., had been killed in East Germany while on an inspection mission in the Soviet zone. I immediately called the President to inform him of the incident, presuming that the Situation Room would call the other White House principals, which was standard operating procedure. Apparently, however, Regan did not learn about the incident until he was on his way to work.

The next morning, I had not been in my office more than a few minutes before I got a call on the hot line from Regan's office. "Get up here right away," Regan ordered, forgoing any greeting.

I made my way to his office after checking with the Situation Room, which verified that no one had called him in the night. This was my error; the Situation Room was under my purview, so if Regan had not been called, the fault was mine. As I stepped into his office, Regan did not wait for me to speak. "This is outrageous," he burst out. "I don't have to learn what's going on from news broadcasts, and I'm not going to put up with this."

I replied immediately. "You're right. I'm sorry. I thought you had been notified, but you hadn't. I take responsibility and I'm sorry."

But Regan had a head of steam going and continued to blow off. His temper flared hotly. "You're goddam right. You'd better be sorry!" he shouted. "I won't take this kind of insubordination."

I was disturbed by the edge of superiority and command that I detected in his voice. I had been wrong, I had said I was wrong, and I had apologized. I tried again to appease him. "Don, you're right. I understand how you feel. It won't happen again." Regan still wasn't going to let go. "You don't seem to realize that you work for me around here."

Enough was enough. "No, I don't," I replied firmly. "I work for the President. It's my job to keep you informed, but I work for the President."

"The hell you do!" Regan roared. "You work for me and everything you do will come through me or you'll be out of here."

At that I stiffened. "You're right again," I said. "I'll be out of the office by the end of the day." And I turned on my heel and walked out. Behind me, Regan was still hollering: "Get back here! I'm not finished with you!"

This, apparently, was Regan's managerial style. I returned to my office and began to prepare for the next meeting, when the hot line rang again. On the other end, Regan sounded much more normal. "All right, let's handle this like grownups," he said. I said nothing. "I shouldn't have gotten so upset," he said.

"If that's an apology, I accept," I said.

We smoothed over this first dispute. I told Regan I would keep him informed of anything that I conveyed to the President, and that if a given matter was not of timely concern, I would send it to the President through him. But there were times, I said, when the job required that I talk directly with the President, and I intended to keep doing that. Regan never was happy about this, but he learned to live with it.

Nevertheless, our relationship had gotten off on the wrong foot, and it was never good after that. As the year progressed, it became more and more fractious. We had several blowups, once over his efforts to reorganize the administration's decisionmaking process for economic policy, once over whether or not President Reagan should endorse the Gramm-Rudman deficit reduction plan. Regan, who had a fiery temper, was rarely shy about holding back.

Our relationship took another bad turn in August. While I was in California with the President, *Parade* magazine published an item about an unnamed White House official and a journalist who were rumored to be having an affair. This rumor actually had been circulating among the White House press corps for some time, and in that circle I was the "unnamed White House official." This rumor was nothing more than a malicious, unfounded piece of gossip. It was bad enough having to hear it floating around the White House; to see it in print was doubly distressing—to me, to the reporter in question, and especially to Jonny.

My press assistant, Karna Small, called me in California to alert me to the *Parade* item and to tell me that the word around the White House was that the rumor had emanated from the office of the Chief of Staff. I decided to tackle the issue frontally. I called Don and asked him to meet with me for lunch. "I want to talk to you about a private matter," I said.

He said fine, and we went up to a little cafe on the road above the

Biltmore Hotel and had lunch. "Don," I began, "I've been told that these false rumors are being put about by you or your people." I didn't wait for him to answer. "If it's true, I'm offended by it," I went on, "and if it isn't true, I wish you'd do something to discount it in the press."

Regan put down his fork. "Bud, that isn't true," he said firmly. "I wouldn't do that, and I don't believe my people would do it, either."

I nodded. "Well, I wish you would check, and if they haven't, then I'm sorry. But if they have, I wish you would deal with it."

"Count on it," he said.

The gossip, however, didn't go away. It appeared again in print, and the rumors continued to circulate. The whole matter seemed to me to be beyond decency. It was a cost of doing business that just wasn't worth it.

—

By autumn, I had decided to resign after the Geneva summit. I wanted to assure that we realized the full potential of that event. But afterward, I was going to leave government.

Added to the friction with Weinberger and Regan, which I thought ultimately could hurt the President publicly, and my bone-weariness, was the sense that it was time I devote more of myself and my energies to Jonny. The children were grown. The twins, Scott and Melissa, were still in college, but Laurie, our oldest, had graduated. I wanted to give Jonny some time, and to provide better financially for her as we moved into our later years. This was something I had thought was in order five years before. I had no reservations about the time I had spent in the Reagan administration. Those years had been the most productive period of my life. I had faced a series of challenges for which I had trained throughout my life, and I thought I had vindicated that training reasonably well. I was especially happy about the grand strategy we had put together to influence change in the Soviet Union; clearly it was working. But now it was time to move on and look to the future again.

I was also concerned about the direction one of our policy initiatives had taken. By October, I had become disillusioned with the Iran initiative. After the first Israeli shipment of TOW missiles to Tehran, I had thought it was time to abort this project. It had too quickly become a trade of Israeli arms for hostages, rather than a serious attempt at identifying a possible successor to Khomeini. Yet I sensed that it was a policy the President would stick with.

In mid-October, Jonny and I invited George Shultz and his wife, O'Bie, to our cabin in the Shenandoah Valley. We were returning their hospitality of the previous month, when they had had us up to their farm near Williamstown, Mass. The weekend was pleasant; we visited a nearby historic plantation and played a few rounds of golf. One evening before dinner, George mixed Manhattans for us from his secret recipe. We sat on the deck, relaxing and talking, watching the sun retreat across the valley and slip behind the Shenandoah Mountains in the distance. In that quiet moment, I shared with George my decision to leave the government at the end of the year.

He was surprised and genuinely dismayed at the news. He had come to rely very heavily on me to make sure that the President was understanding his policy recommendations, he said. Why had I come to this decision, he wanted to know. I told him I believed the time had come to give more time to the family after 30 years in public life, and that the nature of the job inside the White House and the inability to work effectively with Don Regan had become intolerable.

"What would it take to keep you in government?" George asked when I had finished.

"There really isn't anything, George," I said. "I've been privileged to serve, and I think we will have accomplished something, but it's time to go and do something else."

He contemplated that for a moment. "I've always thought you'd make a fine Secretary of Defense," he said.

I smiled. "That's very flattering," I said, pleased at the compliment. "But I expect Cap to be around for a long time. Please understand that I'm telling you these things not to seek accolades or assistance. I just think the time has come." My mind was made up.

After Geneva went off so well, and Jonny and I returned from the victory tour of Europe, I headed out to California, where the President would be spending Thanksgiving. After a few days in San Francisco, where I attended Shultz's 65th birthday bash at the Bohemian Club, I flew down to Santa Barbara. After a week there, the presidential party moved to Los Angeles. Mrs. Reagan wasn't as fond as the President of the slow pace at Rancho del Cielo and it was their habit to spend time in both places. The next day, on December 4, I wrote my resignation letter and slipped it into the binder I gave the President every morning during the daily briefing for him to peruse afterward.

> *Dear Mr. President:*
> *It is with a deep sense of gratitude, sadness and fulfillment that I tender my resignation as your National Security Advisor....*
> *...to have been a part of this national renewal has been an honor and privilege beyond expression. For that I am deeply grateful. In the coming years, as you continue to consolidate this foundation of political, economic and military strength and move beyond it to greater stability in East-West relations, I shall be one of the millions of proud Americans out there in support. Hopefully, there will be a little more time for Jonny and the family. But we won't forget that we were a part of something very important. Thanks, Mr. President.*
> *God bless.*
>
> *Bud*

Half an hour after we finished the daily briefing, the President's assistant, Dave Fisher, called me. "Please come up," he said.

I went back up to the presidential suite in the Century Plaza Hotel, where Reagan was seated on a sofa in the sitting room. He looked genuinely saddened, and as though he had just received a blow.

"I'm just thunderstruck," he said. "I don't know what I'm going to do. I've come to rely on you, and you've really been the only one who's been able to make things work."

I told him again what an honor it had been to work for him, and that I believed that together we had done some useful things. But after 30 years in government, I thought the time had come to look after my family.

Reagan listened quietly and sat silent for a long time. "I can't change your mind?" he asked at last. "Is there anything we can do?"

"No," I said, "I think I owe it to the family to leave."

He nodded, we shook hands and I left. I went downstairs to my suite and called Don Regan, who had gone on to his own vacation home in Florida. When I told him I had tendered my resignation, he reacted with an apparently genuine show of disappointment. "Just when we'd begun to get things moving in the right direction!" he said. We exchanged a few more words and hung up.

Five minutes later, the phone rang. Regan's deputy, Dennis Thomas, was calling to say he had learned from Don about my resignation and to express his dismay. "And by the way, as a matter of housekeeping," he said, "where's the letter?" The body was not even quite cold yet.

I told him the President had it, and he said that he would of course prepare an official acknowledgment, for which I thanked him.

Back in Washington, I urged the appointment of my deputy, John Poindexter, as my successor. Already, however, I was beginning to have a heavy feeling around my heart, as though I had done the wrong thing. A few days earlier, I had learned about the botched Israeli attempt to ship Hawk missiles to Iran. The initiative was badly off course, and I felt a responsibility to try to get it stopped once more. After a Saturday session with the President, Shultz, Weinberger, Regan and Casey, during which the four-month history of the Iran initiative was reviewed, I was charged to fly to London and meet with Ghorbanifar on December 8.

Yet even that meeting and my firm recommendation to the President the following Monday to close down the initiative did not produce the desired effect. As I spent my last few hours at the White House, at a reception the President had given in my honor, I sensed that the Iran initiative was going to go on. I offered the President my assistance if he wanted it. I stayed on the PROFs net, believing I could still make some difference by listening in and offering to be helpful wherever I could.

It was too late to take my resignation back, yet I would have if I could. I said as much to a group of journalists who hosted a dinner for Jonny and me at the International Club about a week after I resigned. CBS's Bill Plante put it to me directly. Did I think I had done the wrong thing in resigning? he asked. And I had to say yes. "Yes, I saw a problem and I walked away from it, and it's a cop-out."

It was more than the Iran initiative that worried me. There, I knew that affairs were going to go off the rails, and that I should have stayed if only to prevent disaster. But in addition, I knew that no one else would be able to handle the Shultz-Weinberger stalemate. I also believed our leverage on defense spending was going to decline because of the turmoil in the Defense Department, a prediction that came true within six months of my departure. Had I stayed on, I could have worked to prevent that.

But I hadn't stayed on. I had left, and I had to look to the future.

As to that future, I had no reason to believe that for me, personally, it would be anything but bright. I was in the prime of life, I had energy to spare, I had a solid career behind me and only the most positive prospects before me. I was well-known, respected, blessed with a wonderful family and many close and caring friends. I was standing on top of the world. Perhaps that's why it seemed such a long way to fall.

PART FOUR

A Public Healing

Chapter 18

COMING BACK

The first thought that came to me as I floated toward consciousness was that it was odd that heaven should be such an organized place. It was not what I would have expected, this sense of efficient bustling amid shining equipment and sterile surroundings that came to me as my eyes opened and my ears became re-attuned to the outside world. And then a voice sounded from beyond the door, a loud voice, strident and commanding—a decidedly unangelic voice—and the realization washed over me that I was not in heaven after all. I was alive, in a hospital bed, with tubes attached to my arms and all the life-sustaining paraphernalia of modern medicine marshaled to keep me from achieving the goal I had set for myself. The final goal.

At that, another realization washed over me. I had failed once again. Even at this! I had failed at the last task I had hoped to perform. I hadn't even managed to take my own life successfully....

Then Jonny was at my side. She looked exhausted, shattered, bruised and anguished. I had never seen her look so bad, and I felt a sharp pang for the wrong I had done to her. As she gazed at me, worry and relief warred with each other for control of her features. All at once, she was smiling and weeping at the same time and embracing me and saying she was sorry, sorry that she had been so absorbed in her own life and hadn't tried to be a better listener, sorry that she hadn't done something to prevent this.

It was ironic, because she had already submitted her resignation—effective that very day—from her teaching position at Bethesda-Chevy Chase High School in order to give me more of her time and support during the period of travail that had overtaken me in the wake of the Iran-contra revelations.

I was in the intensive care unit at Bethesda Naval Hospital. Jonny told me what had happened. The drugs had apparently sent me into a state of deep unconsciousness during the night. My extraordinarily deep breathing and the unresponsiveness of my body had awakened her in the early hours of the morning. She was alarmed at being unable to rouse me, but reassured by the fact that I was breathing evenly. Not wanting to alert the inevitable response from the press that the arrival of an ambulance would bring, she had waited sleeplessly a couple of hours until dawn to call a neighbor who was a physician. He came over immediately when she described my symptoms, which he said sounded like a case of overmedication. He took one look at me and told Jonny to call an ambulance at once. Distressingly, the tape of the phone call she placed to 911 was later released to the news media and replayed over and over, in all its anguish and terror, on local and national television and radio. Public figures are fair game for press scrutiny, but that breach of privacy struck me then and forever after as a stunning example of media insensitivity to the pain of a victim's family and a shocking abdication of responsible reporting.

Jonny had found my letter to her while the paramedics were carrying me down to the ambulance. Now she looked me hard in the eye. Very solemnly and emphatically, she told me that life was not worth living without me, and that nothing could ever possibly compensate for losing me. I knew she meant what she was saying not only as a genuine expression of her feelings, but as an admonition to me never to try this sort of thing again. Then she left, needing to talk to the children before they heard it on the news.

It was a strange day, that February 9, 1987. I still felt groggy and not entirely lucid. Jonny had notified my staff at the Center for Strategic and International Studies and my lawyer, Len Garment, that I was all right, and some dropped by briefly to see me, although I wasn't allowed visitors as yet. Much of my family, including our children, my sister Mary and Jonny's sister Marilyn were on their way to Washington as well. But much of the time I was preoccupied with my thoughts. I reflected on the fact that I had failed at this attempt at suicide, and that there must have been a reason for my failure. My life, apparently, was meant to go on, and slowly I came to accept that it was going to go on, and to think about where I needed to go and what I needed to do from there on out.

The next day, a Tuesday, Jonny told me that Brent Scowcroft had called and asked if he could come to see me. She thought it a good idea, so I agreed. Brent was one of my oldest friends, a colleague with whom I had shared my professional life in public service for almost 20 years, and he was close to my family and children. In many senses, he had been almost like a father to me since I first went to work for him and Kissinger during the Nixon administration. Together, we had worked 364 days a year during the period from 1973-77. And I know Brent had come to trust me absolutely. He hated management and interdepartmental bureaucratics and came to rely on me to tend that side of the National Security Adviser's job so that he could concentrate on his role as Counselor to the President, the role he preferred and in which he was so effective. After four years of working together successfully through the resolution of crises involving military conflict and the constant risk of escalation, we had developed a bond that transcended the normal bounds of friendship. Because of my respect for him, I had been disappointed when he wasn't brought into the Reagan administration in 1981, since he was viewed as a moderate and a friend of Kissinger's who didn't pass the conservative litmus test Reagan's aides applied to most appointments in the early years. But later, I had successfully recommended that President Reagan name him to chair the bipartisan commission on U.S. strategic nuclear policy, and in subsequent months and years I had brought him in whenever the President wanted to hear from scholars on the Soviet Union.

When I decided to resign in the fall of 1985, I had asked Brent to lunch so I could explain my reasons to him. He was dismayed, I remember, and urged me to reconsider. I was the only cabinet-level member of the administration, he said, who could both provide sensible advice and keep U.S. foreign policy on a steady course.

Our meeting at the hospital was profoundly emotional. We talked for a long time, recalling the history we had been through together. At the end, we both broke down in an exegesis of sadness that it had all come to this. Yet I felt Brent's strong friendship and support buoy me even in the darkness of the hour.

Soon, in fact, my melancholy began to be pierced by the public reaction that began to build during the days following my arrival in the hospital and the news that I was on the mend. Distinguished visitors began to come by, and calls and cards began to pour in.

President Reagan was one of the first to call. He spoke unhurriedly and very naturally. He wanted me to know how deeply saddened he was by the turn of events and very deliberately told me again, as he had before, that he had never had anyone work for him in whom he had had more trust, and on whom he had relied more. I said I was sorry I had let him down and created so much turmoil, but he interrupted to contradict me. I hadn't let him down, he said, and he was ready to defend everything we had done.

Right now, Reagan said, I should just concentrate on getting out of the hospital and getting back to work. It was a gracious call, and I was thankful for it.

Henry Kissinger called from Mexico. I thought it an extreme kindness that he should call while on a trip abroad, and, prodded by my Scottish frugality, I strove not to prolong the conversation. But Henry was at pains to continue even as I tried to keep it short. He wanted to make the point that in terms of policy I had not done the wrong thing in the Iran initiative; the effort to reach pragmatists was an entirely sensible course of action. He urged me to get out of the hospital and defend the original concept vigorously. More importantly, though—and it was an extremely gracious thing for him to say—I had to go on to participate in the public policy discourse in the years ahead.

George Bush came to call, having earlier sent a note. The Vice President was another friend of more than 15 years' standing; we had first met during the Nixon years, when he was Ambassador to China and later Director of Central Intelligence. We had talked then whenever he visited the White House. During the Reagan administration, he and I had visited often—our offices were next door to each other—to discuss how we could encourage President Reagan to adopt what both of us felt were sensible courses of action *vis-a-vis* the Soviet Union and other foreign policy issues. The Vice President, unfortunately, is at the mercy of the President in establishing a life and function of his own. Bush and I, both conscious of that, had worked together to develop ways in which he could be helpful in advancing our foreign policy interests through his travel to foreign countries and relationships in the Senate and House of Representatives. He had handled his role superbly, often being the decisive influence on Reagan.

Over time we had become socially friendly as well; periodically, George and his wife Barbara had had Jonny and me over to their home at the Naval Observatory for small dinners; the previous August he had invited us up to spend a weekend at Kennebunkport, although we had been unable to make it. Further, as he began to put together his "brain trust" for the 1988 presidential campaign, he asked me to be his foreign policy guru and to work closely with Ken Duberstein, Craig Fuller and Nancy Reynolds. Now he was coming to see me as a friend, reaching out to support me in a time of distress. He urged me to concentrate on recovering and assured me that I need not worry about the consequences of the Iran scandal. Everything, he believed, would ultimately turn out all right. I had served the President properly, and my service would be vindicated in the end.

On the afternoon of Tuesday, February 17, after I had been in the hospital a week, I had an unexpected and uplifting visitor. Former President Richard Nixon, notwithstanding another phlebitis flareup, got on a plane and flew down from his home in Saddle River, N.J., to pay me a call.

Although I had worked in his administration, I had not really come to know Nixon until the Reagan years, when I had begun a periodic correspondence with him to keep him briefed on administration activities and to seek his counsel on various policy strategies and his help in persuading Reagan to adopt a particular course of action, as in the runup to the Geneva summit. On one occasion, in October 1985, I had traveled to his home to brief him on summit preparations. Afterward, I spent a long evening with him. We talked for three or four hours, through dinner and beyond, about the opportunities at hand regarding the Soviet Union and the historic importance of moving away from building ever larger nuclear arsenals. He was a gracious host as well as a stimulating interlocutor. I remember he served a bottle of 1970 Chateau Lafitte Rothschild; it was his favorite wine and that year's vintage was worth about $300. I was flattered that he chose to share it with me.

Over the course of the past four years, through a half-dozen such meetings and a dozen or so letters, we had developed a working rapport and a relationship of mutual respect and affection. Now, in what was surely the most difficult period of my life, this man who had undergone one of the most traumatic experiences in the history of the presidency, who surely knew what was transpiring in my mind and soul, was extending a hand of friendship and support.

The words and thoughts he shared that day were deeply meaningful to me. He stayed with me for an hour, talking about adversity, adversity in the abstract and his own experience of it. He started by assuring me that the idea of trying to connect with Iranians who might one day succeed Khomeini was a very sensible one. In the long reach of history, he believed, people would understand that. The initiative may have gone off course when arms were introduced prematurely, but my own motives, he knew, had been sound and one day would be vindicated. What made my difficulty worse was that I was dealing with a political culture that was vastly different from the one that had prevailed when he and my father had gone into politics. Then, the press had been willing to yield a large measure of trust to public officials, along with the flexibility they needed to carry out their jobs in often risky and fluctuating circumstances. Today, however, after Vietnam and Watergate, and the more competitive climate among journalists, that presumption of trust and respect for the importance of privacy in conducting foreign policy no longer existed. In short, the kind of thing I had been trying to do was no longer feasible.

"But," he said, "your motives were right and your concept was sound, and you mustn't let this defeat you and end your career. You were the only solid thinker on foreign affairs in the Reagan administration, and you still have a lot to contribute to the country."

Then he invoked his own case. "Look at me," he said. "I've made a lot of mistakes in my life, Bud, and if I had it to do again I would do things differently. But you don't get that chance.

"There was a time after Watergate when I thought there was nothing to live for because of the gravity of what I had done. But I came to believe that the only course I could follow was to do better. I'm not exactly a public hero, but I've kept on saying what needs to be said, and you have to do that, too."

He was speaking as the central figure in the largest scandal of my life. In its aftermath, he had shown tremendous strength, proving that the prescription he offered was a good one. I don't dismiss what Richard Nixon did; his weaknesses and insecurities led to enormous damage to the country. Yet I had always thought that, purely as a matter of fairness, he had been abused. I knew of enough examples of far more serious sins on the part of Presidents Johnson and Kennedy that made it easier for me to at least forgive, if not absolve, the errors of Watergate.

Johnson, through deception and distortion of events, had gotten us into a war that had led to massive loss of life. Yet he was never impeached or prosecuted or forced to resign. Kennedy had been a fundamentally deceptive person, a man who flaunted his personal breaches of trust and fidelity without regard to consequences. I had never believed that you can draw a line between personal breaches of trust and professional behavior; if a person behaves deceptively and without integrity in his private life, then he will behave deceptively and without integrity in his public life as well.

However history finally judges Richard Nixon, I will personally be forever grateful to him for coming forward at a time when I most needed help.

Many other good friends called or visited or wrote: Tom Korologos, an old friend from the Nixon days; Mike Deaver, who came to the hospital twice; Al Keel, of the NSC staff; Marine General John Grinalds and his wife, Norwood; Ken Duberstein, Reagan's Deputy Chief of Staff; and Navy Secretary John Lehman, who flustered the staff at the hospital by coming "aboard ship" unannounced to visit me.

Indeed, the amount and type of support I received at this critical time was an illuminating phenomenon. What was most surprising— but strangely and deeply reassuring—were the confessions of perhaps a dozen prominent people, some of the most prominent in Washington, that they, too, had been where I now was, had stood in my shoes and ventured down the road I had ventured down. In person and in writing, these people opened up doors to the deepest, most intimate secrets of their lives. They, too, had tried to commit suicide. They, too, had had to overcome the depression that had led them to that point and continue living. It was true that my actions had become public, where theirs had not, and this made my road more difficult. But life, they assured me, was not over; like them, I could pick up the pieces and go on.

I was profoundly grateful for these expressions of friendship and comradeship. Most of all, the willingness of these people to be so candid helped somehow to relieve the burden I had been carrying, the burden of having both failed my country and having failed to atone for that failure.

Yet now I began to hear a chorus of the voices that said I had not failed my country. Over the course of the ten days I spent in the hospital, thousands upon thousands of cards and letters of support for me poured into the hospital. Perhaps fifty to a hundred were from people whom I knew, but the vast majority came from strangers, people who knew me from reading about me in the newspapers, people who said they admired me, believed I had done the best I could under the circumstances and respected me for telling the truth.

The mail brought many interesting and touching items. There were sacks of get-well cards, humorous and serious, bouquets upon bouquets of flowers, Bibles and chocolate truffles, a room-wide computer message signed by nearly every member of our church, and personal mementos people I didn't know wanted me to have.

One correspondent from New York sent a simple admonishment—"Watch this!"—attached to a videotape of Frank Capra's *It's a Wonderful Life*. Incredible as it may seem in an age when that movie seems to run on television in a continuous loop during the Christmas season, I had never seen this poignant film about an angel who saves a depressed and beleaguered small-town banker, played by Jimmy Stewart, from killing himself by showing him the ways in which his life has affected and assisted all those around him. Jonny and I watched it with tears in our eyes. Its simple message went straight to my heart: professional success was not the only measure of a man's worth. What really counted were the values he carried in his personal life and passed on to his loved ones and all those with whom he came into contact. This was a truth I had misplaced in the last two months.

Responding to all these good wishes was a gargantuan task, but it was beautifully and conscientiously handled by Jonny, my tireless executive assistant, Caroline Scullin, and my eldest sister, Mary Pitcock, who had flown up from Graham to spend a week writing notes and acknowledging hundreds of letters. Mary is our family role model, a woman with a boundless capacity to love, someone who always has been there for me—and for so many others. To my knowledge, every letter or card or gift I had received was acknowledged.

Len Garment had come to see me on my very first day in the hospital. As much as I needed to see Len, I felt a deep sense of embarrassment at the prospect. For I had truly failed Len in so many ways. It would be difficult to describe a man more wholly generous of spirit, more truly selfless or more capable of unreserved, soul-purging love than Len Garment. A giant intellect whose legal acumen, uncommon humanity and humor had taken him to the heights of his profession, he was, at 60 or so, settling into a new role—a sort of righteous curmudgeon-dom—in which he had decided not to focus on the bottom line anymore. Instead, Len decided to make a

practice of taking on life's lost causes. It is a tribute to his strength
of character that he emerged from so many personal tragedies with
such an unwavering moral compass. Ten years before, his wife,
Grace, had committed suicide, leaving Len devastated—and also a
single parent of two adolescents, both in great inner turmoil.

Although I had known him superficially during the Nixon years
when he was the President's Counselor (and former law partner), I
first landed on Len's doorstep not long after resigning, when I decided to fight the more outrageous libels of those mentioned earlier,
alleging personal indiscretions. I had no money. Len took the case
without even asking when, whether or how he might ever get paid.
In little time, he and his partner, now Deputy Associate Attorney
General Roz Mazer, secured a full retraction and a public apology
from the magazine. Our friendship deepened and before long, I was
back at his door again, this time on the Sunday after the Iran story
broke, asking for his help—without any money. Again he took the
case—on an entirely *pro bono* basis—and over the ensuing two
months had guided me through the politico-journalistic jungle of
scandal which he had negotiated so successfully with so many
before me.

Our families became close. Len's second wife, Suzanne
Garment, and their daughter, Annie—both smarter than Len and I
combined—are wonderful people and unique among everyone we
know. The five of us have remained great and good friends through
the years. Now, my friend, advocate and father confessor—a man
who had been through the kind of crisis from which I had emerged
and didn't deserve to have to go through it again—was coming to
see me. After he arrived, we shared a few moments of anguish over
how we both had failed to avert the breakdown that had occurred—I
by not sharing with him, my counselor, the depths of my despair,
and he by not foreseeing the possibility of my acting as I had. Both
of us broke down. After a while, we began to want to change the
subject and began to focus on what comes next. Len said that some
would portray my attempt at suicide as an attempt to escape responsibility for Iran-contra. I understood that, but it pained me to think
that people would misread my motives in that fashion.

When Len said that the Tower Commission had asked him when
it would be convenient for them to continue questioning me, I told
him to set something up immediately. I had not been trying to

escape; I wanted to demonstrate that by meeting with the board as quickly as possible.

The Tower Board came to the hospital to interview me. We met twice, once for a half-day session on Thursday, February 19, and for two more hours on the morning of Saturday, the 21st. The interviews were held in the hospital's presidential suite, and I went to them fully dressed. The only people in the room were the members of the commission—Senator John Tower, Brent Scowcroft, former Secretary of State Ed Muskie, Commission staff director Rhett Dawson and myself. The interviews were straightforward and uneventful. There was no rancor on the part of the board members toward me, nor any sense that they felt I was not being fully responsive. I finished with the Tower Board with the strong sense that I had come clean on everything and my story had been heard and understood. Secretary Muskie made the generous, public comment that I had been the most credible witness to appear before them.

Meanwhile, I was concentrating most of my energies on my recovery. Within a day or two of my admission, I had been moved out of the intensive care unit and into the cardiac care unit of the hospital. This was a very thoughtful gesture on the part of the admiral in charge of the hospital, and my Navy doctors, because it spared me the onus of being placed in the psychiatric ward. Nonetheless, therapy was the order of the day for me.

Having determined to go on living, I concentrated on doing what the doctors instructed me to do both out of a genuine wish to learn what had gone wrong with my thinking, and out of a desire to get myself through the system as fast as possible. I have always been able to deal with systems, and the system at the hospital was predictable. I had to show a certain amount of progress by a certain amount of time; I had to give the right answers to a certain list of questions, and I had to make the proper physical progress. Fill in all the squares and you get out.

I was diagnosed with clinical depression, and I made it my business to understand the problem and to cooperate in all phases of my recovery. The doctors prescribed imipramine, and I talked daily with a therapist who prepared my psychoanalytic history. I also embarked on a physical program of rehabilitation, running daily with this same therapist.

The minimum stay for psychiatric patients at Bethesda was generally two weeks, but I progressed rapidly enough that the hospital released me in 10 days—without officially signing me out—so that I could have a quiet weekend with my family without being hounded by the press.

I went down to our cabin in the Shenandoah Valley with Jonny and our daughter Melissa, who had come home from Chicago to be with us while I recuperated. It snowed heavily all weekend, and we had a peaceful, happy time together. I will forever hold dear the memory of those days with Melissa, whose gift for nurturing and selfless love was such a treasure.

A few weeks later, Texas businessman Ross Perot called and offered us his home in Eagle, Colorado, for a week's skiing. Ross had been one of my earliest visitors in the hospital and had offered his generous support; his kindness during that period meant a great deal to both Jonny and me. We accepted his offer, and Melissa, who was still home, Jonny and I spent a restorative week on the slopes. Never had sunshine and snow, and clear, cold weather, been so completely invigorating.

These quiet interludes were helpful in restoring my strength and energy, and I came back to Washington in mid-March feeling refreshed and hopeful about confronting the future once again. I was buoyed by the sense of forgiveness that had come to me in all the outpourings of support that had reached me in the hospital and since. I began to feel relief from the sense of shame I had felt at having done something unforgivable and having embarrassed my country. And I derived real optimism from the words of those who had tried, like me, to end their lives, failed, and gone on to continue serving the country in public life.

Unlike me, however, these men had had their crises in private. Mine had played out on the public stage, and that made all the difference. Gradually, over time, as I returned to work and business, it began to become clear that the way in which I was regarded had changed forever. Henceforth, my life would always be viewed through the prism of this episode.

For the next year, I continued to see a psychiatrist. I met for weekly sessions with Walter Reich, an eminent doctor affiliated with the National Institute of Health and, as a writer, with the Woodrow Wilson International Center for Scholars. Many times, we discussed the effects of a suicide attempt on a person's subsequent life and career.

The inescapable conclusion for me was that as someone who had tried to take my life, I was suddenly heir to a whole new image, an image as a weak person, mentally unstable and unable to deal with stress.

Even then, so close to the experience, I did not feel like that person. I wanted people to see beyond this invisible disguise and remember me as they had known me before the highly publicized suicide attempt. Many found that difficult—even impossible—at the time. Their transparent feelings affected me on every level: politically, socially, and in my business dealings. I felt their lack of respect keenly, but I knew only one way to deal with it. I had to continue to meet the challenges of life as I always had, to love, to share, to build. Never feeling that I was a victim, I would refuse to act like one. The only way to convince the world that I was still the man I had been was to be that man, comfortable and assured.

To a great extent, this has worked for me. Contentment and success have been among my rewards. Certainly my credibility is as high as it ever was, overseas. In virtually every country I have visited on business since—Russia, Pakistan, China, Malaysia—I have met with genuine enthusiasm and respect for my point of view and, after six years, a growing international business.

Yet in Washington, remaking oneself after such a public crisis is exceedingly hard. People are not as willing to let go of the negative impressions they have received and the automatic prejudices toward those who have suffered psychological trauma or the effects of depression. And yet it is in Washington especially that people ought to think hard about these prejudices and their consequences. It would be a stunning revelation to many to know that there are dozens of public figures in Washington who have privately tried and failed to take their own lives, but have recovered from their traumas and continue to govern and run the country successfully.

An episode of depression should not be considered disqualifying in an intellectual—or any other—sense. Had it been, the wartime service of Winston Churchill and virtually the entire adult legacy of Thomas Jefferson would have been forfeited.

Six weeks after my suicide attempt, I resumed my normal life. By March 1st, I was back at CSIS and I took up the burden of the continuing Iran-contra investigations. For me as for everyone else involved, the scandal was far from over. A long road still lay ahead.

Chapter 19

TRUTH AND LIES

In May, I appeared before the public hearings being conducted by the congressional select committees investigating the Iran-contra affair. Over five days, on nationwide television, I laid out yet again the history of the Iran initiative to the best of my recollection and answered detailed questions from committee counsel regarding the administration's support of the Nicaraguan freedom fighters, including the question of the Saudi contributions, never stinting on information and detail where I had it at my disposal. I testified without a grant of immunity, as openly and honestly as I could, and wholly prepared to bear whatever consequences would result. I should point out, however, that at no point, from the time the scandal broke in November 1986 through my testimony before the committees seven months later, or during the long, seven-year investigation of Independent Counsel Lawrence Walsh, was I ever granted access to any of my White House records—notes, memos, minutes or anything else that would have jogged or bolstered my memory of events that had occurred nearly two years earlier. If my testimony was sometimes uncertain, it was due to the lack of these source documents to help me in my account of events. In sum, however, I took the attitude that being accountable, telling the truth and expecting the system to respect that approach would lead to justice being done. That turned out to be a bad idea.

With my own testimony over, I waited, like all the rest of the country, to watch the testimony of key Iran-contra figures who thus far had refused to make any comment on their role in the affair. I waited to see what Ollie North, at long last, would have to say to the American people about his part in both the Iran initiative and the support of the Nicaraguan contras. I had found his behavior disappointing since the scandal had broken—refusing to testify before the Tower Board or the Senate and House intelligence committees, citing the Fifth Amendment, and now demanding immunity before agreeing to appear before the select committees.

But I was totally unprepared for what happened when he took the stand on July 6th. He was everything I would have expected him to be: forceful, telegenic, articulate. He was also a few things I had never dreamed it possible for him to be: deceitful, mendacious, and traitorous.

Watching his performance on television, I felt as though I were being stabbed, over and over again, straight in the heart. Revelation followed revelation until my head was swimming. North's testimony revealed, first of all, that he had lied to me, all through 1984 and 1985. When he had flat-out denied raising money for the contras, he had lied. Willfully and knowingly. He had not only raised money for them, he had set up, without my approval or my knowledge, an off-the-shelf enterprise with Dick Secord to funnel funds and weapons to the contras.

But the worst, the unkindest cut of all, was that he claimed he had done all this with my knowledge and approval. That I had backed him up and given him the green light. That I had masterminded things like the coverup of the November Hawk shipments by telling everyone to refer to them as shipments of oil drilling parts. It was the worst act of betrayal I have ever experienced in my life.

I told Len Garment of my reactions to North's testimony, and he in turn took my concerns to the committee counsel. They asked whether I would be willing to testify again, to the specifics about which North had lied. So I appeared a second time before the select committees on July 14.

In a statement, I gave my views of the strengths and weaknesses of covert operations, and the difficulties in conducting such operations under conditions of partisan conflict between the White House and the Congress. I also stated my belief in presidential accountability in conducting foreign policy. Then I refuted the specific charges that North had made against me:

• That I had given him general authority to conduct covert operations for the contras involving widespread military and paramilitary operations based upon the position that the Boland Amendment did not apply to the NSC staff, and that he had kept me advised of all his activities. I had given him no such general authority, and on the several occasions when he asked for approval on activities that went beyond political support for the contras, I had disapproved them. The Committee could see those disapproved memos in front of them.

• That he and Bill Casey had agreed upon a "full service" operation to support the contras, using non-appropriated funds, implying that I had concurred in this. I had never heard of this full service operation until his testimony, and most certainly would never have approved had I known of it. Neither North nor anyone else produced any evidence that I had.

• That he did not recall my ever directing him not to solicit funds to support the contras. I had so directed him, and all my staff, on repeated occasions.

• That in September 1985, I had instructed him to "fix" some memos that raised doubts about his compliance with the Boland Amendment. It was, in fact, he who suggested that he revise the memos; when I received his revisions, I not only did not approve them, I rejected them out of hand. As became clear during North's testimony, all of North's shredding and revisions took place in 1986, a year after I had left government.

• That I had directed that the White House chronologies be altered to say that everyone in the government had believed that oil drilling parts were being shipped by the government of Israel in November 1985. This was untrue. It was North, not I, who invented the "oil drilling" story and though he urged me to adopt it, I refused to put it into my version of the chronology.

"There are a number of other factors upon which Colonel North's recollection differs from mine, but they are marginal to our basic disagreement," I said. "That disagreement involves a clear implication from his testimony that I authorized an operation involving pervasive disregard of statutory restraints, that I permitted, with knowledge, the creation of a separate, clandestine and far-reaching network of private operations that involved private profits and which was to be concealed even from other members of the administration, officials who were entitled to know the details of an authorized covert operation.

"It is true that the conduct of a covert operation consistent with the narrow and changing restrictions of the various Boland Amendments required determinations of authority that were difficult and debatable and in the long run could even be dangerous. But this is a far cry from saying that I or other members of the administration authorized what was clearly beyond anyone's power to authorize, specifically the so-called 'full service' off-shore operation of Messrs. Secord, Hakim, Ghorbanifar and their associates. This is untrue because it is unthinkable. It violates every tenet of my political beliefs, everything I've sought, throughout my career, to sustain and advance. These are my beliefs in the rule of law and the doctrine of political accountability.

"These are the essence of the constitutional form of government I have fought in war to defend, which I worked in Congress to carry out and which were part of my deepest beliefs when I served in the executive branch as Counselor to a Secretary of State and National Security Adviser to the President of the United States."

I let it go at that and didn't go on to diagram for the Committee my own "theory of the case," a theory to which North himself had given credence in his testimony. And that is that it was Bill Casey and North, operating out of Casey's office in the White House complex at the Executive Office Building, who put together the Hakim-Secord "off-the-shelf" contra-support operation. Casey was a Cabinet officer, the Director of Central Intelligence and a right thinker. That was good enough for North—indeed, faced with my disapproval, it was the essential support he needed from a superior. The fact that Casey had no authority to approve such an operation was immaterial to North. Casey gave him the ability to say, "I was just following orders."

And Casey fully understood the deal. Faced with the unwillingness of his own deputy, John McMahon, to go along with continued support of the contras after the Boland amendment passed, and with the prospect of sustained congressional flyspecking of CIA operations even if authority were someday to be restored, Casey was searching for an alternative basis for conducting covert operations in Central America. North provided it.

Bill Casey was a determined, intelligent, wily fighter in the cold war struggle against communism. He had been in that fight and in the intelligence business since his earliest days in the Office of Strategic Services during World War II. Now, knowing that he was nearing the end of his life—based upon his doctor's diagnosis in late 1984—his passionate desire was not to miss an opportunity to contribute to the final collapse of the scourge he had fought against for so long. He knew that what he was doing with North was illegal, but he must have believed that Ronald Reagan would have approved it or at least approved of it. Finally, he probably assuaged his lawyerly soul with the thought that at least he would be taking the rap. I like to think so anyway.

In my testimony, I had attempted to set the record straight. And with that, the most intense period of my focus on Iran-contra was over. The scrutiny and the intense investigative spotlight were momentarily turned off.

———

Just before my last appearance on the Hill, on July 12, Jonny and my assistant Caroline threw a 50th birthday party for me. It was an amazing effort—a fantastic event at Wolf Trap to which at least 100 people came. The guests included Vice President Bush, Commerce Secretary Mac Baldrige, Brent Scowcroft, Paul Nitze, Navy Secretary John Lehman, Secretary of Agriculture Jack Block, Admiral Jim Watkins, who was Chief of Naval Operations, Zbigniew Brzezinski, and just about every friend I had ever had in public and private life including a number of journalists. My sisters Mary and Barbara came from Texas and New Jersey, respectively. The popular group The Capitol Steps, which does satirical song and dance spoofs on Washington issues and personalities, waived their fee and performed for costs. After a long evening of laughter and fun, Army General Ed Rowny brought the party to a close by playing *The Marine Corps Hymn* on his harmonica.

This rallying of people on my birthday lifted my spirits to a high I had not experienced in many, many months. After six months of absorption with scandal and interrogation, it meant more than words could say to know that there were still so many people who would call me friend, and who were willing to come out and show their support publicly.

It is a Washington truism that in times of trouble, one's "friends" will disappear, but we were exceedingly lucky in that regard. We were fortunate to have lived most of our lives in this city and, as a result, were surrounded by many friends who went back as far as high school. These people had known us for 40 years and knew for certain what kind of people we are. There were some, to be sure, who crossed us off their lists, but in the end, that was perhaps for the best.

In the same way, it was revealing to see how the media reacted to Iran-contra and to compare how some reporters treated me before the scandal and afterward. During my White House tenure, the press had been generous toward me. I had been the subject of a number of laudatory stories in the press, including a *New York Times Magazine* cover story and other favorable pieces. In these I was seen as strong, in command of the national security apparatus, a power in the Reagan administration, one of the few people who thought conceptually and knew how to run a decent foreign policy for a President with no sense of history and no interest in foreign affairs.

After Iran-contra, there was a sea change in that view. Suddenly, I was portrayed as an over-reaching know-nothing who had hopelessly tried to emulate Henry Kissinger and Zbigniew Brzezinski. After the suicide attempt, I became a weak and unstable figure to boot. Many of the most critical stories were written by the same reporters who had earlier been most fulsome in their praise. On the other hand, other reporters, who had been more guarded in their assessments of me while I was in the White House, maintained an even-handed, reasonable approach to my story after Iran-contra broke. Lou Cannon of the *Washington Post* comes particularly to mind. His stories post-Iran-contra were thoughtful and insightful.

In an excerpt of his new book, *News and the Culture of Lying*, which recently appeared in *The New York Times*, Paul Weaver summed up the condition of political discourse in our country better than I could: "On television and in newspapers, reality and truth have long since fallen by the wayside, replaced by what can be called a culture of lying... The media are less a window on reality than a stage on which officials and journalists perform self-scripted, self-serving fictions."

In the end, unlike Ollie North, I just wasn't a "performer."

Meanwhile, Iran-contra was once again about to invade my life. Trouble was brewing on another front. In October 1987, Independent Counsel Lawrence Walsh, after first saying that I would not be a target of his criminal investigations of the Iran-contra affair, abruptly changed his mind.

Chapter 20

THE PRICE OF POWER

After months of anxiety and nervous waiting, Judge Lawrence Walsh had reached a decision on the disposition of my case. One day in early February 1988, he called in my lawyer, Len Garment, and Len's partner, Peter Morgan, to inform them of what he intended to do about charging me in the Iran-contra affair.

A poker-faced, taciturn man, Walsh dispensed with most of the formalities and pleasantries and got right to the point. "McFarlane is a patriot," he said soberly, "quite different from the others. He has been extremely helpful and ought not be put in the same category. But he still stepped over the line. He got too close to the flame."

He would have to charge me with one count of perjury and perhaps several other felonies.

I was to be indicted on the basis of the letters I had sent to Congressmen Lee Hamilton and Mike Barnes in 1985, saying that the NSC staff had not engaged in any illegal activities in support of the Nicaraguan contras, and my failure to disclose my knowledge of the Saudi Arabian contributions to the contras in 1984 and 1985.

Len's jaw, as he told me later, dropped. What he was hearing seemed unbelievable. Since October, we had presumed that there was still a possibility that I would not be charged at all. In working with me, Walsh had expressed more than once his belief that my behavior had been admirable throughout. He had sympathized with my situation at the White House, where he was astounded at the outrageous behavior of George Shultz and Cap Weinberger and conceded that I had been operating in a "snakepit." At worst, we had believed, I would be charged with a single misdemeanor. But felonies!

Len launched into a 45-minute recapitulation of all the reasons—in law as well as equity—why it would be harmful to the national interest for me to be indicted. In the history of the republic, no cabinet-level official had ever been prosecuted on any charge related to his correspondence with or testimony to the Congress. Letters did not have the status of sworn testimony, and to suggest that any or all of a cabinet officer's correspondence might one day be used as evidence against him would almost certainly lead either to its discontinuation or to its reduction to such sterile content as to make it of dubious value. And that restriction of executive-legislative dialogue would make it more, not less likely that we would face this kind of problem again.

Secondly, I had set a precedent with my pattern of cooperating with all the investigatory bodies looking into the Iran-contra affair. Mine was the kind of behavior Justice Department officials should want to encourage among the career services and among government employees generally. If I were not treated fairly in the end, my case would only serve to send the signal that it did not pay to cooperate.

Finally, purely on the merits, my testimony and my record were eminently defensible. Even where questions could be raised, such as over my seeking to avoid public exposure of Saudi Arabia's support of the contras, my motive was clear. I was trying to prevent damage to an important foreign relationship. Similarly, when I made the categorical denials in my letters regarding NSC staff support for the contras, I had only been repeating what Ollie North had told me to be true. I had not lied; I had believed I was telling the truth.

None of these arguments, however, appeared to make the least impression on the silent judge. Len, growing ever more agitated, finally rose to his feet and offered the most powerful summation to his arguments he could muster: "For McFarlane to be indicted would be a national f---ing outrage!" And he stormed out of the room.

Judge Walsh and Peter Morgan sat silently for a moment. Then Peter got up and began to pack up his papers. Judge Walsh also rose, gave a gentle tug to his vest, and, as though nothing at all had happened, said mildly to Peter: "I hope we can look forward to seeing you and Len tomorrow morning. I just know we can find a suitable arrangement."

———

The news that Walsh had decided to make me a target of his investigation had not at bottom surprised me when it came, but it had angered me greatly. From the beginning of the Iran-contra investigations, I had proceeded under the apparently misguided impression that if I were accountable and told the truth, and if I hadn't broken the rules—the political rules of conduct—then the principles of fair play and these same political rules would lead me, albeit through great turmoil, finally to atonement and reconciliation.

I had acknowledged error and held myself accountable. I did not believe that I had broken the rules. And, above all, I could not imagine that even in the most extreme interpretation, what I had done could possibly measure up to the actions of men who had gone before me, men like Lyndon Johnson and Henry Kissinger, who had never been charged with any violations of law or the public trust.

The notion of special trust and confidence is the doctrine that governs the performance of public officials in a representative democracy. This trust is a bilateral one. The electorate, for its part, must yield its sovereign right to judge public policy to its representatives. It also gives these representatives the latitude to take risks, to use discretion, and to choose the right course of action in any given situation. The reciprocal trust, flowing from the official, is that he or she will act legally, not in self-interest, and in good faith toward the citizens he or she represents.

Over the years, this high-sounding doctrine has had its ebbs and flows; there have been times in our history when our public officials have breached it, other times when they have exploited it and taken the country in extraordinarily successful directions. The state of the doctrine in my lifetime has been basically healthy, although not without blemish. Its zenith probably came in the Eisenhower years, when a Republican President and Democratic congressional leaders fashioned a *modus vivendi* whereby the congressional leaders, respecting the constitutional authority of the President to conduct foreign policy, would accede to his chosen course and behave as a loyal opposition. In his turn, however, the President would show respect for the Congress's legitimate role in governing the country. It is this good faith and mutual respect practiced constantly between every President and congressional leader that is the glue which holds the executive-legislative framework together.

If this foundation exists, then as a practical matter, each side can do things expedient to its partisan or constituent interest, which may seem to depart from the strict standard of putting everything into a letter. It was on this basis that I had sent the letters to Hamilton and Barnes with their categorical (perhaps too categorical, I can see in retrospect) denials of wrongdoing, but then followed up with candid private meetings to flesh out the precise nature of what I believed my staff was doing.

At all times, I had adhered to the one enduring rule of this political process: I had not lied. Some of the most prominent figures of our day could not say the same. Think of Lyndon Johnson's distortion of events, including the Gulf of Tonkin episode, in both public statements and responses to Congress, that led us into a tragic war. His sins were magnified by Robert McNamara, who by his own admission lied about the situation in Vietnam and our intended courses of action. Later, their successors, Richard Nixon and Henry Kissinger, at the very least countenanced the falsification of records on the bombing of Cambodian targets.

In contrast to these men, I believed, I had adhered to the rules of the game. Certainly I had adhered to a far higher standard than any of them. Yet Watergate and Vietnam had eroded trust. Partisan criticism and press scrutiny were far more severe in 1986 and 1987 than at any previous time. Moreover, I was the recipient of the legacy of Ronald Reagan.

Reagan was a man who did not want to engage with the Congress. He lacked the confidence to be able to sustain his position in the give and take of rigorous argument, whether the subject was federal housing policy, health care, or, above all, foreign policy, of which he had only a superficial grasp. But he recognized that he could overcome those shortcomings and outflank the system by going directly to the people and exploiting his strong suit of persuasive communication and salesmanship.

To me, this was irresponsible. There is nothing wrong with going to the people as a tactic, as long as you respect the institutions of governance. But if you show a lack of respect for either the Congress or the press by refusing to deal with them, then slowly and inexorably, you generate rage.

By 1986, in the Democratic leadership of Congress and the entire Washington press corps, Reagan had created two constituencies looking for revenge. I should have recognized that their rage would overcome whatever vestigial respect any Democrats might have retained for accountability and a willingness to cooperate. But I did not.

Further, I had misread the forces that drove the Independent Counsel. It was naive of me to expect that Judge Walsh would see his role as trying to identify lessons from the Iran-contra scandal, to propose corrective measures, and, in sum, to advance the national interest.

Judge Walsh had come to Washington to prosecute. So had the battalion of lawyers he had recruited. The Judge personally may have had a superficial perception of the larger purpose of his inquiry, but in two years and 300 hours of interviews, there was never the slightest hint that any of his lawyers wanted to do anything except indict as many people as they could, hang as many scalps as they could on the wall, and enhance their own personal standing in the legal community.

Grasping all this would not have changed my behavior. But learning it did lower my expectations.

———

On March 11, 1988, in Federal District Court for the District of Columbia, I entered a plea of guilty to four misdemeanor counts of unlawfully withholding material information from Congress.

After considerable legal wrangling, Walsh had agreed to lower the charges to misdemeanors in exchange for my agreement to testify at the subsequent trials of those charged with criminal violations of the law in the Iran-contra affair.

Accepting a plea bargain had been a difficult decision to make. Jonny and I had talked about it for days. Len, his wife and young daughter were living in an apartment in our basement at the time while their own house was being renovated. Endlessly, the four of us worried the bone of what it would mean to bargain for a reduced charge. Ultimately, we came to several conclusions. In the climate that prevailed in Washington, I could not expect any favors for simply being accountable and doing the right thing. I would have to look out for myself. In that light, I should drive the best bargain I could with the prosecutors and then do my best in testimony to assure against a conviction of any of the others.

At one point, Walsh had urged Len to persuade me to agree to "cooperate fully" in my testimony against all the leading figures, in exchange for which all charges against me would be lifted at the conclusion of the trials. Len and I were both outraged at this suggestion, and never even seriously considered it. Instead, we accepted the reduced counts on a guarantee that the sentence would not include any period of imprisonment and that I would be sentenced before the other trials began, to avoid any appearance that my testimony would be colored in any way to affect my sentence.

The day my plea bargain was announced, Ollie North voiced his reaction to the final disposition of his old boss's case in the Iran-contra affair. *"This* Marine will never cop a plea," North announced. He didn't need to. He had found he could beat the system on his own.

But my sense of personal betrayal and hurt did not matter. I would not vent my anger by allowing another injustice to be perpetrated against North. To this day I believe that all of us involved in Iran-contra, as public servants, should have been accountable and explained what we did and why, all the way up to the President. Iran-contra was at heart a political disagreement. We should have expected that the Congress would be angry and disagree with our actions. But since those actions had been taken in good faith and with the President's approval, they should never have led to criminal prosecution.

The President of the United States is ultimately accountable for whatever happens in his administration, and his subordinates should not be held criminally to account for a political disagreement. They never have been before. And they should not have been in 1986. But Ronald Reagan lacked the moral conviction and intellectual courage to stand up in our defense and in defense of his policy.

A political disagreement can only be resolved if political leaders argue about it, present their positions, make their cases, and seek the support of the American people. President Reagan had shown himself unwilling to take the charge for his subordinates, to step up to Congress and say "This was my decision, and this is why I did it." And the Congress, recognizing his popularity and his communication skills, never challenged him directly.

The President—probably at the urging of Mrs. Reagan and his counsel—had shown himself unwilling to be accountable, and I did not believe therefore that Ollie North should have been charged and prosecuted. Whatever he did when I was his superior had been my responsibility, and I would do my part to prevent his conviction.

———

The movement to trial, however, was glacier-like.

North's trial did not open until February 21, 1989, almost a year after I had made my plea. My sentence was handed down on March 3, 1989. Judge Aubrey Robinson sentenced me to two years probation, 200 hours of community service, and a $20,000 fine. I was fortunate to have two good friends, Tom Korologos and Christine Vick, who organized an effort to help pay the fine in very little time, and I was warmed by how many people wanted to help.

As for the community service, I applied myself wholeheartedly to what I found to be fulfilling work. One of my assignments was helping a small foundation for disabled persons gain eligibility to federal programs providing volunteer assistance in the home and the workplace. The foundation was headed by a woman named Louise McKnew, whose son, Donny, was the quadriplegic victim of an automobile accident. Louise and I worked with Senators Sam Nunn and Ted Kennedy and Representative Dave McCurdy of Oklahoma to develop a pilot program whereby young people volunteering for public service under the National Service Act would be assigned to assist the disabled in their homes, helping them to wash, get dressed, perform all the daily chores of life and be productive citizens.

I also spent several weeks working to create a computer database at the Washington YMCA of all the summertime athletic, artistic, musical and other public programs available for youngsters in the District of Columbia. Afterward, I helped man the phones and respond to calls from parents looking for good programs to keep their children off the streets. It was a far cry from my days as a White House mover and shaker, but no less meaningful, I came to see, in the larger scheme of things.

Meanwhile, I had testified at North's trial on March 13 and 14, well after my own sentence had been handed down, as I had requested. I was the lead witness for the prosecution. But the prosecution, I'm sure, could have wished for a far more cooperative witness than I turned out to be.

I was determined to help, not hurt, North, and all my testimony was designed to assume responsibility for whatever he had done on my watch. I was careful to present him in the best light, to give him strong positive character references whenever suitable. It did not matter that he was not quite the wholesome, hard-charging figure I had thought him to be when we worked together in the White House. I saw the larger context of what Ronald Reagan had wanted done, what his goals had been and what sorts of actions he had countenanced and encouraged, and I couldn't say that North had done anything the President hadn't wanted him to do. And I thought there was more of a lesson to be learned from Iran-contra than simply that you should prosecute the most junior subordinate involved.

As the trial unfolded, though, and in the years that have passed since, I came to see that in fact Ollie himself never seemed to get the point that however a public servant may feel about what is right in the policy sense, he still must work within a legal framework. Ollie and a lot of other people in this town of Washington approach the political milieu from a "them and us" perspective, a belief that when it comes to ideological struggle, what's right is determined by who wins. All's fair in that contest, they say, and to believe otherwise is naive.

North was convicted on April 22, 1989, of obstructing Congress, destroying official documents, and accepting an illegal gratuity. He was acquitted of six other charges. By anyone's measure, it was far less than the government had hoped to get him on, and it was undeniable that my testimony had made the difference. I never received a word of thanks or acknowledgment.

Three months later, the U.S. Court of Appeals for the District of Columbia set aside North's convictions. In May of 1991, Judge Gerhard Gesell, who had presided over the original trial, held a hearing to determine whether North's congressional testimony, which he had given under immunity, had affected the outcome of his trial. Again, I was the lead witness.

The proceeding seemed ridiculous to me, since my testimony had had little relevance to the charges on which North was ultimately convicted. But my motive, as I have said, was to get North off, and this was the opportunity. I testified that not only had my trial testimony been "colored" by North's immunized congressional testimony, I had also been deeply affected by it. Which was certainly true, but not, I'm sure, in the sense that the law has in mind.

Ollie North went scot-free. He never went to jail, and never paid a fine, largely due to my testimony. And from that day to this, I have never heard another word from Ollie North.

The man I had thought was patriotic, self-sacrificing and loyal was revealed to be devious, self-serving, self-aggrandizing and true first and foremost to himself. At every turn in the Iran-contra scandal, he had sought to protect himself at the expense of others, acting out of self-interest and expediency. That is the wrong criterion to apply when you are given the honor of serving in government. Then, your criterion must be to vindicate the people's trust.

I believe that Ollie North served his country well for a time. But somewhere along the way, through a combination of hubris, lack of character and pride, he lost his moral compass. He violated the special trust. It's astounding that today, having relegated Iran-contra to the shelf of "ancient history," he could have the audacity to ask to have that special trust reposed in him again.

Audacity, however, is something Ollie North has never had in short supply.

———

By 1992, life had taken several turns for the better. Since leaving the Center for Strategic and International Studies, I had established my own company and had begun to take on a number of business ventures around the world, in Russia, Malaysia, Pakistan and several other countries. Jonny and I bought a house in Georgetown—a small house with a river view, just as we had always dreamed. Leaving behind the Bethesda house, with all the unhappy recent associations that clung to it, had been a positive move and a big step in returning to normalcy.

I had lived and breathed Iran-contra for the better part of six years. Just when I might have thought it was receding into the past, there came another call from the White House. There was a move afoot in the Bush administration, the caller said, to obtain pardons for those involved in the Iran-contra scandal. Did I want to sign on and be included?

"No," I said, without hesitation. "I don't think the President needs to incur the inevitable criticism on my account that would come from that. I would never seek a pardon."

Jonny thought I was wrong, but I didn't change my mind. And yet, on December 24th of that year, President George Bush, to the predicted outcry from Democrats in Congress, issued pardons to me and five other Reagan administration officials who had been convicted, indicted or stood to be indicted in the Iran-contra scandal. It was a nice Christmas present, and I thanked him for it. But in the final analysis, as I wrote to Bush, what had begun as a political fight was simply ending as a political fight.

"What have Americans seen happen in this tawdry episode?" I wrote. "They've seen a President (who approved every single action I ever took in this matter) refuse—from lack of intellectual and moral fiber—to defend his point of view; refuse to support or even to acknowledge the truthfulness of those who acted in his behalf, and escape completely from any measure of accountability. They have seen some who were sworn to uphold the Constitution take the Fifth Amendment and evade responsibility. And they have seen the only one who was accountable and who took responsibility spend six years in the dock, dogged by six investigating bodies, testifying more than all others combined and end up more discredited than anyone."

In light of all that, it was hard to derive any sense of moral vindication from a pardon.

———

The ball had one last pathetically ironic bounce to take. In August 1993, Lawrence Walsh issued the final report on his investigation into Iran-contra matters. The report, while terribly weak in most respects, was gratifying, and gave me a stronger feeling of vindication than any I had experienced heretofore. Walsh had finally uncovered the existence of George Shultz's and Cap Weinberger's contemporaneous notes on the entire Iran initiative and knew the extent to which Weinberger, Shultz and others had lied or downplayed their roles and their awareness in the affair.

"...in testimony regarding the 1985 Iran arms sales, McFarlane contradicted other senior officials on critical points," Walsh's report stated. "McFarlane repeatedly testified that he kept the NSC principals briefed and was insistent that the President had approved the 1985 shipments. It was not until Independent Counsel in 1990, 1991 and 1992 obtained previously unproduced notes from [Caspar] Weinberger, [Don] Regan and others that the truthfulness of many of McFarlane's statements regarding the early shipments could be proven."

It warmed my heart to read those words. At last, the truth was acknowledged. Moreover, the Walsh report as first circulated recognized another reality of the Reagan administration response to the Iran-contra scandal: "...that the President's most senior advisers and the Cabinet members on the National Security Council participated in the strategy to make National Security staff members McFarlane, Poindexter and North the scapegoats whose sacrifice would protect the Reagan administration in its final two years."

I had not seen myself as a scapegoat, merely as someone willing to tell the truth. But the men above me had not been willing to do that, and so the burden of their lack of accountability had fallen on my shoulders.

The media dutifully carried stories on the Walsh report, and for one day, Iran-contra was back in the news. The next day, it was gone again, relegated by the modern media world of high-speed technology and 15-second attention spans to the back shelves of history.

Others may have put it aside long before, but for me, Iran-contra had been a constant presence, a rock I had carried with me for the last seven years of my life. Yet mine was a life that had had much good to show for it, I believed. It was time to remember that. Even Jacob served only seven years for Rachel. Seven years' penance was, finally, enough.

It was time to put down the rock, and move on.

AFTERWORD

In the *Preface,* I referred to the wisdom of our forefathers expressed in the idea of "resposing special trust and confidence" in a few worthy and able individuals to lead us in the affairs of state. I have tried, throughout the book which followed, to describe how that trust has been breached but also vindicated in my lifetime. We've experienced truly historic victories—such as winning the cold war and putting a man on the moon. We've also suffered defeats—such as the Vietnam war and the political scandals of Watergate and Iran-contra.

My concern is that our reaction to these events has been to focus too heavily on the losses, to undervalue the gains, and to conclude too quickly that the basic idea was unsound—that the machinery of governance was broken and needed fixing. And I am concerned that in our zeal to fix it, we may have made it more difficult for the original idea—of reposing special trust in those we ask to serve—to function.

There are four parties to this compact of governance—the Presidency, the Congress, the press and the people. Each of them has specific responsibilities, but in order for the system to work, they must engage in a civil manner. There must exist among them a spirit of comity—a willingness to work courteously and respectfully together. Naturally, there will be tensions. The President's desires will not always be supported by the other three groups. Criticism from the press will anger Congress or the President. The public will deny office to those who it no longer feels are worthy or capable. But each group must understand its responsibility to the whole.

The President must inform both the public and the Congress, whenever possible, of his agenda. The Congress must acknowledge that the President has won office by gaining the support of the majority of the public. The press must acknowledge that also, and extend that understanding to the Congress. And the public must do its part by studying, thinking and voting. Democracy is not a spectator sport; it requires participation from all of us, and as in any sport, the players must adhere to the rules of the game. Sportsmanlike conduct results in an outcome that, win or lose, all can accept.

If we can understand how absolutely vital the re-emergence of comity is, and work to re-establish it as the cornerstone to our national conversation, we will once more be able to make public service the noble—and satisfying—undertaking it was before it became so adversarial. I can think of no more worthwhile goal for the last years of this century.

In my view, however, our destiny as a nation of nations will ultimately be determined by the acknowledgment by each citizen of his or her obligation to God: to do our best in all that we do—as we raise our families, care for our communities, elect qualified leaders, and support them.

For my own part, there is an abundance of opportunity waiting. In 30 years of public service, I've accumulated a great deal of knowledge concerning other cultures. Now, with the cold war behind us, there is great need to help the developing nations of the world grow—not with foreign aid, but with shared knowledge and sensible investment. After five years of working with governments and private investors from Siberia to Malaysia to Pakistan and China, I've gotten pretty good at developing large projects that will benefit both the struggling peasant populations and U.S. investors. And I have enjoyed vast satisfaction from translating the results of the special trust I have received over the years to benefit others.

How about you? How much of the enormous trust of talent and opportunity invested in you are you giving back? Twenty years from now, who is going to be better off for having known you? At the end of the day, the larger trust is not to a chosen few, but to all of us.

Appendices

THE WHITE HOUSE

WASHINGTON

May 27, 1975

Dear Bud:

You made a tremendous contribution to our successful effort to recover the ship and crew of the <u>Mayaguez,</u> and I want to express my gratitude.

You performed with great skill and dedication through a difficult period. The outcome itself is the best testimony to the contribution you made.

Thank you for all you did.

Sincerely,

Jerry Ford

Major Robert C. McFarlane, USMC
Military Assistant to the Assistant to
   the President for National Security Affairs
The White House

Letter from President Gerald Ford concerning the *SS Mayaguez.*

SYSTEM II
91001

THE WHITE HOUSE

WASHINGTON

SECRET   SENSITIVE

January 17, 1983

Declass :ed/Released   7/16/94
under provision:.   E.O. 12356
by D. Van Tassel, National Security Counc
F94-1102

National Security Decision
Directive Number 75

U.S. RELATIONS WITH THE USSR   (S)

U.S. policy toward the Soviet Union will consist of three
elements: external resistance to Soviet imperialism; internal
pressure on the USSR to weaken the sources of Soviet imperialism;
and negotiations to eliminate, on the basis of strict reciprocity,
outstanding disagreements. Specifically, U.S. tasks are:

1.   To contain and over time reverse Soviet expansionism by
     competing effectively on a sustained basis with the Soviet
     Union in all international arenas -- particularly in the
     overall military balance and in geographical regions of
     priority concern to the United States. This will remain
     the primary focus of U.S. policy toward the USSR.

2.   To promote, within the narrow limits available to us, the
     process of change in the Soviet Union toward a more plura-
     listic political and economic system in which the power of
     the privileged ruling elite is gradually reduced. The U.S.
     recognizes that Soviet aggressiveness has deep roots in the
     internal system, and that relations with the USSR should
     therefore take into account whether or not they help to
     strengthen this system and its capacity to engage in
     aggression.

3.   To engage the Soviet Union in negotiations to attempt to
     reach agreements which protect and enhance U.S. interests
     and which are consistent with the principle of strict
     reciprocity and mutual interest. This is important when
     the Soviet Union is in the midst of a process of political
     succession. (S)

In order to implement this threefold strategy, the U.S. must convey
clearly to Moscow that unacceptable behavior will incur costs that
would outweigh any gains. At the same time, the U.S. must make
clear to the Soviets that genuine restraint in their behavior
would create the possibility of an East-West relationship that
might bring important benefits for the Soviet Union. It is
particularly important that this message be conveyed clearly during
the succession period, since this may be a particularly opportune
time for external forces to affect the policies of Brezhnev's
successors. (S)

SECRET   SENSITIVE
Declassify on: OADR      cy 16 of 12 copies

National Security Decision Directive Seventy-Five, January 17, 1983.

SECRET   SENSITIVE   2

Shaping the Soviet Environment: Arenas of Engagement

Implementation of U.S. policy must focus on shaping the environment in which Soviet decisions are made both in a wide variety of functional and geopolitical arenas and in the U.S.-Soviet bilateral relationship. (S)

A.   Functional

1.   Military Strategy: The U.S. must modernize its military forces -- both nuclear and conventional -- so that Soviet leaders perceive that the U.S. is determined never to accept a second place or a deteriorating military posture. Soviet calculations of possible war outcomes under any contingency must always result in outcomes so unfavorable to the USSR that there would be no incentive for Soviet leaders to initiate an attack. The future strength of U.S. military capabilities must be assured. U.S. military technology advances must be exploited, while controls over transfer of military related/dual-use technology, products, and services must be tightened. (S)

In Europe, the Soviets must be faced with a reinvigorated NATO. In the Far East we must ensure that the Soviets cannot count on a secure flank in a global war. Worldwide, U.S. general purpose forces must be strong and flexible enough to affect Soviet calculations in a wide variety of contingencies. In the Third World, Moscow must know that areas of interest to the U.S. cannot be attacked or threatened without risk of serious U.S. military countermeasures. (S)

2.   Economic Policy: U.S. policy on economic relations with the USSR must serve strategic and foreign policy goals as well as economic interests. In this context, U.S. objectives are:

--   Above all, to ensure that East-West economic relations do not facilitate the Soviet military buildup. This requires prevention of the transfer of technology and equipment that would make a substantial contribution directly or indirectly to Soviet military power.

--   To avoid subsidizing the Soviet economy or unduly easing the burden of Soviet resource allocation decisions, so as not to dilute pressures for structural change in the Soviet system.

--   To seek to minimize the potential for Soviet exercise of reverse leverage on Western countries based on trade, energy supply, and financial relationships.

--   To permit mutual beneficial trade -- without Western sub- sidization or the creation of Western dependence -- with the USSR in non-strategic areas, such as grains. (S)

SECRET   SENSITIVE

The U.S. must exercise strong leadership with its Allies and others to develop a common understanding of the strategic implications of East-West trade, building upon the agreement announced November 13, 1982 (see NSDD 66). This approach should involve efforts to reach agreements with the Allies on specific measures, such as: (a) no incremental deliveries of Soviet gas beyond the amounts contracted for from the first strand of the Siberian pipeline; (b) the addition of critical technologies and equipment to the COCOM list, the harmonization of national licensing procedures for COCOM, and the substantial improvement of the coordination and effectiveness of international enforcement efforts; (c) controls on advanced technology and equipment beyond the expanded COCOM list, including equipment in the oil and gas sector; (d) further restraints on officially-backed credits such as higher down payments, shortened maturities and an established framework to monitor this process; and (e) the strengthening of the role of the OECD and NATO in East-West trade analysis and policy. (S)

In the longer term, if Soviet behavior should worsen, e.g., an invasion of Poland, we would need to consider extreme measures. Should Soviet behavior improve, carefully calibrated positive economic signals, including a broadening of government-to-government economic contacts, could be considered as a means of demonstrating to the Soviets the benefits that real restraint in their conduct might bring. Such steps could not, however, alter the basic direction of U.S. policy. (S)

3.   Political Action: U.S. policy must have an ideological thrust which clearly affirms the superiority of U.S. and Western values of individual dignity and freedom, a free press, free trade unions, free enterprise, and political democracy over the repressive features of Soviet Communism. We need to review and significantly strengthen U.S. instruments of political action including: (a) The President's London initiative to support democratic forces; (b) USG efforts to highlight Soviet human rights violations; and (c) U.S. radio broadcasting policy. The U.S. should:

--   Expose at all available fora the double standards employed by the Soviet Union in dealing with difficulties within its own domain and the outside ("capitalist") world (e.g., treatment of labor, policies toward ethnic minorities, use of chemical weapons, etc.).

--   Prevent the Soviet propaganda machine from seizing the semantic high-ground in the battle of ideas through the appropriation of such terms as "peace." (S)

B.   Geopolitical

1.   The Industrial Democracies: An effective response to the Soviet challenge requires close partnership among the industrial democracies, including stronger and more effective collective defense arrangements. The U.S. must provide strong leadership

and conduct effective consultations to build consensus and
cushion the impact of intra-alliance disagreements. While Allied
support of U.S. overall strategy is essential, the U.S. may on
occasion be forced to act to protect vital interests without
Allied support and even in the face of Allied opposition; even in
this event, however, U.S. should consult to the maximum extent
possible with its Allies. (S)

2.   The Third World: The U.S. must rebuild the credibility of
its commitment to resist Soviet encroachment on U.S. interests
and those of its Allies and friends, and to support effect.vely
those Third World states that are willing to resist Soviet pressures
or oppose Soviet initiatives hostile to the United States, or are
special targets of Soviet policy. The U.S. effort in the Third
World must involve an important role for security assistance and
foreign military sales, as well as readiness to use U.S. military
forces where necessary to protect vital interests and support
endangered Allies and friends. U.S. policy must also involve
diplomatic initiatives to promote resolution of regional crises
vulnerable to Soviet exploitation, and an appropriate mixture of
economic assistance programs and private sector initiatives for
Third World countries. (S)

3.   The Soviet Empire: There are a number of important weaknesses
and vulnerabilities within the Soviet empire which the U.S.
should exploit. U.S. policies should seek wherever possible to
encourage Soviet allies to distance themselves from Moscow in
foreign policy and to move toward democratization domestically.
(S)

(a)   Eastern Europe: The primary U.S. objective in Eastern
      Europe is to loosen Moscow's hold on the region while promoting
      the cause of human rights in individual East European countries.
      The U.S. can advance this objective by carefully discriminating
      in favor of countries that show relative independence from
      the USSR in their foreign policy, or show a greater degree
      of internal liberalization. U.S. policies must also make
      clear that East European countries which reverse movements
      of liberalization, or drift away from an independent stance
      in foreign policy, will incur significant costs in their
      relations with the U.S.   (S)

(b)   Afghanistan: The U.S. objective is to keep maximum pressure
      on Moscow for withdrawal and to ensure that the Soviets'
      political, military, and other costs remain high while the
      occupation continues.   (S)

(c)   Cuba: The U.S. must take strong countermeasures to affect
      the political/military impact of Soviet arms deliveries to
      Cuba. The U.S. must also provide economic and military
      assistance to states in Central America and the Caribbean
      Basin threatened by Cuban destabilizing activities. Finally,
      the U.S. will seek to reduce the Cuban presence and influence
      in southern Africa by energetic leadership of the diplomatic
      effort to achieve a Cuban withdrawal from Angola, or failing
      that, by increasing the costs of Cuba's role in southern
      Africa. (S)

(d) <u>Soviet Third World Alliances</u>: U.S. policy will seek to limit
the destabilizing activities of Soviet Third World allies
and clients. It is a further objective to weaken and, where
possible, undermine the existing links between them and the
Soviet Union. U.S. policy will include active efforts to
encourage democratic movements and forces to bring about
political change inside these countries. (S)

4.   <u>China</u>: China continues to support U.S. efforts to strengthen
the world's defenses against Soviet expansionism. The U.S.
should over time seek to achieve enhanced strategic cooperation
and policy coordination with China, and to reduce the possibility
of a Sino-Soviet rapprochement. The U.S. will continue to pursue
a policy of substantially liberalized technology transfer and
sale of military equipment to China on a case-by-case basis
within the parameters of the policy approved by the President in
1981, and defined further in 1982. (S)

5.   <u>Yugoslavia</u>: It is U.S. policy to support the independence,
territorial integrity and national unity of Yugoslavia. Yugoslavia's
current difficulties in paying its foreign debts have increased
its vulnerability to Soviet pressures. The Yugoslav government,
well aware of this vulnerability, would like to reduce its trade
dependence on the Soviet Union. It is in our interest to prevent
any deterioriation in Yugoslavia's economic situation that might
weaken its resolve to withstand Soviet pressure. (S)

C.   <u>Bilaterial Relationships</u>

1.   <u>Arms Control</u>: The U.S. will enter into arms control negotiations
when they serve U.S. national security objectives. At the same
time, U.S. policy recognizes that arms control agreements are not
an end in themselves but are, in combination with U.S. and Allied
efforts to maintain the military balance, an important means for
enhancing national security and global stability. The U.S.
should make clear to the Allies as well as to the USSR that U.S.
ability to reach satisfactory results in arms control negotiations
will inevitably be influenced by the international situation, the
overall state of U.S.-Soviet relations, and the difficulties in
defining areas of mutual agreement with an adversary which often
seeks unilateral gains. U.S. arms control proposals will be
consistent with necessary force modernization plans and will seek
to achieve balanced, significant, and verifiable reductions to
equal levels of comparable armaments. (S)

2.   <u>Official Dialogue</u>: The U.S. should insist that Moscow
address the full range of U.S. concerns about Soviet internal
behavior and human rights violations, and should continue to
resist Soviet efforts to return to a U.S.-Soviet agenda focused
primarily on arms control. U.S.-Soviet diplomatic contacts on
regional issues can serve U.S. interests if they are used to keep
pressure on Moscow for responsible behavior. Such contacts can

also be useful in driving home to Moscow that the costs of
irresponsibility are high, and that the U.S. is prepared to work
for pragmatic solutions of regional problems if Moscow is willing
seriously to address U.S. concerns. At the same time, such
contacts must be handled with care to avoid offering the Soviet
Union a role in regional questions it would not otherwise secure. (S)

A continuing dialogue with the Soviets at Foreign Minister
level facilitates necessary diplomatic communication with the
Soviet leadership and helps to maintain Allied understanding and
support for U.S. approach to East-West relations. A summit
between President Reagan and his Soviet counterpart might promise
similarly beneficial results. At the same time, unless it were
carefully handled a summit could be seen as registering an improvement in U.S.-Soviet relations without the changes in Soviet
behavior which we have insisted upon. It could therefore generate
unrealizable expectations and further stimulate unilateral Allied
initiatives toward Moscow. (S)

A summit would not necessarily involve signature of major
new U.S.-Soviet agreements. Any summit meeting should achieve
the maximum possible positive impact with U.S. Allies and the
American public, while making clear to both audiences that improvement in Soviet-American relations depends on changes in Soviet
conduct. A summit without such changes must not be understood to
signal such improvement. (S)

3.   U.S.-Soviet Cooperative Exchanges: The role of U.S.-Soviet
cultural, educational, scientific and other cooperative exchanges
should be seen in light of the U.S. intention to maintain a strong
ideological component in relations with Moscow. The U.S. should
not further dismantle the framework of exchanges; indeed those
exchanges which could advance the U.S. objective of promoting
positive evolutionary change within the Soviet system should be
expanded. At the same time, the U.S. will insist on full
reciprocity and encourage its Allies to do so as well. This
recognizes that unless the U.S. has an effective official framework for handling exchanges, the Soviets will make separate
arrangements with private U.S. sponsors, while denying reciprocal
access to the Soviet Union. U.S. policy on exchanges must also
take into account the necessity to prevent transfer of sensitive
U.S. technology to the Soviet Union. (S)

Priorities in the U.S. Approach: Maximizing Restraining Leverage
over Soviet Behavior

The interrelated tasks of containing and reversing Soviet
expansion and promoting evolutionary change within the Soviet
Union itself cannot be accomplished quickly. The coming 5-10
years will be a period of considerable uncertainty in which the
Soviets may test U.S. resolve by continuing the kind of aggressive
international behavior which the U.S. finds unacceptable. (S)

The uncertainties will be exacerbated by the fact that the Soviet
Union will be engaged in the unpredictable process of political
succession to Brezhnev. The U.S. will not seek to adjust its
policies to the Soviet internal conflict, but rather try to
create incentives (positive and negative) for the new leadership
to adopt policies less detrimental to U.S. interests. The U.S.
will remain ready for improved U.S.-Soviet relations if the
Soviet Union makes significant changes in policies of concern to
it; the burden for any further deterioration in relations must
fall squarely on Moscow. The U.S. must not yield to pressures to
"take the first step." (S)

The existing and projected gap between finite U.S. resources and
the level of capabilities needed to implement U.S. strategy makes
it essential that the U.S.: (1) establish firm priorities for
the use of limited U.S. resources where they will have the greatest
restraining impact on the Soviet Union; and (2) mobilize the
resources of Allies and friends which are willing to join the
U.S. in containing the expansion of Soviet power. (S)

Underlying the full range of U.S. and Western policies must be a
strong military capable of action across the entire spectrum of
potential conflicts and guided by a well conceived political and
military strategy. The heart of U.S. military strategy is to deter
attack by the USSR and its allies against the U.S., its Allies,
or other important countries, and to defeat such an attack should
deterrence fail. Although unilateral U.S. efforts must lead the
way in rebuilding Western military strength to counter the Soviet
threat, the protection of Western interests will require increased
U.S. cooperation with Allied and other states and greater utili-
zation of their resources. This military strategy will be combined
with a political strategy attaching high priority to the following
objectives:

--   Sustaining steady, long-term growth in U.S. defense spending
       and capabilities -- both nuclear and conventional. This is
       the most important way of conveying to the Soviets U.S.
       resolve and political staying-power.

--   Creating a long-term Western consensus for dealing with the
       Soviet Union. This will require that the U.S. exercise
       strong leadership in developing policies to deal with the
       multifaceted Soviet threat to Western interests. It will
       require that the U.S. take Allied concerns into account, and
       also that U.S. Allies take into equal account U.S. concerns.
       In this connection, and in addition to pushing Allies to
       spend more on defense, the U.S. must make a serious effort
       to negotiate arms control agreements consistent with U.S.
       military strategy and necessary force modernization plans,
       and should seek to achieve balanced, sigificant and verifiable
       reductions to equal levels of comparable armaments. The
       U.S. must also develop, together with the Allies, a unified
       Western approach to East-West economic relations, implementing
       the agreement announced on November 13, 1982.

-- Maintenance of a strategic relationship with China, and
   efforts to minimize opportunities for a Sino-Soviet
   rapprochement.

-- Building and sustaining a major ideological/political
   offensive which, together with other efforts, will be
   designed to bring about evolutionary change of the Soviet
   system. This must be a long-term and sophisticated program,
   given the nature of the Soviet system.

-- Effective opposition to Moscow's efforts to consolidate its
   position in Afghanistan. This will require that the U.S.
   continue efforts to promote Soviet withdrawal in the context
   of a negotiated settlement of the conflict. At the same
   time, the U.S. must keep pressure on Moscow for withdrawal
   and ensure that Soviet costs on the ground are high.

-- Blocking the expansion of Soviet influence in the critical
   Middle East and Southwest Asia regions. This will require
   both continued efforts to seek a political solution to the
   Arab-Israeli conflict and to bolster U.S. relations with
   moderate states in the region, and a sustained U.S. defense
   commitment to deter Soviet military encroachments.

-- Maintenance of international pressure on Moscow to permit
   a relaxation of the current repression in Poland and a
   longer-term increase in diversity and independence throughout Eastern Europe. This will require that the U.S. continue
   to impose costs on the Soviet Union for its behavior in
   Poland. It will also require that the U.S. maintain a U.S.
   policy of differentiation among East European countries.

-- Neutralization and reduction of the threat to U.S. national
   security interests posed by the Soviet-Cuban relationship.
   This will require that the U.S. use a variety of instruments,
   including diplomatic efforts and U.S. security and economic
   assistance. The U.S. must also retain the option of using
   of its military forces to protect vital U.S. security
   interests against threats which may arise from the Soviet-
   Cuban connection. (S)

**Articulating the U.S. Approach: Sustaining Public and Congressional
Support**

The policy outlined above is one for the long haul. It is
unlikely to yield a rapid breakthrough in bilateral relations
with the Soviet Union. In the absence of dramatic near-term
victories in the U.S. effort to moderate Soviet behavior, pressure
is likely to mount for change in U.S. policy. There will be
appeals from important segments of domestic opinion for a more
"normal" U.S.-Soviet relationship, particularly in a period of
political transition in Moscow. (S)

SECRET   SENSITIVE   UNCLASSIFIED

It is therefore essential that the American people understand
and support U.S. policy. This will require that official U.S.
statements and actions avoid generating unrealizable expectations
for near-term progress in U.S.-Soviet relations. At the same
time, the U.S. must demonstrate credibly that its policy is not
a blueprint for an open-ended, sterile confrontation with Moscow,
but a serious search for a stable and constructive long-term
basis for U.S.-Soviet relations. (S)

Ronald Reagan

SECRET   SENSITIVE

cy __1G__ of __12__ copies

SECRET

Ronald Reagan

President of the United States of America

To — Robert Carl McFarlane, of Maryland — Greeting:

Reposing special trust and confidence in your Integrity, Prudence, and Ability, I do appoint you — Assistant to the President of the United States of America for National Security Affairs, — authorizing you, hereby, to do and perform all such matters and things as to the said place, or office, do appertain, or as may be duly given you in charge hereafter, and the said office to hold and exercise during the pleasure of the President of the United States for the time being.

In testimony whereof, I have caused the Seal of the United States to be hereunto affixed.

Done at the City of Washington this — seventeenth — day of October — in the year of our Lord one thousand and nine hundred and — eighty-three — and of the Independence of the United States of America the two hundred and eighth. —

By the President:

Ronald Reagan

George P. Shultz
Secretary of State.

Commission of Robert C. McFarlane from President Ronald Reagan
to be National Security Adviser.

THE WHITE HOUSE

WASHINGTON

Nov. 4 '85

Bud

I wanted you to have in writing
what I've already told you about the
the "Achille Lauro" affair — "well done."
The extraordinary synergism of our
diplomatic, defense, and intelligence communities
during this protracted terrorist incident
reflects your stewardship as National
Security Advisor. Your accurate, timely,
and succinct advice was invaluable.

Once again you have well served
our great nation. Thank you and
God bless you for your tireless efforts.

Sincerely

Ron

Note from President Reagan regarding the
recovery of the *Achille Lauro*.

THE SECRETARY OF STATE'S
DISTINGUISHED SERVICE AWARD

Established by George P. Shultz 1985

For Distinguished Contribution to the Development, Management,
or Implementation of American Foreign Policy

Robert C. McFarlane

For extraordinary and dedicated service to the Nation and the President; for brilliant management of the policymaking process at a time of unprecedented new challenges to American diplomacy; and for a major creative contribution to the achievements and successes of American policy in an historic period.

January 1986

                Secretary of State

Secretary of State's Distinguished Service Award.

RICHARD NIXON

26 FEDERAL PLAZA
NEW YORK CITY
1-22-'87

Dear Bud,

I thought your recommendations on arms control + other initiatives the administration might take in its last two years were right on target.

My problem is - putting it bluntly - who in the hell can carry them out. a letter to the President would probably go to Regan who knows very little about arms control or Carlucci who is a first class bureaucrat but not a strategic thinker. Schultz believes he knows all the answers already.

Let me know if you have a candidate!

Sincerely, Dick

President Nixon's reaction to the foreign policy initiatives
Robert McFarlane proposed to President Reagan in January 1987.

RICHARD NIXON

26 FEDERAL PLAZA
NEW YORK CITY

2-10-'87

Dear Bud,

Get well. The nation needs you.

The amateurs who are trying to advise the President on foreign policy couldn't even shine your shoes.

Let Len know as soon as you could spare me the time for a visit. I need your advice on a trip I am planning to take —

With warm regards

RN

Note from President Nixon following Robert McFarlane's
attempted suicide.

ZBIGNIEW BRZEZINSKI
1800 K STREET, N. W., SUITE 400
WASHINGTON, D. C. 20006
(202) 833-2408

2/11/87

Dear Bud —

Old National Security Advisors just keep plugging on .... You have much to contribute to our national security — so don't let the current difficulties divert you from thinking about the future because you will be very much part of it.

Cordially,

Zbig.

Note from Zbigniew Brzezinski, National Security Adviser to President Carter.

PERSONAL

10 DOWNING STREET

THE PRIME MINISTER   19 February 1987

Dear Bud

I just wanted to say that you have been very much in my thoughts recently. All your many friends over here wish you well.

Warm regards.

Yours sincerely

Margaret Thatcher

Mr. Robert McFarlane

PERSONAL

Note from Prime Minister Margaret Thatcher.

GERALD R. FORD March 4, 1987

Dear Bob:

I have been terribly negligent in not writing sooner following your hospitalization and apologize for this indefensible failure. I hope you will understand. For the past month both Betty and I have been terribly overcommitted with the publication of her new book and the David Wolper movie and a surge of my own commitments.

Both of us were saddened and shocked by your illness and hospitalization. We are now encouraged by your recovery. We trust future developments will all be most favorable.

I admire your forthright appearances in various forums which is quite a contrast with the actions of others. It angers me that some who were knowledgeable or involved ducked or fudged. We have full faith in your integrity and patriotism.

As you know I will be forever grateful for your many kindnesses, sound advice and dedicated loyalty. You were an invaluable member of the Ford Administration White House staff. I thank you for being so constructive at all times. I deeply treasure your friendship.

Betty and I hope and pray all will go well in the future. Warmest regards.

Jerry Ford

Letter from President Ford.

RICHARD NIXON

February 28, 1991

Dear Bud

577 CHESTNUT RIDGE ROAD
WOODCLIFF LAKE, NEW JERSEY

Events have moved so fast in the Gulf that they have overtaken your observations with which I found myself in complete agreement. Winning the war has been much easier than was expected. You know better than I do that winning the peace will be more difficult than some of the foreign policy pundits have speculated.

One of the down sides of the war in the Gulf has been that attention has been distracted from a far more important arena -- the developments in the Soviet Union. I was particularly interested in your observations about Yeltsin, and I agree, incidentally, with your implication that Gorbachev may turn out to be a transitional figure. I only hope that those in the foreign policy establishment and in the Administration who contend that Gorbachev's initiative in the Gulf has been "useful" are saying that for diplomatic reasons and not because they believe it. I'm sure you would be the first to agree that Soviet and U.S. goals in the Gulf are as different today as they were before the Cold War was supposed to have ended.

I found your observations on Japan fascinating. Except for Yoshida and possibly Kishi and maybe Nakasone, whom I did not know well, I agree that virtually all Japanese leaders in government and business tend to be parochial with very little understanding or interest in geopolitical issues which do not directly impinge Japanese security. I think you are rendering a very constructive service by trying to get some of the leaders to recognize that an economic superpower should play a far more responsible role on the world stage.

One of these days, when you are in this area, I hope we can get together for a good chat. It will be like preaching to the choir, but I always enjoy our meetings!

With warm regards,

Sincerely,

Honorable Robert C. McFarlane

President Nixon's response to Robert McFarlane's letter of January 1991 regarding Boris Yeltsin and issues in U.S.-Japanese relations.

INDEX

ABC News, 94
Acheson, Dean, 137
Achille Lauro hijacking, 41, 103, 314
Adams, Tom, 266
Adelman, Kenneth, 302
Adenauer, Konrad, 136
Assad, Hafez al-, 90, 237-239, 242-243, 246-248, 251, 252-253, 273, 310
Al Shiraa newspaper, 89
Allen, Richard, 173-174, 188
Alsop, Joseph, 144
Andropov, Yuri, 293, 296-297, 301
Angerman, Dr. and Mrs. Jack, 120, 123
Annenberg, Walter, 303
Arafat, Yasser, 206
Arbatov, Georgi, 318
Argov, Shlomo, 206
Armacost, Michael, 50
Arms Control and Disarmament Agency, 198
Arms Control Information Working Group, 198
Armstrong, Sir Robert, 267
Aspin, Les, 160, 234

Baker, Howard H., 264-265
Baker, James A., III, 29, 172, 193, 199-200, 254, 259,-260, 283, 305, 326
Baldrige, Malcolm "Mac," 353
Barnes, Michael, 77, 83-85, 355, 357
Barrow, General Robert, 229
Bartholomew, Reginald, 38, 63
Begin, Menachem, 187, 188, 205-206, 208-210, 240
Beirut, see also Lebanon, 6, 20-21, 24, 37-38, 206-212, 245, 247, 249-257, 262-263, 309-310, 326; Marine barracks bombing, 262, 267-273; U.S. embassy bombing, 240-241
Berri, Nabih, 309-310
Bethe, Hans, 232
Bethesda-Chevy Chase High School, 14, 120, 337
Biden, Joe, 297
Billington, James, 277
Birkelund, John, 11
Bishop, Inez, 116-118
Bishop, Maurice, 256, 261
Block, John, "Jack" 353
Boland amendment, 267, 273, 281, 312, 350-352
Boland, Edward, 67, 281
Botha, P.W., 311
Botha, Roelof "Pik," 311
Boverie, Dick, 231
Bradley, Ann, 177
Brady, Nicholas, 260-261
Bremmer, Jerry, 204
Brezhnev, Leonid, 151, 296
Brokaw, Tom, 93-94
Brown, Harold, 216
Brzezinski, Zbigniew, 60, 177, 353-354
Buckley, William, 21, 38
Budd, Ed, 11
Bundy, MacGeorge, 177
Burt, Richard, 176, 178, 182, 196-198, 206, 232, 286
Bush, Barbara, 90, 340
Bush, George H. W., 9, 24, 28, 33, 51, 90, 168-169, 176, 181, 261-262, 295-296, 301, 307, 340, 353, 363
Byrd, Robert, 264

Calero, Adolfo, 70, 72-73, 75-76
Calvert, Admiral James, 120,
Camp David, 31, 177, 194, 207,
    295, 306
Cannon, Lou, 354
Caribbean Basin Initiative, 180,
    219
Carl, Dr. and Mrs. Frank, 115
Carlucci, Frank, 242
Carter, Jimmy, 22, 59, 90, 165,
    168-169, 171, 177, 218, 220,
    223, 229, 275,
Casey, William J., 28-30, 32-35,
    46, 51, 68, 96, 172, 174-175,
    211, 259, 263, 279, 283-284,
    292, 302, 323, 332, 351, 352
Castro, Fidel, 178, 257
Cave, George, 54, 55, 61
CBS Morning News, 6
Center for Strategic and
    International Studies (CSIS),
    338, 348, 363
Central America, see also
    Nicaragua, 9, 66, 68-69, 72,
    76, 83, 107, 174, 175, 177-
    178, 180, 184, 186, 278-282,
    284, 352
Central Intelligence Agency, 18,
    21, 28-30, 32, 38, 46, 53-56,
    63, 66-67, 72, 75, 96-97, 103,
    150, 154, 156, 172, 174, 178-
    180, 184, 195, 197, 199, 216,
    263, 267, 270, 279-281, 283,
    302, 308, 352
Charles, Eugenia, 261, 266
Cheney, Richard, 84, 165
Chernenko, Konstantin, 291, 296-
    299, 301, 302, 307
Chevy Chase Presbyterian
    Church, 130
China, 77, 142, 161, 166, 177,
    239, 277, 285, 348, 368; Nixon
    opening to, 92-93, 146, 150-
    151, 155-156,
Choate, Mary Jane, 115

Church, Frank, 154
Cisneros, Henry, 152, 282
Clark, Don, 126
Clark, William P., 78, 188-189,
    193-194, 200-201, 203-205,
    211, 219, 226, 229-230, 242-
    244, 249, 251, 254-255, 257-
    260, 276, 292, 323-325
Cohen, William S., 224
Colby, William, 150, 154
Cole, Nat King, 118
Congress, U.S., 8-9, 27, 32, 35,
    52, 67, 69-71, 73-75, 77-78,
    82-83, 86-88, 92-93, 100, 104-
    108, 114, 144, 149, 151-152,
    154, 157, 159, 163, 168, 174-
    175, 178, 209, 223, 226-227,
    232-234, 248, 277, 280-284,
    286, 307, 311-313, 325, 350,
    352, 355-360, 362, 363, 367
Connally, John, 169
Contras, see also Nicaragua, 6,
    13, 68, 70, 72-73, 75-77, 83,
    84, 85-87, 89-90, 93, 101-102,
    104, 107, 269, 280-281, 284,
    337, 345, 348-349, 352-353,
    354-356, 358-360, 362-367
Cooper, Charles, 99
Cooper, Ford, 180
Counihan, Gene, 98
Coy, Craig, 95
Craxi, Bettino, 196, 314
Crisis Pre-Planning Group
    (CPPG), 194-195
Crocker, Chester, 175, 300
Cuba, 300; Haig's desire to
    invade, 177-180; presence in
    Grenada, 257

Darman, Richard, 260
Dawa prisoners, 39, 62
Dawson, Rhett, 168, 346
Deaver, Michael, 9, 29, 172-173,
    182, 193-194, 199-200, 209,
    254-255, 269, 295, 319, 343

Defense, U.S. Department of, 7, 19, 72, 75, 156, 169, 172, 178, 180, 186, 199, 213, 242, 276, 280-281, 305, 312, 316, 323,-324, 333
Dillon, Robert, 245-246
Dillon Read, 11
Dobrynin, Anatoly, 292-293, 297-298
Draper, Morris, 205
Duberstein, Kenneth, 341, 343
Dur, Commander Phil, 244, 270

Eagleburger, Larry, 175, 182, 204, 292
Earl, Robert, 95
Eckstine, Billy, 118
Eisenhower, Dwight D., 126-127, 136, 248, 261, 357
Eisenhower, Susan, 234
Ellinger, Dick, 119
El Salvador, 67, 278-279, 281-282
Enders, Tom, 175, 280

Fahd, King of Saudia Arabia, 69, 71, 74, 243
Fairbanks, Richard, 244, 246
Fascell, Dante, 84
Fazio, Vic, 234
Feith, Doug, 205
Fiers, Alan, 72
Fisher, Dave, 320, 331
Ford, Gerald R., 7, 80, 120, 145, 149-151, 157-167, 180, 188, 220, 222, 285, 302
Fortier, Donald, 74, 97, 277
Foster, Jodie, 181
Foster, Johnny, 232
Freymond, Jacques, 137
Friedman, Tom, 252
Fuller, Craig, 341
Fuller, Graham, 19, 30

Gabriel, General Charles, 229

Gadhafi, Moammar, 260
Gaithersburg Chamber of Commerce, 98
Gantt, Florence, 97, 244
Garment, Leonard, 13, 14, 338, 344-345, 350, 355
Garment, Suzanne, 345
Garner, John Nance, 114
Gemayel, Amin, 240, 243-247, 249, 252-254, 260, 268, 273
Gemayel, Bashir, 210-212, 237
Geraghty, Colonel Timothy, 251
Gergen, David, 193, 198, 232
Gesell, Gerhard, 362
Ghorbanifar, Manucher, 25, 29, 36-38, 41, 47, 48, 49,-50, 52, 56-60, 62, 64-66, 96, 185, 332, 351
Gibson, Bob, 167
Giscard d'Estaing, Valery, 217
Goldberg, Woody, 204
Goodman, Lieutenant Robert, 272
Gorbachev, Mikhail, 24, 40-41, 44-45, 96, 300,-302, 306-309, 313-322
Gorbachev, Raisa, 320-321
Gore, Al, 234
Gorman, General Paul, 179, 292
Gossett, Edward, 113-114, 121
Gray, Major General Alfred, 269
Greenfield, Mary Ellen "Meg," 14, 91
Grenada, 257-261, 263-267, 269, 276, 298
Grinalds, Major General John, 79, 343
Gromyko, Andrei, 291, 297, 299, 302, 304-306, 308-309, 313
Guggenheim, Paul, 136
Gulf of Tonkin Resolution, 134, 158, 358

Habib, Philip, 199, 205-207, 209-212, 238, 240-241, 243, 246
Haddad, Wadi, 243

Index

Haig, Alexander M., 18, 20, 122, 154-156, 169, 172-173, 175-184, 188-189, 194, 199-201, 203-205, 248, 293, 323

Haldeman, H.R., 156

Hall, Fawn, 95

Hall, Wilma, 176-177, 189, 244

Halle, Louis, 136-137

Hamilton, Lee, 77, 83, 353, 357

Harris, Maggie, 112,

Hartmann, Arthur, 320

HAWK missile shipments, 42-43, 46-47, 50, 53, 55, 58, 60, 96-97, 99-100, 332, 350

Helms, Richard, 150

Hezbollah (Party of God), 21, 49, 60, 62, 249

Hinckley, John, 181

Hostages. see also Lebanon and individual hostages, 6-7, 10, 20,-27, 32-33, 37-40, 42-43, 46-49, 52-55, 58, 60-66, 82, 84, 89-90, 94, 106, 169, 262, 309-310, 330

House of Representatives, U.S., 10, 112, 158, 307, 340; Foreign Affairs Committee, 84; Judiciary Committee, 156-157; Select Committee on Intelligence, 67, 83, 104

Howe, Jon, 150, 153

Humphrey, Hubert, 160

Huntington, Sam, 277

Husayni Suicide Forces, 270

Hussein, King of Jordan, 184, 207-208

Hyde, Henry, 83-84

Ikard, Frank, 121

Ikle, Fred, 292, 317

INF, 197, 260, 275, 291, 293-294, 296,-298, 300, 313, 319

Inman, Admiral Bobby, 184

Iran, 6,-8, 10-14, 17-21, 23, 26-28, 30, 32-38, 40-46, 48, 50-59, 61-66, 84, 87-96, 98, 100-102, 104, 106-107, 169, 177, 186, 195, 269, 270, 310-311, 323, 332-333, 337, 340-341, 345, 348-349, 353-356, 358-360, 362-365, 367

Iran initiative, 6-10, 14, 19, 23, 26, 28, 30-31, 33-36, 42-47, 50-53, 64, 88-89, 91-92, 94-96, 98, 101, 106-107, 323, 330, 332-333, 340, 342, 349, 364

Iran-contra scandal, 6, 13, 84, 87-88, 93, 101-102, 104, 107, 269, 337, 345, 348-349, 353-356, 358-360, 362-365, 367

Iraq, 18, 20, 34, 48, 55, 59, 186, 270, 310-311

Israel, 26, 62-63, 65, 101, 169, 177, 242, 309-310, 351; war with Lebanon, 199, 205-213, 237, 239-241; strategic partnership with U.S., 18, 20-21, 23-24, 32-35, 42, 55, 68, 183-188,

Jabotinsky, Ze'ev, 187

Jackson, Henry "Scoop," 160, 168, 281

Jaruzelski, General Wojciech, 201, 202

Jastrow, Robert, 232

Jenco, Father Lawrence Martin, 22

Johnson, Lyndon B., 104, 114, 134, 152, 158, 342, 357, 358

Joint Chiefs of Staff (JCS), 24, 28, 75, 134, 155-156, 178, 180, 195, 197, 228-230, 250-251, 268, 272, 302

Jumblatt, Walid, 272

KAL shootdown, 275, 294-295, 297, 300

Kamal, Majid, 270

Kampelman, Max, 197, 293

Karch, Brigadier General F.J., 135

Keel, Alton, 97, 168, 343

Kelley, Marine Commandant General P.X., 81-82
Kemp, Geoff, 207, 244
Kennan, George F., 137, 176
Kennedy, Richard, 172
Kennedy, Edward M., 361
Kennedy, John F., 89, 133, 137-138, 160, 177, 180, 342
Kennerly, David Hume, 163
Kent, Art, 94
Keyworth, Jay, 232
Khamenei, Ali, 20, 54
Khomeini, Ayatollah, 6, 12, 17-21, 25, 29, 34, 46-47, 64, 66, 89, 94, 104, 195-196, 278, 310-311, 330, 341
Kimche, David, 17, 19-25, 28, 30-34, 36-37, 40, 47, 48, 56, 99, 186-187, 311
Kirkland, Lane, 282
Kirkpatrick, Jeane, 282
Kissinger, Henry, 79, 92-93, 145-146, 149-169, 172, 176, 183, 201, 213, 238-239, 241, 282, 339-340, 354, 357-358
Klinghoffer, Leon, 41, 314
Kohl, Helmut, 314
Kokoshin, Andrei, 235
Kondrashev, Sergei, 293
Koppel, Ted, 94
Korologos, Tom, 167, 343, 361
Kraemer, Sven, 197, 198
Kristol, Irving, 277

Lalive, Pierre, 136
Lane, Ruth, 118
Lange, Lieutenant Mark, 272
Lebanese Armed Forces (LAF), 244, 250-251
Lebanon, see also Beirut, 126-127; war with Israel, 187-188, 195, 199, 204-212, 237, 239-241, 243-245, 247-250, 253, 262, 267-269, 271-273, 276-277, 298, 310, 326; hostages in, 7, 20-21, 53, 60, 62, 82, 89
Ledeen, Michael, 17, 19, 25, 31, 36-38, 41, 184-185
Lehman, John, 104, 167-168, 231, 345, 353
Lehman, Ronald, 168
Linhard, Colonel Bob, 197
Lord, Winston, 150
Luce, Clare Boothe, 101
Lukhin, Vladimir, 235

Madden, Nancy, 127
Madden, Captain Robert, 127-128
Marine Corps, U.S., 3, 5-6, 8, 12-13, 64, 79-82, 86,-88, 105, 118, 122, 129-132, 134-135, 138, 140, 152, 155, 166-168, 184, 209, 228, 240, 253, 269, 270, 315, 353
Martin, William, 278
Martin, Graham, 145-147
Matlock, Jack, 294, 296, 298, 308, 314, 319
Maverick, Maury, 114
Mayaguez, SS, seizure of, 161-163
Mazer, Roz, 345
McCurdy, Dave, 361
Macdonell, Rev. Dr. James, 253
McFarlane, Alma (Alma Ellen Carl), 111
McFarlane, Barbara, 116-118, 353
McFarlane, Betty, 118
McFarlane, Bill, 118, 125
McFarlane, Jonda, see also Jonda Riley, 3-4, 10, 12-16, 38, 44-45, 47, 55, 62, 90, 95, 103-104, 120, 123, 127-131, 134, 166, 231, 242, 253-254, 258-259, 261, 312, 321-322, 328,-332, 337-338, 340, 344, 347, 353, 359, 363
McFarlane, Lauren, 132, 329
McFarlane, Mary Ellen, see also Mary Pitcock, 112, 118, 338, 344, 353

McFarlane, Melissa, 134, 329, 347

McFarlane, Robert C. "Bud," xi, 11, 29, 89, 94, 101, 121, 128-129, 132, 166, 189, 312, 317, 355-356, 364

McFarlane, Robert W., 112

McFarlane, Scott, 105, 122, 134, 136, 329

McFarlane, William Doddridge, 5, 10, 12, 82-83, 102, 104, 111-117, 119, 121, 124-125, 155, 159-160, 246, 342

McGovern, George S., 160

McKnew, Louise, 361

McMahon, Bernard, 103

McMahon, John, 46, 352

McNamara, Robert S., 142-143, 158, 217, 358

Meese, Edwin, 29, 32, 98-101, 172-173, 182, 193-194, 211, 259

Meir, Golda, 187

Menges, Constantine, 258

Menshikov, Stanislav, 296, 298, 314

Michel, Robert, 264-265

Mitterrand, Francois, 196, 272, 314

Mondale, Walter, 285

Morgan, Peter, 353, 356

Motley, Tony, 258, 280

Moynihan, Daniel Patrick, 283, 285

Mubarak, Hosni, 103

Mulroney, Brian, 314

Murphy, Dan, 292

Musawi, Abu Haydar, 270

Muskie, Edmund, 346

Musavi, Hussein, 54

MX missile (Peacekeeper), 222-224, 226, 229, 234, 281, 307

National Security Act, 175

National Security Council (NSC), 17, 29, 41, 55, 75, 76-77, 85, 95, 150, 154, 172, 175, 188-189, 196-199, 203, 205, 207, 219, 244, 258, 260, 294, 311, 343, 350, 355-356, 364

National Security Planning Group (NSPG), 28, 36, 68, 96, 174, 251, 259, 263, 267, 270

Naval Academy, U.S., 4, 5, 79, 105, 118, 120-122, 124, 126-130, 140, 167, 283, 322

Najafabadi, Mohammed Ali Hadi-, 59-66

National War College, 166

NBC News, 93-94

Negroponte, John, 72

New Jersey, USS, 249, 253, 273

New York Times, 43, 163, 174, 176, 252, 317, 323, 354

Nicaragua, 10, 33, 67, 70, 72, 75-77, 84, 101, 175, 194, 217, 222, 278, 279-282, 284, 298, 312, 349, 355

Nicholson, Major Arthur D. Jr., 327

Nightline, 6, 94

Nimrodi, Yaakov, 37, 47

Nir, Amiram, 56, 61, 65-66, 96

Nitze, Paul H., xii, 137, 197, 353

Nixon, Richard M., 80, 83, 120, 149, 150-156, 158-159, 161-173, 177, 201-202, 220, 248, 256, 302, 316, 319, 339, 340-343, 345, 358

Noriega, Manuel, 184

North, Oliver L., 7, 36-38, 41, 45, 47, 49-50, 53, 55-58, 64, 66, 68, 70, 72-89, 94-102, 104-105, 258, 266, 282, 284, 312, 349-352, 354, 356, 360-364

Nuclear freeze movement, 197, 223, 279

Nunn, Sam, 9, 160, 168, 224, 325, 361

Obando y Bravo, Cardinal, 84

O'Leary, Pat, 141

Olmsted, General George, 136
O'Neill, Thomas P. "Tip," 230,
   264, 266, 280, 284
Organization of East Caribbean
   States (OECS), 261, 266
Orlov, Yuri, 297
Ortega, Daniel, 67

Parade Magazine, 328
Patton, Captain George S. III, 122
Peres, Shimon, 25, 30
Perle, Richard, 196-198, 232-233,
   286, 305, 317, 322
Persian Gulf, 18, 57, 195, 278
Perot, Ross, 347
Phillips, Jack, 140
Pike, Otis, 30, 154
Pipes, Richard, 219
Pitcock, Mary, see also Mary
   Ellen McFarlane, 112, 344
Pitts, Milton, 120
Plante, Bill, 311, 332
Poindexter, Vice Admiral John, 7,
   36, 41-2, 46-47, 50, 52-53, 58,
   60, 63, 66, 68, 77, 86-88, 90-
   91, 95, 98, 100-102, 104-105,
   226, 229, 231, 263, 273, 311,
   332, 364
Poland: martial law in, 177-179,
   195, 201-202, 324; Ford gaffe
   on, 165
Pollock, Ray, 231
Pope John Paul II, 45
Powell, Charles, 306
Powell, General Colin, 152
Powell, Roger, 253
Price, Charles, 265

Qaboos, Sultan of Oman, 184

Rabb, Maxwell, 254
Rabin, Yitzhak, 42
Rafsanjani, Hashemi, 25, 54, 57,
   59-60, 64, 310

Reagan doctrine (NSDD 75), 219-
   220
Reagan, Dorrie, 288
Reagan, Nancy, 22, 26, 199-200,
   254-255, 261, 269, 288, 295,
   320, 330, 341, 360
Reagan, Ron Jr., 288
Reagan, Ronald W., 5-10, 14, 17,
   19-47, 49-56, 61, 63, 66-75,
   77-79, 85-90, 93, 95-100, 102,
   105-107, 169, 171-176, 178,
   180-184, 187-188, 193-195,
   198-201, 203-205, 207, 209,
   211-213, 219-220, 228-235,
   239, 244, 247-249, 251, 253-
   255, 257-277, 280, 282-283,
   285-288, 291-293, 295-299,
   302-303, 306-308, 310-314,
   316-320, 323-332, 339-341,
   345, 354, 360-361, 363-364
Regan, Donald, 7, 26, 28, 33-34,
   43, 47, 51, 91, 95, 98, 100,
   102, 260-261, 276, 305, 308,
   320, 325-330, 332, 364
Reger, Brenda, 85
Reich, Walter, 347
Reiling, Florence, 114
Reiling, Herman, 114
Revolutionary Guards, see also
   Iran, 58, 250, 270
Ridgway, Rozanne, 305, 322
Riley, Jonda, see also Jonda
   McFarlane, 120, 127
Robinson, Aubrey, 360
Robinson, Gil, 198
Roche, James, 185
Rodman, Peter, 287
Roepke, Wilhelm, 136
Rogov, Sergei, 312
Roosevelt, President Franklin D.,
   111, 114-115
Ross, Christopher, 244
Rowen, Henry S. "Harry," 216, 222
Rowny, General Ed, 197, 353
Rumsfeld, Donald, 162-163

Sabra and Shatilla massacre, 211
Sadat, Anwar, 184, 187
Sagdeev, Roald, 234-235, 301
Sakharov, Andrei, 297
Sanchez, Nestor, 72
Sandinistas, see also Nicaragua, 67, 71, 75, 84, 175, 278-279, 281-282, 284
Santa Barbara, California, 36-37, 77-78, 91, 288, 291, 311-312, 330
Saudi Arabia, 68-69, 184, 212, 246, 284, 355-356
Scowcroft, Brent, 7, 91, 156-157, 161-163, 165, 167, 188, 224, 229, 231, 281, 296, 298, 326, 338, 346, 353
Schlesinger, James, 162-163
Schmidt, Helmut, 217
Schwenk, Lieutenant General Dolf, 166, 167
Schwimmer, Adolf, 25, 31, 37, 47
Scullin, Caroline, 55, 94, 344
Secord, Richard, 47, 50, 55-56, 86, 350-352
Senate, U.S., 85, 102, 168, 182, 188, 223-224, 282, 340; Armed Services Committee, 9, 168, 218, 224, 281; Intelligence Committee, 103, 283-284; Select Committee on Iran-Contra, 104, 349
Shamir, Yitzhak, 30
Sharon, Ariel, 186-187, 205-206, 208
Shcharansky, Anatoly, 294, 297
Shevardnadze, Eduard, 40, 313
Shultz, George P., 7, 9-10, 19, 26-30, 32, 34-35, 41, 43-44, 46, 50, 51, 53, 70-72, 74, 99-100, 195, 201, 205, 207, 211-212, 215, 222, 232, 240, 242-244, 248-249, 255, 259-263, 268, 273, 276-277, 281, 286-287, 291-293, 295, 297-298, 302-305, 308-309, 314-317, 320-321, 323-324, 326, 330, 332-333, 355, 364
Shultz, O'Bie, 330
Small, Karna, 328
Smith, William French, 99
Socialist International, 17
Solomon, Richard, 277
Sonnenfeldt, Helmut, 176
South Africa, 219, 300; sanctions against, 36, 311
Soviet pipeline project, 202-203, 221, 293, 324
Soviet Union, 11-12, 24, 33, 48, 59, 62, 71, 107, 126, 143, 150, 151, 155-156, 165, 171, 175-178, 182-183, 193-194, 196, 201-202, 212, 215-222, 224-225, 233, 239, 255, 277, 279, 291-292, 295-296, 298, 300, 304-305, 307, 313-317, 320-321, 329, 339-341
Speakes, Larry, 181, 193, 311
Special Situations Group (SSG), 194-195, 199, 261
State, U.S. Department of, 18-19, 28, 137, 155, 161, 172, 174-177, 181-183, 186, 196, 199, 204-205, 240-241, 243-244, 249, 251, 268, 277, 279, 281, 298, 308, 317, 324-325
Steiner, Steve, 197-198
Stennis, John, 160
Stethem, Robert Dean, 21-22, 309
Stiner, General Carl, 250
Stockman, David, 193
Stoessel, Walt, 175, 204
Strategic Defense Initiative, 12, 227-235, 291-293, 299, 301, 303-307, 315-320
Sultan, Prince Bandar bin, 69-70, 73-75, 243
Suq al-Gharb, seige of, 250, 252, 268

Tehran, see also Iran, 18, 20, 22, 29, 42-43, 47, 49-50, 52-54, 56-57, 59-60, 62-63, 65-66, 88-90, 94, 96, 270, 310, 330
Teicher, Howard, 55, 95, 97, 207, 244
Teller, Edward, 105, 232
Tet offensive, 144, 252
Thatcher, Prime Minister Margaret, 45, 196, 234, 265, 266, 267, 300-302, 305-307, 314
Thomas, Dennis, 332
Thompson, Paul, 85
Tillman, Jackie, 282
Timmons, William, 152, 155
Today show, 6
TOW missile shipments, 25-26, 28, 37-38, 46, 97, 330
Tower Board, 6-7, 14, 16, 35, 346, 349
Tower, John, 102, 168-169, 224, 325, 345, 346
Travelers Insurance, 11
Truman, Harry S, 104
Tuttle, Admiral Jerry, 270
TWA Flight 847 hijacking, 21-22, 84, 311

Ulam, Adam, 277
United Nicaraguan Opposition, 75
United States Information Agency, (USIA), 198

Vance, Cyrus, 220
Veliotes, Nick, 175, 207
Vessey, General John "Jack," 23, 28, 32, 34-35, 211, 229-230, 249, 264, 273
Vick, Christine, 361
Vietnam, 8, 33, 64, 71-72, 75, 78, 81, 91, 93, 107, 132-135, 137-146, 149-150, 152, 155-156, 158, 160-161, 175, 220, 241, 252, 258, 269, 342, 358, 367

Waite, Terry, 62
Wallison, Peter, 102
Wall Street Journal, 93
Walsh, Lawrence, 102, 349, 354-356, 358-359, 364-365
War Powers Resolution, 159
Washington Post, 14, 91, 174, 354
Watergate scandal, 91, 93, 95, 150, 154, 156-157, 159, 342, 358, 367
Watkins, Admiral James, 227-229, 353
Weinberger, Caspar "Cap," 7, 10, 19, 23, 26, 28-29, 32, 35, 43-44, 46, 50-51, 53, 68, 70-71, 75, 172, 182, 186-187, 195-196, 203, 209-212, 223-224, 232, 242, 248-249, 255, 259, 264, 268, 270-273, 276, 281, 286-287, 302-303, 314, 316-317, 323-326, 329, 332-333, 355-356, 364
Weir, Rev. Benjamin, 37-40
Weir, Carol, 38-39
Wick, Charles Z., 198, 221
Wickham, General John, 229
Wilson, James Q., 282
Wolfowitz, Paul, 175-176, 178, 182, 185, 207
Worldnet, 221
Wright, Jim, 264

Zagladin, Vadim, 296
Zawawi, Qais, 184
Zia-ul-Haq, General M., 184